The Critical Response to Ralph Ellison

Edited by
Robert J. Butler

Critical Responses in Arts and Letters, Number 35
Cameron Northouse, Series Adviser

GREENWOOD PRESS
Westport, Connecticut • London

Library of Congress Cataloging-in-Publication Data

The critical response to Ralph Ellison / edited by Robert J. Butler.
p. cm.—(Critical responses in arts and letters, ISSN 1057–0993 ; no. 35)
Includes bibliographical references and index.
ISBN 0–313–30285–5 (alk. paper)
1. Ellison, Ralph—Criticism and interpretation. 2. Afro-Americans in literature. I. Butler, Robert, 1942– . II. Series.
PS3555.L625 Z635 2000
818′.5409—dc21 00–020767

British Library Cataloguing in Publication Data is available.

Library of Congress Catalog Card Number: 00–020767
ISBN: 0–313–30285–5
ISSN: 1057–0993

First published in 2000

Greenwood Press, 88 Post Road West, Westport, CT 06881
An imprint of Greenwood Publishing Group, Inc.
www.greenwood.com

Printed in the United States of America

The paper used in this book complies with the Permanent Paper Standard issued by the National Information Standards Organization (Z39.48–1984).

10 9 8 7 6 5 4 3 2 1

Copyright Acknowledgments

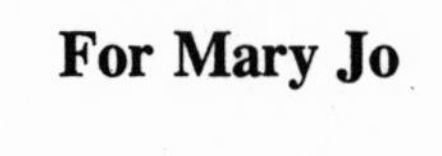
For Mary Jo

Contents

Ellison's Non-Fiction

Posthumous Assessments

Series Foreword

Critical Responses in Arts and Letters is designed to present a documentary history of highlights in the critical reception to the body of work of writers and artists and to individual works that are generally considered to be of major importance. The focus of each volume in this series is basically historical. The introductions to each volume are themselves brief histories of the critical response an author, artists, or individual work has received. This response is then further illustrated by reprinting a strong representation of the major critical reviews and articles that have collectively produced the author's, artist's, or work's critical reputation.

The scope of *Critical Responses in Arts and Letters* knows no chronological or geographical boundaries. Volumes under preparation include studies of individuals from around the world and in both contemporary and historical periods.

Each volume is the work of an individual editor, who surveys the entire body of criticism on a single author, artist, or work. The editor then selects the best material to depict the critical response received by an author or artist over his/her entire career. Documents produced by the author or artist may also be included when the editor finds that they are necessary to a full understanding of the materials at hand. In circumstances where previous isolated volumes of criticism on a particular individual or work exist, the editor carefully selects material that better reflects the nature and directions of the critical response over time.

In addition to the introduction and the documentary section, the editor of each volume is free to solicit new essays on areas that may not have been adequately dealt with in previous criticism. Also, for volumes on living writers and artists, new interviews may be included, again at the discretion of the volume's editor. The volumes also provide a supplementary bibliography and are fully indexed.

While each volume in *Critical Responses in Arts and Letters* is unique, it is also hoped that in combination they form a useful, documentary history of the critical response to the arts, and one that can be easily and profitably employed by students and scholars.

Cameron Northouse

Acknowledgments

Bringing this book to a successful conclusion would not have been possible without the generous support and assistance of many people. I wish to give special thanks to Dr. Ellen Conley and Dr. Herbert Nelson of Canisius College for supporting my research with a sabbatical and summer fellowship. I am also deeply grateful to Mrs. Lucy Jagodzinski and Ms. Moira Ragan who word processed and formatted the manuscript and faithfully saw it through so many revisions. Their tireless work, patience, and expertise were absolutely crucial to the book's success. I am also very much in debt to my research assistants, Kevin Jones and Marisa Loffredo, whose skilled and steady work were enormously helpful in all stages of the book's development. My deepest thanks go to my students at Tougaloo College and Stillman College who first made visible to me the wonders of Ellison's art and also to my students at Canisius College, Collins Correctional Facility, Attica Correctional Facility, and Wyoming Correctional Facility, who over the years have enabled me to see more fully the richness and complexity of Ellison's great novel, *Invisible Man*. I would also like to thank Professor John F. Callahan of Lewis and Clark College for his generous support and encouragement.

But most of all, I want to express heartfelt thanks and appreciation to my wife, Mary Jo, and my children, Becky, Geoff, Mike, and Eric. As always, their high spirits, encouragement, and belief were vital resources that magically increased the more I drew from them.

Introduction

Since the publication of *Invisible Man* in 1952, Ralph Ellison has been perceived by a wide variety of critics, scholars, and novelists as a major writer who has made important contributions to American, African American and modernist traditions. Early reviewers, such as Saul Bellow and Alain Locke, immediately sensed that *Invisible Man* was a seminal work which would provide many fruitful new directions for an entire generation of post-World War II writers. Even a superficial examination of books like Ken Kesey's *One Flew Over the Cuckoo's Nest*, Joseph Heller's *Catch-22*, and Sylvia Plath's *The Bell Jar* indicates the remarkably immediate effect which Ellison's novel had on his contemporaries. In succeeding years Ellison's fiction has continued to influence strongly a broad spectrum of important novelists and short story writers, including Ernest J. Gaines, Ishmael Reed, James Alan McPherson, Clarence Major, Toni Morrison, Charles Johnson, Sherley Anne Williams, and Randall Kenan. In Keith Byerman's words, *Invisible Man* has become a "paradigmatic work"[1] which has inspired, fascinated, and sometimes angered several generations of writers and critics. Its importance as a landmark cultural document and a literary masterwork is firmly established.

The critical response to Ellison's work can be roughly divided into four main periods: 1) the early reviews, 2) scholarly articles and chapters in books written from the mid-fifties to the mid-sixties, 3) commentary produced from the late sixties to the late seventies, and 4) critical and scholarly work from the early eighties to the present. As is always the case, these "periods" should be seen as helpful but somewhat arbitrary markers which can help us to detect trends in Ellison scholarship. They are not by any means objective and empirically reliable boundaries which can allow us to categorize the critical response into neat and absolutely clear patterns. Certain continuities remain in all phases of Ellison scholarship and overlappings of critical interests and judgments are more the rule than the exception. (As Ellison himself has vividly reminded us, the end can often be found in the beginning and reality moves more like a boomerang than an arrow.) Nevertheless, the critical response to Ellison has developed in roughly discernible phases producing patterns which, however shifting and blurry, still have meaning.

****

Ellison's career as a writer began quite modestly in 1937 with the publication of his review of Waters Edward Turpin's *These Low Grounds* in the leftist journal *New Challenge*. For the next fifteen years he published ten short stories and thirty-seven essays on literature, music, culture, and politics, none of which drew much attention from scholars and critics. But when *Invisible Man* was published in 1952 it drew a variety of spirited and sensitive responses from a broad spectrum of important figures. Indeed, very few first novels written by an American writer have received more enthusiastic praise in major critical journals. Many of these reviews were written by highly influential critics who hailed Ellison as a writer of genuine importance who was destined to make substantial contributions to American and African American literary traditions. Although most reviewers were careful to point out what they felt were flaws in the novel (what reviewer, after all, can resist this impulse?), the great majority of them argued that these faults paled in significance when balanced against the book's extraordinary strengths. Only a few reviews can be considered negative assessments of the novel.

Saul Bellow's "Man Underground" (*Commentary*, June 1952) characterized *Invisible Man* as "a book of the very first order, a superb book" which "is immensely moving and has greatness." Bellow was particularly impressed with the novel's unique style and voice, what he praised as its "very significant kind of independence" from the limited realism and dreary pessimism of much contemporary fiction. He also found this fledgling novel remarkable for its "maturity," its ability to project American experience in terms which were "enormously complex" and "intellectually responsible." Moreover, Bellow, himself a Jewish-American writer, supported Ellison for not adopting "a minority tone"; that is, transcending a narrowly racial vision of American life and instead tapping into what is "universal" in experience. Bellow concludes by claiming that *Invisible Man* offers impressive evidence that the novel is alive and well and not "dying" as many critics of the time had proclaimed. Indeed, Bellow sees Ellison's novel as a text which gives proof of a "resurrection" for the novel in particular and modern literature in general.

Richard Chase makes precisely the same point in his review of *Invisible Man* and Paul Bowles's *Let It Come Down*. While he cites the latter book as a painful example of the novel's decline due to a needless obscurity and a glaring lack of content, he sees Ellison's book as a bright example of the novel's persistent vitality. Impressed by *Invisible Man's* "sheer richness of invention" (*The Kenyon Review*, Autumn 1952), Chase praises the novel for its "many memorable episodes," extraordinary characterizations, and its "vigorous, witty, and sinuous language." Comparing Ellison with Faulkner, Dickens, Kafka, and Dostoevski, he regards Ellison as fruitfully positioned in the main traditions of the British, American, and European novel whose "central plot has been the passage, or failure of passage, from innocence to experience."

R.W.B. Lewis was equally enthusiastic in welcoming *Invisible Man* as an important literary achievement. In a general review which included assessments of Flannery O'Connor's *Wise Blood* and Ernest Hemingway's *The Old Man and the Sea*, Lewis ranked *Invisible Man* above these two novels, arguing that it matched Faulkner's best work in artistic quality: "It is not easy to name a work of fiction since *Light in August* which gives us so much and holds itself so well" (*The Hudson Review*, Spring 1953). Noting Ellison's "fierce power of imagination," he locates *Invisible Man* squarely within the tradition of the American novel, a body of literature centering on heroes who are "propelled by some lonely, personal, and self-generated power," outsiders who are "makers of their own conditions." Like Bellow, he praises the novel for transcending the limits of race, claiming that *Invisible Man* is not a "Negro novel" but instead is a book which explores broadly American and modernist themes.

William Barrett makes a similar point, observing that Ellison brilliantly explores the perennial American problem of how to define oneself in "a new, evolving, and fluid society" (*American Mercury*, June 1952). He connects *Invisible Man* to important masterworks of European modernism such as Céline's *Journey to the End of Night* and Dostoevski's *Notes from the Underground*. Like many other early reviewers, he found the novel's surrealistic style to be a special strength, stressing that "the book conveys more than any flatly reportorial or naturalistic fiction would do." Summing up, Barrett predicts a bright future for Ellison: "I do not see that we can set any limits now to how far Ellison may yet go in the novel. He has already written a book that just misses greatness."

Alain Locke, likewise, forecasts a brilliant career for Ellison on the strength of a first novel which he considers a major landmark in black American literature. Pointing out that in his thirty years of reviewing he has seen "three points of peak development" (*Phylon*, Spring 1953) in Negro literature, he ranks *Invisible Man* with Jean Toomer's *Cane* and Richard Wright's *Native Son* as seminal works. Regarding *Invisible Man* as "a great novel" which is in "both style and conception a new height of literary achievement," he praises Ellison for his three-dimensional characterizations, his brilliant use of irony, and his comprehensive and penetrating vision of race in America. Indeed, he considers the novel as "one of the best integrated accounts of interaction between whites and Negroes in American society that has yet been presented."

Orville Prescott joined in this chorus of praise, describing Ellison as "a richly talented writer" (*New York Times*, 16 April 1952) whose work surpasses in literary quality all previous fiction by black American authors:

> Ralph Ellison's first novel, *The Invisible Man* [sic] is the most impressive work of fiction by an American Negro which I have ever read. Unlike Richard Wright and Willard Motley, who achieve their best effects by overpowering their readers with documentary detail, Mr. Ellison is a finished novelist who uses words with great skill, who writes with poetic intensity and immense narrative drive.

Like Bellow and Barrett, Prescott senses that Ellison's unique blending of realistic and surrealistic styles enables him to produce a mode of literature which is well suited to capture the richness and complexity of post-war American experience.

It is important to realize, however, that the early reviews of *Invisible Man* were not without criticism. Even the very positive reviews cited above remarked that the novel had substantial weaknesses. Prescott, for example, noted that he found "many flaws" in the book, particularly its "flair for gaudy melodrama" and its "feverishly emotional" pace. He found parts of the book "overwritten" and feared that Ellison's "torrent of rhetoric" would obscure its meanings and clog its narrative. Even a reader as enthusiastic as Saul Bellow remarked that *Invisible Man* was "not by any means faultless," objecting to the imaginative flatness of the Brotherhood chapters. Locke complained about Ellison's "lack of restraint" and was troubled by parts of the novel in which Ellison's "talent" was "smothered with verbosity and hyperbole." Barrett was worried that the novel's affirmations were asserted but not adequately dramatized since Ellison was not able to bring his hero out of the underground. And Lewis felt that the book's overall excellence was marred by the fact that "It is occasionally melodramatic and self-indulgent, and it is a trifle too long."

These criticisms, however, must be put into context as relatively minor objections within otherwise glowingly positive assessments. For reviews which make fundamental criticisms of *Invisible Man*, one must refer to pieces written either by Marxist critics who faulted the novel for its political vision (or lack thereof) and some African American reviewers who saw the novel as presenting an inadequate or warped vision of black life in America. Lloyd Brown, a black novelist writing for the leftist journal *Masses and Mainstream*, made both objections in an extremely pointed way. He characterized Ellison as a sort of "Judas" who has betrayed his people by writing a novel which is "profoundly anti-Negro" (*Masses and Mainstream*, June 1952) because it shows a contempt for the Negro working masses. Aligning Ellison with white modernists like T.S. Eliot and deeply alienated writers in exile such as Richard Wright and Chester Himes, Brown criticizes Ellison for being "cut off from the mainstream of Negro life." For Brown, Ellison's stance of alienation prevents him from either portraying the positive features of black cultural life or suggesting ways in which blacks might liberate themselves from the oppression of the capitalist system.

Abner Berry makes similar complaints, charging Ellison with not only presenting a crudely stereotyped view of the Negro masses but also unfairly vilifying the Communist Party (*The Worker*, 1 June 1952). Roi Ottley objects to what he feels is a one-sided portrayal of Negro life which overemphasizes its "defeats and frustrations" (*Chicago Sunday Times*, 11 May 1952). Marguerite D. Cartwright, likewise, accuses Ellison of "defaming" Negroes by providing an excessively negative picture of black males (*Amsterdam News*, 7 March 1953). John O. Killens is so offended by what he feels is Ellison's "vicious distortion of Negro life" that he concludes "The Negro people need Ralph Ellison's *Invisible Man* like we need a hole in the head or a stab in the back" (*Freedom*, June 1952).

In all fairness, however, it must be pointed out that some African American critics responded to the novel in a very different way, celebrating it as an important achievement which was not only an artistic triumph but also successfully portrayed black life in America. Alain Locke, in the *Phylon* review cited above, ranked *Invisible Man* as a landmark work in black fiction and was particularly pleased with the novel's vision of racial relationships. Langston Hughes described *Invisible Man* as "deep, beautifully written, provocative, and moving" (*New York Age*, 28 February 1953). And Henry Winslow found the novel to be an artistically satisfying work which explored American racial problems in a penetrating way (*Crisis*, June-July 1952).

Perhaps the most comprehensive early review of *Invisible Man* was Irving Howe's "A Negro in America" which appeared in *The Nation* on May 10, 1952. Howe's essay contains many elements found in all of the reviews previously analyzed, expressing a deep admiration for *Invisible Man* as a work of art while also pointing out what he feels are serious defects in the novel. His summing up of the novel's strengths reiterate much of the praise contained in reviews by Bellow, Lewis, Locke, and Prescott:

> For Ellison has an abundance of that primary talent without which neither craft nor intelligence can save a novelist; he is richly, wildly inventive; his scenes rise and dip with tension; his people bleed, his language stings. No other writer has captured so much of the confusion and agony, the hidden gloom and surface gaiety of Negro life. His ear for Negro speech is magnificent. . . .

Howe also defends Ellison against the charge that *Invisible Man* is not sufficiently "black" by stressing that the novel is "drenched in Negro life, talk and music" and that "no white writer could have written it."

But Howe also has strong reservations about *Invisible Man*. Like many leftist critics, he was uncomfortable with Ellison's depiction of the Communist Party, insisting that the Brotherhood chapters are "not quite true" because they reduce communists to stereotyped "clowns." He also agrees with the leftist complaint that Ellison's is excessively individualistic in outlook, lacking a strong social vision. Aesthetically, he finds *Invisible Man* suffers from "structural incoherence " and stylistic excesses which lead Ellison to "overwhelm" the reader with a narrative that sometimes becomes "feverish," even "hysterical." Finally, he shares Barrett's worry that the novel asserts affirmations which it does not concretely dramatize. Howe sees little evidence for the "infinite possibilities" which invisible man celebrates at the end of the novel.

****

This extraordinary series of early reviews set up the basic framework for the lively critical debate about Ellison's work which continues to the present day. Taken as a whole, they raise many of the fundamental questions which have driven Ellison scholarship for over forty-five years. To what extent is *Invisible Man* a seminal work which has reinvigorated American, African American, and modernist traditions? How successfully has Ellison absorbed and then portrayed the experience of black people in America? Has he been able to connect black experience to the experience of other cultures, thus "universalizing" it, broadening and deepening its significance? Or has Ellison's attempt to achieve the universal diluted his vision, ultimately leading him to betray his responsibilities as a black artist?

The early reviews also raise important aesthetic questions about Ellison's work which continue to intrigue us. Is *Invisible Man* what Bellow and others claim it is, a "great" novel which masterfully fuses sophisticated technique with a deep, rich, and resonant vision of modern life? Or is it, as others have maintained, an "uneven" book which frequently degenerates into stylistic pyrotechnics which dazzle the reader but leave us finally more confused than illuminated? Like many other American masterworks such as Twain's *Adventures of Huckleberry Finn*, Dreiser's *Sister Carrie*, and Wright's *Native Son*, *Invisible Man* exhibits an enormous vitality by the energy, diversity, and acumen of the critical responses it has inspired. The early reviews of the novel clearly demonstrate that the publication of the novel in 1952 was an event of great cultural and literary importance. If Howe would later claim that with the publication of *Native Son* in 1940 American life was "changed forever,"[2] we might claim today that with the publication of *Invisible Man* American literature was likewise changed forever. For nearly fifty years critics, scholars, and writers have engaged in a spirited and fruitful debate over the precise nature of the extraordinary impact of *Invisible Man*.

The next phase of this critical debate extends roughly from the appearance of scholarly articles on *Invisible Man* in the mid-1950s to the end of the Civil Rights Movement in the late 1960s. For the most part, Ellison's critical stock rose steadily during this period as a significant volume of articles in journals and chapters in books explored the subtlety of Ellison's craft and the depth and resonance of his vision. A few negative estimates emerged during this time but they were as yet in a distinct minority. Most students of Ellison's work were in solid agreement that *Invisible Man* was an important, perhaps great, American novel which opened up exciting new directions for the post-World War II writer. Not only did the novel win the National Book Award for Fiction in 1953 but a national poll sponsored by *Book Week* in 1965 selected *Invisible Man* as the most distinguished American novel to appear since 1945. Many other important honors were awarded to Ellison during this period, including a Rockefeller Foundation Award in 1954, the Prix de Rome Fellowship in 1955, and the Medal of Freedom in 1969.

One clear measure of the immediate and widespread acceptance of *Invisible Man* as an important American novel is how quickly it gained extremely favorable treatment in some of the most influential studies of American literature emerging from the mid-1950s to the early 1960s. R.W.B. Lewis's seminal work *The American Adam* (1955) concludes by ranking *Invisible Man* with Salinger's *Catcher in the Rye* and Bellow's *The Adventures of Augie March* as examples of "the truest and most fully engaged American fiction after the second war"[3] Robert Bone's groundbreaking *The Negro Novel in America* (1958) describes Ellison as "a writer of the first magnitude" and characterizes *Invisible Man* as "quite possibly, the best American novel since World War II."[4] Leslie Fiedler's *Love and Death in the American Novel* (1960) cites Invisible Man as an example of the persistent vitality of the gothic tradition in American literature and its special relevance for black writers. Fiedler praises the novel not only for being a "technical achievement" but also for providing a compelling vision of American life unsurpassed by previous black writers.[5]

A number of scholarly articles praising various aspects of *Invisible Man* also begin to appear shortly after the novel's publication and steadily increase in volume and complexity during this period. Charles I. Glicksberg's "The Symbolism of Vision," published in 1954, is an astute analysis of Ellison's artful use of symbols pertaining to "light, color, perception, sight, insight"[6] Glicksberg argues cogently that Ellison uses this pattern of images to explore the unique dilemmas of black Americans in ways which are both pointed and subtle. Esther Merle Jackson's "The American Negro and the Image of the Absurd" also scrutinizes networks of imagery and symbolism as a way of focusing on the novel's central themes. Arguing that Ellison envisions the Negro as "a symbol, a sign of the total alienation of man in the twentieth century," Jackson compares invisible man with Faulkner's Joe Christmas and Wright's Bigger Thomas as "studies in the phases of the absurd sensibility." Whereas Christmas represents the first phase of absurdity, entrapment, and while Bigger is seen as exemplifying the second phase, revolt, Ellison's hero transcends both conditions in achieving existential freedom, undergoing a "journey of the fragmentary self through experience to knowledge and, ultimately, to being."[7]

Two other early studies of *Invisible Man* carefully examine its comic vision, Earl Rovit's 1960 essay "Ralph Ellison and the American Comic Tradition" describes *Invisible Man* as "a profoundly comic work" which is deeply rooted in masterpieces from our classic literature such as Whitman's "Song of Myself," Melville's *The Confidence Man* and Emerson's *Essays*. As such, the novel adopts a "comic stance"[8] which acknowledges the rich doubleness and fruitful incongruities of American life, recognizing both the absurdities of our history and the ability of the individual to triumph over these absurdities through acts of will and consciousness. Three years later, an equally revealing analysis of Ellison's comic art appeared but it stressed the author's profound connection to the African American folk tradition. Floyd R. Horowitz' "Ralph Ellison's Modern Version of Brer Bear and Brer Rabbit in *Invisible Man*" is the first in a long line of studies which would explore Ellison's deep understanding and skillful use of his folk roots. For Horowitz, the central task for invisible man is to become like Brer Rabbit, a trickster figure who uses superior knowledge and guile to outwit physically stronger opponents like Brer Bear. Although for most of the novel he repeatedly blunders when he tries to enact the role of Brer Bear in his search for outward wealth and power, he finally achieves a comic triumph by going underground (his briar patch) where he finally becomes a trickster hero who can achieve a "victory of perspective" with "a knowledge of self."[9]

More clear evidence of the extremely positive critical response to Ellison's work during this period is the fact that several influential books on post-war American fiction devoted whole chapters to detailed analyses of *Invisible Man*. Ihab Hassan's *Radical Innocence* (1961) argued that "the novel is neither comic nor tragic" but instead describes its central character as in "a state of suspension"[10] producing a condition of isolation and impotence, a feeling of *anomie* which he can not overcome but can only describe in his blues-like rendition of his own story. Jonathan Baumbach's *The Landscape of Nightmare* (1965) places Ellison in the tradition of absurdists such as Joyce, Kafka, West, Camus, and Faulkner, minimizing his connections with African American novelists such as Baldwin and Wright. Baumbach envisions *Invisible Man* as an intricate set of variations on the absurd quest which the hero undertakes in the Battle Royal, resulting finally in the central character admitting defeat by withdrawing into the mad world of the underground. Although Baumbach makes several sharp criticisms of the book, especially its "curiously static quality," he does conclude that "Ellison has written a major novel, perhaps one of the three or four most considerable novels of the past two decades."[11] Marcus Klein's *After Alienation* (1964) devotes a seventy-six page chapter to Ellison, using his work as an illustration of his thesis that the most significant American fiction of the postwar era has rejected the radical alienation of the twenties and thirties and has attempted to seek an "accommodation" with social reality." For Klein, *Invisible Man* does not end with the hero escaping into self but instead trying to integrate himself with American and African American "community."[12]

Ellison's reputation therefore rose steadily in the years following the publication of *Invisible Man*, firmly establishing him as an important figure in American literary culture. But in the Autumn of 1963 Irving Howe published an article in *Dissent* entitled "Black Boys and Native Sons" which would reactivate the doubts raised eleven years earlier by some Marxist and African American reviewers. A re-working of Howe's initial review of *Invisible Man*, it praised Ellison faintly for his stylistic achievements but then chided him for abandoning the tradition of black protest literature brought to a culmination by Richard Wright in favor of a form of literature which was "literary to a fault." For Howe, Ellison's novel is "marred" by the "ideological delusions" of the 1950s; that is, it recoils from exploring in a responsible way the social suffering and political dilemmas of American blacks and retreats instead into an aestheticism and individualism which Howe finds self-indulgent. For Howe, the racial injustices of American life literally force the black writer to adopt a stance of militant protest:

> How could a Negro put pen to paper, how could he so much as think or breathe without some impulsion to protest, be it harsh or mild, political or private, released or buried? . . . The 'sociology' of his existence forms a constant pressure on his literary work, and not merely in the way this might be true of any writer, but with a pain and ferocity that nothing could remove.[13]

Ellison was quick to respond to Howe in two brilliantly argued essays which appeared in the December 1963 and February 1964 issues of *The New Leader*. (Both were later conflated into a single essay entitled "The World and the Jug" which was included in *Shadow and Act*.) Ellison defended himself and his art from Howe's charges in several important ways. First, he reminds Howe of the irony of a white critic who with "confident superiority" takes it upon himself to tell a black writer "the meaning of Negro life" while never "bother(ing) to learn how varied it really is." He then points out that black writers, like all writers, have literary options which range well beyond the limits of protest fiction because black life in America contains many positive dimensions which enable black people to transcend the sufferings imposed upon them by a racist environment. Sharply contesting Howe's claim that unrelieved suffering is the only "real" Negro experience, Ellison reminds Howe that there is a long "American Negro tradition" of mastering pain by transforming it into "art." Such art, which Ellison finds not only in black musical forms such as the blues but also the religious rituals of the black church, produces a "fullness" and "richness" of Negro life which emphatically demonstrates the "humanity" of black people in America.

At the heart of Ellison's quarrel with Howe is a strong rejection of the social and political determinism which underpins protest fiction. Ellison stresses that American racism was never able to destroy the humanity of black people by reducing them to the status of simple victims. Quite to the contrary, the harshness of the American social environment produced in black people a "discipline" which enabled them to overcome their "burden" and then to build a culture of remarkable depth and beauty. Ellison therefore insists that for art to capture the full range of black experience, both its pain and achievements, it must go beyond political propaganda and literary protest. Art is not merely a "weapon" but a celebration of life in all of its complexity:

> Wright believed in the much abused idea that novels are "weapons" . . . But I believe that true novels, even when most pessimistic and bitter, arise out of an impulse to celebrate human life and therefore are ritualistic and ceremonial at their core. Thus they would preserve as they destroy, affirm as they reject.[14]

It is important here to emphasize that Ellison is not rejecting the validity of social and political protest (as Howe and many others have claimed) but rather is arguing that such protest is only one dimension of art just as pain is only one part of human life. He does insist that art can indeed "reject" and "destroy" what is unjust in a given society and later in the essay he emphasizes his own outrage at the racism which has afflicted black people throughout American history. He stresses that true art must be as richly multifaceted as life itself--it must not "retreat from reality" but must engage the world in a comprehensive way, acknowledging its complexities. Ellison finally describes his own art as centered in a "complex double vision" which both affirms what is good in American life and also rejects what is bad in American life. For Ellison protest can be an important element in art but art itself is never reducible to protest.

****

In the next phase of the critical response to Ralph Ellison, which runs roughly from the late sixties to the late seventies, the kind of objections made by Howe became more prominent. An obvious reason for this can be found in the political and social changes occurring in this very turbulent period. As American society experienced the severe disruptions brought on by the Vietnam War, a series of political assassinations, and the countercultural revolution, Ellison's very complex and nuanced vision of American life was rejected by many readers seeking simpler solutions to complicated problems. Political dissidents, for example, began to read *Invisible Man* with some dismay because it did not offer them clear and programmatic answers to the difficult questions raised during this period. Moreover, the novel did not seem to provide a course of action to solve personal and cultural problems but seemed to valorize a kind of philosophical brooding leading to paralysis.

Furthermore, the mid- to late-sixties witnessed a profound shift in black liberation strategies, moving from a Civil Rights Movement centered in a nonviolent quest for full integration of black people into American society to a black power movement of younger, more militant people intent on achieving the goals of black nationalism, even if a violent revolution were necessary to secure these aims. Because *Invisible Man* fully embraced the core values of the Civil Rights Movement, emphatically rejecting violence and celebrating the ideal of a fully integrated American where all would be "visible" to each other, the novel enjoyed great popularity during the heyday of the Freedom Movement, a political movement which Ellison clearly endorsed. But the novel's rejection of black nationalism and its deep suspicion of power politics in any form made it a book which drew heavy criticism from a new generation of militants who often vilified the book as irresponsibly a-political and labeled its author as one who had aligned himself with the white establishment.

Perhaps the clearest example of this extremely hostile response to Ellison's work is a 1967 piece by Ernest Kaiser entitled "Negro Images in American Writing." Kaiser takes Ellison to task for being a novelist who positions himself in the mainstream of Western culture and who believes that American blacks must achieve their identity within that tradition. For Kaiser, Ellison is a part of a corrupt system which not only reduces literature to an empty formalism but also victimizes blacks and other non-white people:

> Following André Malraux, the existentialists, the disillusioned or clever, opportunistic attackers of the left and the New Critics who emphasize form as supreme, even determining content, Ellison has become an establishment writer, an Uncle Tom, an attacker of the sociological formulations of the civil rights movement, a defender of the criminal Vietnam war of extermination against the Asian (and American Negro) people, a denigrator of the great tradition of Negro protest writing and, worst of all, for himself as a creative artist, a writer of weak and ineffectual fiction and essays mostly about himself and how he became an artist.[15]

This image of Ellison as a politically disengaged and self-indulgent writer who has betrayed his people by retreating into the alienation of high modernist writing appears frequently throughout the late sixties and seventies. And, as unfair and simplistic as this criticism is, it lingers even to the present moment as a cloud of suspicion over Ellison's otherwise superb reputation as a writer.

Another clear index to this shift in the critical response to Ellison's work can be found in a poll taken in 1968 by *Negro Digest* which substantially revised the findings of the poll taken by *Book Week* three years earlier praising *Invisible Man* as the most significant American novel to appear in the post war period. *Negro Digest*'s poll was addressed to young black writers who were asked to comment on their relationship to black writers of previous generations. Although some of the authors polled expressed positive views of Ellison and cited *Invisible Man* as an influential work, the majority of them were critical of Ellison and saw themselves as much more strongly influenced by Richard Wright. According to John Reilly, most of these younger writers "did not speak of Ellison as an author to be emulated" and several regarded Ellison as "irrelevant."[16]

Larry Neal's comments on Ellison in the "Afterword" to *Black Fire* (1968), likewise, characterizes Ellison's writing as outdated. Identifying himself as part of the Black Arts Movement which had gone beyond the identity crises afflicting previous generations of black intellectuals and artists, Neal states:

> . . . The things that concerned Ellison are interesting to read, but contemporary black youth feel another force in the world today. We know who we are, and we are not invisible, *at least not to each other*. We are not Kafkaesque creatures stumbling through a white light of confusion and absurdity.[17]

In a similar way, Addison Gayle makes a serious complaint against *Invisible Man*, describing it as out of touch with current thinking about race in America. He faults Ellison's fiction for being centered in the assimilationist hopes of the forties and fifties rather than endorsing a vision of "racial unity" proclaimed by writers associated with the Black Arts Movement. Like Kaiser, he sees Ellison as someone who has been overpraised and led astray by "white critics and academicians" who require that black art chase the bluebird of the "universal" instead of capturing what is unique in black experience. For Gayle, Ellison's failure lay in the fact that he, like his protagonist, is suspended ambiguously between white and black worlds, refusing to "emerge as a black man.[18]

It is important to realize, however, that all black writers and critics of this period did not share this negative assessment of Ellison's writing. Novelist James Alan McPherson, in a widely reprinted article published in 1970, expressed deep admiration for Ellison's ability to describe African American experience in a broad, balanced way, emphasizing both its distinctively black characteristics and its ties to American culture in general. Arguing that Ellison's achievements are "too enormous to be reduced to a sociological cliché," he defends Ellison against politically oriented critics. He also admires Ellison for his "healthy stubbornness," an independence of mind which allows him to think beyond the orthodox positions coming either from black critics who try to move him toward an "enforced cohesiveness" or white critics who attempt to lead him toward a nihilistic vision of life. McPherson notes that "a growing number of young black writers," including Michael Harper, Ernest Gaines, Ishmael Reed, and Al Young, show a deep respect for Ellison's work.[19]

A year later, George E. Kent, in an essay published in a special number of the *College Language Association Journal* devoted to Ellison, approved of Ellison's resistance to narrowly political notions of race, praising him for transcending a "rhetorical" grasp of blackness which he sees in much "radical" writing of the period. He finds Ellison's reading of black experience to be much truer because it is more complex, expressing both a "deep sense of the beauty as well as the terror of Black tradition.." Indeed, Kent ascribes an "almost god-like knowledge of Blackness" to Ellison. Although Kent expresses "a certain unease" about Ellison's hesitance to explore the African roots of black American experience, he nevertheless regards him as a major writer who has done a superb job of exploring the "power" and "complexity" of black American life, decoding its "cryptic messages" in ways which should intrigue rather than offend his readers.[20]

In 1970 Larry Neal dramatically revised his negative estimate of Ellison's writing in an article published in *Black World* entitled "Ellison's Zoot Suit." Arguing now that "much of the criticism directed against Ellison is either "personal and oversimplified" or rooted in a "specific body of Marxian and Black Neo-Marxist thought," he rejects the "ideological sources" of his earlier criticism of Ellison and describes "*Invisible Man* as "one of the world's greatest novels." He sees Ellison as one of the most engaging of the older generation of black writers and argues that "all Black creative artists owe Ellison a special gratitude." Like Kent, he expresses some concern over Ellison's apparent indifference toward the African roots of black American culture. But he clearly acknowledges that Ellison is a major force in Afro-American literature because he developed a mature art which was based upon "form, content, craft, and technique" rather than "fashionable political attitudes." Such a black art "sticks to the ribs" because it utters truths about the specific nature of African American experience as well as the life of "Man on the planet."[21]

In 1974 Houston H. Baker, Jr. described Ellison as one of the many black American novelists who can be "identified as culture builders and historians of a distinctive, whole way of life." He characterized *Invisible Man* as "a rich and complex work of art" which is part of a long tradition of African American works dating back to early slave narratives and including such twentieth century masterpieces as Du Bois' *The Souls of Black Folk* and Johnson's *The Autobiography of an Ex-Colored Man*. Far from being a conservative document written to please the white establishment, Ellison's novel is for Baker a distinguished book which portrays both "the spirit of black American culture and the liberation of its citizens."[22]

If the critical response to Ellison's writing by black critics during this period is a fascinating mixture of conflicting attitudes, the reactions to Ellison's work by other writers at this time was nearly unanimous in its praise. Many of these studies examine the formal artistry and thematic complexity of *Invisible Man*. William Schafer's 1968 article, "Ralph Ellison and the Birth of the Anti-Hero," for example, carefully explores the novel's intricate plot patterns as a four-part spiritual quest beginning with the hero's false sense of emancipation and ending with a disintegration of the self. Comparing the book's complicated narratives to a blues performance, Schafer concludes that Ellison achieves the highest levels of formal excellence:

> Technically, *Invisible Man* is a *tour de force*, using a whole spectrum of fictional techniques to convey a complex authorial attitude and build a fictional world which transcends realistic description or simple probability . . . It is a virtuoso performance, moving from unsophisticated methods to highly complex and subtle modes of narration; Ellison especially reveals his craftsmanship in language which builds from colloquial idioms and maintains its rhythms and texture of speech throughout. It is an extended jazz performance . . . with fluid improvisations on simple themes coalescing into a polished organic unity.[23]

Thomas Vogler is in agreement with Schafer about the mastery of form demonstrated in *Invisible Man* but sees a different meaning emerging from its narrative structure and imagery. He argues that the Battle Royal is artfully varied in the novel's major scenes, not to produce the erasure of self which Schafer detects, but rather to produce a deepening of the hero's consciousness, culminating in a new sense of "identity."[24]

Tony Tanner's 1971 study of the contemporary American novel, *City of Words*, devotes a full chapter to *Invisible Man*, claiming that it is "the most profound novel about American identity written since the war."[25] He too analyzes the book's narrative structure, envisioning it as a journey which takes place on geographical, social, historical, and philosophical levels. Like Vogler, he interprets the ending optimistically as signaling a rebirth, resulting in the creation of a self which mediates intelligently between a mechanical identity which would reduce the hero to a robot and a purely improvisional identity which would make him an opportunist like Rhinehart. For Tanner, the novel is about a search for empowerment in which the central character finally rejects outward forms of power which will destroy him and then embraces psychological and moral forms of power which will help him to understand his world and create a genuinely human self.

Roger Rosenblatt's *Black Fiction* analyzes the plot structure of *Invisible Man*, concluding that it is a powerful inversion of most heroic narratives:

> The novel may be categorized in a number of ways, but it is above all else the celebration of disappearance, of nothingness . . . As a romance, nothing is at the end of the quest, as a bildungsroman, nothing is the product of the education; as a tour de force, nothing is the vehicle. The hero progresses from South to North to nothing; from capitalism to communism to nothing.

For Rosenblatt, Ellison's novel is the most brilliant example of texts in black American literature like Ward's *Day of Absence*, Kelley's *A Different Drummer*, and Williams' *The Man Who Cried I Am* which are about the disappearance of black characters in plot patterns which entrap them in "cyclical" nightmares culminating in "self-disintegration."[26]

Many other excellent studies produced during this period focus on how Ellison has made skillful artistic use of American and European traditions. Michael Allen's 1969 article carefully explores Faulkner's influence on Ellison, arguing persuasively that both writers employ an "internal language"[27] to probe deeply into the consciousness of their central characters. Three years later Leonard Deutsch examined how Ellison's moral vision was rooted in his life-long fascination with Emerson's essays. Deutsch builds a solid case for the idea that Emerson's notions of self are one of the "major thematic concerns"[28] in *Invisible Man*. Martin Bucco's "Ellison's Invisible West" probes the author's Oklahoma background and discusses how western imagery and symbols are used in *Invisible Man*.[29]

Valerie Bonita Gray's 1978 book *Invisible Man's Literary Heritage: "Benito Cereno" and Moby Dick* is a detailed analysis of how Melville's fiction influenced Ellison.[30]

Many other critics were equally intent on defining how Ellison used European masterworks in fashioning his vision of life. Archie Sanders draws revealing parallels between Homer's *The Odyssey* and *Invisible Man*, stressing important similarities in narrative structure, conceptions of the hero, and minor characters. For Sanders, Emerson is a kind of Circe who tempts the hero with self-destructive debauchery and Jack is a version of Polyphemous who tries to intimidate invisible man into an equally self-destructive submission to authority.[31] Charles Scruggs makes an equally revealing argument for Ellison's self-conscious use of Virgil's *The Aeneid*.[32] Scruggs points out how Ellison ironically inverts certain aspects of Virgil's epic, for example, in the character of Sybil who is portrayed as a false prophet who mires Ellison's hero in his "underworld." But Scruggs also stresses how Ellison also made very affirmative use of other motifs from Virgil, especially in the search for "home" which centers both *The Aeneid* and *Invisible Man*.

Marcia Lieberman studies revealing parallels between *Invisible Man* and Voltaire's *Candide*, arguing that both works are grounded in a sharply qualified but nevertheless real hope. Ellison's protagonist, like Candide, begins in youthful illusion, flirts with despair, but ultimately "matures into skepticism, avoiding cynicism."[33] John Hersey's 1974 interview with Ellison surveys the author's interests in a wide variety of modern writers, including Joyce, Eliot, Hemingway, Stein, and Malraux and then focuses sharply on Ellison's admiration for nineteenth century Russian fiction. In that interview Ellison made an illuminating comparison between the cultural situation faced by writers such as Dostoevski and the cultural problems faced by contemporary American novelists:

> Such disruption of the traditional ordering of society, as in our own country since 1954, made for an atmosphere of irrationality, and this created a situation of unrestrained expressiveness. Eyeballs were peeled, nerves were laid bare, and private sensibilities were subjected to public laceration. In fact, life became so theatrical that Dostoevski's smoking imagination was barely able to keep a step ahead of what was actually happening in the garrets and the streets. Today, here in the United States, we have something similar . . . [34]

Ellison's complex use of the literary traditions of America and Europe, so thoughtfully probed by critics of the fifties, sixties, and seventies, laid a solid foundation for more elaborate and detailed studies which would emerge in later decades. By the late seventies, however, it was clear that reviews, scholarly articles, special numbers in journals, and chapters in books were not sufficient to grasp the full range, complexity, and depth of Ellison's art. Book-length studies of the sort which were published in the 1980s and 1990s were needed to bring Ellison scholarship to full maturity.

****

The first full study of Ellison's life and works was Robert E. O'Meally's *The Craft of Ralph Ellison*. Published in 1980, it is an incisive, balanced, and nuanced examination of Ellison's fiction and essays from apprentice pieces of the late 1930s to work-in-progress of the late 1970s. Containing a wealth of previously undisclosed biographical information, this book laid the groundwork for much further study and remains today one of the most valuable accounts of Ellison's career. O'Meally argues persuasively that the most distinctive feature of Ellison's writing was his masterful combining of black folk expression with the sophisticated techniques of modernist art:

> In Ellison's fiction, folklore, stylized and transformed by modernist techniques, gives special resonance and power to his language as it frees his characters to fly toward the moon, dive unmarked into the briarpatch, or become invisible and sail through the air unseen. Here the vernacular and the symbolist traditions in American literature converge.

O'Meally's early chapters narrate the main features of Ellison's life growing up in Oklahoma City, attending Tuskegee Institute, and eventually moving to New York where he studied music and sculpture and soon became a writer. Ellison's literary apprenticeship is carefully detailed, tracing his remarkable development from a proletarian writer using naturalistic techniques to articulate political views to a much more sophisticated artist who blended a variety of realistic and surrealistic styles to express an existential vision centered in consciousness and free will. The central chapter, a close reading of *Invisble Man*, explores how "an intricate pattern of folk forms," including blues, gospel music, sermons, toasts, and boasts, is "woven through the fabric"[35] of the novel to produce a complex and tough-minded celebration of African American experience. O'Meally's book also contains perceptive analyses of the short fiction which Ellison wrote at all points in his career and also makes astute speculations about his unpublished writings, especially the "big" novel which he hoped would follow, and perhaps surpass, *Invisible Man*. He concludes with a sensitive analysis of Ellison's aesthetics, especially as they are expressed in *Shadow and Act*.

Several other important books on Ellison were published in the 1980s. Robert N. List's *Daedalus in Harlem: The Joyce-Ellison Connection* (1980) is an extremely valuable study of Joyce's pervasive influence on Ellison's fiction. List explores in a very detailed way important parallels between Joyce's situation as an Irish writer in a culture dominated by the British and Ellison's condition as a black writer in a society dominated by whites. He is careful to point out that both writers were careful to avoid ethnic and racial chauvinism and instead developed visions which were broadly international and cosmopolitan. They were able to do this by skillfully using archetypal patterns from ancient literature as touchstones of value which could enable them to discover universal meanings in the ordinary events of modern life. List's book also offers important insights into how Joyce's complex uses of musical technique and Irish folklore inspired Ellison to make similar use of black music and folk materials. Finally, List builds a lucid and convincing case that Ellison's concept of the hero is rooted, at least in part, in Joyce's notion of the hero as artist and trickster.

Rudolf O. Dietze's *Ralph Ellison: The Genesis of an Artist* (1982) examines a variety of literary influences on Ellison and is particularly strong in demonstrating how he was powerfully influenced by Malraux's conception of the modern artist. Kerry McSweeney's *Invisible Man: A Student's Companion to the Novel* (1988) combines a detailed and sensitive formalist reading of the novel with an intelligent discussion of its critical reception and cultural background.

Alan Nadel's *Invisible Criticism* (1988) makes extensive use of postmodernist critical theory to reveal how *Invisible Man* deconstructs twentieth century notions of American tradition, culture, and identity which reduce minorities to "invisibility" and marginality. For Nadel, the novel's elaborate patterns of allusions function to redefine the "canon" of American literature and the cultural and political assumptions which underpin this canon. Stating that the "central aim" of his book is to explore how "*Invisible Man* is deeply informed by the issue of canonicity," he stresses that "my larger purpose is always to expose some of the ways Ellison situates *Invisible Man* in regard to the American literary tradition, comments on that tradition, and in so doing, alters it." Nadel finally argues that in redefining the American canon Ellison created space in modern American literary culture for blacks and other minorities, thus "opening up literature to the vitality of other voices" and providing us with a "means that may permit us to hear the voices of otherness."[36] Central to this process is Ellison's artful use of works by Emerson, Melville, and Twain. For these nineteenth century writers, unlike their counterparts in the first half of the twentieth century, endorsed broadly humanistic and democratic values which embraced black people as integral parts of American culture. By recovering the social and moral vision which is at the heart of nineteenth century masterpieces such as *Representative Men*, "Benito Cereno," and *Adventures of Huckleberry Finn*, Ellison reinvigorates twentieth century American literature.

Mark Busby's *Ralph Ellison* (1991), likewise, makes a strong case for Ellison as an important shaping influence on American literary tradition, claiming that "Ellison charted new frontiers in American literature" and that *Invisible Man* is probably the most important post-1950 American novel." For Busby, Ellison's genius lay in his "integrative imagination"; that is, his ability to draw skillfully from a wide variety of literary and folk traditions to produce works of art endowed with unusual power, technical brilliance, and resonance. Busby lays particular stress on Ellison's use of geography as a way of integrating American experience:

> Geography influences his writing so completely that the symbolic values of the three primary locations where he spent his life provide a metaphor that permeates his work: thesis/antithesis=synthesis. His southwestern background provided him with freedom and possibility; the South offered restriction and limitation; the North allowed a mature synthesis. Writing requires constant interaction with the shadow of the past--with one's geography and history--to produce the synthesis of art, which, Ellison emphasizes, imagination offers: "As I say, imagination itself is *integrative*, a matter of making symbolic wholes out of parts."[37]

Busby's book offers a particularly thoughtful discussion of Ellison's conscious use of the comic techniques of nineteenth century frontier humor and also contains sensitive analyses of his short fiction and essays.

Edith Schor's *Visible Ellison: A Study of Ralph Ellison's Fiction* (1993) is a close reading of Ellison's short stories and *Invisible Man*, demonstrating Ellison's development as a fictionist. Shor applauds Ellison for using folk materials in such a way as to probe the intricacies of African American experience while also reaching out to concerns and values which are universal. Her final chapter studies the Hickman stories, praising them for their wit and thematic richness.

The most recent book-length study of Ellison is Jerry Gafio Watt's *Heroism and the Black Intellectual: Ralph Ellison, Politics, and Afro-American Intellectual Life* (1994). Offering a "sociological approach" to Ellison, Watt's book does not engage in literary analysis but instead focuses on the author's "views on American society, Afro-American culture, the political situation of black Americans, and the black writer's relationship to the other three." His fundamentally negative assessment of Ellison's achievements as a black intellectual mainly reiterates complaints which can be traced back to some early reviews, the Ellison-Howe quarrel, and objections raised by several militants of the 1960s and 1970s. Like John O. Killens, he objects to what he regards as Ellison's misreading of black American experience. He also shares Howe's objections to Ellison's individualism, seeing it as politically and culturally irresponsible. And he agrees with Marxist readers who have accused Ellison of an "elitism" and "establishmentarianism" which they feel have separated him from the plight of the black masses. Contrasting him with a politically engaged novelist like Wright and a publically committed poet like Hughes, Watts finds

Ellison wanting and diagnoses him as suffering from "a rather typical black intellectual disease" which he labels as "the elitism of heroic individualism."[38]

This sort of negative criticism of Ellison's intellectual stance and artistic achievement is clearly a minority view in the 1980s and 1990s. The vast majority of scholars, critics, and writers responding to Ellison's work during this period praise it strongly. This is particularly true of a younger generation of African American novelists who see Ellison as a writer to be emulated, one who has created many new directions which they have explored in their own fiction. Charles Johnson, for example, regards *Invisible Man* as "something of the modern Ur-text for black fiction"[39] which has, along with the Black Arts Movement, defined one of the two major directions for contemporary African American writing. Ishmael Reed, Leon Forrest, Clarence Major, and Randall Kenan have also expressed admiration for and indebtedness to Ellison for breaking away from the limits of mimetic fiction and opening up new technical and thematic possibilities for black fiction writers.

Many critics during this period also stress Ellison's importance as an innovator who enriched American and African American literary traditions. Keith Byerman in *Fingering the Jagged Grain* (1985) examines in meticulous detail the dialectical narrative patterns in *Invisible Man*, arguing for their ability to generate new ideas:

> Within and between the layers of the story in *Invisible Man* new meanings constantly open. Thus the telling of the story becomes a way of resisting closure. Even when the narrator attempts to explain his meanings, as he does in the epilogue, his comments are tested against the scenes he has presented. The concrete experiences, not the abstractions from them, are the test of meaning. And because those experiences work on a number of levels, the tale refuses to be reduced to a system.

Byerman sees the open narrative as "non-Hegelian" because it does not culminate in a stable synthesis of opposite ideas but concludes instead with "disruption," an active ferment of ideas which are forever generating new concepts. Narrative patterns of this kind suggest that the hero has a radically protean identity which is always in the process of becoming, never resting in a stable condition of "being."[40]

Valerie Smith's *Self-Discovery and Authority in Afro-American Literature* (1987) offers an extremely subtle discussion of how first person narration is used in *Invisible Man* to dissolve fixed, stereotyped notions of self and to move toward a more open, indeterminate identity created and controlled by the narrator. Melvin Dixon's *Ride Out the Wilderness* (1987) explores how Ellison's fiction employes imagery of flight and underground settings to dramatize the unresolved identity problems of Ellison's protagonists. Dixon claims that such characters are doomed to a life of "inertia and inaction" because their attempts to fly away from inhibiting environments "boomerang," sending them into underground worlds of "hibernation and stasis"[41] Thomas Schaub discusses Ellison's "invention of a form" that can make us experience invisible man's sense of the world as "chaos" and his sense of his own identity as a series of "masks"[42] which provide him with a way of operating within that world. This led Ellison to reject conventionally realistic modes of fiction in favor of a radically surrealistic novelistic form which undercuts any objective interpretations of life.

The 1980s and 1990s are also a time when many excellent studies of Ellison's literary foregrounding continue to be written. Joseph T. Skerrett, Jr. profitably re-opened the investigation into Ellison's relationship with Richard Wright, concluding that the two writers, however different in some respects, were remarkably similar in certain important ways. Skerrett argues brilliantly that Ellison's work is not a "negation" of Wright's work but is instead an attempt to "complete" it; that is, it builds upon the foundation Wright built and then transcends it. But Skerrett rightly stresses "the central agency" of Wright in the formation of Ellison's artistic sensibilities, however much Ellison was anxious to deny this influence.[43] In a series of articles, Robert J. Butler has studied how *Invisible Man* was shaped by the American picaresque tradition, Dante's *Inferno*, and Bergson's theories of time.[44] Mary Ellen Williams Walsh examined Eliot's influence on Ellison[45] and Robert O'Meally took a careful look at Hemingway as one of Ellison's important literary "ancestors."[46]

Dostoevski's strong influence on Ellison is carefully documented in important article by Joseph Frank. Frank draws revealing parallels between the cultural sources of alienation expressed in *Notes from the Underground* and *Invisible Man*. He also suggests that Dostoevski's deeply sympathetic response to Russian peasant culture in *The House of the Dead* parallels Ellison's equally affirmative vision of black folk life. Frank, however, cautions readers not to conclude that Ellison slavishly imitated Dostoevski but instead made intelligent artistic use of him while fashioning his own unique vision of African Americna life: "Ellison took from Dostoevski what he needed but used it in his own way."[47]

One of the most penetrating discussions of the richly varied combination of influences found in Ellison's work is Berndt Ostendorf's "Ralph Waldo Ellison: Anthropology, Modernism, and Jazz." He envisions Ellison's art as deeply rooted in three factors: modernist literary theory, African American and American folklore, and jazz. Whereas Ellison's commitments to modernism and folklore are a source of possible conflict, even contradiction, because they place him between elitist and popular notions of art, jazz supplies him with a rich "synthesis" since it is centered in folk roots and also involves great formal complexity and sophisticated kinds of experimentation. Playing upon these "three encompassing frames" as a jazz musician might improvise "chord progressions," Ellison is able to harmonize modernist techniques to express an affirmative vision of life which springs out of the richness of black folk experience. Using jazz as a mediating art form, Ellison can "square the circle of intellectual excellence and group loyalty." He can be true to the exacting demands of his craft as a modern artist while affirming his African American identity. In the process, he is able to transcend the limits of white "angst" as well as "black anger."[48]

John F. Callahan's *In the African-American Grain* (1988) provides another provocative and nuanced probing of Ellison's sophisticated use of black folk art to enrich twentieth century writing. *Invisible Man* uses not only thematic motifs from the blues and folk tales but also skillfully employs a "call" and "response" technique which is central to black sermons and vernacular speech. This rhetorical strategy is based upon an organic connection between an individual who "calls" and a community which "responds." Seen in this way, *Invisible Man*'s prologue is a "call" of a "disembodied voice" which is ultimately answered by the epilogue's "response" portraying the hero as building a "bridge of words and actions between the self and American democratic ideals." Unlike critics who quarrel with Ellison for constructing a world view which is excessively individualistic and dooms the hero to narcissicism and inaction, Callahan argues convincingly that Ellison's narrative strategies generate a free discourse between the self and the public world which is essential to the vitality of a democratic society. Ellison's rhetoric uses the "spoken word" to "create bonds and bring about personal and social transformation." Such a "narrative discourse of democratic possibility" endows Ellison's writing with an energy, depth, and resonance usually missing in modern fiction produced by mainstream writers.[49]

Since the early 1980s Ellison studies have benefited greatly from some of the theoretical approaches to literature which have become prominent during this time.

Houston Baker's *Blues, Ideology, and Afro-American Literature* (1984) applies poststructualist methods to a close reading of the Trueblood episode in *Invisible Man*, finding that Trueblood's telling of his story enables him to deconstruct the "systems of signs" which the dominant culture uses to imprison him and this enables him to create a new self which transcends the stereotypes and roles which whites have imposed upon him. Inverting social norms and transgressing social boundaries, he becomes for Baker a "cosmic creator"[50] who can serve as a model for the novel's protagonist. Henry Louis Gates's *Figures in Black: Words, Signs, and the Racial Self* briefly discusses Ellison to illustrate the concept of "signifying," a mode of discourse at the heart of black literary tradition which repeats and artfully revises previous discourse, thereby creating fresh meanings which are distinctively black. Gates characterizes Ellison as "our Great Signifier," someone who consciously signifies on previous texts such as *Their Eyes Were Watching God* and *Native Son* and who in turn is signified upon by younger writers like Ishmael Reed. Gates therefore regards Ellison's fiction as an integral part of African American literary tradition because it builds upon the narrative forms of the past and extends them with a "new way of seeing" and a "new manner of representation."[51]

Feminist scholars have also addressed Ellison's fiction in recent years. Hortense Spillers, for example, objects to the way in which women are portrayed in *Invisible Man*, particularly in the Jim Trueblood episode:

> The entire tale of incest in *Invisible Man* is told by Trueblood . . . For all intents and purposes, the wife/mother Kate and the daughter/surrogate love Mattie Lou are deprived of speech, of tongue, since what they said and did and when are reported/translated through the medium of Trueblood. These silent figures, like materialized vectors in a field of force, are curiously silent in the sense that incest fiction, even by women, never, as far as I know, establishes the agency of the incestuous act inside the female character.[52]

Mary Rohrberger, for the most part, agrees with this assessment, faulting Ellison for what she feels is a consistently negative portrayal of women in *Invisible Man*:

> Nowhere in *Invisible Man* is there a woman not characterized as automaton-prostitute or mother. From the blond woman in the opening scene, through the innocent and nameless black girls who dream of romantic love and marriage, to Sybil, subsumed by fantasies of rape, to Mary, the "good mother," who sustains as well as destroys, the women are one-dimensional figures playing roles in a drama written by men.

Rohrberger finds that Trueblood's wife is the only woman who edges beyond stereotype because she is the only female character with "any semblance of real power." The rest of the novel's women she characterizes as stereotyped whores, mother-figures, and "hangers-on of men."[53]

Claudia Tate, on the other hand, takes a very different view of the matter, insisting that female characters in *Invisible Man* only appear to be marginalized by stereotyping. A closer reading of the novel reveals that Ellison starts with stereotyped images of women but transcends them to dramatize their humanity and also to show how these women highlight the "broader aspects of the humanity of all of us." For Tate, the stages of invisible man's human development are triggered by his encounters with a number of women who teach him a series of "lessons" about himself and the world. By confronting outwardly stereotyped women who often reveal to him human qualities beneath their stereotypes, he becomes more fully aware of how he has been labelled by a society which refuses to see his humanity. The slave woman at the beginning of the novel teaches him about the true nature of freedom, the blonde at the Battle Royal gives him a lesson in "ambivalence," and Mary Rambo revives him by reconnecting him to the nourishing values of his racial past. The human identity he achieves by the end of the novel is signalled by his refusal to stereotype and victimize Sybil. Indeed, he sees her in human terms as "his last teacher" who helps him to become free by making him understand that he can make his "invisibility" a strength by using it for his own purposes.[54]

Throughout the eighties and nineties, therefore, the centrality of Ellison's place in American literary tradition has been powerfully documented by a broad range of writers, scholars, and critics. Saul Bellow, whose review of *Invisible Man* opened the critical discussion of that novel, observed a year after Ellison's death that Ellison's masterpiece "holds its own among the best novels of the century."[55] Poet Michael Harper, in an important festival devoted to Ellison at Brown University, praised Ellison for a career centered in "imaginative freedom"[56] which has enriched American and African American traditions. Mark Busby has recently described *Invisible Man* as a book which has had "a profound effect on American literature, both mainstream and African-American."[57] Stanley Crouch, in a powerful essay written shortly after Ellison's death, eulogized him as a writer of great national importance who transcended boundaries of race, class, gender, and religion to "make us all Americans." He admires Ellison for an integrity which enabled him to avoid the oversimplifications and narrowness which have plagued lesser writers:

> Alone of the internationally famous Negro writers of the past half century, Ellison has maintained his position as a citizen of the nation . . . This champion of democratic narrative wasn't taken in by any of the professional distortions of identity that have now produced, not the astonishing orchestra of individuals our country always promises, but a new Babel of opportunism and naiveté, one we will inevitably defeat with a vital, homemade counterpoint.

Writing with a pen which Crouch describes as "both a warrior's lance and a conductor's wand" Ellison imagined a rich vision of American life in the twentieth century which is remarkable for its breadth, complexity, and hope. Crouch rightly observes that Ellison's "knowledge of race in conflict" is, in the final analysis, a "wildly orchestrated metaphor for all of human life."[58]

****

Yet much work remains to be done if we are to gain a truly comprehensive understanding of Ellison's remarkable achievement. As John Callahan has reminded us,. . . there's work to be done, facts to be tracked, stories to be gathered and preserved, connections to be made, interpretations to be offered . . . [59] Critics have barely scratched the surface of Ellison's considerable achievements as a non-fiction prose writer. His essays have recently been collected and deserve serious study. Ellison's short stories, ranging from recently uncovered apprentice pieces like "Boy on a Train" and "I Did Not Learn Their Names" to accomplished masterpieces like "Flying Home" and "King of the Bingo Game," have also been posthumously collected but need to be critically assessed, and related to Ellison's overall canon. Ellison's extraordinary second novel, *Juneteenth* has recently been published and awaits careful scrutiny. This important book, which has been hailed in an early review "as a visionary tour de force" [60] can only add to Ellison's reputation as a major American writer. Moreover, the substantial amount of unpublished fiction and non fiction now located in the Library of Congress should be carefully examined and the most significant pieces published. And *Invisible Man*, as closely as it has been studied over the past forty-seven years, is far from exhausted--it still offers fresh and expansive "territory" which critics have either left unexplored or poorly mapped. Certainly much more needs to be said about Ellison's envisioning of female experience and how feminine values are an important part of his vision. Postmodern critical approaches such as New Historicism and reader response criticism also provide promising, but as yet underutilized, perspectives on Ellison's many-layered and historically situated novel. And, of course, biographical studies are greatly needed. We must know much more about his Oklahoma background, his years at Tuskegee, his involvements with leftist politics, the interval in Dayton, and his life after he had achieved world-wide acclaim.

By providing a detailed account of the critical response to Ellison, this book is an attempt to provide one more tool to assist in this further study of his life and work. The pieces collected in this volume provide a clear track record of where Ellison scholarship has been and, more importantly, they also lead the way to further study. The first section, consisting of early reviews of *Invisible Man*, establishes a framework which raises many of the important questions which have driven Ellison scholarship. Since these questions have never been adequately answered, they must be freshly probed by current scholars in an open, vigorous way. The second section focuses on previously published and newly commissioned studies of *Invisible Man*. Again, these essays stress the extraordinary richness of Ellison's masterwork and are intended as openings for further investigation rather than "definitive" studies which can settle matters absolutely. The next two sections concern themselves with Ellison's essays and short stories, two woefully understudied dimensions of his career. And the final section of the book, entitled "Posthumous Assessments" provides a series of new essays which attempt to sum up Ellison's achievement and suggest further areas of study. The net effect of this book, therefore, is both to survey the critical response to Ellison over a period of nearly fifty years and also to stress that the real work of understanding and assessing Ellison's genius is just beginning. As Ellison himself has observed, "the territory ahead is an ideal place--ever to be sought, ever to be missed, but always there."[61] The literary frontier he opened up during his remarkable career is still a wide open space awaiting exploration, not a dusty museum awaiting cataloguing.

NOTES

1. Keith Byerman. *Fingering the Jagged Grain: Tradition and Form in Recent Black Literature* (Athens and London: The University of Georgia Press), 1985.

2. Irving Howe, "Black Boys and Native Sons" in *Twentieth Century Interpretations of Native Son*, ed. Houston Baker (Englewood Cliffs: Prentice Hall, 1972), 65.

3. R.W.B. Lewis. *The American Adam: Innocence, Tragedy, and Tradition in the Nineteenth Century* (Chicago: The University of Chicago Press, 1955), 197.

4. Robert Bone. *The Novel in America* (New Haven and London: Yale University Press, 1958), 212.

5. Leslie Fiedler. *Love and Death in the American Novel* (New York: Dell Publishing, 1969), 501. *Invisible Man* is also favorably mentioned in two influential surveys of American literature which were published in the early 1960s. Willard Thorpe's *American Writing in the Twentieth Century* (Cambridge: Harvard University Press, 1960) includes Ellison as among a new generation of black writers who have emancipated themselves from the formulas of conventional protest fiction and are making fresh contributions to post-war American literature. Leon Howard's *Literature and the American Tradition* (Garden City, N.Y.: Doubleday, 1960) singles out *Invisible Man* as the pre-eminent American novel about Harlem.

6. Charles I. Glicksberg. "The Symbolism of Vision." *Southwest Review*, XXXIX (Summer 1954), 261.

7. Esther Merle Jackson. "The American Negro and the Image of the Absurd." *Phylon* XXIII (Winter 1962), 360, 361, 367.

8. Earl Rovit. "Ralph Ellison and the American Comic Tradition." *Wisconsin Studies in Contemporary Literature*, I (Fall, 1960), 34, 34.

9. Floyd R. Horowitz. "Ralph Ellison's Modern Version of Brer Bear and Brer Rabbit in *Invisible Man*." *Midcontinent American Studies Journal* IV, No.2 (1963), 25.

10. Ihab Hassan. *Radical Innocence* (Princeton: Princeton University Press, 1961), 175, 175.

11. Jonathan Baumbach. *The Landscape of Nightmare: Studies in the Contemporary American Novel* (New York: New York University Press, 1965), 85,85.

12. Marcus Klein. *After Alienation* (Cleveland: World Publishing Co., 1965), 85, 85.

13. Irving Howe. "Black Boys and Native Sons" in *A World More Attractive* (New York: Horizon press, 1963).

14. Ellison, Ralph. "The World and the Jug" in *Shadow and Act* (New York: Signet Books, 1966), 115-16, 119, 119,119,121,130,137.

15. Ernest Kaiser. "Negro Images in American Writing." *Freedomways* VII (Spring 1967), 152-63. In *Twentieth Century Interpretations of Invisible Man*. John Reilly, ed. (Englewood Cliffs, N.J.: Prentice Hall, 1970), 111.

16. John M. Reilly. *Twentieth Century Interpretations of Invisible Man*. (Englewood Cliffs, N.J.: Prentice Hall, 1970), 8.

17. LeRoi Jones and Larry Neal, *Black Fire: An Anthology of Afro-American Writing* (New York: William Morrow and Co., 1968), 652.

18. Addison Gayle. *The Way of the New World: The Black Novel in America* (Garden City, N.J.: Doubleday, 1975), 212, 204, 212. It should be noted here that Gayle's harsh criticism of Ellison's "political beliefs" (213) are qualified by his admiration for other aspects of his work. He praises *Invisible Man* for its stylistic virtuosity and its ability to recreate "the immense color and pageantry of black life" (209). He characterizes the novel as "remarkable" (213), ranking it as "among the twenty best novels written in the last thirty years" (210).

19. James Alan McPherson. "Indivisible Man." *The Atlantic*, Vol. 226, No. 6 (December, 1970).

20. George E. Kent. "Ralph Ellison and the Afro-American Folk and Cultural Tradition." *CLA Journal*, Vo. XII, No. 3 (March 1970),

21. Larry Neal. "Ellison's Zoot Suit." *Black World*, Vol. XX, No. 2 (December 1970), 31, 50, 48, 41.

22. Houston A. Baker, Jr. *Singers at Daybreak: Studies in Black American Literature* (Washington, D.C.: Howard University Press, 1974), 18, 28, 30.

23. William J. Schafer. "Ralph Ellison and the Birth of the Anti-Hero." *Critique* X, (1968), 83.

24. Thomas Vogler. "Invisible Man: Somebody's Protest Novel." *Iowa Review*, I (Spring 1970), 81.

25. Tony Tanner. *City of Words: American Fiction, 1959-1970* (New York: Harper and Row, 1971), 51.

26. Roger Rosenblatt. *Black Fiction*. (Cambridge, Mass.: Harvard University Press, 1974), 185, 199.

27. Michael Allen. "Some Examples of Faulknerian Rhetoric in Ellison's *Invisible Man*" in *The Black American Writer, Vo. I,* edited by C.W.E. Bigsby (Baltimore: Penguin Books, 1971), 144.

28. Leonard Deutsch. "Ralph Waldo Ellison and Ralph Waldo Emerson: A Shared Moral Vision." *CLA Journal* 16 (1972), 160.

29. Martin Bucco. "Ellison's Invisible West" *Western American Literature* (1975), 237-38.

30. Valerie Bonita Gray. *Invisible Man's Literary Heritage: "Benito Cereno" and Moby Dick* (Amsterdam: Editions Rodopi, N.V., 1974).

31. Archie D. Sanders. "Odysseus in Black: An Analysis of the Structure of *Invisible Man*" *CLA Journal* 13 (March 1970), 217-28.

32. Charles W. Scruggs. "Ellison's Use of *The Aeneid* in *Invisible Man*." *CLA Journal* 17 (March 1974), 368-78.

33. Marcia Lieberman. "Moral Innocents: Ellison's *Invisible Man* and *Candide*." *CLA Journal* 15 (September 1971), 79.

34. Hersey, John. "A Completion of Personality." in *Ralph Ellison: Collection of Critical Essays* (Englewood Cliffs, N.J.: Prentice Hall, 1974), 16.

35. Robert O'Meally. *The Craft of Ralph Ellison* (Cambridge, Mass.: Harvard University Press, 1980), 2, 79.

36. Alan Nadel. *Invisible Man: Ralph Ellison and the American Canon* (Iowa City: University of Iowa Press, 1988), XII, XIII, 116.

37. Mark Busby. *Ralph Ellison* (Boston: G.K. Hall, 1991), 144, 141, 141, 1. The quote from Ellison is from an interview contained in *Chant of Saints,* edited by Robert B. Stepto and Michael S. Harper (Urbana: University of Illinois Press, 1979), 458.

38. Jerry Gafio Watts. *Heroism and the Black Intellectual: Ralph Ellison, Politics, and Afro-American Intellectual Life* (Chapel Hill: The University of North Carolina Press, 1994), 14, 32-33, 47, 46, 119.

39. Charles Johnson. *Being and Race: Black Writing Since 1970* (Bloomington and Indianapolis: Indiana Unversity Press, 1990), 15.

40. Byerman, Keith. *Fingering the Jagged Grain: Tradition and Form in Recent Black Fiction*. (Athens, Georgia: The University of Georgia Press, 1985), 38-39, 12, 12.

41. Dixon, Melvin. *Ride Out the Wilderness: Geography and Identity in Afro-American Literature* (Urbana and Chicago: University of Illinois Press, 1987), 75, 74.

42. Thomas Schaub. "Ellison's Masks and the Novel of Reality" in *New Essays on Invisible Man,* edited by Robert O'Meally (Cambridge, England: Cambridge University Press, 1988), 127, 126, 127.

43. Joseph T. Skerrett, Jr. "The Wright Interpretation: Ralph Ellison and the Anxiety of Influence" in *Speaking for You: The Vision of Ralph Ellison,* edited by Kimberly W. Benston (Washington, D.C.: Howard University Press,1990), 225, 228.

44. See "Patterns of Movement in *Invisible Man*." *American Studies* XXI (Spring 1980), 5-21; "Dante's *Inferno* and Ellison's *Invisible Man*: A Study in Literary Continuity." *CLA Journal* XXVIII (Sept. 1984), 57-77; and "The Plunge into Pure Duration." *CLA Journal* XXXIII (March 1990), 260-79.

45. Mary Ellen Williams Walsh. "*Invisible Man*: Ralph Ellison's Wasteland." *CLA Journal* 28 (1984), 150-58.

46. O'Meally, Robert G. "The Rules of Magic: Hemingway as Ellison's 'Ancestor.'" In *Speaking for You: The Vision of Ralph Ellison,* edited by Kimberly W. Benston (Washington, D.C.: Howard University Press, 1990), 752.

47. Joseph Frank. "Ralph Ellison and a Literary 'Ancestor'" in *Speaking for You: The Vision of Ralph Ellison,*" edited by Kimberly W. Benston (Washington, D.C., Howard University Press, 1990), 233.

48. Berndt Ostendorf. "Ralph Waldo Ellison: Anthropology, Modernism and Jazz" in *New Essays on Invisible Man,* edited by Robert O'Meally (Cambridge, England: Cambridge University Press, 1988), 96, 117, 108. Susan Blake in the late 1970s expressed a very different view, chiding Ellison for sacrificing the power and richness of black folk tradition in order to achieve a "universality" acceptable to a mainstream audience ("Ritual and Rationalization: Black Folklore in the Works of Ralph Ellison." *PMLA* 94 (1979), 121-36.)

49. John F. Callahan. *In the African-American Grain: The Pursuit of Voice in Twentieth Century Black Fiction* (Urbana and Chicago: University of Illinois Press), 1988, 151, 168, 115, 257.

50. Houston A. Baker, Jr. *Blues, Ideology, and Afro-American Literature: A Vernacular Theory* (Chicago: The University of Chicago Press, 1984), 176, 183.

51. Henry Louis Gates, Jr. *Figures in Black: Words, Signs, and the Racial Self* (New York and Oxford: Oxford University Press, 1987), 244, 246.

52. Hortense J. Spillers. "The Permanent Obliquity of an In(pha)llibly Straight: In the Time of the Daughters and the Fathers" in *Black Literature Criticism, Volume I,* edited by James Draper (Detroit: Gale Research Inc.), 1992, 706.

53. Mary Rohrberger. "'Ball the Jack': Surreality, Sexuality, and the Role of Women in *Invisible Man*" in *Approaches to Teaching Ellison's Invisible Man*, edited by Susan Resneck Parr and Pancho Savery (New York: The Modern Language Association of America, 1989), 130, 131.

54. Claudia Tate. "Notes on the Invisible Women in Ralph Ellison's *Invisible Man*," in *Speaking for You: The Vision of Ralph Ellison*, edited by Kimberly W. Benston (Washington, D.C.: Howard University Press, 1987), 167, 166, 170.

55. Saul Bellow. "Preface." The Collected Essays of Ralph Ellison, ed. John F. Callahan (New York: Random House, 1995), 1X.

56. Michael Harper. "Introduction." *The Carleton Miscellany* 18 (1980), 7.

57. Busby, 142.

58. Stanley Crouch. "The Oklahoma Kid." *The New Republic* (May 9, 1994), 23, 24.

59. John F. Callahan. "The American Scholar(s): Inaugural Address of the Morgan S. Odell Professorship in the Humanities," March 14, 1995, 12.

60 *Juneteenth, Publisher's Weekly*, March 22, 1999, p. 68.

61. Quoted in Callahan, "The American Scholar(s)," 12.

Chronology

1914 — Ralph Waldo Ellison born 1 March in Oklahoma City. His father, Lewis Ellison, was an independent businessman selling coal and ice and his mother, Ida Milsap Ellison, a church steward and a social activist, was a strong supporter of Eugene Debs's Socialist Party. Ellison's parents had left Georgia in search of a freer life for themselves and their family in the West. Unlike African American writers such as Richard Wright and Zora Neale Hurston, who grew up in rigidly segregated parts of the Deep South which confronted them with harsh social environments and extreme economic hardship, Ellison was raised in a southwestern state which was only seven years removed from its status as a territory. Such a world, although far from being a model of democratic fairness and racial justice, was in Ellison's view, a world of "possibility" encouraging him to pursue many options which would have been denied to him had he grown up in the South.

1917 — Ellison's father dies, plunging the family into poverty. His mother works as a maid to support the family. Although Ellison faced economic hardship for much of his childhood, his mother provided him and his brother Herbert with books and magazines from the white houses in which she worked and strongly encouraged both sons to excel in school and pursue higher education. Ellison remembered his childhood as deeply influenced by his mother's social activism and her respect for education.

1920-1929 — Growing up in Oklahoma City, Ellison reads widely in books borrowed at the Paul Laurence Dunbar Library, works many odd jobs as a waiter, elevator operator, newspaper boy, shoeshine boy, and drug store clerk. He develops what would become a life-long fascination with oral story-telling, listening with keen ears to the yarns and tall tales told by people he encountered at work and in his neighborhood.

1929-1933 — Attends Frederick Douglass High School, whose principal Inman Page was the first black person to receive a doctorate from Brown University. He plays varsity football and becomes an accomplished trumpeter in the school band. (By the time he was eighteen, Ellison had spent twelve years studying and playing music ranging from classical works to jazz.) Ellison's keen interest in music is further intensified by Oklahoma City's unusually rich jazz culture. Ellison hears at various local theaters and night spots many important jazz musicians, including Jimmy Rushing, Lester Young, King Oliver, Ida Cox, and "Hot Lips" Page. He plays trumpet for several jazz combos and sits in during rehearsals with Page's Old Blue Devil's band.

1933-1935 He leaves Oklahoma City to pursue a degree in music and music theory at Tuskegee Institute, one of the major centers for the study of music in the South. Pursuing his ambition to be a composer of symphonies, Ellison studies with composer Walter L. Dawson. While at Tuskegee, however, Ellison experiences first-hand the full severity of southern segregation and this leaves a lasting impression on him.

Ellison's college years were also a time when he immersed himself actively in a variety of other arts, including painting, sculpture, and poetry. He takes English classes from Morteza Drexel Sprague (to whom he later dedicates *Shadow and Act*) and becomes seriously interested in modern literature. During his second year at Tuskegee he develops a particularly keen interest in James Joyce's fiction and T.S. Eliot's poetry, both of which suggest to him ways of integrating classical mythology and folk art with complex modernist techniques. He is particularly influenced by Eliot's *The Waste Land* and "Tradition and the Individual Talent."

1936 After having completed his junior year at Tuskegee, Ellison is forced to leave college when technical difficulties with his scholarship leave him without sufficient funds for his senior year. He goes to New York in hopes of studying sculpture and earning enough money as a musician to return to Tuskegee to complete his education.

The Harlem which Ellison experienced was an extremely rich cultural environment, a thriving center of African American art, music, and literature. In his second day in Harlem Ellison meets Langston Hughes, with whom he develops a close friendship. Hughes introduces him to novelist Richard Wright who encourages him to become a writer. Ellison also studies sculpture with Richmond Barthe and studies symphonic music with Walter Riegger. He also immerses himself enthusiastically in the jazz culture of Harlem, forming a close friendship with Teddy Wilson and regularly attending performances at the Savoy Ballroom and Mintons where he hears the music of jazz performers such as Charley Parker, Dizzy Gillespie, Charlie Mingus and Duke Ellington.

1937 He publishes his first piece, a review of Waters Edwards Turpin's *These Low Grounds* which appeared in the leftist journal *New Challenge*. He goes to Dayton, Ohio to attend his mother's funeral and remains in Dayton with his brother Herbert for seven months. His mother's death plunges

Ellison into a period of considerable grieving and introspection. Ellison writes to Richard Wright that his mother's death marked the end of his childhood.

In Dayton Ellison renews his study of modernist writers such as Hemingway, Dostoevski, Stein and Joyce, committing himself to a career as a fiction writer. He writes several short stories in the manner of Hemingway and begins work on a novel, part of which survives as the story "Slick Gonna Learn."

1938 After returning home to New York, Ellison receives, with Wright's assistance, a job as a researcher in the Federal Writer's Project and works in that job for four years. His work puts him in regular contact with professional writers and deepens his interest in African American folk art and history. One of his projects consists of serious and sustained research on the history of black people in New York and another project focuses on urban folklore. Ellison's work requires him to interview many Harlem residents as a way of documenting their personal histories, songs, tales, toasts, and boasts. His four years of work with the WPA in Harlem convinces him that black folk art provides an important key to understanding African American experience.

1939 He publishes his first short story, "Slick Gonna Learn" in the September issue of *Direction*. This story is written in a "hard-boiled" realistic style in the manner of Hemingway, Wright, Dreiser, and Farrell.

1940 Ellison publishes "The Birthmark" in *The New Masses*, another story employing a harshly realistic style to express proletarian themes. This story is selected by John O'Brien to appear in the volume *The Best Stories of 1940*.

1942 Ellison quits the Federal Writer's Project and becomes managing editor of *Negro Quarterly*. This move reflects his growing dissatisfaction with radical leftist politics and his growing desire to explore black American culture independently from any political ideologies or agendas which might narrow his focus or distort his findings.

1943 He covers the Harlem riot for the *New York Post*, a historical event which later becomes the basis for the riot sequence in *Invisible Man*.

Because he wanted to contribute to the war effort but did not want to serve in the segregated armed forces, Ellison joins the Merchant Marine. During his two-year stay there, he found substantial time for writing and began a novel entitled "In a Strange Country." This book centered on a black pilot imprisoned in a German concentration camp.

1944 Ellison publishes two of his finest short stories, "King of the Bingo Game" and "Flying Home," in *Cross Section*. These stories represent a significant break from his earlier published fiction since they employ complex mixtures of realism and symbolism to explore existentialist rather than naturalistic themes. They clearly show Ellison moving toward a distinctive voice and vision which he will later use in *Invisible Man*.

1945 Contracting a kidney disease and suffering from exhaustion, Ellison takes sick leave and spends the summer at a friend's farm in Waitsfield, Vermont. He stops work on his war novel and begins writing *Invisible Man*. He receives a Rosenwald Grant which allows him to work full-time on the novel.

1946 He marries Fanny McConnell, a graduate of Fick University and the University of Chicago who had worked for the Urban League in New York and was Executive Director of the American Center for Burma at the time of their marriage.

1947 What would later become the "battle royal" episode of *Invisible Man* is published in the October issue of *Horizon*. For the next five years he works steadily on *Invisible Man*.

1952 'Invisible Man: Prologue to a Novel" is published in the January-February issue of *Partisan Review* and the entire novel is published later that year. Reviews are largely positive, hailing Ellison as an important new voice in postwar American fiction.

1953 *Invisible Man* receives the National Book Award. The jury, which included Irving Howe, Howard Mumford Jones, and Alfred Kazin, cited Ellison for possessing an "exuberance of narrative gifts" and breaking away from "the conventions and patterns of the well-made novel." They also praised Ellison for having "the courage to take many literary risks" and succeeding with them. Ellison also wins the Russwurn Award and The Certificate of Award from the *Chicago Defender*.

1954 Ellison wins a Rockefeller Foundation Award and is selected to give a lecture tour in Germany. He also lectures at the Salzburg Seminar in Austria.

1955-1956 Ellison is awarded the Prix de Rome Fellowship from the American Academy of Arts and Letters. He spends two years touring and lecturing in Italy.

1958-1961 He teaches Russian and American literature at Bard College. He works on the Hickman stories, intending them to be parts of an ambitious novel of

American and African American life from approximately 1920 to 1960. "And Hickman Arrives" is published in *Noble Savage* and "The Roof, the Steeple and the People" is published in *Quarterly Review of Literature*. Over the next fifteen years Ellison publishes six more Hickman stories but is unable to complete the novel for which they were intended.

1964 *Shadow and Act*, a collection of essays on literature, music, art, and American culture, is published. Ellison teaches at Rutgers and Yale Universities.

1965 *Invisible Man* is selected in a *Book Week* poll as the most distinguished post-World War II American novel.

1967 The 368-page manuscript of the Hickman novel is destroyed by a fire in Ellison's summer home in Plainfield, Massachusetts.

1969 Ellison receives the Medal of Freedom from President Lyndon B. Johnson. But he also comes under increasing attack from younger black writers and critics for not opposing the Vietnam War and for not endorsing the Black Power and Black Arts movements.

1970 André Malraux, the Minister of Cultural Affairs in France, awards Ellison the Chevalier de l'Order des Artes et Lettres. Ellison becomes the Albert Schweitzer Professor of Humanities at New York University, a chair he occupies for ten years.

1971 He receives honorary doctorates from Adelphi University and Long Island University.

1973 Cadillac Flambé is published in *American Review*.

1974 He is awarded honorary doctorates from The College of William and Mary, Harvard College, and Wake Forest University.

1975 He is elected to the American Academy of Arts and Letters.

1986 *Going to the Territory*, a series of essays on American and African American culture, is published.

1994 Ellison dies on 16 April.

Overview: A Conversation with Ralph Ellison

Study and Experience: An Interview with Ralph Ellison

Robert B. Stepto and Michael S. Harper

Stepto: Both you and Wright strove to read, and strove to write, but I think the situations were quite different. What we see sometimes is that people have the theory, an ancient one, of sons wanting to slay the fathers....

Ellison: Well, Wright and I were of different backgrounds, different ages, and from different regions. What united us was our mutual interest in ideas and the craft of fiction, not some fanciful notion of father and son. I've heard the metaphor used in justification of actions taken after the disruption of friendships between younger and older writers, and inevitably it is the younger who uses it in his own defense. I don't buy it because it misnames a complicated relationship.

S: What do you mean?

E: For one thing, I mean that writers as artists are sons of many fathers, or at least the sons of many writers' *styles.* This was true even of Dostoyevsky and Henry James, and no matter what the personal relationship between two writers happens to be, unless the younger writer is a mere imitator his style will diverge from, and often negate in certain aspects, the style of his older friend. That's where the important conflict takes place and it's more or less inevitable and it only obscures matters when we drag in the father-son metaphor. Rather than a case of the son slaying the father, such rows are more like those instances wherein an unwedded mother gives her unwanted baby over for adoption. And then, after the child has been brought through the precarious period of infancy, toilet-training and whooping cough, she discovers that she has safely weathered the terrors of shame and uncertainty of her maternity and proceeds to demand the return of the child. In doing so she makes noble noises about the sacredness of motherhood and the imperiousness of the maternal instinct, and has nasty things to say about the manners, morals, and low human quality of those into whose hands she has thrust her squirming infant. Neither metaphor is really adequate, but sometimes a young writer seeks to place his infant talent in the care of an older writer whom he hopes will nurture, instruct and protect it and himself against the uncertainties that are a necessary phase of his development. But then, after he has gained confidence and achieved a sense of his own identity as a writer, he seeks to reclaim his psychological independence. Thus it seems to me that instead of seeking for a father principle, the writer, as *writer*, is seeking ways to give birth to books. And what if during his formative period a male writer is given support by a writer who is female? When he asserts values that are in conflict with hers shall we say that the son must slay the mother and thus brand him a "Mother"? Or if both writers are women do we say that the younger mother of books is slaying another mother? Seriously, a writer learns (and quite early, if he's lucky) to depend upon the authority of his own experience and intuition. He must learn to dominate them, but these are his capital and his guide, his compass and crud-detector, his sword and his cross; and he defers to the authority of others at the peril of his artistic individuality. His drive is to achieve his own artistic possibilities by whatever artistic means necessary. Of course a young writer may have feelings of dependency that have their source in areas of his personality that are not necessarily linked to his drive toward expression and would be present even if he were without artistic talent. But in the writer, in the artist, such feelings of dependency find relief in the action of creation.

S: So how do you view the relationship between a younger and older writer where one is established and the other just beginning?

E: If we stick to the father-son metaphor I'd say that, given a reasonable degree of psychological independence on the part of the younger man, it would be difficult to decide who at any given moment is in the position of "father," who of "son." Such relationships are dramatic; it is a matter of give and take. Insight is determined less by chronological age than by the density of one's felt experience and by one's consciousness of implication. A younger man whose adolescence was spent in a big city might well possess insights of which an older man whose formative period was spent in a small town may be innocent. I speak of possibilities, and of course the reverse is often true, with the small town providing experiences and insights difficult to come by in densely structured cities. Anyway, I would think that when a younger man designates an older writer as his symbolic father he would keep his projection subjective, miming it rather than giving it utterance.

Because to name his attitude would be to concede far more to another than most assertive young men (and writers are very assertive types, at least psychologically) would wish to admit. What Kenneth Burke terms "courtship" is implicit in friendship, which is a relationship between, shall we say, two consenting adults who "woo" one another. In such relationships there are risks for both participants. For awhile the older writer might consider it flattering to be elected the "father" of a gifted symbolic "son," there is also the possibility that he might be repelled by the responsibility of that role. Remember that both Hawthorne and Henry James regarded the imposition of one's will upon the freedom of another as a sin against democratic individuality and gave considerable attention to the theme in their fiction. The lessons of his own experience, his own apprenticeship, might lead the older writer to feel that his young friend should undergo the risks that are part of the task of achieving an artistic identity. These risks are a part of his extended initiation. And if he is in fact psychologically mature enough to act out the "father" role he will have learned that artists are self-creating types--or at least that they tend to *pretend* that they are--and thus in their efforts in this direction they're apt to savage those into whose hands they've delivered themselves. Then there is a wavery line between the pieties of friendship and the subjective compulsion which writers feel to project their individual visions. Each writer interprets life as he sees it, and in the conflict of passion and insight which occurs when writers strive to project their individual visions, the son-slaying-the-father metaphor becomes a source of needless confusion. Writers of different backgrounds and generations often disagree because they seek to make unique works of art out of the subjectivity of diverse experiences which are connected objectively by duration and by issues arising from within the social scene in which they find themselves. If friendships between writers are not strong enough to overcome these built-in sources of conflict and competition, they fail, but if the relationship has been fruitful it finds continuity in the works of art that came into being during the quiet moments of antagonistic cooperation which marked the relationship.

S: Still the father/son metaphor persists . . .

E: Yes, but let's not forget that often it isn't the self-justifying younger writer who drags it in, it is done by outsiders; this, perhaps, because it seems to simplify the relationship between an older and younger artist. It allows for a facile sense of continuity between the generations of artists and does away with the mystery surrounding the nature of artistic influence. This is especially true of those who look at culture in strictly racial terms; people, let us say, who don't know what to make of Richard Wright's early apprentice relationship with James T. Farrell. Here I'm reminded of an incident that occurred back when I still thought of myself as a musician.

Shortly after arriving in New York from Tuskegee I wrote one of my teachers, that among other exciting developments, I had made the acquaintance of a famous artist. In return I received an enthusiastic letter in which my teacher said in effect, "Isn't it wonderful to be sitting at the feet of such an artist and to have the privilege of breathing in the intellectual atmosphere which he exudes?" Oh, Lord! My reaction was to hit the ceiling. I wasn't particularly overt in my youthful arrogance, but my teacher's well-meaning interpretation of that relationship outraged me. For awhile I realized that the man had much to teach me about art (far more, in fact, than most of the older writers whom I found incapable of discussing writing techniques with any precision). I also realized that he was far from being an intellectual. Not only was he innocent of a serious interest in ideas, but he hadn't *begun* to read the books that I had read, even before entering college.

And yet in the romantic imagination of my delighted teacher this man had been cast in the role of my intellectual "father"--simply because he had achieved a fairly broad reputation and was some years my senior. So given such misinterpretations the objective complexity of such relationships can get lost and can happen whether the younger individual is *looking* for a "father" or not.

But then again, most friendships have their vague areas of mystery and the older member of a relationship between writers might himself project the younger in a role which obscures the extent of his intellectual maturity or the extent and variety of his experience. One of my early experiences with Dick Wright involved such an underestimation, with him assuming that I hadn't read many books with which I was, in fact, quite familiar.

S: What sorts of things did he assume you hadn't read?

E: Well, among others, he assumed that I hadn't read any of Marx . . . Conrad . . . Dostoyevsky . . . Hemingway--and so on. I was somewhat chagrined by his apparent condescension, but instead of casting him in the role of misunderstanding "father," I swallowed my pride and told myself, "Forget it, you know what you know; so now learn what he thinks of in terms of his Marxism and the insights he's gained as a developed writer of fiction." And that was the way it went. At the time he was already working on *Native Son* and possessed a conscious world view, while I had only begun to write, had no consciously formulated philosophy or way of structuring what I had read and experienced. So I listened and learned even when I disagreed. Speaking of fathers: I lost my own at the age of three, lost a step-father when I was about ten, and had another at the time I met Wright. I was quite touchy about those who'd inherited my father's position as head of my family and I had no desire, or need, to cast Wright or anyone else, even symbolically, in such a role.

However, his underestimation did make for a certain irony in our relationship; because sometimes, thanks to my own reading and quite different experience, I was in a position to have made suggestions for solving problems from which he might have benefited. But since I recognized that his subjective image of me did not encourage the acceptance of certain levels of advice, I usually kept my opinions to myself.

S: To what extent does Wright's essay, "Blueprint for Negro Literature," represent his thinking when you were seeing him in New York in the late thirties and early forties?

E: That essay was written rather early. Wright had come to New York in June, 1937 and I met him the day after. He was preparing it for the first issue of *New Challenge,* of which he was an editor. Yes, I think it was a projection of his current thinking. It was polemical in relationship to the current line of the Communist Party, and his emphasis on nationalism, on how to deal with "Negro nationalism" (or "black chauvinism" as it was termed) was influenced by Joseph Stalin's pamphlet on the *National Question.* Wright was attempting to square the official communist "line" with certain resentments entertained by black communists as a result of their experience of American racism, some of which they found within the party. And as a writer he was struggling to work out an orientation for himself as one whose background lay in certain areas of Afro-American culture.

S: One thing that has troubled me about that essay, and I wonder if it troubled you, is the extent to which "folk materials" fall under the rubric of nationalism for him. That seems to me to be a rather limiting term for our various cultural traditions.

E: Actually, he was trying to work within the definitions of the Communist Party, which viewed Afro-Americans officially as a "nation" with geographical roots in the Black Belt of the South; a line which led some critics to hold that ultimately the white communists planned to segregate the blacks by herding them into the South and isolating them. I think that Wright was actually trying to deal with the confusion between race and culture within the limitations of communist theory. He held that "nationalism" was not the "black chauvinism" for which it was taken by white communists, and defined it as an "emotional expression of group feeling." However, I can't be too certain, since it's been years since I was familiar with the essay. I do know that Wright's attitude toward our Afro-American background was mixed. As a communist intellectual he appeared to consider Afro-American culture "naive" and "humble." But then, in *Twelve Million Black Voices,* he makes lyrical use of certain folk materials. It isn't an easy question because at the time Wright was so embattled; fighting the official line of the Communist Party, defending himself against the anti-intellectual attacks of certain black communist leaders, attacking in turn those writers and intellectuals whom he considered "bourgeois Negroes." On a more objective level, however, his *Blueprint* was a projection of his own plan for action and, I would suggest, a manifesto through which he was announcing his authoritative assumption of literary and intellectual leadership. He was utterly serious in this independent assertion of leadership, but just as serious in his effort to maintain party discipline while remaining loyal to his racial experience.

Perhaps the last was why he was so embattled with those he considered bourgeois Negroes. He had little tact in dealing with them and I don't think that he was aware that his failure to communicate was often his own fault. He told me of an incident in which he went to a party at one of the colleges near Chicago where he was outraged to see that the black students were attired in tuxedos and evening dresses. As far as Wright was concerned, this alone marked them as "bourgeois" and I'm sure that his attitude made for the poor communication which resulted. His sartorial distrust of the group was reinforced by his communist ideology. However, Bill Attaway, the novelist, was present and although Attaway was not the intellectual that Wright was, he was certainly close to our Afro-American folk tradition--perhaps even closer than Wright--and a rather marvelous teller of folktales and a serious writer in his own right. I suppose it was a matter of Wright's having seen the clothing and missed the people, a matter of an ideology-grounded, "trained-incapacity" to respect or communicate with Negroes who were formally educated. Perhaps it is one of the purposes of ideology to render it unnecessary to deal with human complexity. At any rate, you've raised questions that require scholary investigation. In his essay on T. E. Lawrence, Malraux has stated that in revolutionary histories what runs counter to revolutionary convention (here let us say "ideology") is suppressed more imperiously than embarrassing episodes in private memoirs. I've always been struck by the fact that in the account which Wright gives in *Black Boy* of his running away from Mississippi he fails to reveal that the boys who helped him steal the canned goods and other articles with which he made his escape were, in fact, Zack and Wilson Hubert, the sons of the late President Hubert of Jackson College. This was a rather interesting detail to omit, I thought, from the account of one who was usually so sensitive to the class divisions within the Afro-American group. I happened to have known Zack and Wilson at the time their father was president of Langston University out in Oklahoma and found them rather lively and attractive young men. But perhaps it was a matter of conscious selectivity, of Wright's keeping his class views neat by filtering out certain contradictions that might have embarrassed his ideologically structured projection of experience. Perhaps their having been, or become, in his estimation "middle class" was inconvenient to the larger point he was making.

S: I guess one reason I have been thinking more and more about Wright is because we seem to be in a period of renewed interest in him. Why do you think this is so? Is this merely something cyclical, or is it something akin to the temper of the times?

E: Basically it's because he was a powerful writer and even though many of the solutions he offered were obviously inadequate, the issues which he explored haven't gone away. But I think much of it was stirred up by the Black Aesthetic people, who are *badly* in need of a hero, and an answer to James Baldwin's criticism of Wright. Now with Wright safely out of the way they can shape him and his work to their own convenience. Some of them would make him an outright cultural racist by way of giving authority to their own biases and confusions. But I think there is another reason: By now several generations of young people have been taught *Native Son* and *Black Boy* in high schools and colleges. After all, given a decade of emphasis upon "blackness" and "militancy," how many writers of Wright's stature are there to conjure with? It doesn't matter to the "Black Aesthetic" crowd that in tailoring him to suit their own threadbare arguments they are forced to overlook the fact that he was more concerned--at least during the period when his most powerful books were written--with Marxist-Leninist-Stalinist ideology than with even his own version of "black nationalism." He wasn't, as they say, in their "bag" at all; yet that's where they've sought to cram him, no matter that his head and limbs refuse to accommodate their efforts.

It would seem that these black "Black Aestheticians" are so hung up on race and color that they tend to imitate that species of worm which maintains its ranks by following a scent laid down by the leader. Introduce them to the rim of a swill barrel, let the leader negotiate one circle of the rim and even though you remove him the rest will continue to circle the swill indefinitely. It doesn't matter that the leader might have been taken off and gone on to become metamorphosed into a butterfly and flown away, they keep on circling. Frequently it appears that somebody or some thing has staked off a certain area of thought and endeavor and said, "Here, this is yours; this is where you're to stay and we've marked it 'Black' so that you can be safe and comfortable. Therefore you stay right there and everything will be O.K.--You hear?" And oh, how so many Afro-American would-be intellectuals agree. They can't seem to imagine that books or authors that fail to mention "Black" explicitly might be of crucial importance in dealing with their own racial, cultural, and individual dilemmas. Thus it's ironic to see these people embracing Wright, because his was anything but such an attitude. In his effort to make some sort of intellectual *Gestalt* for himself, he read all kinds of books, entertained all kinds of ideas. And during the days when I knew him well he certainly didn't allow racial considerations to limit the free play of his intellect. After all, most of his friends, like both of his wives, were white.

S: Well, you mention the Black Aesthetic crowd: On the one hand, we have their interest in Wright, yet on the other we have very little fiction produced by these writers, these writer-critics. Why, in your opinion, don't they write fiction? Is it because of conventional notions of the novel being a bourgeois art form, or is it because a novel is so damn hard to write (laughter)?

E: I can tell you this: they're damn hard for me! As for the others, I have no idea. I don't know most of those people, even though many seem to feel that we have a personal quarrel. But to put it into the vernacular, I would think that there's a heap of shucking going on and none of it stacks. They find it easier to issue militant slogans while remaining safely in the straight-jacket of racist ideology--the ideology that has been made of what they call "Blackness"--than to deal with either the beautiful and confounding complexities of Afro-American culture or the difficulties that must be faced by those who would convert experience into the forms of the novel. If they can't grasp the meaning of what they live and read because their obsession with the mysticism of race and color has incapacitated their ability to see, then they certainly can't subject themselves to the discipline demanded by the novel. Which, after all, is a product of the *integrative* and *analytical* play of the imagination as it seeks to convert experience into forms of symbolic action. How can one abstract Afro-American experience from that of the larger culture of which it is so important a part without reducing it, in the name of "Blackness," to as vapid a collection of stereotypes as those created in the name of whiteness? As I say, imagination itself is *integrative,* a matter of making symbolic wholes out of parts. Afro-American culture is itself a product of that process carried on under the most difficult social and political conditions. Thus it would seem to me that any objective approach to its dynamics would lead to the basic conclusion that, here in the U.S. at least, culture has successfully confounded all concepts of race. American culture would not exist without its Afro-American component, or if it did, it would be quite different. Yet, certain people who are fixed on the concept of race at the expense of culture would claim Alexander Dumas as a true blue "Boot," "Race Man," or what not, but this is to ignore his achievement, the language in which he thought and wrote, and the image which he held of himself. All this by way of elevating a part of his blood line to a position of total (really totalitarian) importance.

But not only was Dumas culturally a Frenchman, he was a Frenchman who worked and achieved himself in the novel, a literary form which in itself was influenced by developments taking place in England, in Germany and in Russia. Such people also claim Pushkin as their own, and not because of the fact that he was the father of modern Russian literature, but because there was an African or Ethiopian in his background. The relationship between biology and culture is mysterious; perhaps General Hannibal's sperm was precisely what was needed to release the greatness of Russian literature. But although he was a distinguished military man and engineer in his own right, we know of him mainly because of his great-grandson's *literary* achievements, not for his influence upon the Russian racial mixture. I suppose what I'm saying is that an over-emphasis on our own racial origins in Africa (an origin which is only partial) at the expense of the way in which our cultural expression has transcended race, our present social status and our previous condition of servitude, is to ignore much of what is most intriguing and admirable in Afro-American experience. Worse, it is to miss the fact that American culture owes much of its distinctiveness to idioms which achieved their initial formulation through the cultural creativity of Afro-Americans. White Americans have put tremendous energy into keeping the black American below the threshold of social mobility but they still had to descend to see what Negroes were making of the new democratic experience, in order to know what to make of their own. This was especially true of the vernacular idiom in the arts, where lessons were to be learned in everything from power to elegance.

S: So what are we to make of people who say, in echo of a certain black poet, that the black masses are uninterested in elegance?

E: To accept that notion you've got to have a tin ear and absolutely no eye for style. Elegance turns up in every aspect of Afro-American culture, from sermons to struts, pimp-walks and dance steps. Listen to a sermon by Howard Thurman or the Reverend Franklin, father of the famous singer. Listen to Jimmy Rushing sing the *How Long Blues.* Listen to Basie, listen to Ellington; watch 0. J. Simpson slice through an opposing line with a dancer's slithering grace. And doesn't all that Afro-American adoration of the Cadillac speak of elegance? Look at the elegance with which the dedicated worshiper of the Cadillac sits at the steering wheel of his chariot. If Bill Robinson and Honi Coles weren't elegant tap dancers, I don't know the meaning of the term. And if Louis Armstrong's meditations on the "Potato Head Blues" aren't marked by elegance, then the term is too inelegant to name the fastidious refinement, the mastery of nuance, the tasteful domination of melody, rhythm, sounding brass and tinkling cymbal which marked his style. Aesthetically speaking, when form is blended successfully with function, elegance results. Black Americans expect elegance even from prizefighters and basketball players and much of the appeal of Jack Johnson and Joe Louis sprang from the fact that each was as elegant as the finest of ballet dancers.

Such statements are products of ideological foolishness and are efforts to palm off sloganeering doggerel as poetry. Surprisingly, the verse of some of these people gives the lie to their assertions, for it reveals as much of the influence of e. e. cummings and Emily Dickinson as of Langston Hughes or Sterling Brown. Blacks alone didn't invent poetics any more than they invented the American language; and the necessary mixture of cultural influences that goes into creating an individual poetic style defies the neat oversimplifications of racist ideologies. Some of the "Black Aesthetic" people say that nothing written before 1967 is of any value, but I'm pretty sure that those who do would *not* say that nothing done in surgery or law before that date was valueless; but then such people don't chatter about law or surgery because they recognize that they are too difficult to be reduced to empty verbalizing. An unserious familiarity with literature breeds contempt, so they feel that they can get away with any kind of irresponsible statement. Perhaps they'd feel less secure if our people were as interested in literature as they are in music. The Kansas City physician who accidently severed the jugular of band leader Benny Moten while performing a tonsillectomy was almost lynched by his own people in their outrage over the discovery that inept medical technique could end the life of a musician whom they revered for his musical excellence. I quote an extreme instance, but sometimes Afro-Americans have been known to call their own irresponsibles to account.

S: What did you think of the *Black World* issue on your work?

E: Hell, man, what would you expect? It was obvious that I couldn't have a fair exchange of opinion with those who used the issue to tee off on me, so there was nothing to do but treat them as I had bad dogs and bigoted whites down South: Mentally, I walked away from it. Long before that issue was published they had been banging away at a hateful straw man whom they'd labeled "Ellison" and were using it as a scapegoat for their discontents and disappointments, and it appeared that the more I refused to be provoked the more strident they became. I was amused by the time they wasted attacking me when it was really a couple of *books* that were making them mad, and the only way to win a fight with a book is to write a better book. I could have respected them had they done that, but I saw little evidence that this was going to happen. However, I did appreciate the essays by those who used the issue to express serious disagreement with my work and my position on social issues. I hoped that younger writers would read them as antidotes to the rantings of those who tried to reduce literary discussion to the level of the dirty dozens. I was also amused by the extent of the bad-mouthing because the editor of *Black World* was so persistent in his attempt at scapegoating, while I continued to function very much as I had always done. Even having a bit of influence. His conception of the cultural reality of the U.S. was puzzling because he appeared to have no idea of how books can reach beyond the boundaries of the black community. He seemed to think that he could kill the influence of a novel by attacking its author. That struck me as strange, since his organ reached but a few thousand readers while my books were being read by *many* thousands.

Then there was the other contributor to the issue who gave the impression of being as eager to burn books as any Nazi *gauliter*--which was rather obscene, considering that the man is an old communist and has spent a good part of his life working in a library. His example and that of a like-minded fellow contributor demonstrated that they could be just as vehement, provincial, and totalitarian in the name of "Black Militancy" and "Black Aesthetics" as they had been in the name of "Soviet Communism" and "Socialist Realism." I guess it's a case of Reds infiltrating Blacks, running into a stubborn Negro and turning blue in the face. But I can say this for them: Safe behind the fence provided by a black capitalist, they had one big "barking-at-the-big-gate" go at me. They even managed to convince a few students that I was the worst disaster that had ever hit Afro-American writing. But for all their attacks I'm still here trying--while if I'm asked where is *Black World* today my answer is: Gone with the snows of yester-year/ down the pissoir--Da-daa, Da-daaa--and good riddance!

S: Our talk about groups reminds me of something Leon Forrest once said. He was asked if he belonged to a group or crowd, and I believe his response was, "I guess you might say that McPherson, Toni Morrison, Albert Murray, Ralph Ellison and I might constitute a crowd." Now what is your response to that?

E: It's an interesting grouping of writers whom I respect; still I am by instinct (and experience) a loner. There is no question, however, but that we share what Malraux has termed a "collectivity of sensibilities" and a high regard for the artistic potential of Afro-American experience. And certainly we're all more concerned with art than with ideology or propaganda. But as to our constituting a school, that kind of thing--no. I don't think it desirable even though it offers some relief from the loneliness of the trade. For when writers associate too closely there is a tendency to control one another's ideas. I'm not implying that association is itself necessarily a negative matter, but I suspect that the loneliness of writing causes us to seek for a kind of certainty among our peers--when very often it's the *uncertainty* of the creative process which leads to new insights and to unanticipated formulation. Nevertheless, I share ideas and certain goals with such people as Forrest and McPherson, just as I do with a number of white writers, and certainly with Al Murray, whom I've known since our days at Tuskegee; but they do their own thinking and I do mine. (I don't know Miss Morrison personally.) Perhaps Forrest was really describing a collectivity of outsiders who are united by a common attitude toward the craft.

S: He is also describing a group of *fiction* writers, and I can't help but continue to link this issue to genre . . .

E: I agree, because a writer's point of view is determined to a large extent by the form in which he works. The form shapes his sensibility, it structures his emotions, and guides his imagination and vision. That's most important: The novel is a complex agency for the symbolic depiction of experience, and it demands that the writer be willing to look at both sides of characters and issues--at least while he's working. You might say that the form of the novel imposes its morality upon the novelist by demanding a complexity of vision and an openness to the variety and depth of experience.

Kenneth Burke says that language "moralizes" both mankind and nature, thus the novel "moralizes" the novelist. Dostoyevsky could be pretty rabid in some of his ideological concerns, pretty bigoted in his attitudes toward the members of certain groups, but when he chose to depict characters identified with such groups he gave them all the human complexity that the form and action of the novel demanded. I don't think that you can do this if your mind is made up beforehand. You end up creating stereotypes, writing propaganda.

Harper: Is there any sort of organization that you now see in the fiction you've published over the years since *Invisible Man?* I've put together the fiction I've seen in various places and it seems to me that it is all of one piece--that is, I see certain kinds of relationships. For example, could one go out and collect "Song of Innocence" and "Juneteenth" and make a case for works-in-progress being sections of the same novel?

E: Yes, they *are* parts of the same novel, but whether they will remain in that relationship I don't know, because, you know, I lost a good part of the novel in a fire. It's a long manuscript, and it just might be two books.

H: I remember talking with some students at Harvard and two of them were offended by "Juneteenth" where Hickman says that Africans were heathens who didn't have any souls. They said this is a terrible thing! You got to get him up here!

E: They went on to say other things, didn't they? Did they read what was *there?*

H: Yes, but they were bothered by "heathen." Again, this is the old question of ideology. I think the source of their agitation was that they thought you were making a statement to the effect that when Americans came to this country they were soulless.

E: Oh, for God's sake! I didn't make that statement, *Hickman* did. He was preaching about transcendence; about the recovery from fragmentation; about the slave's refusal, with the help of God, to be decimated by slavery. He was speaking as a Christian minister of the role his religion had played in providing a sense of unity and hope to a people that had been deliberately deprived of a functional continuity with their religions and traditions. Hickman didn't attend college but, hell, he knew that all of our African ancestors didn't belong to the same tribe, speak the same tongue, or worship the same gods....

H: If they had proposed the argument that either Bliss or Hickman was the persona of Ralph Ellison *that* might have been debatable--it probably wasn't *right,* but it might have been debatable. The one-dimensional character, the way they view literary creation, is what bothered me. We got in a similar row over "Song of Innocence." In the mind of some students who are not familiar with literary convention and the whole business of creation, anything you write is autobiographical, it's about you.

S: This reminds me of students who write papers for me about *The Autobiography of an Ex-Coloured Man,* and begin, "When *Johnson* gets off the train in Atlanta.... [Laughter]

H: Do you get many inquiries about the chapter deleted from *Invisible Man* that appears in *Soon, One Morning?* Did you willingly cut it out?

E: Well, the book was long and they wanted cuts, and I found a better way than just cutting was to restructure. So, instead of that particular handling of the narrative sequence I just took it out. I think it would have probably worked better in.

H: Why isn't "Society, Morality and the Novel" in *Shadow and Act?* It came before.

E: I wanted to put it in but my editor said no. I think it was because we already had enough material.

S: Can you tell us about your teaching experiences? I'm especially interested in experiences resulting from attempts to teach certain texts side by side. For example, in

1970, I once began a course on the Harlem Renaissance by assigning *The Great Gatsby.* I still think it was a great idea, but the students couldn't get with it--even on the level of establishing a milieu, or "countermilieu."

E: I have had the same trouble getting that across with *Gatsby.* For instance, I find it significant that the character who saw who was driving the "death car" was a Negro; and yet, some students resist when I tie that in with Tom Buchanan's concern over the rise of the colored races, the scene in which blacks are being driven by a white chauffeur, and the characterization of the Jewish gangster. They miss the broader context of the novel that is revealed in the understated themes of race, class, and social mobility. The novel is set in what was called the Jazz Age, but what is the difference between Fitzgerald's Jazz Age and that of Duke Ellington and Louis Armstrong? I point out that Fitzgerald was familiar with Brick Top's nightclub and was often at the Harlem Cotton Club, and I suggest that after reading what Fitzgerald made of the experience the student should take a look at what Langston Hughes and other writers of the Harlem Renaissance made of it. It's ironic that some of the white writers were more open to knowledge relating to the Harlem of that period than are the black kids who refuse to study it seriously because they feel that they know it through their genes. They think affirmations of "Blackness" resolves all mysteries of time and place, circumstance and personality. But for a writer like Fitzgerald, Harlem was one of the places where the action was, so, being a good novelist, with an interest in people and an eye for exciting new developments in the culture, he went where the action was unfolding. Now we don't have to like what white writers, musicians, and dancers made of what went on, but I do think we should recognize that across the division of race they were attempting to absorb and project some of the cultural complexity of the total American scene. They were responding in their individual ways to the vitality of the Afro-American cultural idiom. The "Black Aesthetic" crowd buys the idea of total cultural separation between blacks and whites, suggesting that we've been left out of the mainstream. But when we examine American music and literature in terms of its themes, symbolism, rhythms, tonalities, idioms and images it is obvious that those rejected "Neegroes" have been a vital part of the mainstream and were from the beginning. Thus, if a student is to grasp the complex sources of American cultural tradition he should assume that a major part of that tradition springs from Afro-America; because one of the few ways the slaves and their descendants had of expressing their inner sense of identity was by imposing their own aesthetic will upon those who assumed that they would have nothing to do with defining American experience. Today sociologists, many of them the first members of immigrant families to attend college, and who now teach at universities and advise politicians, are telling us that the American melting-pot didn't melt. But despite discrimination and other inequities in the society, its various cultural idioms did, indeed, melt and are continuing to do so.

H: Don't you teach a course in the vernacular?

E: Yes, from a base in American lit. I teach a course which allows me to touch many areas of American culture. American literature grew out of the development of American vernacular speech as it asserted its modes against European tradition and proper English usage. As the young nation achieved coherence, the very pressures of Nature, of the New World "scene," forced Americans to create a flood of new terminologies: for naming the newly created social forms, the nuances of the individualism that was spreading throughout the young society, and the relationships between diverse groups. Out of the democratic principles set down on paper in the Constitution and the Bill of Rights they were improvising themselves into a nation, scraping together a conscious culture out of the various dialects, idioms, lingos, and methodologies of America's diverse peoples and regions. In this effort the English language and traditional cultural forms served both as guides and as restraints, anchoring Americans in the wisdom and processes of the past, while making it difficult for them to perceive with any clarity the nuances of their new identity. Given the reality of slavery and the denial of social mobility to blacks, it is ironic that they were placed by that very circumstance in the position of having the greatest freedom to create specifically *American* cultural idioms. Thus the slaves had the unnoticed opportunity to be culturally daring and innovative because the strictures of "good taste" and "thou shall-not" of tradition were not imposed upon them. And so, having no past in the art of Europe, they could use its elements and their inherited sense of style to improvise forms through which they could express their own unique sense of American experience. They did so in dance, in music, in cuisine and so on, and white American artists often found the slaves' improvisations a clue for their *own* improvisations. From the very beginnings of the nation Afro-Americans were contributing to the evolution of a specifically *American* culture.

H: Are you happy with your students at N.Y.U. ?

E: With some of them; you know, the quality varies from class to class. I am unhappy with the numbers who can't write. I consider myself as having had a fairly incomplete education, but as I look back I realize that even in high school there were a number of us who could write rings around some of my graduate students. Most of my students are white. I haven't had many black students, but when I work with those who are having difficulty I say to them, "All right, you are here now, so recognize that you have certain disabilities which I can't ignore. So let's not kid ourselves but face the fact that there's some catching up to be done. There's nothing wrong with your mind but there is a lot wrong with the kind of training you've had, if not then with the kind of attention you've given to learning. Face that fact and allow your experience to feed your study and you'll be surprised at how fast you can come up to par." Fortunately, a few understand that this isn't a put-down, but the truth.

The other day I had to tell a black student who wants to substitute militancy for study and who came up with an easy criticism of George Washington Carver that I didn't like Dr. Carver either, but for a specific and personal reason: At Tuskegee he was always chasing me out of Rockefeller Hall where I'd go to work out my harmonic exercises on the piano. My investigations into the mysteries of harmony interfered with his investigations of the peanut, and to me harmony was more important. But today I realize that not only did a large industry draw upon his experiments but by manipulating strains of peanuts he was growing himself an American President! Dr. Carver has been called an "Uncle Tom," but I keep looking at the announcement of prizes given in such fields as science and architecture, in biology and electronics and I'm chagrined over the fact that few of our students are getting them. Sheer militancy isn't enough, and when used as an excuse to avoid study it is disastrous. Today we're in a better way to learn and participate in the intellectual life of this country than ever before, but apparently we're taking fewer advantages of our opportunities than when we were limited to carrying bags and waiting tables. The availability of ideas and culture means little if we don't take advantage, participate, and compete with the best in our elected fields.

H: Bob and I know a folklorist who thinks you are one of the few people who really understand what folklore is and how it ought to be used. Would you care to comment on that?

E: Folklore has been such a vital part of American literature that it is amazing that more people (and especially writers) aren't aware of it. Constance Rourke points out that there are folk motives even in the work of Henry James. I guess one of the difficulties here is that people think of folklore as "quaint," as something that is projected in dialect, when in fact it is its style and wisdom that count. The same problem arises when you speak of

American folklore in the general sense and overlook the complex influence of vernacular idioms, the mixture of vernacular styles, that operate in American culture. Considering the social condition of the slaves, what is to be made of their singing a comic song which refers to a black girl's dancing "Taglioni" in the street? Or what are you going to do with fairly illiterate jazz musicians who interpolate phrases from the likes of Bach, Verdi, or Puccini in their improvisations on the Blues or popular melodies? In this country it is necessary to redefine what we mean by folklore, because, culturally, Americans are heirs to the culture of all the ages, and it is through the vernacular process that we blend folk and classical modes into an art that is uniquely American. Thus I believe it a mistake to think of the slaves as having been separate from the eclectic processes, the general culture, when in fact they were participating in it in many unexamined ways. Art was an inseparable part of their African forebearers' lives, and they did, after all, do most of the building of Monticello! They made the bricks and did the carpentry and cabinetry. Recently *The Crisis* published an article calling attention to the manner in which historians tend to omit the slave craftsmen when describing the "cultural activities" of Thomas Jefferson, but my God, somebody was there doing the work and receiving the instructions necessary for carrying it to completion. If there are doubts as to this, all one has to do is observe the demonstrations down at Colonial Williamsburg. Slaves were craftsmen and artists as well as field hands and as such they absorbed and mastered the styles and techniques around them. That's how I see it and I can't imagine a human situation that would *not* be like that.

Perhaps we have too damn much of a wound-worshiping investment in the notion that the slaves were brutalized beyond the point of exercising their human will to survive. Which reminds me of an aspect of the uproar centering around *Time on the Cross.* Whatever the viability of their methods, the authors were saying that slavery wasn't as brutalizing as the usual view would have it. They held that the slaves were *not* reduced to a gas-oven state of docility, a view that would see each and every slave master as a Hitler and American slavery as a preview of the Holocaust. I'm no historian, but their view seems to offer a more adequate accounting for the character of the ex-slaves whom I knew in Oklahoma and Alabama. After all, I did see my grandaddy and he was no beaten-down "Sambo." Rather he was a courageous, ingenious old guy who owned property, engaged in the Reconstruction politics of South Carolina, and who stood up to a mob after they had lynched his best friend. When ordered to leave town, he told the lynchers, "If you're gonna kill me, you're gonna kill me here where I've got my family, and my property and my friends." He died there years later, in his own bed, and at the age of 76. I also knew one of his friends who, after years of operating a printing business for a white man, came north and set up his own printing shop in Harlem.

The other argument that I find interesting in *Time on the Cross* is the author's statement that, while the slaves in the Caribbean and Brazil died off every ten years and had to be replaced from Africa, those in the United States managed to reproduce themselves. And of course they did! There were times when native-born blacks outnumbered native-born whites. Unlike the slaves of the other Americas, they had a good injection of white European chromosomes which made them immune to many European diseases. (Laughter!) They also became "Indianized," and certainly these biological facts show in our faces. Still, many historians and sociologists act as though these factors are irrelevant, and by ignoring them they contribute to the divisive mystification of race.

S: I pointed that out to an historian the other day, and I could tell by the look on his face that I was embarrassing him! (Laughter)

E: Then Fern Brodie published a biographical account of Jefferson's long affair with his black mistress. Why don't the historians allow these people their human complexity?

H: Well, we did!

E: That's right! (Laughter) It's amusing the way this thing works. In my class I get raised eyebrows by pointing out that race is always at the center of our uneasy preoccupation with American identity. It is as abiding as our concern with the principles of freedom and equality. Thus, when you read American literature and fail to see the words "Black" or "Negro" or "Afro-American" in a given work, it doesn't mean that they are not operating there symbolically. The old phrase "There's a nigger in the woodpile" was more fact than fantasy. Just examine the logic of a work's symbolism and you'll discover that there are surrogates for Blacks and the hierarchal motives they symbolize; just as Negroes are often surrogates for the American Indian. Once we were discussing the tragedy of the Indian, and someone said, "Yeah, the Indian, he stood up to the white man; he didn't take that crap." This went on until someone got serious and said, "Yeah, but look here man, what *happened* to them damn Indians?" And I said, "Well, don't you know? You became the damn Indians!" They laughed but I don't think that it really got across. As a child watching cowboy and Indian movies I frequently pulled for the Indians to win, but as you know, they seldom did.

H: What would you like to see people researching and writing that would begin to correct things?

E: Well, I would really like to see more studies that deal with the actual pre-Emancipation scene; works that would place people. Who was doing what jobs? And what happened to them after Emancipation, and later after the betrayal of Reconstruction? Where did people go? I'd like to see more done on the role of geography in American Negro history. Many black cowboys were slaves who, after their owners moved west, were taken out of the cotton patch and put on horses. Many Afro-American characteristics that are assumed to spring from the brutality of slavery are partially the results of geography, of the localities in which they were enslaved. Some of this is suggested by the phrase "sold down the river." The Mississippi was as tremendous a force in Afro-American history as it was in the vision of Mark Twain. The geographical division of the country into political districts and regions with complementary agricultural and economic systems underlies much of Afro-American poetic symbolism. That the star points north is not important because of some abstract, mystical or religious conception, but because it brought into conjunction Biblical references, concrete social conditions and the human will to survive including the fact that if you got safely across certain socio-geographical boundaries you were in freedom. Writers have made much of the North Star but they forget that a hell of a lot of slaves were running away to the West, "going to the nation, going to the territory," because as Mark Twain knew, that too was an area of Negro freedom. When people get to telling stories based on their cooperate experience, quite naturally such patterns turn up. Because as significant scenes in which human will is asserted, they help organize and focus narrative. They become more poetic the further we are removed from the actual experience, and their symbolic force is extended through repetition.

I'd also like to see someone write about jazz in such a way that they cover those people who are the intermediaries, the mentors, the teachers, the transmitters of classical tradition. All around the country there were musicians, bandmasters, etc. who disapproved of the jazz life but who, nevertheless, were training people to read music and to perform on instruments. People who taught voice and staged operettas, and so on. You still have them in the colleges, you have them in the towns, giving piano lessons, teaching harmony. These are the links between the classical and folk traditions and jazz.

H: Thanks for letting us visit with you this afternoon.
E: It's been my pleasure. I enjoyed it.

From *The Massachusetts Review* 18:3 (Fall 1977), 417-435.

Early Reviews of *Invisible Man*

A Review of *Invisible Man*

Orville Prescott

Ralph Ellison's first novel, *Invisible Man* is the most impressive work of fiction by an American Negro which I have ever read. Unlike Richard Wright and William Motley, who achieved their best effects by overpowering their readers with documentary detail, Mr. Ellison is a finished novelist who uses words with great skill, who writes with poetic intensity and immense narrative drive. *Invisible Man* has many flaws. It is a sensational and feverishly emotional book. It will shock and sicken some of its readers. But, whatever the final verdict on *Invisible Man* may be, it does mark the appearance of a richly talented writer.

Ralph Ellison was born in Oklahoma and educated at Tuskegee Institute. He has shined shoes and played the first trumpet in a jazz orchestra. He has studied music and sculpture, lectured on Negro culture and James Joyce, written short stories and literary criticism. In *Invisible Man* he has written a book about the emotional and intellectual hazards which beset the educated Negro in America. He has written it on two levels. The first is the level of story-telling, the second that of exaggeration, suggestion and symbolism.

Invisible Man is much more successful in the first respect, it seems to me, than in the second. Mr. Ellison has a grand flair for gaudy melodrama, for savage comedy, for emphatic characterization. He is not interested in literal, realistic truth, but in an emotional, atmospheric truth which he drives home with violence, writing about grotesquely violent situations. With gruesome power he has given *Invisible Man* the frenzied tension of a nightmare.

This is the story of the adventures, shocks, and disillusionments of a young Southern Negro, a naive idealist with a gift for spontaneous oratory, who journeys--almost like Bunyan's pilgrim--through Harlem's slough of despond, but who never reaches the other side. It is told in the first person and is divided into a series of major episodes, some lurid and erotic, some ironic and grotesque. The breathless excitement and coldly sardonic humor of many of these are superb.

The nameless narrator learns his first important lesson in disillusionment at a Southern Negro college when he discovers that the president he admired humbly is a cynical hypocrite. He learns more in a surrealistic horror of a paint factory on Long Island; more still during his service in the "Brotherhood."

The " Brotherhood" is Mr. Ellison's euphuistic synonym for the Communist Party. Why he does not call the party by its real name is a mystery. But the identification is exact, and his befuddled hero's adventures among the brothers are a fine demonstration of what he is talking about, and it is not pleasant. His hero experienced a brief hour of glory as an orator and then a permanent state of humiliation and despair. And the Harlem riot which the "Brotherhood" provoked makes a theatrical climax of looting and arson for Mr. Ellison's book.

Invisible Man is undoubtedly melodramatic; but each melodramatic incident represents some aspect of the Negro's plight in America, or of his response to it. To this extent Mr. Ellison's novel is sharp and clear. But *Invisible Man* is not all melodrama. Parts of it consist of long and impassioned, sometimes hysterical, reveries which are frequently highly obscure. Other parts still seem grotesquely exaggerated or repetitious. And these strange interludes are overwritten in an ultra pretentious, needlessly fancy way. Spasms of torrential rhetoric, they obscure the point of some of Mr. Ellison's symbolical incidents and check temporarily the swift course his story.

The bewildered and nameless hero of *Invisible Man* longs desperately to achieve a personal success and to help his people. But his role as a man acted upon more often than acting, as a symbol of doubt, perplexity, betrayal and defeat, robs him of the individual identity of the people who play a part in his life. These, while not subtly portrayed, have a vibrant life which makes them seem real and interesting. They include Dr. Bledsoe, the sanctimonious and unscrupulous college president; Mr. Norton, the Boston millionaire benefactor of the college; Lucius Brockway, psychopathic engineer in the paint factory; "Ras, the Exhorter," rabble-rouser and street prophet; Brother Jack, one-eyed and ruthless member of the "Brotherhood" committee.

Invisible Man is tough, brutal and sensational. It is uneven in quality. But it blazes with authentic talent. No one interested in books by or about American Negroes should miss it.

From *The New York Times* (April 16, 1952), 23.

A Negro in America

Irving Howe

This novel is a searing and exalted record of a Negro's journey through contemporary America in search of success, companionship, and, finally, himself; like all our fictions devoted to the idea of experience, it moves from province to city, from naive faith to disenchantment; and despite its structural incoherence and occasional pretentiousness of manner, it is one of the few remarkable first novels we have had in some years.

The beginning is a nightmare. A Negro boy, timid and compliant, comes to a white smoker Southern town: he is to be awarded a scholarship. Together with several other Negroes he is rushed to the front of the ballroom, where a sumptuous blonde tantalizes and frightens them by dancing in the nude. Blindfolded, the Negro boys stage a "battle royal," a free-for-all in which they pummel each other to the drunken shouts of the whites. "Practical jokes," humiliations, terrors—and then the boy delivers a prepared speech of gratitude to his white benefactors.

Nothing, fortunately, in the rest of the novel is quite so harrowing. The unnamed hero goes to his Southern college and is expelled for having innocently taken a white donor through a Negro gin-mill; he then leaves for New York, where he works in a factory, becomes a soapboxer for the Harlem Communists, a big wheel in the Negro world, and the darling of the Stalinist bohemia; and finally, in some not quite specified way, he "finds himself" after witnessing a frenzied riot in Harlem.

Though immensely gifted, Ellison is not a finished craftsman. The tempo of his book is too feverish, and at times almost hysterical. Too often he tries to overwhelm the reader, and usually he does; but when he should be doing something other than overwhelm, when he should be persuading or suggesting or simply telling, he forces and tears.

Because the book is written in the first person singular, Ellison cannot establish an ironic distance between his hero and himself, or between the matured "I" telling the story and the "I" who is its victim. And because the experience is so apocalyptic and magnified, it absorbs and then dissolves the hero; every minor character comes through brilliantly, but the seeing "I" is seldom seen.

The middle section of the novel concerns the Harlem Stalinists, and it is the only one that strikes me as not quite true. Writing with evident bitterness, Ellison makes his Stalinists so stupid and vicious that one cannot understand how they could have attracted him. I am ready to believe that the Communist Party manipulates its members with conscious cynicism, but I am certain that this cynicism is both more guarded and complex than Ellison assumes; surely no Stalinist leader would tell a prominent Negro member,

"You were not hired to think"—even if that were what he secretly felt. The trouble with such caricature is that it undermines the intention behind it, making the Stalinists seem not the danger they are but mere clowns.

Equally disturbing is Ellison's apparent wish to be intellectually up-to-date. As his hero quits the Communist Party, he wonders: "Could politics ever be an expression of love?" This portentous and perhaps meaningless question, whatever its place in a little magazine, is surely inappropriate to a character who has been presented mainly as a passive victim of experience. Nor am I persuaded by the hero's final discovery that "my world has become one of infinite possibilities," his refusal to be the invisible man whose body is manipulated by various social groups. Though the unqualified assertion of individuality is at the moment a favorite notion of literary people, it is also a vapid one, for the unfortunate fact remains that to define one's individuality is to stumble over social fences that do not allow one "infinite possibilities." It is hardly an accident that Ellison's' hero does not even attempt to specify those possibilities.

These faults mar "Invisible Man" but do not destroy it. For Ellison has an abundance of that primary talent without which neither craft nor intelligence can save a novelist; he is richly, wildly inventive; his scenes rise and dip with tension; his people bleed, his language stings. No other writer has captured so much of the confusion and agony, the hidden gloom and surface gaiety of Negro life. His ear for Negro speech is magnificent: a sharecropper calmly describing how he seduced his own daughter, a Harlem street-vender spinning jive, a West Indian woman inciting her men to resist an eviction. The rhythm of the prose is harsh and tensed, like a beat of a harried alertness. The observation is expert: Ellison knows exactly how zoot-suiters walk, making stylization their principle of life, and exactly how the antagonism between American and West Indian Negroes works itself out in speech and humor. For all his self-involvement, he is capable of extending himself toward his people, of accepting them as they are, in their blindness and hope. And in his final scene he has created an unforgettable image: "Ras the Destroyer," a Negro nationalist, appears on a horse dressed in the costume of an Abyssinian chieftain, carrying spears and shield, and charging wildly into the police—a black Quixote, mad, absurd, yet unbearably pathetic.

Some reviewers, from the best of intentions, have assured their readers that this is a good novel and not merely a good Negro novel. But of course, "Invisible Man" is a Negro novel—what white man could ever have written it? It is drenched in Negro life, talk, music; it tells us how distant even the best of whites are from the black men that pass them on the streets; and it is written from a particular compound of emotions that no white man could possibly simulate. To deny that this is a Negro novel is to deprive Negroes of their one basic right: the right to cry out their difference.

From *The Nation* (May 10, 1952), 454.

Black and Blue: A Negro Céline

William Barrett

Because of his achievements in popular music, jazz and spirituals, we must count the Negro as perhaps the greatest artistic potential in America today. In literature, the obstacles to his self-expression have been greater, in good part because of the stereotypes of character the white man has forced upon him, so that thus far we have had only premonitory flashes, brilliant but brief, as in the touching and amusing pathos of a Langston Hughes, or in the thunderous--but also somewhat abstract--social protest of a Richard Wright. Now, however, a new novel has just appeared, Ralph Ellison's *Invisible Man*, which marks a sensational entry by the Negro into high literature.

There is social protest in Ellison's book, to be sure--how could one write honestly about the Negro and avoid this?--but it differs from Richard Wright in grappling with the whole inner problem of the Negro as a human person; rather than as a mere social abstraction symbolizing an exploited class, and with a hero immensely more complex and intellectual than Wright's Bigger Thomas. Apart from Ellison's artistic and technical powers, which are considerable, it is just this unflinching spiritual search on his part to find out what it really means to be a Negro that makes his book, to my mind, the first considerable step forward in Negro literature.

Ellison calls his hero an "Invisible Man" because he cannot be seen by other people in our society--neither by the whites nor by his fellow blacks, neither by reactionaries nor by Communists. And they do not see him for what he is because they refuse to see him. Which is to say; they refuse to grant him his own identity, or even the possibility of one. Ellison's novel, told in the first person, is a record of the search by this "I" for his denied identity.

Here the author has got hold of a theme as big as America itself, certainly a theme larger than the "Negro problem" alone, however special a slant the Negro may have upon it. It is a fact, perhaps the basic fact, of our national psychology that the American, in general, is not yet quite sure of his own identity. And the Negro, as *the* insulted and injured of our society, has only experienced this drama of the national soul in a more abysmal way than the rest of us. People in older civilizations--say, the Englishman or the Frenchman--have behind them centuries of a settled and defined culture, which serves as a mirror in which they can see their own features and find their own identity. The American, on the contrary, exists in a new, evolving and fluid society that does not offer him any external image of his own individual possibilities and meaning. He and his new civilization are adventurers on the surface of the planet; and like all adventures, in history or in legend, his adventure is a quest, and in the last analysis every quest is a quest for oneself.

Thus it is no paradox to maintain, as one well-known authority on Negro culture has done, that the Negro really represents the American in his pure state. America, after all, is made up of immigrant stocks, and the Negro is only one among these groups, the most discriminated against and therefore, too, the group that faces the possibilities of American life more nakedly than the rest. If an American is first-, second-, or even third-generation Italian, Irish, Jewish, or what have you, he is bound to feel the drag of this foreign past upon him as he confronts life in this country; at the same time, he is so alien from his ancestors that he can never again hope to take their identity upon himself. This leaves him something of a divided being (and the division may be all the sharper for being buried deeper in the unconscious), torn between his ancestral past and his American future. He tries desperately to find himself in the New World by losing every trace of the Old Country. But that past is still there, troubling or exalting him. For the Negro, however, the past has receded farther than for any other stock, and consequently he is more naked in the present, and therefore more typically American. Hence too, he experiences the anguish of the search for himself in the most direct and brutal American fashion.

No doubt, because he is the most persecuted, the Negro is the outsider and the stranger in the midst of American life. But this does not mean that he may not express the American character at a more subterranean level. Remember that the scapegoat in primitive communities was sacrificed to expiate the sins of the group. By taking the sins of the others upon himself, the scapegoat experienced their guilt for them; he, the outcast, expressed the deeper and darker parts of their soul.

The best proof of all this is Ellison's story itself, which as a parable of the alienated individual in search of himself belongs in the mainstream of recent American fiction. The typical hero of modern American fiction--as in Hemingway, Faulkner, Nelson Algren--is the lonely figure existing on the shady side of the law, the tough guy or outcast who cannot hunt with the pack; and this image, or archetype, goes far back in the American tradition to the solitary heroes of J. Fenimore Cooper pitting their skill against the wilderness. Thus, in telling a story of contemporary American life, Ellison has plunged into the center of an American tradition; and though the particular events of this story are the kind of things that could have happened only to a Negro, I, as a white, was able to identify myself completely with the hero's frantic search.

The story opens in the South. The hero, still a boy, has won a prize for public speaking, a leather briefcase; but the whites of the town will award it to him only after he has been subjected to the ordeal of the "smoker" and a free-for-all in which all the local Negro boys are pitted, blindfold, against each other in a boxing ring, for the white man's sport. Thus, the nightmare touch asserts itself right at the beginning, and grows as the story unfolds. The book has an uncanny power from this combination of nightmare and realism, which partly suggests Faulkner but can only be compared with the Frenchman Céline's *Journey to the End of the Night*, that great poem of nihilism of the 1930's. The details of life are only too real and actual but heated in the furnace of Ellison's imagination, they expand to the grotesque and distorted proportions of a nightmare. And this nightmare is simply the life of the Negro in America; so that, even as a social protest, the book conveys more than any flatly reportorial or naturalistic fiction could do.

That night the hero has a real nightmare: he dreams that his grandfather, who had been born a slave, returns and tells him to open his prize brief case, inside which he finds a letter: *"Keep this nigger boy running!"* During the rest of the story he never stops running. Everybody in the world--whites, blacks, reactionaries, Communists--seem to be in a conspiracy to keep him on the move, in the inexorable and unending journey toward a self.

Another set of nightmarish encounters (where Ellison's bold imaginative gifts are at the top of their bent) involving a white trustee gets the hero dismissed from college. He goes to Harlem, drifts into and out of job and hospital, and then is picked up by the Communists and becomes a valuable minor functionary in the Party. For a while he goes great guns. But the good fortune cannot last, for he is also "invisible" to the Communists, who are interested in the Negro only as a tool for their own purposes.

The main drama toward the end of the book concerns the hero's two-front battle with the Party and with a Negro racist group headed by Ras, the Exhorter, a grotesque rabble-rouser. This works up into the final apocalyptic climax of a Harlem riot, which reads like the end of the world or the destruction of Valhalla, with people running wild and smashing everything in sight. Fleeing through the streets, first from Ras's men and then from some street thugs, the hero falls into an open manhole. Here the story ends in a merciful gesture of symbolism: the Invisible Man is the Underground Man of Dostoevski, the dark smoldering rejected figure of modern civilization, and his only salvation therefore is to go underground and remain out of sight.

Ellison has all the gifts a novelist could ask for: a command of impassioned rhetoric and language (which may turn out to be as native to the Negro as his genius for rhythm); the gift of telling a story whose pace never lags; intelligence to know exactly what he is about artistically. And, above all, he has the born novelist's gift of characterization. At first glance, his portrait of Dr. Bledsoe, the head of the Negro college, looks like something that has been done before—the unctuous, bowing, but deadly aggressive Negro; but Ellison has done it so sharply and individually that the character emerges as something really new in our fiction. Unfortunately, however, Ellison is too sparing with this gift of characterization, and in the struggle to make his story symbolic, rather than purely naturalistic, fiction, he has also made it somewhat abstract. As soon as he moves into the Communist Party, we begin to draw blanks as characters. The nervous vitality of Harlem comes through, but not enough of its richness in individual characters. Ellison is too furiously driven by his theme to take time to look lingeringly and appreciatively at the deeply human individuals he must have found there.

The trouble would seem to be that Ellison is divided within himself about his theme. The Underground man has been treated by Dostoevski and Céline, and though it is a mark of Ellison's achievement that he deserves comparison with these masters, he has nevertheless not resolved this difficult theme as satisfactorily as either. Céline committed himself to his revolt against mankind, taking the train of disgust to its last stop; Ellison is much too warmly attached to life for any such ultimate commitment. On the other hand, unlike Dostoevski, he has not risen beyond the Underground Man in himself to a level of richer and deeper human perception. A man who has been treated as socially "invisible" for so long cannot easily be reconciled to the purely human side of this invisibility. Thus, though it happens in an altogether different way than Richard Wright, in the end the protesting Negro does take some precedence over the novelist. Considering the almost inhuman obstacles in his way, this may be a fate inevitable for the Negro writer.

But this is Ellison's first novel, and while prophecy is customary on such occasions, here the promise cannot be empty when the performance is already so imposing. Luck is an especially capricious goddess to writers, but granting him just a little of it, I do not see that we can set any limit now to how far Ellison may yet go in the novel. He has already done a book which just misses greatness.

From *American Mercury* 74:342 (June 1952), 100-104.

Man Underground

Saul Bellow

A few years ago, in an otherwise dreary and better forgotten number of *Horizon* devoted to a louse-up of life in the United States, I read with great excitement an episode from *Invisible Man*. It described a free-for-all of blindfolded Negro boys at a stag party of the leading citizens of a small Southern town. Before being blindfolded the boys are made to stare at a naked white woman; then they are herded into the ring, and, after the battle royal, one of the fighters, his mouth full of blood, is called upon to give his high school valedictorian's address. As he stands under the lights of the noisy room, the citizens rib him and make him repeat himself; an accidental reference to equality nearly ruins him, but everything ends up well and he receives a handsome briefcase containing a scholarship to a Negro college.

This episode, I thought, might well be the high point of an excellent novel. It has turned out to be not *the* high point but rather one of the many peaks of a book of the very first order, a superb book. The valedictorian is himself Invisible Man. He adores the college but is thrown out before long by its president, Dr. Bledsoe, a great educator and leader of his race, for permitting a white visitor to visit the wrong places in the vicinity. Bearing what he believes to be a letter of recommendation from Dr. Bledsoe he comes to New York. The letter actually warns prospective employers against him. He is recruited by white radicals and becomes a Negro leader, and in the radical movement he learns eventually that throughout his entire life his relations with other men have been schematic; neither with Negroes nor with whites has he ever been visible, real. I think that in reading the *Horizon* exerpt I may have underestimated Mr. Ellison's ambition and power for the following very good reason, that one is accustomed to expect excellent novels about boys, but a modern novel about men is exceedingly rare. For this enormously complex and difficult American experience of ours very few people are willing to make themselves morally and intellectually responsible. Consequently, maturity is hard to find.

It is commonly felt that there is no strength to match the strength of those powers which attack and cripple modern mankind. And this feeling is, for the reader of modern fiction, all too often confirmed when he approaches a new book. He is prepared, skeptically, to find what he has found before, namely, that family and class, university, fashion, the giants of publicity and manufacture, have had a larger share in the creation of someone called a writer than truth or imagination--that Bendix and Studebaker and the nylon division of Du Pont, and the University of Chicago, or Columbia or Harvard or Kenyon College, have once more proved mightier than the single soul of an individual; to find that one more lightly manned position has been taken. But what a great thing it is when a brilliant individual victory occurs, like Mr. Ellison's, proving that a truly heroic quality can exist among our contemporaries. People too thoroughly determined--and our institutions by their size and force too thoroughly determined--can't approach this quality. That can only be done by those who resist the heavy influences and make their own synthesis out of the vast mass of phenomena, the seething, swarming body of appearances, facts, and details. From this harassment and threatened dissolution by details, a writer tries to rescue what is important. Even when he is most bitter, he makes by his tone a declaration of values and he says, in effect: "There is something nevertheless that a man may hope to be." This tone, in the best pages of *Invisible Man*, those pages, for instance, in which an incestuous Negro farmer tells his tale to a white New England philanthropist, comes through very powerfully; it is tragicomic, poetic, the tone of the very strongest sort of creative intelligence.

In a time of specialized intelligences, modern imaginative writers make the effort to maintain themselves as *un*specialists, and their quest is for a true middle-of-consciousness for everyone. What language is it that we can all speak, and what is it that we can all recognize, burn at, weep over; what is the stature we can without exaggeration claim for ourselves; what is the main address of consciousness?

I was keenly aware, as I read this book, of a very significant kind of independence in the writing. For there is a "way" for Negro novelists to go at their problems, just as there are Jewish or Italian "ways." Mr. Ellison has not adopted a minority tone. If he has done so, he would have failed to establish a true middle-of-consciousness for everyone.

Negro Harlem is at once primitive and sophisticated; it exhibits the extremes of instinct and civilization as few other American communities do. If a writer dwells on the peculiarity of this, he ends with an exotic effect. And Mr. Ellison is not exotic. For him this balance of instinct and culture or civilization is not a Harlem matter; it is *the* matter, German, French, Russian, American, universal, a matter very little understood. It is thought that Negroes and other minority people, kept under in the great status battle, are in the instinct cellar of dark enjoyment. This imagined enjoyment provokes envious rage and murder; and then it is a large portion of human nature itself which becomes the fugitive murderously pursued. In our society Man--Himself--is idolized and publicly worshipped, but the single individual must hide himself underground and try to save his desires, his thoughts, his soul, in invisibility. He must return to himself, learning self-acceptance and rejecting all that threatens to deprive him of his manhood.

This is what I make of *Invisible Man*. It is not by any means faultless; I don't think the hero's experiences in the Communist party are as original in conception as other parts of the book, and his love affair with a white woman is all too brief, but it is an immensely moving novel and it has greatness.

So many hands have been busy at the interment of the novel--the hand of Paul Valéry, the hands of the editors of literary magazines, of scholars who decide when genres come and go, the hands of innumerable pipsqueaks as well--that I can't help feeling elated when a resurrection occurs. People read history and then seem to feel that everything has to conclude in their own time. "We have read history, and therefore history is over," they appear to say. Really, all that such critics have the right to say is that fine novels are few and far between. That's perfectly true. But then fine anythings are few and far between. If these critics wanted to be extremely truthful, they'd say they were bored. Boredom, of course, like any mighty force, you must respect. There is something terribly impressive about the boredom of a man like Valéry who could no longer bear to read that the carriage had come for the duchess at four in the afternoon. And certainly there are some notably boring things to which we owe admiration of a sort.

Not all the gravediggers of the novel have such distinction as Valéry's, however. Hardly. And it's difficult to think of them as rising dazzled from a volume of Stendhal, exclaiming "God!" and then with angry determination seizing their shovels to go and heap more clods on the coffin. No, theirs unfortunately isn't often the disappointment of spirits formed under the influence of the masters. They make you wonder how, indeed, they *would* be satisfied. A recent contributor to *Partisan Review,* for instance, complains that modern fiction does not keep pace with his swift-wheeling modern consciousness which apparently leaves the photon far behind in its speed. He names a few *really* modern writers of fiction, their work unfortunately still unpublished, and makes a patronizing reference to *Invisible Man*: almost, but not quite, the real thing, it is "raw" and "overambitious." And the editors of *Partisan Review* who have published so much of this modern fiction that their contributor attacks, what do they think of this? They do not say what they think; neither of this piece nor of another lulu on the same subject and in the same issue by John Aldridge. Mr. Aldridge writes: "There are only two cultural pockets left in America, and they are the Deep South and that area of northeastern United States whose moral capital is Boston, Massachusetts. This is to say that these are the only places where there are any manners. In all other parts of the country people live in a kind of vastly standardized cultural prairie, a sort of infinite Middle West, and that means that they don't really live and they don't really do anything."

Most Americans thus are Invisible. Can we wonder at the cruelty of dictators when even a literary critic, without turning a hair, announces the death of a hundred million people?

Let us suppose that the novel is, as they say, played out. Let us only suppose it, for I don't believe, it. But what if it is so? Will such tasks as Mr. Ellison has set himself no more be performed? Nonsense. New means, when new means are necessary, will be found. To find them is easier than to suit the disappointed consciousness and to penetrate the thick walls of boredom within which life lies dying.

From *Commentary*, XIII (June 1952), 608-610.

The Deep Pit

Lloyd L. Brown

"Whence all this passion toward conformity?" asks Ralph Ellison at the end of his novel, *Invisible Man.* He should know, because his whole book conforms exactly to the formula for literary success in today's market. Despite the murkiness of his *avant-garde* symbolism, the pattern is clear and may be charted as precisely as a publisher's quarterly sales report.

Chapter 1: A 12-page scene of *sadism* (a command performance of 10 Negro youths savagely beating each other for the Bourbons' reward of scattered coins), *sex* (a dance by a naked whore with a "small American flag tattooed upon her belly"), and *shock* (literally applied to the performers by an electrically charged rug.)

Chapter 2: Featuring a 14-page scene in which a poor Negro farmer tells a white millionaire in great detail how he committed incest with his daughter; and the millionaire, who burns to do the same to his own daughter, rewards the narrator with a hundred-dollar bill.

And so on, to the central design of American Century literature--anti-Communism.

Author Ellison will reap more than scattered change or a crumpled bill for *his* performance. *Invisible Man* is already visible on the best-seller lists. The quivering excitement of the commercial reviewers matches that of the panting millionaire.

Strangely, there is much truth in their shouts of acclaim: "It is a sensational and feverishly emotional book. It will shock and sicken some readers ... the hero is a symbol of doubt, perplexity, betrayal and defeat ... tough, brutal and [again] sensational," says Orville Prescott in the New York *Times* about "the most impressive work of fiction by an American Negro which I have ever read."

"Here," writes Daniel James in the war-mongering *New Leader,* "the author establishes, in new terms, the commonness of every human's fate: nothingness."

"Authentic air of unreality," exults the reviewer in the Sunday *Times,* about the part dealing with the "Brotherhood" (Ellison's euphemism for the Communist Party).

The Sunday *New York Herald Tribune* man knows what he likes too:

> "For a grand finale there's the hot, dry, August night of the big riot when the hungry looted, when Ras the destroyer—of white appeasers—alone was out for blood; when Sybil, the chestnut-haired nymphomaniac, was raped by Santa Claus, and when the Invisible Man, still clutching his briefcase, fell through an open grill into a coal cellar—and stayed there to write a book..."

The *Saturday Review of Literature* is also impressed with this work that is as "'unreal' as a surrealist painting ... It is unlikely that *Invisible Man* is intended to be a realistic novel, although the detail is as real as the peeling paint on an old house."

At this point a reviewer in *M&M* might very well say "Amen!" and leave the unpleasant subject. But the commercial claque does more than extol Ellison's "surrealist horror," "well-ordered dissonance," "Dostoyevskianism," and thrill to "Harlem's slough of despond." We see that the same *Saturday Review* critic who is happily certain that this is not a realistic novel insists that "... *here, for the first time, is the whole truth about the Negro in America.*"

The mind reels before a statement such as that, compounded as it is of an ignorance so stupendous that it can only be matched by its arrogance.

Ostensibly set in Negro life, the novel is profoundly anti-Negro and it is this quality which moved several of the chauvinist critics to say that its author has "transcended race" and "writes as well as a white man"—the highest accolade they can bestow!

Here, as in James Jones' whine *From Here to Eternity,* is the one-man-against-the-world theme, a theme which cannot tell the "whole truth" or any part of the truth about the Negro people in America or about any other people anywhere.

Ellison's narrator-hero is a shadowy concept, lacking even the identity of a name, who tells of his Odyssey through a Negro college in the South, then to Harlem where he is hired by the Communists as their mass leader ("How would you like to be the new Booker T. Washington?") for $300 cash advance and the munificent, depression-period pay of $60 per week; he is quickly disillusioned and, battered in body and soul, finds refuge down a man-hole from whence to write a book about it all.

It would not be in order here to speak of responsibility, for the writer has anticipated and answered that objection in the prologue: "I can hear you say, 'What a horrible, irresponsible bastard!' And you're right. I leap to agree with you. I am one of the most irresponsible beings that ever lived."

Nor will I here attempt to refute the particular variations of the anti-Communist lie that Ellison tells. Some idea of his writing on this subject can be gained when we see the *New Leader,* second to none in Redbaiting viciousness, complaining that "Ellison's Communists are hard to believe, they are so unrelievedly humorless, cynical, and degenerate (including the black Communist)." And the *Nation's* reviewer--who says he is "ready to believe" the worst about "Harlem Stalinists"--grumbles: "The trouble with such caricature is that it undermines the intention behind it." (Nevertheless, he finds the book "exalted.")

And just as the author makes his irresponsibility undebatable, so does he help establish the fact that his work is alien to the Negro people and has its source in upper-class corruption. According to an interview in the *Saturday Review* it was "T.S. Eliot's 'The Wasteland' which ... changed the direction of his life: 'Eliot said something to my sensibilities that I couldn't find in Negro poets who wrote of experiences I myself had gone through.'"

Indeed, there is nothing in common between the wailing eunuchs of decay on the one hand, and the passionate strength and beauty of Negro poetry on the other. One can only speculate as to what it was in Ellison's "sensibilities" that drew him to Eliot and away from his people. But the result of the infection is a tragedy: the first-born of a talented young Negro writer enters the world with no other life than its maggots.

Ellison is also a disciple of the Richard Wright-Chester Himes school and shares with these writers their bitter alienation from the Negro people, their hatred and contempt of the Negro working masses, their renegades' malice—and their servility to the masters. Cut off from the surging mainstream of Negro life and struggle and creativity, they stagnate in Paris, wander on lonely crusades, or spit out at the world from a hole in the ground.

But against them and their inspirers is the growing renaissance of the Negro people's culture-writers, playwrights, poets, singers, musicians, dancers, artists, and actors, who are linked with their people, who *love* their people and who sing with the Negro poet of long ago:

"Lord, I don't want to be like Judas in my heart...."

From *Masses and Mainstream*, 5 (June 1952), 62-64.

A Novel Is a Novel

Richard Chase

At one point in Mr. Paul Bowles's new novel, the hero basks comfortably in the sun and reflects that "life is not a movement to or away from anything; not even from the past to the future, or from youth to old age, or from birth to death. The whole of life does not equal the sum of its parts. It equals any one of its parts; there is no sum. The full-grown man is no more deeply involved in life than the new-born child; his only advantage is that it can occasionally be given to him to become conscious of the substance of that life, and unless he is a fool he will not look for reasons or explanations. Life needs no clarifying, no justification. From whatever direction the approach is made, the result is the same: life for life's sake, the transcending fact of the living individual. In the meantime you eat." These perilous words invite a variety of meditations. If, for example, the novelist has come to believe that this idea of the human situation is an adequate basis for fiction, then surely that tiresomely heralded catastrophe, the death of the novel, must be at hand. For look at it how you will, a major theme of the novel has always been innocence; usually it has been *the* theme. And innocence, of course, has meant to the novelist a lack of involvement in life and has implied the possibility of a deeper involvement. The novel has shown a marvelous variety, but its central plot has been the passage, or the failure of passage, from innocence to experience. Its assumption has always been that life is in need of "clarifying"–that is, of being clearly seen in its reality and its complication--and of "justification"–that is, of being grasped in its inner meaning and fashioned into a controlling image by the imagination. Are these opinions too "rationalistic," too deficient in the theological *éclat,* too little cognizant of the horror and the glory, too poor to merit the splendid language of modern criticism, too little conversant with the rhetoric of motive and the dialectic of incarnation? My defense for a "rationalistic" interpretation of the novel must on this occasion be, first, history, and, second, Mr. Ellison.

One has no trouble at least in discerning that Mr. Ellison's *Invisible Man* shows far more knowledge of mystery, suffering, transcendent reality, and the ultimate contradictions of life than most of the modern novels which, like that of Mr. Bowles, declare themselves for a vitalist philosophy shading off at the edges into a theology. Yet Ellison's theme is the classic novelistic theme: the search of the innocent hero for knowledge of reality, self, and society. The story begins in the South and traces the career of a promising Negro youth, with his illusions about becoming a new Booker T. Washington, as he passes from a Negro college to Harlem, as he finds his way into and out of the Communist Party, and then to his final condition as an "underground" but incipiently emergent man.

The novel has many memorable episodes, the first being the death-bed scene of the hero's grandfather, who had been a slave and who leaves the injunction, resonantly developed throughout the novel, "to keep up the good fight. I never told you, but our life is a war and I have been a traitor all my born days, a spy in the enemy's country ever since I gave up my gun back in the Reconstruction. Live with your head in the lion's mouth. I want you to overcome 'em with yeses, undermine 'em with grins, agree 'em to death and destruction." There is the lurid episode of the white business men's smoker, which though hardly convincing by itself nevertheless finds its place in the whole pattern of the novel, with its account of how the boy who had been asked to deliver a speech on "social responsibility" was first forced to confront a naked white woman and then engage in a "battle royal" or mass boxing match with several other colored boys, followed by a frantic scramble to pick fake gold pieces off an electrified rug. There is the scene in which the young man involuntarily gets Mr. Norton, a northern white trustee of the college, involved with a local Negro who has had a child by his own daughter and then, equally involuntarily, introduces the trustee into a drinking and whoring establishment magnificently called the Golden Day and frequented by the inmates of a hospital for insane Negro veterans–an episode in which Mr. Ellison successfully practices the arts of Faulkner, Dickens, and Dostoevski. There is the striking revelation of the cynicism of Mr. A. Herbert Bledsoe, the revered president of the college, who exclaims to our fledgling Booker T. Washington, "My God, boy! You're black and living in the South–did you forget how to lie .... the only way to please a white man is to tell him a lie," and who abruptly dismisses the young man from the college, though not before giving him several letters to potential white employers in the North, each of which (the young man does not know it) asks that he be given no employment and ends with the mellifluous injunction "to help him continue in the direction of that promise which, like the horizon, recedes ever brightly and distantly beyond the hopeful traveler." There is the somewhat Kafkaesque episode of the employment in the paint company in New York, where the bewildered hero is painfully caught between a Stalinist labor union and a viciously insecure Negro boss who functions in the dark and noisy underground of the paint factory. There is the extended involvement with the Communists and their betrayal of Harlem and of the still innocent hero. There is the wonderful invention of Rinehart, the Negro bookie, gambler, briber, lover, and preacher–a sort of semi-mythic combination of Harlem trimmer and Panurge, who helps the hero to dispell his own illusions as well as those of the Party dialectic and to see, for the first time, the extraordinary wealth and wonder of the world. And there is finally the climactic rioting and looting in Harlem during which the Negro nationalist, Ras the Exhorter, appears on a black horse and dressed like an Abyssinian chieftain; the riot drives the hero into a more than slightly symbolical coal cellar, wherein, however, he is able to arrive at those reaffirmations of the restless human mind and some tentative and difficult resolutions of the dilemmas posed by his life.

I have thought it proper to summarize at such length because one of the virtues of Mr. Ellison's novel is its sheer richness of invention. So great an imaginative feat entails, to be sure, several incidental errors. Mr. Ellison is a very literary man, and his mind bears the imprint of the literary preoccupations of the 1940's. He is sophisticated, sometimes even slick. Yet most of his errors are, one might almost say, gratifyingly amateurish and gross (not all of them; one or two seem merely *chic*–he does after all make his hero print a humorous legend in lipstick on the stomach of an intoxicated white woman). His failures are not usually the product of his interest in symbol, myth, and linguistics; they are the product of the total imaginative quality of his mind. There is something positively engaging in the fact that he calls two of his northern white gentlemen Mr. Emerson and Mr. Norton (Charles Eliot Norton, one presumes). As for Mr. Norton who gazes "at the long ash of his cigar, holding it delicately in his slender, manicured fingers," he is so entirely disembodied–indeed so "invisible" to the author—as to be quite incapable of smoking a cigar or of being a character in a novel. Hardly less probable, except as an interesting idea, is Mr. Emerson, Jr., who complains to the raw youth from the South that "I had a difficult session with my analyst last evening" and who says, "I'm Huckleberry, you see .... with us it's still Jim and Huck Finn." Not all of Mr. Ellison's Communists escape cliché, and sometimes his vigorous, witty, and sinuous language frays out into irrelevancy which is inclined to be either colloquial and jazzy or to echo Eliot and Joyce. Also disconcerting, but partly justified by what is happening to the "seeing" powers of the hero, is Mr. Ellison's picture of Harlem taken in winter, a Harlem so unpeopled that it resembles North Dakota.

Like so many recent novels, *Invisible Man* is rather thickly endowed with symbols. Apart from the great number of meaningful pigeons flying around, the symbols have mostly to do with visibility, invisibility, and color. For example, the motto of the paint company is "Keep America Pure with Liberty Paints" and its chief product is "Optic White." Then there is the blind Reverend Mr. Barbee, the Communist official with the glass eye, and so on. Yet the symbols, like the other elements of the novel of which one is wary--the tendency toward surrealism and jazz culture--are not asked to carry more weight than they can. The real weight of meaning is carried by the profound underlying metaphor of "invisibility" which Mr. Ellison derives from his idea that the white man cannot or does not *see* the Negro as an individual and that by extension this invisibility is in our time the fate of all individuals. And this idea is not only a social comment, for Mr. Ellison is able to give it metaphysical, psychological, and moral meanings. Invisibility becomes for the hero both a plight and a device, like Hamlet's madness.

By contrast to Mr. Ellison's significant book, Bowle's *Let It Come Down* seems pallid and futile, despite its carefully contrived violence, its efforts at philosophy, and its occasional real triumphs of characterization and, especially, of scenery painting. That which one is exhorted to let come down is Ultimate Doom, and this is one of those novels, the distant offspring of Spengler, and of Hemingway and Lawrence, whose energy, such as it is, is derived from the prospect of the annihilation of the West. The disadvantage for the novelist of such a theme is of course that Annihilation becomes the only interesting thing in the book, all the characters being necessarily bores by comparison. . . .

From *The Kenyon Review*, XIV (Autumn 1952), 678-684.

Eccentric's Pilgrimage

R.W.B. Lewis

. . . *Invisible Man* by Ralph Ellison is the most impressive work of fiction in a number of years. It is occasionally melodramatic and self-indulgent, and it is a trifle too long. But the book is a great solid chunk of fictional reality; it has a tremendous sheer existence; its core is inviolable and can stand any amount of scrutiny. The chunk is made up of all kinds and conditions of things, all of them held together by a fierce power of imagination. Melville is Mr. Ellison's major ally; and like *Moby-Dick*, *Invisible Man* contains sermons and songs and mediations and prayers, dreams and jokes and reminiscent anecdotes; it has fights and funerals and political meetings; it enters colleges, offices, bars, brothels, factories, private homes and star-chambers. The artistic ambition, like Melville's, is to suggest by a circus-vision of the world that reality is to be sought for everywhere and only everywhere, by multiplication rather than by reduction. (It is such a notion, I take it, that led Mr. Ellison back to the widely-ranging novel of the nineteenth century, for comfort and guidance, as against the sparse reductiveness of the Hemingway school.)

The circus-vision is appropriate to the story Mr. Ellison has to tell, for it is a contemporary, Negro version of the clown's grail. His hero is a Negro Charlie Chaplin, skidding around corners and dashing down alleys, endlessly harried by the cops and the crooks of the world, endlessly hurrying in search of whatever it is that can sanctify human existence. On the run, Mr. Ellison's nameless hero is defrauded, betrayed and beaten, as all innocents and fools are born to be; yet, in the great tradition, he acquires a tough, private conscience as a result. *Invisible Man* is not ultimately a "Negro novel"; for just as the odyssey of the eccentric is an account of the condition of human life seen in American perspective, so *Invisible Man* simply passes that condition through yet another perspective, that of the Negro. Its young seeker is the modern hero as American Negro.

His adventures are too numerous for summary, but they share the common element of a droll reversal whereby he invariably achieves the opposite of what he aims at. Hoping to impress a trustee of his college, for example, he exposes the fellow instead to a Negro farmer, about to have children simultaneously by wife and daughter. He is swept into service by the communistic "Brotherhood"' after starting a riot with a speech intended to prevent one. His best efforts to gain honor with the Brotherhood get him promptly and severely punished; his lectures to women on the improvement of their estate win him instant invitations to their beds. His grand mission to rise in the political and social world concludes with a dive down a manhole: where he decides to hibernate for a while, assessing the value of his clownish quest.

The world Mr. Ellison has contrived for his hero is pictured as a vast, disorderly and utterly spurious ritual, something designed not to bring the seeker into the center of valid energy and to show him its sacred treasures: but to keep him out, to keep him running. College president, industrial magnate, political organizer, libidinous *hausfrau*: all connive to guard the secret of their own emptiness. But while the ritual hawked about by the book's confidence-men is spurious, the experience itself has the form of a genuine rite of passage. The adventures have passed the young man through a series of trials, to the moment of profound change anticipated in the climax. He acknowledges his moral and psychological invisibility, while asserting in darkness an achieved identity. I should say that the ritual is larger than the experience, like a shoe a couple of sizes too big for the foot. Melville admitted some allegorical intention or other, but he could not remember it very clearly; Mr. Ellison appears to have been reading up on his allegories, and the one he wants us to notice is not quite a perfect fit. But wherever the events and the hero's response to them give off their own formal suggestiveness, the novel has that life beyond life which is the nature of art. It is not easy to name a work of fiction since *Light in August* which gives us so much and holds itself so well...

From *The Hudson Review* VI:1, (Spring 1953), 148-49.

From *Native Son* to *Invisible Man: A Review of the Literature of the Negro for 1952*

Alain Locke

...In the thirty years' span of my active reviewing experience, there have been in my judgment three points of peak development in Negro fiction by Negro writers. In 1923 from a relatively low plateau of previous problem fiction, Jean Toomer's *Cane* rose to unprecedented artistic heights. Not only in style but in conception it raised a new summit, as it soared above the plane of propaganda and apologetics to a self-sufficient presentation of Negro life in its own idiom and gave it proud and self-revealing evaluation. More than that, the emotional essences of the Southland were hauntingly evoked in an impressionistic poetic sort of realism; it captured as well some of the more distinctive tone and color of Negro living. Its only shortcomings were that it was a series of character sketches rather than a full length canvas: a succession of vignettes rather than an entire landscape–and that its author chose not to continue. In 1940, Richard Wright's skillful sociological realism turned a hard but brilliant searchlight on Negro urban life in Chicago and outlined the somber tragedy of Bigger Thomas in a well-studied setting of Northside wealth and Southside poverty. Artistically not the equal of the more masterful series of short stories, *Uncle Tom's Children*, that preceded it, *Native Son's* narrative was masterful and its character delineation as skillful as any work of Dreiser's or Farrell's. The book was marred only by Wright's overreliance on the communist ideology with which he encumbered his powerful indictment of society for Bigger, the double pariah of the slum and the color-line. Wright was essentially sound in his alignment of the social forces involved, but erred artistically in the doctrinally propagandist tone which crept into his novel chapter by chapter until the angry, ineffective end. The greater pity it was–and is–that later he disavowed this ideological commitment that cheated him of an all-time classic of American fiction. Despite this, *Native Son* has remained all these intervening years the Negro novelist's strongest bid for fiction of the first magnitude.

But 1952 is the significant year of Ellison's *Invisible Man*, a great novel, although also not without its artistic flaws, sad to say. Ralph Ellison is a protege of Wright, who predicted for him a bright literary future. Written in a style of great force and originality, although its talent is literally smothered with verbosity and hyperbole, *Invisible Man* is both in style and conception a new height of literary achievement. The life story of its hero, obviously semi-autobiographic, ranges from the typical South of a few years back to the metropolitan North of New York and vicinity. Conceptually it runs also almost the whole gamut of class in American society and is interracial at all stages, even in the deep South from the benefactor patron of the college visiting for Founders Day to the sinister "crackers" of the rural backwoods. It is in fact one of the best integrated accounts of interaction between whites and Negroes in American society that has yet been presented, with all characters portrayed in the same balance and perspective. Ellison's philosophy of characterization, incisive, realistic, unsparing of physical and psychological detail–all his major characters are stripped bare to the skin and bone, so to speak–is close to the best European realism in that it is so three-dimensional. We see a grand caravan of types, all registered first person on the sensitive but rather cynical retina of the young Negro protagonist. In the South, the patronizing but well-intentioned school trustee, the piously hypocritical Negro school principal, the gauche, naive but not too honest students, the disillusioned, institutionalized war veterans, the townsfolk, the peasants of the countryside, white and black, and most particularly the unforgettable earthy peasant character of Jim Trueblood. In the North, the pageant resumes with all sorts and manner of men and women: the financiers of Wall Street and their decadent jazz-loving sons, factory workers, pro and anti-union varieties, the urban peasants and their homely oddities, parlor-pinks and hard inner-core communists, race leaders, educated and illiterate, each after his kind–and the Harlem community generally displayed finally at frenetic tension in its one big authentic riot. Stylistically all this unrolls in a volcanic flow of vivid, sometimes livid imagery, a tour de force of psychological realism. A double symbolic meaning piled on top of this realism gives the book its distinctive and most original tone and flavor: *Invisible Man* is actually a surrealistic novel because of this, and but for its lack of restraint would rank among the very best of the genre. But the unrestrained bravado of treatment, riding loose rein at full gallop most of the time and the overprecious bravura of phrase and diction weight it down where otherwise it would soar in well-controlled virtuosity. Many readers will be shocked at Ellison's daring franknesses and dazed by his emotional intensity but these are an integral part of the book's great merit. For once, too, here is a Negro writer capable of real and sustained irony. *Invisible Man,* evidently years in the making, must not be Ralph Ellison's last novel...

From *Phylon: The Atlanta University Review of Race and Culture* XIV (Spring 1953), 34-35.

Seminal Studies

Ralph Ellison's Modern Version of Brer Bear and Brer Rabbit in *Invisible Man*

Floyd R. Horowitz

Mr. Ellison's Invisible Man is an intelligent, young Negro attuned to what he considers the clarion philosophy of the white world--"keep this nigger boy running." At first we find him like a bear, by his own admission, hibernating, unknown to anyone in a Harlem tenement basement. There he reflects upon his past experience, which soon, like Dante's travail to the blinding light of knowledge, is to be recounted. We can meanwhile understand symbolically one of his preoccupations. Around him in this dark basement he has rigged electric fixtures. He has tapped a power line and currently is stealing the electricity that illuminates his hibernation. On the ceiling and walls there are now 1369 lighted bulbs. Such enlightment metaphorically sets the tone of the book. It is from one frame of reference a psychological study, impressionistically told.

So begins the story. In the South, once, a Negro boy was awarded by the whites a scholarship to a Negro state college. He was to learn the tradition of Booker T. Washington--practical service to the Negro community, humble dignity (at least in public), intellectualized acceptance of white authority. And naively on that foundation he frames his goals, and affixes in the rafters the hopeful branch of religion. Diligently and in innocence he learns to conform. As a reward, in his third year, he is chosen to chauffeur a visiting white trustee of the college.

The day is a disaster. Taking a back road he allows the delicately sensitive trustee to see the Negro in all his squalor. Following a conversation with a farmer who is known to have committed incest, the trustee faints and is carried to the only available haven, a saloon and brothel just then at the height of its weekly business with the Negro ambulatory Vets of a mental institution. Within the day our hero is dismissed from the college of conformity, on the morrow traveling North to the expectation of greater freedom.

In short order, thus upon the verge of manhood, other disillusionments follow. The letters of recommendation which he carries from the college president prove treacherous. In the North he is economically exploited. Because of his skill as a public speaker he is enlisted by the Communists and later duped. In the shadow of each rebuff he distinguishes his grandfather's enigmatic smile and hears his words: "overcome 'em with yesses." Accordingly, the race of his experience in the South and North exhausts his consciousness of self. He finds that in running he is nowhere. Like a continually endangered Odysseus under the polyphemal white eye of society, he is Noman. The whites are blind to him, he is invisible to himself, having failed in a succession of roles. While in itself this is a kind of knowledge by suffering, it is more than he can bear. His self-imposed basement exile is therefore an escape from responsibility, if also from the inequity of a hostile world. The winter of his discontent, he knows, must come to its hibernative end, and he must chance the new spring, yet for the time--and for the emphasis of the novel--his past disillusioning experience must be narrated.

Because the mode of that narration is impressionistic, Ellison takes the opportunity to convey the largest part of the novel's meaning via a quite imaginative, often bizarre range of imagery. In that way the logic of image associations sets out the basis of thematic implication. This may come as a new idea to the historian and litterateur alike, especially because the social and political significance of Mr. Ellison's book seems conclusively to derive from its open drama, colorful vignettes, and frank appraisals. Yet it may not be amiss to demonstrate that there is a good deal more social and political commentary being effected in the work via a highly planned if somewhat covert structure.

This means several things. Such a demonstration is necessarily involved with its own tools, the logic of interpolation as well as the more generally understood judgment of interpretation. Further, the story is not always told literally, but rather is rendered by symbols and images that have something like a life of their own. At an extreme (the Invisible Man's experience while in shock), the literal result takes the form of an impenetrable impressionistic morass, and the reader must agree to witness rather than to understand in the traditional sense. Other times a logical association can be drawn from similar instances: at the beginning of the novel the Invisible Man comes to a southern "smoker" where he will enter the prizefight ring, and while there he sees a nude dancer who has an American flag tattooed on her belly: at the end of the book he is described as a "black bruiser" who is "on the ropes" and "punch drunk," and he scrawls another distortion of another American message across the belly of another nude: "Sybil, you were raped by/Santa Claus/Surprise." Such devices as these form the texture (albeit an ironic one) of the American meanings which the hero experiences, and which no less importantly the reader is invited to experience with him.

As we do so we may trace the Invisible Man as a Christ-like figure, sacrificed and sacrificing. Many of the symbols by which he is described are distinctly Christian symbols, many of his actions are analogues of Biblical events. Or, psychologically considered, he is the dramatic vortex of Negro neuroticism: so extensive is the imagery here that we must read and interpret with the aid of an unabridged Freud. Historically and politically, too, he is beset by a cavalcade of American symbols and images which are in the wrong places, a sometimes subtle, sometimes raucous debunking of the names and institutions which Americans are supposed to hold so dear: the American flag upon her belly undulates to the shimmy of a nude, the identity of Jefferson is an illusion in the mind of a shellshocked veteran, the Statue of Liberty is obscured in fog while liberty is the name applied to a corporate enterprise, Emerson is a businessman, the Fourth of July is Jack the Communist's birthday as well as the occasion of a race riot.

Based fairly closely upon the folklore motif of Brer Rabbit and Brer Bear, the line of imagery discussed in this paper is as ironic as such other patterns of meaning, and perhaps even more so because of its Negro origin. Like the novel's fifty or perhaps seventy-five other motifs, it is not especially extensive, nor does it so closely effect an analogy that it admits of no other meaning for its individual parts. Quite the opposite. The bear and the rabbit are sometimes psychologically one and the same, as in Jack the Rabbit, Jack the Bear. But it would seem that the rabbit can be Peter as well. Or he is called Buckeye, which describes Jack the Communist later on. Or he is about to be peppered with BUCKshot. Or there is a pun on bear, so that the hero can not bear his existence. There is, in short, a rich language play which intertwines this motif with many others, which, perhaps too gratuitously on occasion, identifies rabbit with Brer Rabbit, which makes literary explication not the easiest of pursuits. Yet, for all that, the point of Ellison's use of this motif seems plain enough. Though they are sometimes friendly enough, less than kin and more than herbivorous quadrupeds, rabbit and bear are naturally irreconcilable. More, we know from Uncle Remus that soon they will match wits.

This makes for a good metaphor in which to cast the Invisible Man, since, interestingly enough, for Ellison, wit is not the same as intelligence. His protagonist is not a victor. Early in his education the Invisible Man discovers that. While he is chauffering Mr. Norton, the trustee of the college, they approach Jim Trueblood's backroad shack. The Invisible Man mentions that Trueblood has had relations with his own daughter. Norton demands that the car be stopped. He runs over to Trueblood, accosts him, wants his story. While the amazed and morally upright Invisible man looks on, Trueblood complies in full detail. Ellison already has described him "as one who told the old stories with a sense of humor and a magic that made them come alive." And again, as one "who made high plaintively animal sounds." Now this story: sleeping three abed because of the extreme cold, his wife, daughter and himself, as if in a dream well beyond his control, just naturally, incest occurred. The story is a colloquial poetic. Before the act Trueblood has been nothing, but now he freely admits: "But what I don't understand is how I done the worst thing a man can do to his own family and 'stead of things gittin bad, they got better. The nigguhs up at the school don't like me, but white folks treats me fine."

This irony is the key to Ellison's entire treatment of Brer Rabbit and Brer Bear's relationship. Here the issue is moral. Trueblood, in the middle of the night which he describes "Black as the middle of a bucket of tar," has given his daughter a baby. For this he is rewarded. Norton gives him a hundred-dollar bill. "You bastard," says the Invisible Man under his breath, "You no-good bastard! You get a hundred-dollar bill!" Playing the bear, the Invisible Man is fooled, of course; thrown out of school in a hurry. In vain he objects to the college president: "But I was only driving him, sir. I only stopped there after he ordered me to. . . ." "Ordered you?" retorts the president, "He *ordered* you. Dammit, white folks are always giving orders, it's a habit with them. Why didn't you make an excuse? Couldn't you say they had sickness--smallpox--or picked another cabin? Why that Trueblood shack? My God, boy! You're black and living in the South--did you forget how to lie?"

This is the form of the anecdote. Brer Bear is outwitted by Brer Rabbit in a first encounter. So the Invisible Man travels to the North. There on the streets of New York City he meets the second rabbit man, in this instance named Peter. Of course, exactly considered, Peter Rabbit is not the same as Brer Rabbit, yet he belongs to the same tradition. He knows how to escape the McGregors of the world. Here in Harlem he looks like a clown in baggy pants, wheeling a cart full of unused blue-prints. Says Peter, "Man, this Harlem ain't nothing but a bear's den." The Invisible man then completes the bridge of logic to the original analogy: "I tried to think of something about bears to reply, but remembered only Jack the Rabbit, Jack the Bear." Peter needs no social reinforcement, however. He proffers his key to success: "All it takes to get along in this here man's town is a little shit, grit, and mother-wit. And man, I was bawn with all three." So the friendly side of the rabbit's personality, advising the Invisible Man what to expect from the city, the North, the white world. But it is no use, for the bear must always be tricked--and soon he is.

He has heard of a job at Liberty Paints and hurried to apply. The scene depicts a patriotic devotion to the free enterprise system: flags flutter from the building tops. A screaming eagle is the company's trade mark. Liberty Paints covers America with what is advertised as the whitest white possible, a defective shipment just then being sent out for a Washington national monument. The bear is sent down, down, down, to help the irascible Negro, Lucius Brockway.

"Three levels underground I pushed upon a heavy metal door marked 'Danger' and descended into a noisy, dimly lit room. There was something familiar about the fumes that filled the air and I had just thought *pine,* when a high-pitched Negro voice rang out above the machine sounds." In an image which we may recall, the first rabbit, Trueblood, has already dreamed of such machinery. And his black as tar description is taken up now by the Invisible Man's thought of *pine,* and by Ellison's pun "high-pitched." So the hero encounters Lucius, the next Brer Rabbit, who defends himself by biting, and whose coveralls covered by goo bring the image of Tar Baby to the Invisible Man's mind.

Against Lucius's grit and mother-wit there is barely any defense. It turns out that Lucius alone has the secret of America's whitest white paint. He and no one else knows the location of every pipe, switch, cable and wire in the basement heart of the plant. Only he knows how to keep the paint from bleeding (whereas Trueblood does actually bleed for his moral smear), only he knows how to mix the base. He has helped Sparland, the big boss, word the slogan "If it's Optic White, It's the Right White." And he knows his worth: "caint a single doggone drop of paint move out of the factory lessen it comes through Lucius Brockway's hands." So in the matter of economics as before with morals, Brer Bear can not win. As Lucius's assistant he tends the steam valves, and when they pass the danger mark, burst, Brockway scrambles for the door and escapes while the Invisible Man attempts to shut them off and is caught in the steam. Again we may remind ourselves that the concepts of machinery and scalding have been united in Trueblood the rabbit's dream. Brer Bear can not win no matter how hard he tries.

In this case, moreover, his efforts are naive, short of the hypocrisy which alone means survival for the natively talented Negro. While he struggles for consciousness and self in the company hospital, that fact of Negro existence is brought out. A card is placed before him: "What is your name?" Under the bludgeoning of experience he has lost his identity, "I realized that I no longer knew my own name. I shut my eyes and shook my head with sorrow." The fantasy of his impression continues. Other cards are submitted, finally the question: "Boy, who was Brer Rabbit?" Soon after, he is released in a daze, finds his way to Harlem and collapses on the sidewalk.

Here Ellison has been portraying the New Negro intellectual. What has this Invisible Man learned?--that in the South, in the course of enlightenment he is pitted against his fellow Negro, farmer and college president alike; that Negro inured to the quasi-slavery practiced by the white. And in the North little better: survival in a slum, a bear in a bear den. Yet defeat is a realization, and a realization is a victory of perspective. In short, he is no simple Brer Bear. It is Ellison's intention to have him learn what the young intellectuals must learn--that as long as narrow self-interest motivates him he can have no peace. He must be the realm of the universal. That becomes the next phase, not with a rush of empathy, but as before, through trial, defeat, through knowledge of self.

One day, when he has recovered from his ordeal in the paint factory, he comes upon the Harlem eviction of an aged Negro couple. Their meagre possessions on the sidewalk, the wife attempts to return into their apartment to pray. When the marshals in charge refuse permission, the crowd riots. Suddenly in the melee the Invisible Man hears himself yelling, "Black men! Brothers! Black Brothers!" His further role as Brer Bear has begun. Under the aegis of his colloquial eloquence the crowd returns the furniture to the apartment. Then, in another moment, the police have arrived and he searches for a way of escape. A white girl standing in the doorway accosts him, "Brother, that was quite a speech you made," directs him to the roof. He hurries across to a far corner. But as he waits for the light to change there comes the quiet, penetrating voice beside his ear, "That was a masterful bit of persuasion, brother." The biggest, most persistent rabbit of all has just tracked him, Brer Jack the Communist, alias Buckeye the one-eyed international hopper. Brer Bear is wanted for the organization. Will he listen over coffee?

Says the Invisible Man, "I watched him going across the floor with a bouncy rolling step." Again: "His movements were those of a lively small animal." And Jack's pitch is short: "Perhaps you would be interested in working for us. We need a good speaker for this district. Someone who can articulate the grievances of the people. They exist, and when the cry of protest is sounded, there are those who will hear it and act." Communism is the answer to his needs, for as many reasons as it is advertised to have. It offers him a cause, social equality and a job. It fulfils what must seem the generic destiny of a Brer.

What informs the Communist policy is the scientific attitude, however, not the man but the mass. To this positivistic philosophy the Invisible Man must immediately be trained, for in the course of change to the new brotherhood, he is told by Hambro the Communist philosophe, certain sentimental ideas will have to be sacrificed. The very idea of race, that core and defense of Negro unity, must be sublimated. Nor is there place in the Brotherhood's teaching for emotion, for psalms singing, yam-eating, Tuskegee zeal. All is to be logical: the answers to the woman question, the rational youth groups, the organization of labor, even the public rallies. At least this is the theory, and if like Liberty Paints it is myopic and actually tinged with grey, if the women take him to bed to answer their political questions, if the youth are too easily frantic, if the public is still strong for the gospel and labor distrusts the Negro as scab; if these realities, the Invisible Man's idealism draws him into the bear trap, Brother Jack his foil.

His *is* a persuasive skill. Soon he is known, liked, trusted, powerful, confident that the Brotherhood is leading the Negro aright. Now he is willing to fight Ras the Exhorter, leader of the Negro-only movement. But as quickly, the trap springs: the internationally directed Brotherhood changes its Harlem policy. Indefinitely, there will be an interdiction of its plan to better the Negro's social condition. Unless the Invisible Man is willing to sacrifice the trust, the hopes of his fellow Negro, he must renounce identity once more.

In a scene which proves the Brotherhood's shortsightedness--Brer Jack, it turns out, actually has but one eye--there comes the break. But now, unallied, the Invisible Man must reckon with Ras the Destroyer, who in a Fourth of July flash electrifies Harlem as the nationalist leader of a super race riot. This is no time for intellectualism, nor this the place. Pursued, to survive, our hero has no choice but to hide in an underground cavern. There we find him when the novel begins: "Call me Jack-the-Bear, for I am in a state of hibernation." That is the pattern, from rural copse to cosmopolitan forest.

From *Midcontinent American Studies Journal* 4:2 (1963), 21-27.

Ralph Ellison and the Afro-American Folk and Cultural Tradition

George E. Kent

Ralph Ellison stressed connections between Afro-American folk and cultural tradition and American culture, since "The heel bone is, after all, connected, through its various linkages, to the head bone," and not to be ignored is" the intricate network of connections which binds Negroes to the larger society."[1] Mindful of this pronouncement I shall sketch in some of Ellison's ideas concerning the value of the folk tradition, explore representative techniques in *Invisible Man,* and offer suggested comments concerning the value and limitations of his method.

Pressed toward a bag of pure Blackness, Ellison was capable of minimizing folk tradition's value for the self-conscious writer, as he does in "Change the Joke and Slip the Yoke," an essay in response to Stanley Edgar Hyman's attempt to create achetypes of Blackness.[2] In "Change the Joke," he contended that the Black writer was "heir to the human experience which is literature," an inheritance which might be more important to him than his own living folk tradition. As for himself, Black folklore became important through literary discovery. Seeing the uses to which folklore is put in the works of James Joyce and T.S. Eliot, Ellison saw the folk tradition, the spirituals, blues, jazz and folk-tales as a stable factor in "the discontinuous, swiftly changing, and diverse American culture"[3] It expresses qualities needful in a world which exemplifies to a considerable degree a blues-like absurdity. It offers much to the writer, who can "translate its meaning into wider, more precise vocabularies."[4]

Actually, Ellison usually gave greater emphasis to folk traditions, and some allowance should be made for the fact that the primary goal of "Change the Joke" is to correct Stanley Edgar Hyman's concept of Black folklore. Since 1940, Ellison had been stressing its *ultimate* importance. In "Stormy Weather," a review of Langston Hughes's *The Big Sea,* which was critical of Hughes on other grounds, Ellison commended him for developing the national folk sources of his art.[5] Ellison's essay "Recent Negro Fiction" praised Hughes and Wright: Hughes for taking note of folklore and seeing the connection between his efforts and symbols and images of Negro forms; Wright, for attention to the Southern Negro folk.[6] In 1944, Ellison's short story, "Flying Home," made elaborate use of the Black folklore motif of the Black character who comes to grief in heaven for flying too imaginatively with his angel's wings. The main character, a Black aviator, finds peace only when he comes to term with the survival values of folk tradition.[7]

In 1945, Ellison's essay entitled "Richard Wright's Blues," [8] revealed a profound understanding of the *blues* as a folk cultural form and the value of its *forms* of response to existence for the self-conscious writer. He also analyzed the oppressive weight of American culture upon the folk, argued their complexity, and made a widely publicized definition of the *blues:*

> The blues is an impulse to keep the painful details and episodes of a brutal experience alive in one's aching consciousness, to finger its jagged grain, and to transcend it, not by the consolation of philosophy but by squeezing from it a near-tragic, near-comic lyricism. As a form, the blues is an autobiographical chronicle of personal catastrophe expressed lyrically.[9]

Later in the same essay, he points out that the blues express "both the agony of life" and the possibility of overcoming it through sheer toughness of spirit. The blues are a valuable form also, in that they emphasize self-confrontation.

Comments upon the folk tradition are scattered among several essays in *Shadow and Act.* Perhaps the most emphatic occurs in Ellison's responses during the 1955 Paris Interview.[10] He called attention to several functions of folklore and described some ways in which folklore worked dramatically in *Invisible Man.* Offering the first drawings of a group's character, preserving situations repeated in the history of the group, describing the boundaries of thought and feeling, projecting the group's wisdom in symbols expressing its will to survive, embodying those values by which it lives and dies, folklore seemed, as Ellison described it, basic to the portrayal of the essential spirit of Black people. In general, Ellison noted that great literature of France, Russia, and Spain was erected upon the humble base of folklore. Folk symbols serve Picasso as an annihilator of time through the use of simple lines and curves, and, for the viewer, a whole culture "may resound in a simple rhythm, an image." But most important, in its relationship to Black experience is Ellison's belief that the Black's folklore "announced the Negro's willingness to trust his own experience, his own sensibilities as to the definition of reality, rather than to allow his masters to define these crucial matters for him." Black American folklore, nonetheless, represents for Ellison an American and Western experience--"not lying at the bottom of it, but intertwined, diffused in its very texture."

Ellison also emphasizes the special qualities of a Black tradition in confronting reality and describes them at some length in his essay, "The World and the Jug."[11] Suffice it here to say that they cover the gamut of attitudes for defining life positively, surviving oppression and extracting from existence many of its joys.

II

In *Invisible Man,* the whole gamut of Ellison's descriptions of the functions of folklore find their place. However, to be fully suggestive of their power is to bear in mind some specifics concerning the total reach of the novel. In the first place the novel's title is *Invisible Man,* not THE *Invisible Man.* In relationship to its nameless protagonist, the story delivers itself through at least three wave-lengths, none in the form of the novel, completely separable from another: the hero as cosmic man, with the inescapable duty to gather up and affirm *Reality,* despite social oppression; the hero as victim, struggling with a cultural machinery that would reduce him to negative sign; and the hero as an allegory of Black struggle in American history.

Black cultural and folk tradition frequently involves more than one of the wave-lengths.

In simplest form, we may see the interaction through several characters, who, in varying degrees, are folk or are a part of cultural tradition. In more complex form, the interaction of folk and cultural tradition ranges from motifs to situations, symbols, and strategic appearances of folk art forms: blues, spirituals, and folk rhymes.

The characters contrast with the lostness of the invisible narrator, since they represent Reality confronted. Thus the slave woman envisioned singing spirituals in the prologue is used to comment upon the pain of victimization, but she and her sons also define *freedom,* a basic theme of the novel, as the ability to articulate the self, and as a question that can be answered only by each individual's confrontation with the self. Louis Armstrong and his jazz reflect an articulated self and a mode of breaking through the ordinary categories of Western clock time. The grandfather who appears at strategic points throughout the novel is a reflector of bitter past and continuing victimization. On the other hand, he is, in Ellison's words, the "ambiguity of the past," a sphinx-like riddle which must be approached creatively and not in the literal minded fashion which actually makes of the invisible narrator an accessory to the Brotherhood's crime of provoking a riot in Harlem. Yet the destruction of whites by yessing and confirming their false sense of reality, which the invisible narrator has imitated with nearly fatal consequences, was a solid survival technique of his grandfather and the folk.

Trueblood and Mary, who have assimilated both folk and general Black cultural tradition, play the most powerful dramatic roles among the folk figures. Trueblood, with whom the invisible narrator inadvertently confronts philanthroper Norton, is several roles. On the simple folk level, he is a person who can face the results of his humanity: becoming an expectant father by both his wife and his daughter.

He achieves a conclusion, which the brainwashed and pragmatic invisible narrator requires most of the novel to grasp: "I ain't nobody but myself." His achievement is dramatized through the rituals of first singing spirituals--and then the blues. Singing the spirituals dramatizes his struggle and pain. But it is the singing of the blues, the folk form which Ellison has celebrated for its ritual of self-confrontation, that enables Trueblood to get himself together. In Chapter Nine, the blues *forms of response* to existence become meaningful to the invisible narrator as a street singer celebrates the *absurdity* of a self committed passionately to a woman with "feet like a monkey" and "legs like a frog," and the narrator, realizing how Bledsoe has duped him, can laugh bitterly at himself by singing, "they picked poor robin clean." But it is Trueblood who exemplifies the real toughness of the tradition, the highly flavored speech, and the capacity for enjoyment of life.

But Trueblood is also interconnected with American and Western tradition. He is, on one hand, the testimony to the destiny of reality that Western rationalism evades. And he is, on the other, American and Western scapegoat, frankly admitting the sins of the flesh, the full acknowledgment of which the philanthroper Norton dodges by Platonic and puritanical sublimation. For Norton too has committed incest with his daughter but mentally, rather than physically. And the white Southern community acknowledges its secret sexual longings and Trueblood's role as their substitute bearer of sin by dropping coins into his pocket.

But more broadly still, Trueblood connects finally with Western incest tradition and with Freud.[12] Like Oedipus he has invaded unaware the zone of taboo. For he cohabited with his daughter while dreaming. So, was he guilty? Selma Fraiberg argues persuasively that in Freudian terms he was, since he was the author of the dream which his being conjured up for the purpose of allowing the sexual act. At any rate, Trueblood must bear up while the gods deliberate indefinitely concerning the sins of mortal man.

It will be remembered that Mary Rambo is the Southern migrant,--now New York mistress of a boarding house--into whose hands the invisible narrator falls after barely surviving the allegorically represented attempt of the industrial system to eliminate all potential for individuality and reduce him to anonymity. The elaborate role that Ellison had designed for Mary may be examined in the fragment published in Herbert Hill's anthology of contemporary Black literature, *Soon One Morning.*[13] Mary is the warmth, wit, coping power, and humanity of the folk tradition as it survives in the modern industrial city. And she is the integration of the bitter past with the present, as can be seen by her possession of such purely survival items as the bank topped by a minstrel figure, "a very black, red lipped and wide mouth Negro, his face an enormous grin, his single large black hand held palm up before his chest." In Chapter Fifteen, where he appears, the invisible narrator tries unsuccessfully to drop the symbols of the past, which must be integrated into his being. Unlike Trueblood, Mary makes a strong positive impact upon the invisible narrator, although he must symbolically leave her and become powerless to return as he mounts higher into the abstractions of rationalism through the Brotherhood and as he retreats into the freely imaginative self.

Another folk figure is Dupre, the leader of Harlem rioters who burn down a tenement building. The dramatic and symbolic function of Dupre and his followers is to reflect the folk ability to move with poise amidst chaos and in contradiction to the flat rational assumptions of the Brotherhood concerning its mission as planners for others. The rioters move with a plan that directly confronts Reality.

The discussion of the foregoing characters illustrates, rather than exhausts, the role of folk or folkish characters. We must turn now to scenes that are informed with folk motifs. Ellison himself has commented upon the early Battle Royal scene as one that he lifted from living rituals and placed in a context of larger meaning.[14] It and the invisible narrator's speech comprise on one wave length the ultimate in oppression and self-victimization, as the invisible protagonist tries to be pragmatic and economic man. In the highest sense of the word, the scene is both horrible and wildly comic.

It involves several motifs from folk tradition, a full explanation of which would comprise a separate essay. On the level of Blackness, there is the manipulation of Blacks to fight each other blindly, education as brainwash, the general white manipulation of reality, and the shaping of misleaders of the people. The narrator, himself, embodies the sardonic folk concept that "what's white is right."

But one of the powerful folk motifs is the racial joke of black man and tabooed white woman. The unwritten folk joke, from which the scene derives, is concerned with a Black looking at a white woman and expressing sexual desire while a white man stands by and replies.

> Black. Oh man, will I ever, ever!
> White. No Nigger, you will never, never!
> Black. As long as there's life there's hope!
> White. Yeah Nigger, and as long as there's trees there's rope.

In the Battle Royal scene, it will be recalled, the Black boys are forced to watch the nude white woman dance, and are abused if they look and abused if they do not look. In terms of Blackness, the ritual is to stamp upon them the symbolic castration they are supposed to experience in the presence of a white woman.

Ellison, however, makes his connections. He dramatizes the perverted responses of the white men, and the American flag tattooed upon the nude woman's belly as satire upon American corruption of sexuality. He unites the invisible narrator and the nude blonde as victims and makes out of her a symbol implying the mystery of freedom, similar to James Joyce's use of woman in *A Portrait of the Artist as a Young Man:* "She seemed like a fair bird-girl girdled in veils calling to me from the angry surface of some gray and threatening sea."[15]

Perhaps enough attention has been given to the unconstrained density of reality represented by people, folk and non-folk, of the Golden Day, the sporting house where the philanthroper Norton is faced with all the reality that his rational categories have suppressed. I focus instead upon the vesper scene in Chapter Five, a poem really, in which folk, Black cultural tradition in general, and Western mythology merge. Ellison, in this chapter, is not without humor, but he extracts, at times tenderly, a deep pathos for the uplift dreams that somehow ought to be true. The narrator looks upon them as his investment in identity. The folk motif is the remembered coming of a Moses to bring freedom and richness to the barren land, a ritual and myth delivered in the rich rhetoric of the Black speech tradition. Of course, Homer Barbee, the priest who summons up pictures of ancestors to validate the myth, is blind--a device for undermining his credibility.

Ellison combines the Black Moses myth with the Biblical Moses and the rituals traditionally describing the miraculous birth and survival of the hero. For good measure, the students are also involved in the rites of Horatio Alger. The combination carries the chapter to one of the memorable intensities of the novel. And adding still more to the pathos is the ex-slave matron, Susie Greshman, who brings the warmth and tragic knowledge of the folk--and their high hopes--to this colorful but ineffectual ritual. Anyone who has sat through ceremonies that achieve such a high sense of group communion and shared memories will identify briefly with the invisible narrator despite his terrible delusion.

Such folkish scenes appear also at strategic points in the section of the book devoted to the narrator's Northern experiences, and Ellison exacts from them, at will, humor, pathos, and philosophy. The hero's transition to the impersonal Northern experience evokes memories of folklore deriving from the Southern black's initiation into Northern urban life. The black man-white woman motif arises in a comic scene where the crush of subway traffic jams the narrator against a white woman: "I wanted desperately to raise my hands, to show her it was against my will." I have already referred to the pivotal confrontation with Mary, symbol of all that is positive and something of the negative in folk tradition.

I shall mention briefly additional scenes--all of which function mainly in the exemplification of blackness. In Chapter Eleven, the highly symbolic section which portrays the tendency of industrialism to reduce men to a programmed zero, the Brer Rabbit motif emphasizes the toughness of the Black experience, the indestructibility of a fiber, which is later restored through the care of the folkish Mary Rambo. The numerous folk symbols appearing in different scenes within Chapter Thirteen range in significance from the hero's *elementary* awakening to his heritage through the evoking of the entire Black tradition in the eviction of the ex-slave couple, Mr. and Mrs. Primus Provo, a couple who also embody the bitter fruits harvested by Blacks since securing freedom.

The self-contained and bitter pride of the Provos has an affinity with the feelings evoked in Chapter Thirteen by Brother Tarp, a man who spent nineteen years on the chain gang for opposing white imposition before escaping to New York. Tarp passes on to the invisible narrator a link from the chain broken to secure his freedom. Symbolically, it is a bitter link in the chain of Black tradition, meant to serve as a reminder of roots and inescapable contours in the profile of Black reality. Other images of Blackness appear as warnings as the invisible narrator moves deeper into the Brotherhood: the minstrel fascism of the Brother Wrestrum, who provokes the Brotherhood trial of the narrator; the minstrel dolls manipulated ritualistically to express the youth organizer Todd Clifton's deep sense of betrayal, and the allied image of the zoot-suited Black boys playing their bitter hip satire upon "history" in Chapter Twenty; and perhaps we may include Ras the Exhorter whose existence and strength (Todd Clifton: " . . . it's on the inside that Ras is strong . . . dangerous.") are based first upon the urban folk's hunger for identity and nationhood and second, at least latently, in the breast of every Black conscious of loss and of deep and sustained betrayal. With Rinehart, symbol of possibility through imagination and masking, we are back to Western tradition.

However, Ellison has a deep sense of the beauty, as well as the terror of Black tradition, and therefore acknowledgment of his rendering the rich folk language of the South, the salty speech of the Northern urban areas, and the joyful myth making of urban narrators in the Harlem riot scene is probably the proper note on which to draw toward conclusions.

The first conclusion is that, along with other devices, the folk tradition affords the Black writer a device for instant movement into the privacy, tensioned coherence, toughness, terror, and beauty of Black experience--a method for conjuring up instant Blackness. It is to be noted that Ellison tends to use folk tradition without making outside connections in some scenes emphasizing the height of betrayal of Blackness (as in the Primus Provo eviction), in those portraying dramatic recoil of the narrator from illusions, or in those especially emphasizing a reverential treatment of folk value. But the principle is not fixed: the over-riding guide is utility to theme and dramatic structure. The vesper scene at the Southern college, it will be recalled, derives from Black folklore and Western mythology.

Folklore does not appear then at any point for its own sake, nor is folk vision sentimentalized. As reverently as the folk Mary Rambo is treated, she is not seen as useful to the highest abstract reaches of personality. This view is in line, by extension, with Ellison's concept of Southern folk community as a pre-individual community.[16] So it is not surprising that, once having absorbed what he can from her and having reached for more abstract levels of personality, the invisible narrator cannot return. Another example of the nonsentimental approach is the invisible narrator's newly gained appreciation of soul food, a passage which has been widely quoted for its humor and evidence of acceptance of identity. But the narrator realizes that identity on this level is really too simple. Further, as he continues to eat yams, one turns out to be a frost-bitten--not mere sweetness.

Yet there is something of the great performance, the *tour de force,* in Ellison's use of the folklore and cultural tradition that makes for both enlightenment regarding the literary potential of folklore and a certain unease. This response, I think, is inspired by the elaborate system of interconnection with Western symbols and mythology, and our awareness that Blackness is more in need of definition than Western tradition, which has had the attention of innumerable literary masters. It had to do with the degree of faith that one has in the West, and the suspicion that major literary documents from Melville through Faulkner have been whispering to us of its death. And, in the Black tradition, there has been so frequently an ambivalence and a questioning of the West that go deeper than casting a critical eye upon its technology and rationalism.

The questions raised by Larry Neal regarding Ellison's relationship to the West in his critical essays may well be raised regarding the interconnection system in *Invisible Man,* since there is almost a mathematical consistency between Ellison's critical pronouncements and his creative performance. Writing in *Black Theatre,* Neal credited Ellison with a broad theoretical sense of Black folklore tradition and culture, and an awareness of the "explosive tensions underlying the Black man's presence in the United States," but criticized him for overlaying "his knowledge of Black culture with concepts that exist outside it."[17]

Certainly, the result in *Invisible Man,* if one commits himself to a grasp of the depths of the book, is sometimes simultaneously an awe at sheer brilliance of conjunctions and a hunger for further depths of definition of Blackness which this wily genius obviously has the capacity to make. For make no mistake about it, anyone who could throw in those images of Blackness with such rapidity and apparent ease, who could tone their depths as a gifted musician would do, has, as a pressure behind his imagination, an almost godlike knowledge of Blackness. Make no mistake, Ellison paid his dues to culture. At no time does one run into a Blackness that is rhetorical only, as one still frequently does in even very radical writing. But Ellison, himself, admits that the book would have been better if it had more of Mary Rambo.[18] We would add to Mary, more of Bledsoe, more of the campus dreamers, more of the Harlem rioters, and more even of B.P. Rinehart and Ras, the Destroyer. And we would suppose that it is possible to sound the depths of the universe by a fine excess in the examination of Blackness. A William Faulkner, for example, in making us feel the American and Western aspects of his universe, simply asserts himself as the deepest of Southerners, and communicates through symbols most deeply associated with the South. Perhaps the Faulknerian way is one for the future, since neither the spirit of the 1950's nor the temperament and sensibility which Ellison has frequently and emphatically expounded suggest that earlier, in dealing with Blackness, a Black focus would have been successful or that it would have found an audience.

In the end, it is the great fruits at hand which Ellison harvested, that must be seized upon. For the young writer, his use of folk tradition provides a veritable textbook which can be adapted, according to one's own sensibility and outlook. For more than any other writer, Ellison grappled with its power, its cryptic messages, its complexity. Particularly noteworthy is his realization that folk tradition cannot seem, in a self-conscious artist, to be an end in itself. That is, the writer cannot simply enclose himself within the womb of folkness or content himself with simple celebration of folkness. True folk forms have already celebrated folk life better than the self-conscious artist can hope to do. But the basic *attitudes* and *forms* of response to existence evolved by the folk are abandoned by us only at our peril. These attitudes and forms of response are then of greatest service as flexible instruments for confronting a darkness that is always changing in its complexity. Ellison exemplified a profound knowledge of all such ramifications.

NOTES

1. Ralph Ellison, *Shadow and Act* (New York: Random House, 1964), p. 253.
2. Both authors' essays first appeared in *Partisan Review* (Spring, 1958). Ellison's essay is reprinted in *Shadow and Act,* Hyman's in *The Promised End* (Cleveland: World Publishing Co., 1963).
3. *Shadow and Act,* p. 58.
4. Ibid., p. 58.
5. *New Masses,* 37 (September 24, 1940), 20-21.
6. *New Masses,* 40 (August 5, 1941), 22-26.
7. James A. Emanuel and Theodore L. Gross, *Dark Symphony* (New York: Free Press, 1968), pp. 254-
270.
8. *Shadow and Act,* pp. 77-94.
9. Ibid., p. 78 f.
10. Ibid., pp. 167-186. The entire interview merits careful study.
11. *Shadow and Act,* here and there, pp. 107-143.
12. See Selma Fraiberg, " Two Modern Incest Heroes," *Partisan Review,* XXVIII (1961), pp. 646-661. In this section, I am very much indebted to her essay.
13. Herbert Hill, *Soon One Morning* (New York: Random House, 1963).
14. *Shadow and Act,* p. 174.
15. *Invisible Man,* p. 23.
16. *Shadow and Act,* p. 90.
17. Larry Neal, " Cultural Nationalism and Black Theatre," *Black Theatre,* No. 1, p. 10.
18. See unused section of hospital scene, Herbert Hill, *Soon One Morning* (New York: Random House, 1963).

From *CLA Journal* 13: 3 (March 1969), 265-276.

Contemporary Readings of *Invisible Man*

Luminosity from the Lower Frequencies

Leon Forrest

I should like to discuss certain intellectual, cultural, and historical influences upon Ralph Ellison's sense of the hero's character-in-process and the structure of the major chapters throughout his monumental novel, *Invisible Man.* Several influences come to mind: Kenneth Burke, Lord Raglan, Dostoevsky and Faulkner, as well as the artistic and jazz-like rendering of folkloric sources.

From the literary critic Burke, Ellison came to see the possibility of using a formula to structure a chapter. Burke held that a pattern could be employed to achieve character-in-process progression through the formula of *purpose, passion* and *perception:* each chapter begins with a *purpose* for the hero, but then much of the action of the middle section involves a struggle or *passion,* over this *purpose,* or quest. Out of this mix or confrontation with others and the self, the hero comes away with a heightened *perception,* a keener awareness about his life, so that a metamorphosis, or rebirth is implied. But these moments are stages of his processing into life, and the cycle once completed, unleashes new problems and struggles.

Another literary influence on *Invisible Man* came from Lord Raglan, whose seminal book *The Hero,* argues that a constant pattern of biographical data defines the lives of the heroes of tradition. The heroes Raglan calls forth run a gamut from Oedipus Rex to Elijah, Zeus, Orpheus and Robin Hood. The pattern traces some twenty-two steps from birth to death. But the central constant in Raglan's pattern of heroic dimension is this: that the hero dies, goes through a life underground and is reborn. Raglan's concept meshes neatly with Burke's formula of *purpose, passion* and *perception.* For instance, the passion or conflict is quite similar to the turmoil in the mental Underground and all of the attendant agonies. The idea of a heightened *perception* can be linked to Raglan's concept of rebirth, or even redemption in the Christian sense, and to discovery and self-recognition in the Aristotelian sense.

In the major chapters of his novel, Ellison--a jazz trumpeter who studied musical composition--orchestrates and improvises upon an introductory theme raised through a character at the beginning of a chapter. And he ends the chapter on an up-beat thematic moment (sometimes with an enriching, elusive literary statement, that speaks for the chapter and the intelligence of the novel as a whole "at the lower frequencies") which stands in opposition to the opening thematic idea. Our sense of luminosity is heightened with the hero's, because of the sweeping poles or polar distances traversed from the beginning to the end. These are mini-odysseys of purpose, passion and perception, we might say.

Ellison's arrangement of characters and themes standing in during confrontational moments forms a constant source of instruction, as we see the hero's character-in-process evolve and the novel evolve; and it helps the reader to see how these apparently oppositional forces are really quite closely connected. This device recalls anthropologist Levi-Strauss' concept of *thesis, counter-thesis, synthesis.* And it is related to Dostoevsky's use of doubling and of character. One way of looking at doubling is to see it as a blending of opposites--characters who stand in sharp opposition to each other and yet have much in common.

The novel abounds with instances of this Dostoevskian doubling. There is for example the Norton/Trueblood pairing--a one-to-one confrontation, with the Oedipal desire/act forging a linkage between the rich, white, blue-blood, philanthropist, Norton, and the poor, black, uneducated peasant farmer, Jim Trueblood. In Trueblood's dream, we discover an abundance of underground images indicating that Trueblood lusts for power in the real world as much as the powerful Norton lusts for the body of his own daughter--behind the monument of money he has donated in her honor to the school. Another form of Dostoevskian doubling occurs in the reverberating manner in which characters in apparent oppositional quest, status, or station are paired by a theme at completely different stages and times.

For instance, the theme of *eloquence,* its manipulation, uses and misuses, links the tall, Lincoln-like Hambro, mouthpiece for the Communist-like Brotherhood, with the spokesman-versifier for the Negro college and the American white way, the blind, Founder-celebrating minister, Homer Barbee. Short and ugly like Homer, Barbee gives a high-priest choral-arrangement and tribal eulogy for the Founder that sounds like Whitman praising Abe Lincoln (note Ellison's parody on the great Whitman's grand blindness to Abe's angularity, his blemishes, his body-and-soul torment over slavery, his complexity of motives). Now these two high-powered word artist-cum-magicians in turn, represent two power-mad, master tricksters. For Hambro illuminates the enslaving dogma espoused by the one-eyed, Cyclops, Brother Jack, *Head White Man in Charge* of the Brotherhood. And as Hambro attempts to drop the illuminating (but really enshrouding, and blinding) veil of "*understanding*" over the student-hero's eyes, he also blinds himself to the pranks of public policy that enslave the individual for the public good of this most private, elite of American parties. Thus he is veiled by his own public pronouncements.

And that high-priest of bamboozlement, Odyssey-echoing Homer Barbee, eloquently drops the enslaving veil of intellectual blindness across the students' eyes, to please that manipulator of polished slave chains, the college President Herbert Bledsoe and his captive audience of white trustees, that is, over-seers. For in this situation at least, Bledsoe is not only the *Head Nigger in Charge* (HNIC), but he has actually reversed the plantation system so that he is slave-master on this plantation, with Barbee as slave-driver of history. And Barbee in turn is blinded like the statue of the Founder, as he drops the veil honoring institutional power, which is manifested in the body and soul of the Founder's epic story (not in the student's learning and intellectual development). Barbee participates in his own self-impaling ceremony: he dims the light of his own intellectual and moral vision of history, preferring the luxurious delusion of "sweet harmonies" over the reality of the chaos of African-American life. And as he extinguishes his vision with his words, Barbee recalls Oedipus, who having seen too much, tears out his eyes with the clasps of Jocasta's gown. Barbee's physical blindness seems a fitful banishment from the lost North Star light of daring freedom and progress, or as he himself says at one point, as he recalls the declining luminosity in the Founder's life on the train:

> I remember how I looked out of the frosted pane and saw the looming great North Star and lost it, as though the sky had shut its eye. (99)

In this sense too, the phase-polishing Barbee becomes a kind of scapegoat for Bledsoe, as minister Homer leads the lamb-innocent Negro students to a slaughtered rendering of their history. Yet their only hope for escape is the underground railroad, as it were, and that too on an individual basis. For each must read his or her own way through Barbee's fabulous spiel and the only hope for escape from re-enslavement is to hold fast to the undersides of their history, beneath Barbee's words and memories, and hope that probing questions will ignite a liberating response from their fellow blacks. Indeed they must be ready to commit a kind of "treason" like that "snowy-headed man" at one of the Founder's ceremonial lectures who demands that the Founder cut the accommodationist spiel and

> "Tell us what is to be done, sir! For God's sake, tell us! Tell us in the name of the son they snatched from me last week!" And all through the room the voices arising, imploring, "Tell us, tell us!" And the Founder is suddenly mute with tears (97).

Like Ulysses escaping the Cyclops in the cave, the students must approach Barbee's story with cunning to match the blinding light of his language, and like Ulysses, must catch hold of the sacred and the profaned aspects of their history under-the-belly, and hold on for dear life--as Ulysses says, "so I caught hold of the ram by the back, ensconced myself in the thick wool under his belly and hung on patiently to his fleece, face upwards keeping a firm hold on it all of the time." For the students would need to reverse so much of Barbee's speech and to reveal the truths from oral history handed along by the great story-tellers, truths that he constantly subordinates and countermands. This is a central problem for a young Negro confronted by all of the distortions of that peasant, underground history--a fact that the Klan-beset, snowy-headed man in Homer Barbee's saga-spiel knows only too well.

Ellison is concerned there in the Barbee-Founder-Bledsoe trinity, as it were, with the unquestioned reverence for leadership that still seems to haunt certain groups within the race vulnerable to the cult of the personality, especially when touched by the fires of political-religious enterprise. But there is a yeasty truth in Barbee's saga. Barbee knows the language of power, and he manipulates it as it manipulates him--and in that sense he's masking the wisdom of his peasant tongue. Similarly, it is not so much what Brother Jack says about the party but the fact that he lost his eye which keeps him from facing his underground history. When his false eye drops out into the glass of water in a moment of confrontation with the hero late in the novel (over the Invisible Man's unauthorized speech for Tod Clifton), he must drop the party line that covers his vision and babble back into his peasant tongue or into the obscuring language of power. The dropping out of Jack's eye recalls the revelation of Barbee's blindness at the end of his spiel, as he trips in his darkness after having maintained his verbal high-wire act with such deftness, symmetry of line, and balance of power. It recalls chaos-loving Rhinehart's manipulative spiel of eloquence that extracts handouts from the blinded, lamb-innocent church ladies. Rhinehart's spiel is tied to the profane eloquence of chaos-destroyed, hyper-sensitive Tod Clifton, whose street-corner spiel about the Sambo-doll--that it will be whatever you want it to be--reflects the gist of what the streetcorner hustler tells all slum-dwellers hungry to be recognized or loved.

Even in small segments of the novel we see how these clusters, formulas, and influences operate with Ellison's materials. Chapter Nine starts off soon after the hero gets to Harlem on his way to Mr. Emerson to check out the job reference letter given to him by the powerful black president. The hero was booted out, you will recall, because the black madness manifested as the riotous Golden Day, and showed him as well the base human passions (and by indirection Norton's own purposeful passion) revealed by Jim Trueblood's eloquent saga of incest.

Now our hero starts off with the purpose of finding a job, but early on he runs into a bluesman whose song celebrates the powerful, sexually fulfilling catharsis he achieves from his love-making lady, whose praises he sings, as follows:

> She's got feet like a monkey
> Legs like a frog--Lawd, Lawd:
> But when she starts to loving me,
> I holler Whoo, God-Dog!
> Cause I loves my Baabay,
> Better than I do myself . . . (131)

Now this blues song celebrates the fulfilling sex life of a poor bluesman at the bottom, whose woman's beauty is questionable according to standards of beauty in the upper-world. Yet their sex life is an affirming glory of life at the bottom, and it leads him to swear that he loves her better than he does himself. The second point is this: the blues singer is certain about his identity, about who he is sexually; and as it turns out, he is a fierce individualist who tries to tell the hero to be what he is, not to masquerade himself, not to deny the bluesman.

Now towards the end of the chapter the hero comes to discover and recognize his new fate, when he finds out that the masquerading trickster, Dr. Bledsoe, indeed has written the hero out of history and driven him towards the unattainable horizon, not with a job reference letter as the hero assumed, but rather with a prank piece of paper that says in effect--"To Whom It May Concern, Keep This Nigger-Boy Running." But now at this agony-filled, perception-sharpening junction, another kind of song comes bubbling up to the surface of the hero's consciousness, rescuing him from self-pity--a mock dirge, played traditionally in the Oklahoma area. After a burial, Negro jazz musicians would light up into this dirge once they hit the Negro business section of town. It expresses the attitudes central to the black man's memory of history, that if he is to survive he must not allow himself to wallow in self-pity over death, or over the constant dream-shattering, death - dealing experience that is his fate. His mocked fate. The dirge goes:

> O Well, they picked poor Robin clean
> O Well, they picked poor Robin clean
> Well, they tied poor Robin to a stump
> Lawd, they picked all the feathers 'round from Robin's rump
> Well, they picked poor Robin clean. (147)

The bluesman's song is filled with life, possibility, affirmation of love and identity through fundamental sexual confrontation and confirmation. The dirge stands in apparent opposition, since it comes at the time of a death; yet it is life giving and intelligence heightening, even as it is innocence destroying--mocking our hero's false pride and his naive worship of Bledsoe. The song mocks and thereby instructs him that each person must constantly die, or shed the skin of his innocence, in order to grow. The mock dirge comes after a moment of the hero's mock murder, through the pen of bloody Bledsoe. Finally, the song says that savage experience picks us clean of the plumage-like illusions round our baby-soft, rounded rumps and leaves us picked clean to the bone of our innocence--but then, perhaps that is indeed the necessary price of eating of the forbidden fruit of experience and knowledge. Unlike the blues, "which allows no scapegoat but the self," the dirge allows us to "lighten our load by becoming one with the bird, as he symbolically takes over our bone-picked sorrow."

This pattern of death, agony, and mocking affirmation or momentary re-birth informs the entire novel, but is pointedly suggested in that marvelous skeleton of a call-and-response sermon by the black minister in the Prologue. There, in the cellar of the hero's racial consciousness where Ellison's version of Underground Man is dwelling, the preacher says, "I said black is . . . an' black ain't . . . Black will git . . . you and black won't . . . It do, Lawd . . . an it don't--Black will make you . . . or black will unmake you." (8) Bledsoe, the black president of the college, has undone the hero. And minister Barbee looks through a glass darkly, never face to face. But it is a black dirge that souringly surges forth from the underground racial past and it helps rescue, school, and repair the hero at the junction in chapter nine. Here again the movement from affirmation through denial to affirmation, or from thesis to counter-thesis to synthesis is treated dialectically as it was by the man at the bottom, the bluesman, Peter Wheatstraw.

The bluesman is "doubled" with the hero in the Dostoevskian sense. The street-wise bluesman knows everything about northern idiom and what it takes to get along in this here man's town and on the lower frequencies; and yet Peter Wheatstraw is lost and homeless in the world of power, unable at the higher frequencies to manipulate its symbols or to manifest his vision, and he's uneducated in the school sense. At the other end the Invisible Man is lost in the streets of Harlem and is also homeless in the world of power, indeed the most powerful man in his world has just kicked him out of this world (upstairs, you might say, to the North) to Harlem, which is, of course, *nowhere*. And the Invisible Man is under-educated in the street sense. On the other hand, there is synthesis possible for the hero if he but trusts his underground peasant intelligence and memory. For as the hero reflects upon one riff in Peter Wheatstrw's spiel he thinks,

> I liked his words though I didn't know the answer. I'd known the stuff from childhood, but had forgotten it; had learned it back of school. (134)

But at this junction, too, the hero and the bluesman are tied together again because it is very important to him that this "new-boy" in town not deny him. Peter Wheatstraw's concern is almost prophetic because, at the end of the chapter, the hero is to be denied by his *Peter*, Herbert Bledsoe. Bledsoe is glad to see him at first and then denies him privately. The fear of being denied by race brother, by public power, and by father figures sets the stage for the hero's next confrontation.

In the middle of chapter nine, the hero undergoes the *Passion* phase of Burke's law via a confrontation with young Emerson, a man of shattered dreams, denied personal fulfillment, at the top of the economic spectrum. His sexuality is confused and so is his identity about a host of subjects, ranging from the way he really feels about blacks to the ambivalence about his powerful father, who has figuratively devoured his son, like Cronus did unto Zeus. Young Emerson, a homosexual undergoing a form of psychoanalysis which apparently brings him no affirmation, stands then in direct opposition to the solidly based blues-singing, dirt-poor, black man of the streets at the beginning of the chapter, who knows who he is. Yet this pairing also recalls the Norton-Trueblood pairing and doubling.

And this pairing also recalls the old American story of the man who has everything and nothing; young Emerson is rich, white, free and twenty-one, yet he really has nothing but a world of confusion; and the bluesman has nothing but a batch of blueprints showing his dreams of powerful towns and country clubs that he will never erect. He has everything, though, in a real woman who loves him with a great, sexual power, even though her beauty, at the lower frequencies, is invisible to all but the naked eye. It is young Emerson, the homosexual, who unfolds the truth of the letter to the hero, just as it is the remarkable looking lady of the bluesman who gives him the sexual, naked truth and renders him a celebrant of her naked powers, body and soul. One recalls how it is the blind hermaphrodite, Tiresias, who bears to Oedipus the truth below the king's self-righteous existence. But the homosexual at the top and the bluesman at the bottom are also linked; for both are existential outlaws in our society, yet at the same time both are high-priests from the peripheral underground, warning the hero of hidden reality. (Tangentially, we might reflect here that so many of our current musical dance patterns have their genesis in black bars on the one hand, and gay bars on the other, long before we all began to dance, dance to the music.) Indeed one recalls that young Emerson tells the hero about a kind of peripheral bar, the Club Calamus:

> "You haven't? It's very well known. Many of my Harlem friends go there. It's a rendezvous for writers, artists, and all kinds of celebrities. There's nothing like it in the city, and by some strange twist it has a truly continental flavor." (141)

At this point the hero has undergone a mini-motif of Lord Raglan's pattern in this chapter--he has figuratively died, undergone an underground agony, and been re-born tougher and more perceptive and able to laugh at himself. Finally the wonderful spiel delivered by the bluesman as he is advising our hero has provided the first confrontation the southern-born hero has with a northern black and it is significant that, although they are speaking the same language, he hardly understands the bluesman's transformed tongue, at first. Migrate from one part of America to another and you are often lost in terms of idiomatic meaning. Yet in the case of the black man the genesis of language has an ancestral underground root in the old country of the Southland. To show Ellison's many dimensioned use of idiom, let me now attempt to unravel one of his bluesman's riffs:

> "All it takes to get along in this here man's town is a little shit, grit, and mother-wit. And man, I was bawn with all three. In fact I'm seventhsonofaseventhsonbawnwithacauloverbotheyesandraisedonblackcatboneshighjohntheconquerorand greasygreens," he spieled with twinkling eyes, his lips working rapidly. "You dig me daddy?" (134)

Let me suggest that here Ellison is rendering up the fusion of myth and lore which is the genesis of Negro/Black/white/Afro-American idiomatic versification. "The seventh son of a seventh son" comes from the Scottish-English influence upon the former slaves and suggests how myth-bound and haunted the slave-holders were and refers to one who is born lucky. "Bawn with a caul over both eyes" suggests one who is born with the gift of clairvoyance; and has an Ashanti linkage from the African aspect of the heritage. "Raised on black cat bones" is from the Afro-*American* version of Voodoo and the context is this: in Voodoo, which always reverses meaning (as does so much of Negro idiom), you throw a live black cat into a boiling pot of hot water; after the flesh has fallen away you pick out its bones and gnaw away, and if you are lucky, and gnaw down the right bone, you will become *invisible*. "High John the Conqueror" is a mythical hero from slavery, an invisible hero who sided with the slaves, during bad times, with good advice. And "greasy-greens," of course, refers to African-American cuisine, in the old country Southland.

The hero's presence in the North at this time in the novel recalls the migration from the South to the North of blacks who came, often on the run, pursuing the dream of a peaceful kingdom, jobs and personal fulfillment. But the hero's dream becomes a nightmare through a mocking note that , unbeknown to him, reads: "To Whom It May Concern: Keep This Nigger Boy Running." It is significant, and one of ironies of the meshing of race and class, that (while looking for employment) the hero discovers this dimension of his representative fate in the North from a rich white entrepreneur's son whose mock employment has brought him no fulfillment.

But it is even more significant that the hero first recalls the "Nigger Boy Running" joke via a recalled dream that he has of his grandfather, at the end of Chapter I, just after he wins his scholarship to the Negro college. For in the dream, through his grandfather, the hero is ritually warned and instructed:

> He told me to open my brief case and read what was inside--and I did, finding an official envelope stamped with the state seal; and inside the envelope I found another and another endlessly and I thought I would fall of weariness. "Them's yours," he said, "Now open that one." And I did and in it I found an engraved document containing a short message in letters of gold. "Read it," my grandfather said. "Out Loud!"
>
> "To Whom It May Concern," I intoned, "Keep This Nigger Boy Running." (26)

And there is an underground story beneath this memory. For in the old South, a form of black-baiting which had its genesis in slavery would proceed as follows: a Negro newcomer would arrive upon the scene, looking for gainful employment; he would go to a prospective white employer. This ordinary small-town white businessman would immediately spot the fact that this was not one of the local blacks and would tell the black outsider that he did not have work at this time but that he did know of someone who might have jobs available down the road, perhaps.

The white businessman would then give the horizon-seeking black a sealed letter to take to the next prospective employer. Upon reaching the next white man, the letter would be presented, opened by the white man, read and mused over, and then the Negro would hear the same old story--"No Jobs" here but perhaps "Up the road" and then the white merchant would scribble something on the note, reseal the communiqué (like the Negro's fate) and then hand the letter back to the out-reaching dark hand. This would happen again and again, until the black finally opened the letter and read the message, or got the message, and read out his symbolic fate (or some variation upon the theme): "To Whom It May Concern, Keep This Nigger Boy Running." This brutal joke of course had its antecedents in slavery, when many or most slaves couldn't read or write, and could go only from plantation to plantation with a note signed by the Master, or his *earthly* representative. The slave didn't in fact know what might or might not be written down on that note. And although this tortuous ritual or bad-faith convenant came from the pastoral scenes of the gallant South, actually the "jobs" search and its attendant mocking ceremony were often played out in the industrial North. Or more to the point, the duplicity operative at the Paint Factory in *Invisible Man,* which in fact did hire our nameless hero, but only as a scab (union strike buster), signified the way industrial bosses pitted the racial and ethnic groupings of the underclassed against each other. And when the Invisible Man's day labor was used up, he was discarded and put on tentative welfare after signing some papers which freed him from work--new slave papers meant to quiet his aggressive appetite for employment.

It is structurally salient that Ellison establishes early the ancestral tie with the grandfather's folk voice, via the underground avenue of the dream. For the grandfather's appearance and intelligence in the dream is the deeper Underground Railroad reality beneath the American Dream for the Negro. And the grandfather is the oldest ancestor within the hero's family memory. And who is the *grandfather's* authority? No doubt the oldest member of the tribe in his memory, perhaps *his* grandfather--and then we are back into slavery; so that in a highly oral culture the grandfather is the proper high-priest to pass on mythical reality and survival wisdom from the battle-zone. Throughout the novel, a warning or extolling voice issues forth from underground (often coming to the hero's aid, like Tarp's voice at the bottom of the Brotherhood) during moments of agony, conflict, trial, public and private passion. *And* (like the rescuing dirge, or High John the Conqueror) this intelligence informs his hard-won experience, thereby constantly presenting the reader with a hero's awareness or perception that is heightened. Not all of the underground warning voices confer benefits upon the hero as they warn him, however, as Lucius Brockway, in the underground of the paint factory, demonstrates. Brockway becomes a most trying combination of Tar-Baby and Proteus for the Invisible Man.

Now in some cases the ancestral voice comes directly out of the remembering hero's own past, as did the rescuing dirge. The second kind of ancestral voice issues from the hero's consciousness when he recalls moments from his own personal history, which then leads to racial memory as did the dream of the grandfather. The third kind of historical-ancestral linkage comes from symbols or specific items which don't touch the hero's own past but which form a lucid part of his racial memory and the consciousness of the race, in the Joycean sense, suggesting then a duty and a task and a covenant or responsibility to the ancestral community.

Now these symbolic objects surge forth at moments of passion or trial. For instance, when the hero, late in the novel, discovers another kind of "Keep This Nigger Boy Running" note on his desk at the Brotherhood's office, Brother Tarp, the man at the bottom of the organization, gives the hero a picture of Frederick Douglass, our man at the top of Negro leadership in the 19th century. Later Tarp gives the hero his own leg irons, retained from a chain gang. The hero must learn to trust those symbolic ancestral tokens, voices, or manifestations--yet he must sort out the consulting surge of past and present counsellors. Indeed one of the hero's many agonies is to learn not to accept the advice from authority figures without question and to wrestle with advice until he's made it his own and understood it, or spurned it, or accepted it and by accepting it, made certain he's reshaped the advice to fit his own experience. For the other side of the most profane or the healthiest advice is that it renders the hero somebody's "running boy" and does not allow him to be his own man.

So, motifs involving power, sex, women, images of light and dark, broken taboos, Afro-American folklore papers of importance, quests for identity and responsibility, individualism, music, violence, uses of eloquence, all come in clusters and order the improvisations of Ellison's orchestrated novel. Here we can see the influence of William Faulkner's *Light in August,* in which the major scenes are ordered by the presence of sex, women, food, money and are in turn connected with images of light and dark, religion and slavery, as integrating forces which undergird the associative patterns of each narrative section. In terms of power Ellison is constantly improvising upon the whole plantation system as a metaphor for understanding American institutions. This improvisation on the plantation-like hierarchy can be seen in the "descent" section of the Prologue, in the pecking order at the Paint Factory Scene, in life at Mary Rambo's rooming house, in the Brotherhood, at the college, at the Battle-Royal smoker and at the Golden Day.

Connected with this imagery of the plantation is another, deeper dimension of Ellison's metaphoric patterning, in which he projects a symbolic model of American history--thereby joining the very select company of Melville, Hawthorne and especially Faulkner in this recombining of metaphorical vision with history. All of Faulkner's major works involving the black presence, it seems to me, possess this epic design. For instance in *Absalom, Absalom!* the "design" of metaphor can be read in the following manner: Let the French architect stand for America's "borrowed" French principles of refinement, creativity, artistry, ideals of culture, freedom and liberty (indeed our fitful intellectual indebtedness to the French Revolution) and let Sutpen stand for American know-how, cunning, outlandish daring, bigotry, savage frontiersmanship-hustle, furious energy and industry, and white-ethnic class hatred; and let the Negro slaves of Sutpen's Hundreds stand as the enslaved bases of the American economic order.

Sutpen must reduce all others to "niggers" (blacks, women, his family, outside family, poor whites, his son) as he hacks his insanely ambitious way to the top. The new American Adam must reduce the French architect, at the other end of the social spectrum, to a sub-human, to a nigger, once he has used up the architect's expertise. And he then attempts to free his body from Sutpen's clutches. Sutpen in turn re-enacts a mock French revolution by bringing down the French aristocrat-artist. But the French architect only flees when he discovers that he too is enslaved--thus the synthesis between slave and aristocrat is forged by *slavery's* chains. And the French architect's flight and Sutpen's pursuit of him with hound-dogs recalls that of a runaway slave and the ritual pursuit by hound dogs.

Dostoevsky's hero in *Notes From Underground*, and the illumined Invisible Man of the Ellison Prologue and Epilogue, are manifestations of hyper-awareness and terror concerning the inner meanness of the outer world: they observe it as a treacherous terrain. Structurally, the Prologue contains within it all of the materials needed for Ellison's invention; and the core of the work then goes on to illustrate and orchestrate these materials. In Underground Man's world, Part I is a presentation of the arguments and in Part II we have the illustrations. *Notes From Underground* can be seen as a monologue rich with personal and political commentary. The grand sweep of the many monologues in *Invisible Man* carry a similar personal, political "doubleness." But Ellison's monologues have a kind of epic grandness that go beyond Dostoyevsky. Witness for example, Trueblood's saga and Barbee's sermon.

At every turn in *Notes*, Underground Man is out to shock the reader, to *shock* reason itself. The Invisible Man is out to shake the reader into an awareness that is streaked with a soured humour and a great gift for hyperbole. Both novels are within the tradition of the memoir, and like *Notes, Invisible Man* is seasoned in the tradition of confessional literature of the seductive underground diary.

The Russia of Underground Man's day was highly repressive, and so for Ellison's hyperaware man there is ever the feeling of alienation and dispossession. (And you will recall that the Invisible Man's second public address treats the theme of dispossession and he uses it in his third address at the stadium.) In Dostoevsky's Russia you either accepted your socio-economic status as your fate or you dropped out. No mobility. Faced with the fitful combination of power, race, and wrenching leadership, the Invisible Man faces a comparable terrain, cut off in the cellar from upward movement. Perhaps even more in keeping with the vaulting, scorning attitude of Underground man are the men in the Golden Day, who remain as Afro-American examples of broken men, though madness has consumed their soured brilliance.

Both narrators appear to be on to something concerning the way the normal world of power operates in a system of deceit--especially if you are highly aware, you are apt to be driven to reason. For example after seeing too much, in an ancestral dream of the shattering past in the Prologue, The Invisible Man recalls . . .

> And at that point a voice of trombone timbre screamed at me, "Git out of here, you fool! Is you ready to commit treason?" (8)

Both narrators suggest that the mind of highly aware man contains much spite and even vengeance. Underground Man seeks revenge, not justice. But the Invisible Man would seek both. There is a sense in both works--particularly in *Notes*--that hyperconsciousness leads to paralysis. Therefore the only action issues out of a sense of wilfulness and spitefulness. The Invisible Man though, is obsessed with responsibility, and cultural enterprise, and the rage for freedom that remains a viable ancestral imperative. The Invisible Man however, frets about overstaying his time of contemplation in the underground and knows he is bound to come up; he seeks love, and spite can only lead to disintegration of personality, as in those memorable figures in the Golden Day. Ultimately, of course, going underground is a kind of psychological going within oneself for both narrators,

Ralph Ellison starts out wanting to reverse the idea, current at the time he conceived *Invisible Man,* that the Negro was invisible. The narrator says "I am invisible simply because you refuse to see me." But having committed himself to assaulting the current sociological metaphor of the day, Ellison turns the metaphor into a dialectic vision of modern America as a briarpatch. The metaphor of invisibility is "doubly" enriched by his constant allusions to the plantation system. The logic is as follows: *Thesis:* You (society) say I'm a slave. *Counter-thesis:* but I'm not a slave in my soul, nor in my mind. *Synthesis:* I'll admit that slavery is the system in which I dwell, but I only see myself as slave in that system if you'll accept the metaphor of how the system enslaves us all, Master . . . And because I've lived with this knowledge longer, I've learned how to make the plantation my briar patch; though it enslaves my body I have learned how to keep my mind and spirit free from its damnation of the spirit. And Master, economically your survival depends upon my body's productivity in the slave system that obsesses your mind and spirit. Alternatively, the Invisible Man asks himself, and us, as he weaves through the possible meanings of the grandfather's advice in the Epilogue,

> Was it that we of all, we, most of all, had to affirm the principle, the plan in whose name we had been brutalized and sacrificed--not because we would always be weak nor because we were afraid of opportunities, but because we were older than they, in the sense of what it took to live in the world, with others and because they had exhausted in us, some--not much, but some--of the human greed and smallness, yes, and the fear and superstition that had kept them running. (433-34)

Like Dostoevsky's Underground Man, the Invisible Man puts down the idea of racial invisibility; he embraces the metaphor, assaults it, then reverses it. He discovers at the height of the race riots in Harlem that he cannot return to Mary's either, that he is invisible to Mrs. Rambo as he is to Jack, Ras, and Bledsoe. For like Underground Man, he discovers that statistical computations for the collective good, or institutional asylums for the individual's good or visions of the individual's good by powerful figures and forces constantly leave out one important impulse: man's urge and capacity to conceptualize his humanity beyond statistics and regimentation; his wilfulness to do what he wants, in the underground economy of his imagination, to turn a plantation into an underground briar patch or a hostile terrain into the sources and resource points of escape via the mind's Underground Railroad.

For finally the Invisible Man is underground, indeed; but he has decided that it is time to end his hibernation and come up to meet a new level of experience. And it is plain to me that at the end of the novel, our hero, reborn, is about to emerge from his womb of safety in the underground; and it is also clear that he is trapped in a personal way between two voices. For as he acknowledges:

> Thus having tried to give patterns to the chaos which lives within the pattern of your certainties, I must come out, I must emerge. And there's still a conflict

> within me; with Louis Armstrong one half of me says, "Open the window and let the foul air out," while the other says, "It was a good green corn before the harvest." (438)

Now the "green corn" motif comes from a Leadbelly song and refers to a state of innocence before the harvest of experience. Innocence is beautiful but it carries dangerous naivete with it--a naive skin that our hero sheds.

But first of all the hero hears a lyrical line from the man who makes poetry out of invisibility, Louis Armstrong, a song which suggests the sophisticated, toughened shape the hero's perception of reality has taken on out of the furnace-like bad air of passion and conflict which has been his experience throughout the life of the novel. The line refers to a song by Buddy Bolden which Louis Armstrong--also known as Dipper Mouth and Bad-Air--used to sing:

> I thought I heard Buddy Bolden say,
> Funky-Butt, Funky-Butt, take it away,
> I thought I heard somebody shout,
> Open up the window and let the foul air out.

The Funky-Butt was a powerhouse jazz night club in New Orleans, where the solos on the horns were as furious and glorious as the sex act itself, filled with bad air and ecstatic charges, savage thrusts and stellar flourishes. Armstrong, as a kid of ten used to stand outside the door of the Funky-Butt and listen to Bolden, the great jazz trumpeter who ended up in a madhouse, blowing and singing and wailing. Bolden would sing the song in tribute to the funkiness and the foul air in the dance hall caused by the jelly-tight dancing.

Without the liberating bad air, that riffs through the chamber of the good-bad horn of plenty (which also resembles the chamber from whence all life emerges) you can't have the real music of life, nor the dance. For as the hero comments,

> Of course Louis was kidding, *he* wouldn't have thrown old Bad Air out, because it would have broken up the music and the dance, when it was the good music that came from the bell of old Bad Air's horn that counted. (438)

NOTE

1.Ralph Ellison, *Invisible Man* (New York: Random House, 1952), 99. All subsequent citations in this article are to this edition.

From *The Carleton Miscellany* XVIII, 3 (Winter 1980), 82-97.

To Move Without Moving: An Analysis of Creativity and Commerce in Ralph Ellison's Trueblood Episode

Houston A. Baker, Jr.

> *Them boss quails is like a good man, what he got to do he do.*
> Ralph Ellison
> Trueblood in *Invisible Man*

In his essay "Richard Wright's Blues," Ralph Ellison states one of his cherished distinctions: "The function, the psychology, of artistic selectivity is to eliminate from art form all those elements of experience which contain no compelling significance. Life is as the sea, art a ship in which man conquers life's crushing formlessness, reducing it to a course, a series of swells, tides and wind currents inscribed on a chart."[1] The distinction between nonsignificant life experiences and their inscribed, artistic significance (i.e., the meaning induced by form) leads Ellison to concur with André Malraux that artistic significance alone "enables man to conquer chaos and to master destiny" (*S&A*, 94).

Artistic "technique," according to Ellison, is the agency through which artistic meaning and form are achieved. In "Hidden Name and Complex Fate" he writes:

> It is a matter of outrageous irony, perhaps, but in literature the great social clashes of history no less than the painful experience of the individual are secondary to the meaning which they take on through the skill, the talent, the imagination, and personal vision of the writer who transforms them into art. Here they are reduced to more manageable proportions; here they are imbued with humane value; here, injustice and catastrophe become less important in themselves than what the writer makes of them. (*S&A*, 148-49)

Even the thing-in-itself of lived, historical experience is thus seen as devoid of "humane value" before its sea change under the artist's transforming technique.

Since Ellison focuses his interest on the literary, the inscribed, work of art, he regards even folklore as part of that realm of life "elements . . . which contain no compelling significance" in themselves. In "Change the Joke and Slip the Yoke," he asserts:

> The Negro writer is also an heir to the human experience which is literature, and this might well be more important to him than his living folk tradition. For me, at least, in the discontinuous, swiftly changing and diverse American culture, the stability of the Negro folk tradition became precious as a result of an act of literary discovery. . . .For those who are

> able to translate [the folk tradition's] meanings into wider, more precise vocabularies it has much to offer indeed. (*S&A,* 72-73)

During a BBC program recorded in May 1982 and titled "Garrulous Ghosts: The Literature of the American South," Ellison stated that the fiction writer, to achieve proper resonance, must go beyond the blues--a primary and tragically eloquent form of American expression:

> The blues are very important to me. I think of them as the closest approach to tragedy that we have in American art forms. And I'm not talking about black or white, I mean just American. Because they do combine the tragic and the comic in a very subtle way and, yes, they are very important to me. But they are also limited. And if you are going to write fiction there is a level of consciousness which you move toward which I would think transcends the blues.

Thus Ellison seems to regard Afro-American folklore, before its translation into "more precise vocabularies," as part of lived experience. Art and chaos appear to be homologous with literature and folklore.

To infer such a homology from one or two critical remarks, however, is to risk the abyss of "false distinction," especially when one is faced with a canon as rich as Ralph Ellison's. For it is certainly true that the disparagement of folk expression suggested by these remarks can be qualified by the praise of folklore implicit in Ellison's assertion that Afro-American expressive folk projections are a group's symbolically "profound" attempts to "humanize" the world. Such projections, even in their crudest forms, constitute the "humble base" on which "great literature" is erected (*S&A,* 172).

It does seem accurate, however, to say that Ellison's criticism repeatedly implies an extant, identifiable tradition of Western literary art--a tradition consisting of masters of form and technique who must be read, studied, emulated, and (if one is lucky and eloquent) equaled. This tradition stands as the signal, vital repository of "humane value." And for Ellison the sphere that it describes is equivalent to the *primum mobile,* lending force and significance to all actions of the descending heavens and earth.

Hence, while division between folk and artistic may be only discursive, having no more factual reality than any other such division, it seems to matter to Ellison, who, as far as I know, never refers to himself as a folk artist. Moreover, in our era of sophisticated "folkloristics," it seems mere evasion to shy from the assertion that Ellison's criticism ranks folklore below literary are on a total scale of value. What I argue is that the distinction between folklore and literary art evident in Ellison's critical practice collapses in his creative practice in *Invisible Man's*[2] Trueblood episode. Further, I suggest that an exacting analysis of this episode illuminates the relation not only between Ellison's critical and creative practices but also between what might be called the public and private commerce of black art in America.

The main character in the Trueblood episode, which occupies chapter 2 of *Invisible Man,* is both a country blues singer (a tenor of "crude, high, plaintively animal sounds") and a virtuous prose narrator. To understand the disjunctiveness between Ellison's somewhat disparaging critical pronouncements on "raw" folklore and his striking fictional representation of the folk character, one must first comprehend, I think, the sharecropper Trueblood's dual manifestation as trickster and merchant, as creative and commercial man. Blues and narration, as modes of expression, conjoin and divide in harmony with these dichotomies. And the episode in its entirety is--as I demonstrate--a metaexpressive commentary on the incumbencies of Afro-American artists and the effects of their distinctive modes of expression.

In an essay that gives a brilliant ethnographic "reading" of the Balinese cockfight, the symbolic anthropologist Clifford Geertz asserts:

> Like any art form--for that , finally, is what we are dealing with--the cockfight renders ordinary, everyday experience comprehensible by presenting it in terms of acts and objects which have had their practical consequences removed and been reduced (or, if you prefer, raised) to the level of sheer appearances, where their meaning can be more powerfully articulated and more exactly perceived. ("Deep Play," 443)

Catching up on the themes of Balinese society in symbolic form, the cockfight thus represents, in Geertz's words, "a metasocial commentary . . . a Balinese reading of Balinese experience, a story they tell themselves about themselves" (448). The anthropologist's claims imply that the various symbolic (or "semiotic") systems of a culture--religion, politics, economics--can themselves be "raised" to a metasymbolic level by the orderings and processes of "ritual interactions" like the Balinese cockfight.

The coming together of semiotic systems in ways that enlarge and enhance the world of human meanings is the subject of Barbara Babcock-Abraham's essay "The Novel and the Carnival World." Following the lead of Julia Kristeva, Babcock-Abraham's asserts that a "metalanguage" is a symbolic system that treats of symbolic systems; for example, *Don Quixote* "openly discusses other works of literature and takes the writing and reading of literature as its subject" ("Novel," 912). Both social rituals and novels, since they "embed" other semiotic systems within their "texture," are "multivocal," "polyvalent," or "polysemous"--that is, capable of speaking in a variety of mutually reflexive voices at once.

The multiple narrative frames and voices operative in Ellison's Trueblood episode include the novel *Invisible Man,* the protagonist's fictive autobiographical account, Norton's story recalled as part of the fictive autobiography, Trueblood's story as framed by the fictive autobiography, the sharecropper's own autobiographical recall, and the dream narrative within that autobiographical recall. All these stories reflect, or "objectify," one another in ways that complicate their individual and composite meanings. Further, the symbolic systems suggested by the stories are not confined to (though they may implicitly comment on) such familiar social configurations as education, economics, politics, and religion. Subsuming these manifestations is the outer symbolic enterprise constituted by the novel itself. Moreover, the Trueblood episode heightens the multivocalic character of the novel from within, acting as a metacommentary on the literary and artistic system out of which the work is generated. Further enriching the burden of meanings in the episode is the Christian myth of the Fall and Sigmund Freud's mythic "narrative" concerning incest, which are both connoted (summoned as signifiers, in Babcock-Abraham's terms) and parodied, or inverted. I analyze the text's play on these myths later in my discussion.

For the moment, I am primarily interested in suggesting that the Trueblood episode, like other systematic symbolic phenomena, gains and generates its meanings in a dialogic relation with various systems of signs. The sharecropper chapter as a text derives its logic from its intertextual relation with surrounding and encompassing texts and, in turn, complicates their meanings. The Balinese cockfight, according to Geertz, can only tell a "metastory" because it is intertextually implicated in a world that is itself constituted by a repertoire of "stories" (e.g., those of economics and politics) that the Balinese tell themselves.

As a story that the author of *Invisible Man* tells himself about his own practice, the Trueblood episode clarifies distinctions that must be made between Ellison as critic and Ellison as artist. To elucidate its metaexpressive function, one must summon analytical instruments from areas that Ellison sharply debunks in his own criticism.

For example, at the outset of "The World and the Jug," a masterly instructive essay on the criticism of Afro-American creativity, Ellison asks:

> Why is it so often that when critics confront the American as *Negro* they suddenly drop their advanced critical armament and revert with an air of confident superiority to quite primitive modes of analysis? Why is that sociology-oriented critics seem to rate literature so far below politics and ideology that they would rather kill a novel than modify their presumptions concerning a given reality which it seeks in its own terms to project? (*S&A,* 115-16)

What I take these questions to imply is that a given artistic reality designed to represent "Negro American" experience should not be analyzed by "primitive" methods, which Ellison leaves unspecified but seems to associate with sociological, ideological, and political modes of analysis. In the following discussion I hope to demonstrate that sociology, anthropology, economics, politics, and ideology all provide models essential for the explication of the Trueblood episode. The first step, however, is to evoke the theater of Trueblood's performance.

* * *

Trueblood's narration has an unusual audience, but to the farmer and his Afro-American cohorts the physical setting is as familiar as train whistles in the Alabama night. The sharecropper, a white millionaire, and a naive undergraduate from a nearby black college have arranged themselves in a semi-circle of camp chairs in the sharecropper's yard. They occupy a swath of shade cast by the porch of a log cabin that has survived since the days of slavery, enduring hard times and the ravages of climate. The millionaire asks, "How are you faring now? . . . Perhaps I could help." The sharecropper responds, "We ain't doing so bad, suh. 'Fore they heard 'bout what happen to us out here I couldn't get no help from nobody. Now lotta folks is curious and go outta their way to help" (*IM,* 52). What has occurred "out here"--in what the millionaire Mr. Norton refers to as "new territory for me" and what the narrator describes as a "desert" that "almost took [his] breath away" (*IM,* 45)--is Jim Trueblood's impregnation of both is wife and his daughter. The event has brought disgrace on the sharecropper and has mightily embarrassed officials at the nearby black college.

The whites in the neighborhood town and countryside, however, are scarcely outraged or perturbed by Trueblood's situation. Rather, they want to keep the sharecropper among them; they warn the college officials not to harass him or his family, and they provide money, provisions, and abundant work. "White folks," says Trueblood, even "took to coming out here to see us and talk with us. Some of 'em was big white folks, too, from the big school way cross the State. Asked me lots 'bout what I thought 'bout things, and 'bout my folks and the kids, and wrote it all down in a book" (*IM,* 53). Hence, when the farmer begins to recount the story of his incestuous act with his daughter Matty Lou, he does so as a man who has thoroughly rehearsed his tale and who has carefully refined his knowledge of his audience: "He cleared his throat, his eyes gleaming and his voice taking on a deep, incantatory quality, as though he had told the story many, many times" (*IM,* 53).

The art of storytelling is not a gift that Trueblood has acquired recently. He is introduced in *Invisible Man* as one who "told the old stories with a sense of humor and a magic that made them come alive" (*IM,* 46). A master storyteller, then, he recounts his provocative exploits to an audience that is by turns shamed, indignant, envious, humiliated, and enthralled.

The tale begins on a cold winter evening in the sharecropper's cabin. The smell of fat meat hangs in the air, and the last kindling crackles in the dying flames of the stove. Trueblood's daughter, in bed between her father and mother, sleepily whispers, "Daddy." At the story's close, the sharecropper reports his resolution to prevent Aunt Cloe the midwife from aborting his incestuous issue. At the conclusion of his tale, he reiterates his judgment that he and his family "ain't doing so bad" in the wake of their ordeal.

Certainly the content and mode of narration the sharecropper chooses reflect his knowledge of what a white audience expects of the Afro-American. Mr. Norton is not only a "teller of polite Negro stories" (*IM,* 37) but also a man who sees nothing unusual about the pregnant Matty Lou's not having a husband. "But that shouldn't be so strange," he remarks later (*IM,* 49). The white man's belief in the promiscuity of blacks is further suggested by Mr. Broadnax, the figure in Trueblood's dream who looks at the sharecropper and his daughter engaged in incest and says, "They just nigguhs, leave 'em do it" (*IM,* 58). In conformity with audience expectations, the sharecropper's narrative is aggressively sexual in its representations.

Beginning with an account of the feel of his daughter's naked arm pressed against him in bed, the farmer proceeds to reminisce about bygone days in Mobile when he would lie in bed in the evenings with a woman named Margaret and listen to the music from steamboats passing on the river. Next, he introduces the metaphor of the woman in a red dress "goin' past you down a lane . . . and kinda switchin'' her tail 'cause she knows you watchin'" (*IM,* 56). From this evocative picture, he turns to a detailed account of his dream on the night of his incestuous act.

The dream is a parodic allegory in which Trueblood goes in quest of "fat meat." In this episode the name "Mr. Broadnax" (Mr. Broad-in-acts) captures the general concepts that mark any narrative as allegory. The man whose house is on the hill is a philanthropist who gives poor blacks (true bloods) sustaining gifts as "fat meat." The model implied by this conceptualization certainly fits one turn-of-the century American typology, recalling the structural arrangement by which black southern colleges were able to sustain themselves. In one sense, the entire Trueblood episode can be read as a pejorative commentary on the castrating effects of white philanthropy. Trueblood's dream narrative is parodic because it reveals the crippling assumptions (the castrating import) of the philanthropic model suggested in "Broadnax." The man who is broad-in-acts in the dream is the one who refers to the sharecropper and his daughter as "just nigguhs." Further, his philanthropy--like Mr. Norton's--has a carnal undercurrent: it is dangerously and confusingly connected with the sexuality of Mrs. Broadnax. What he dispenses as sustaining "fat meat" may only be the temporarily satisfying thrill of sexual gratification. The "pilgrim," or quester, in Trueblood's dream allegory flees from the dangers and limitations of such deceptive philanthropy. And the general exposé effected by the narrative offers a devastating critique of that typography which saw white men on the hill (northern industrialists) as genuinely and philanthropically responsive to the needs of those in the valley (southern blacks).

Instructed to inquire as Mr. Broadnax's house, Trueblood finds himself violating a series of southern taboos and fleeing for his life. He enters the front door of the home, wanders into a woman's bedroom, and winds up trapped in the embraces of a scantily clad white woman. The gastronomic and sexual appetites surely converge at this juncture, and the phrase "fat meat" takes on a dangerous burden of significance. The dreamer breaks free, however, and escapes into the darkness and machinery of a grandfather clock. He runs until a bright electric light bursts over him, and he awakens to find himself engaged in sexual intercourse with his daughter.

In *Totem and Taboo,* Freud advances the hypothesis that the two taboos of totemism--the interdictions against slaying the totem animal and against incest--result from events in human prehistory.[3] Following Darwin's speculations, Freud claims that human beings first lived in small hordes in which one strong, jealous man took all women to himself, exiling the sons to protect his own exclusive sexual privileges. On one occasion, however, Freud suggests, the exiled sons arose, slew, and ate the father, and then, in remorse, established a taboo against such slaughter. To prevent discord among themselves and to ensure their newly achieved form of social organization, they also established a taboo against sexual intercourse with the women of their own clan. Exogamy, Freud concludes, is based on a prehistorical advance from a lower to a higher stage of social organization.

From Freud's point of view, Trueblood's dream and subsequent incest seem to represent a historical regression. The sharecropper's dreamed violations of southern social and sexual taboos are equivalent to a slaughter of the white patriarch represented by Mr. Broadnax, who does, indeed, control the "fat" and "fat meat" of the land. To eat fat meat is to partake of the totemic animal. And having run backward in time through the grandfather clock, Trueblood becomes the primal father, assuming all sexual prerogatives unto himself. He has warned away "the boy" (representing the tumultuous mob of exiled sons) who wanted to take away his daughter, and as the sexual partner of both Matty Lou and Kate, he reveals his own firm possession of all his "womenfolks"--his status, that is to say as a sexual producer secure against the wrath of his displaced "sons." Insofar as Freud's notions of totemism represent a myth of progressive social evolution, the farmer's story acts as a countermyth of inversive social dissolution. It breaks society down into components and reveals man in what might be called his presocial and unaccomodated state.

One reason for the sharecropper's singular sexual prerogatives is that the other Afro-Americans in his area are either so constrained or so battered by their encounters with society that they are incapable of a legitimate and productive sexuality. The sharecropper's territory is bounded on one side by the black college where the "sons" are indoctrinated in a course of instruction that leaves them impotent. On the other side lie the insane asylum and the veterans' home, residences of black men driven mad--or at least rendered psychologically and physically crippled--by their encounters with America. These "disabled veterans" are scarcely "family men" like Trueblood. Rather, they are listless souls who visit the whores in "the sun-shrunk shacks at the railroad crossing . . . hobbling down the tracks on crutches and canes; sometimes pushing the legless, thighless one in a red wheelchair" (*IM,* 35). In such male company Trueblood seems the only person capable of ensuring an authentic Afro-American lineage. When he finds himself atop Matty Lou, therefore, both the survival of the clan and the sharecropper's aversion to pain require him to reject the fate that has been physically or psychologically imposed on his male cohorts. He says, "There was only one way I can figger that I could git out: that was with a knife. But I didn't have no knife, and if you'all ever see them geld them young boar pigs in the fall, you know I knowed that was too much to pay to keep from sinnin" (*IM,* 59). In this reflection, he brings forward one of the dominant themes of *Invisible Man.* This theme--one frequently slighted, or omitted, in discussions of the novel--is black male sexuality.

Perhaps critical prudery prevents commentators from acknowledging the black male phallus as a dominant symbol in much of the ritual interaction of *Invisible Man.* In *The*

Forest of Symbols: Aspects of Ndembu Ritual, the symbolic anthropologist Victor Turner provides suggestive definitions for both "ritual" and "dominant symbols." He describes ritual as "prescribed formal behavior for occasions not given over to technological routine, having reference to beliefs in mystical beings or powers. The symbol is the smallest unit of ritual which still retains the specific properties of ritual behavior; it is the ultimate unit of specific structure in a ritual context" (19). For Turner, the most prominent--the "senior," as it were--symbols in any ritual are dominant symbols (20); they fall into a class of their own. The important characteristic of such symbols is that they bring together disparate meanings, serving as a kind of condensed semiotic shorthand. Further, they can have both ideological and sensuous associations; the mudyi tree of Ndembu ritual, for example, refers both to the breast milk of the mother and to the axiomatic values of the matrilineal Ndembu society (28).

Ellison's *Invisible Man* is certainly an instance of "prescribed formal behavior" insofar as the novel is governed by the conventions of the artistic system in which it is situated, a system that resides ludically outside "technological routine" and promotes the cognitive exploration of all systems of "being" and "power," whether mystical or not. The black phallus is a dominant symbol in the novel's formal patterns of behavior, as its manifold recurrence attests. In "The Art of Fiction: An Interview," Ellison writes, "People rationalize what they shun or are incapable of dealing with; these superstitions and their rationalizations become rituals as they govern behavior. The rituals become social forms and it is one of the functions of the artist to recognize them and raise them to the level of art" (*S&A,* 175).

Stated in slightly different terms, Ellison's comment suggests an intertextual (indeed, a connoted) relation between the prescribed formal social behaviors of American racial interaction and the text of the novel. Insofar as Jim Crow social laws and the desperate mob exorcism of lynchings (with their attendant castrations) describe a formal pattern of Anglo-American behavior toward black men, this pattern offers an instance of ritual in which the black phallus gathers an extraordinary burden of disparate connotations, both sensuous and ideological. It should come as no surprise that an artist as perceptive as Ellison recognizes the black phallus as a dominant symbol of the sometimes bizarre social rituals of America and incorporates it into the text of a novel. In "The Art of Fiction," in fact, Ellison calls the battle-royal episode of *Invisible Man* "a ritual in preservation of caste lines, a keeping of taboo to appease the gods and ward off bad luck" (*S&A,* 175). He did not have to invent the ritual, he says; all he had to do was to provide "a broader context of meaning" for the patterns the episode represents.

The black phallus, then, does seem an implicit major symbol in Ellison's text, and prudery aside, there are venerable precedents for the discussion of male sexual symbols in ritual. For example, in "Deep Play" Geertz writes:

> To anyone who has been in Bali any length of time, the deep psychological identification of Balinese men with their cocks is unmistakable. The double entendre here is deliberate. It works in exactly the same way in Balinese as it does in English, even to producing the same tired jokes, strained puns, and uninventive obscenities. [Gregory] Bateson and [Margaret] Mead have even suggested that, in line with the Balinese conception of the body as a set of separately animated parts, cocks are viewed as detachable, self-opinionated penises, ambulent genitals with a life of their own. (417)

Certainly the notion of "ambulent genitals" figures in the tales of the roguish trickster recorded in Paul Radin's classic work *The Trickster.* In tale 16 of the Winnebago trickster cycle, Wakdjunkaga the trickster sends his penis across the waters of a lake to have intercourse with the chief's daughter.[4]

The black phallus as a symbol of unconstrained force that white men contradictorily envy and seek to destroy appears first in the opening chapter of *Invisible Man.* The influential white men of a small southern town force the protagonist and his fellow black boxers in the battle royal to gaze on a "magnificent blonde--stark naked" (*IM,* 18). The boys are threatened both for looking and for not looking, and the white men smile at their obvious fear and discomfiture. The boys know the bizarre consequences that accompany the white men's ascription of an animallike and voracious sexuality to black males. Hence, they respond in biologically normal but socially fearful (and justifiably embarrassed) ways. One boy strives to hide his erection with his boxing gloves, pleading desperately to go home. In this opening scene, the white woman as a parodic version of American ideals ("a small American flag tattooed upon her belly" [*IM,* 191]), is forced into tantalizing interaction with the mythically potent force of the black phallus. But because the town's white males exercise total control of the situation, the scene is akin to a castration, excision, or lynching.

Castration is one function of the elaborate electrically wired glass box that incarcerates the protagonist in the factory-hospital episode: "'Why not castration, doctor?' a voice asked waggishly" (*IM,* 231). In the Brotherhood, the class struggle is rather devastatingly transformed into the "ass struggle" when the protagonist's penis displaces his oratory as ideological agent. A white woman who hears him deliver a speech and invites him home seizes his biceps passionately and says, "Teach me, talk to me. Teach me the beautiful ideology of Brotherhood" (*IM,* 405). And the protagonist admits that suddenly he "was lost" as "the conflict between the ideological and the biological, duty and desire," became too subtly confused (*IM,* 406). Finally, in the nightmare that concludes the novel, the Invisible Man sees his own bloody testes, like those of the castrated Uranus of Greek myth, floating above the waters underneath a bridge's high arc (*IM,* 557). In the dream, he tells his inquisitors that his testes dripping blood on the black waters are not only his "generations wasting upon the water" but also the "sun" and the "moon"--and indeed, the very "world"--of his own human existence (*IM,* 558). The black phallus--in its creative, ambulent, generative power, even when castrated--is like the cosmos itself, a self-sustaining and self-renewing source of life, provoking both envy and fear in Anglo-American society.

While a number of episodes in *Invisible Man* (including Trueblood's dream) suggest the illusionary freedoms and taboo-induced fears accompanying interaction between the black phallus and white women, only the Trueblood encounter reveals the phallus as indeed producing Afro-American generations rather than wasting its seed upon the waters. The cosmic force of the phallus thus becomes, in the ritual action of the Trueblood episode, symbolic of type of royal paternity, an aristocratic procreativity turned inward to ensure the royalty (the truth, legitimacy, or authenticity) of an enduring black line of descent. In his outgoing phallic energy, therefore, the sharecropper is (as we learn on his first appearance in *Invisible Man*) indeed a "hard worker" who takes care of "his family's needs" (*IM,* 46). His family may, in a very real sense, be construed as the entire clan, or tribe, of Afro-America.

As cosmic creator, Trueblood is not bound by ordinary codes of restraint. He ventures chaos in an outrageously sexual manner--and survives. Like the Winnebago trickster Wakdjunkaga, he offers an inversive play on social norms. He is the violator of boundaries who--unlike the scapegoat--eludes banishment.[5] Indeed, he is so essential to whites in his sexual role that, after demonstrating his enviable ability to survive chaos, he and his family acquire new clothes and shoes, abundant food and work, long-needed eyeglasses, and even the means to reshingle their cabin. "I looks up at the mornin' sun," says the farmer, describing the aftermath of his incestuous act, "and expects somehow for it to thunder. But it's already bright and clear. . . .I yells, 'Have mercy, Lawd!' and waits. And there's nothin' but the clear bright mornin' sun" (*IM,* 64-65).

Noting that most tricksters "have an uncertain sexual status," Victor Turner points out that on some occasions

> tricksters appear with exaggerated phallic characteristics: Hermes is symbolized by the herm or pillar, the club, and the ithyphallic statue; Wakdjunkaga has a very long penis which has to be wrapped around him and put over his shoulder in a box; Eshu is represented in sculpture as having a long curved hairdress carved as a phallus. ("Myth," 580)

Such phallic figures are, for Turner, representatives par excellence of what he calls "liminality" (*Forest,* 93-112). Liminality describes that "betwixt and between" phrases of rites of passage when an individual has left one fixed social status and has not yet been incorporated into another. When African boys are secluded in the forest during circumcision rites, for example, they are in a liminal phase between childhood and adulthood. They receive, during this seclusion, mythic instruction in the origin and structures of their society. And this instruction serves not only to "deconstruct" the components of the ordered social world they have left behind but also to reveal these elements recombined into new and powerful components. The phallic trickster aptly represents the duality of this process. In his radically antinomian activities--incest, murder, and the destruction of sacred property--he symbolically captures what Turner describes as the "amoral and nonlogical" rhythms and outcomes of human biology and of meteorological climate: that is, the uncontrollable rhythms of nature (:Myth," 577). But the trickster is also a cultural gift bearer. Turner emphasizes that "the Winnebago trickster transforms the pieces of his broken phallus into plants and flowers for men (580)." Hermes enriches human culture with dreams and music. In a sense, therefore, the phallic trickster is a force that is, paradoxically, both anticonventional and culturally benevolent. The paradox is dissolved in the definition of the trickster as the "*prima materia*--as undifferentiated raw material" from which all things derive (*Forest,* 98). Trueblood's sexual energies, antinomian acts, productive issue, and resonant expressivity make him--in his incestuous, liminal moments and their immediate aftermath--the quintessential trickster.

In his sexual manifestation, Ellison's sharecropper challenges not only the mundane restraints of his environment but also the fundamental Judeo-Christian categories on which they are founded. As I have already noted, he quickly abandons the notion of the knife--of casting out, in Mr. Norton's indignant (and wonderfully ironic) phrase, "the offending eye." His virtual parodies of the notions of sin and sacrifice lend comic point to his latitudinarian challenge to Christian orthodoxy. When his wife brings the sharpened ax down on his head, Trueblood recalls, "I sees it, Lawd, yes! I sees it and seein' it I twists my head aside. Couldn't help it. . . .I moves. Though I meant to keep still, I moves! Anybody but Jesus Christ hisself woulda moved" (*IM,* 63). So much for repentance and salvation through the bloody sacrifice of one's life. But Trueblood goes on to indicate why such sacrifice may not have been required of him: with the skill of a revisionist theologian, he distinguishes between "blood-sin" and "dream-sin" (*IM,* 62) and claims, with unshakable certainty, that only the dream of his encounter at the Broadnax household led to his sexual arousal and subsequent incest.

But while this casuistic claim suffices in the farmer's interaction with the social world, his earlier appraisal of the event suggests his role as a cosmically rebellious trickster. He says that when he awoke to discover himself atop Matty Lou, he felt that the act might not be sinful, because it happened in his sleep. But then he adds, "although maybe sometimes a man can look at a little old pigtail gal and see him a whore" (*IM,* 59). The naturalness, and the natural unpredictability, of sexual arousal implied by "although" seems more in keeping with the sharecropper's manifestation as black phallic energy.

Trueblood's sexual energies are not without complement in the arid regions where the sharecropper and his family eke out their existence. His wife, Kate, is an awesome force of both new life and outgoing socioreligious fury. His yard is filled with the children she has borne, and his oldest child, Matty Lou, is Kate's double--a woman fully grown and sexually mature who looks just like her mother. Kate and Matty Lou--both moving with the "full-fronted motions of far-gone pregnancy" (*IM,* 47)--are the first human figures that Mr. Norton sees as he approaches the Trueblood property. The two bearers of new black life are engaged in a rite of purification, a workaday ritual of washing clothes in a huge boiling cauldron, which takes on significance as the men situate themselves in a semicircle near the porch where the "earth . . . was hard and white from where wash water had long been thrown" (*IM,* 51). In a sense the women (who flee behind the house at Norton's approach) are present, by ironic implication, as the sharecropper once more confessionally purges himself--as he, in vernacular terms, again "washes his dirty linen" before a white audience. Further, Matty Lou, as the object of Trueblood's incestuous desire, and Kate, as the irate agent of his punishment for fulfilling his desire, assume significant roles in his narrative.

The reversal of a traditional Freudian typology represented by Trueblood's dream encounter at the Broadnax Big House is reinforced by an implied parody of the Christian myth of the Fall.[6] For if the white Matty Lou becomes an ersatz Eve, the paradoxical recipient of the farmer's lust. Similarly, if Mr. Broadnax--an inhabitant of the sanctuarylike precincts of a house of "lighted candles and shiny furniture, and pictures on the walls, and soft stuff on the floor"--is the avenging father, or patriarch, of the dream, then the matriarchal Kate replaces him in exacting vengeance. The "fall" of Trueblood is thus enacted on two planes--on a dream level of Christian myth and on a quotidian level of southern black actuality. In its most intensely conscious and secular interpretation, the incestuous act is a rank violation that drives Kate to blind and murderous rage: "I heard Kate scream. It was a scream to make your blood run cold. It sounds like a woman who was watching a team of wild horses run down her baby chile and she caint move. . . .She screams and starts to pickin' up the first thing that comes to her hand and throwin' it" (*IM,* 61).

The "doubleness" of Kate and Matty Lou is felt in the older woman's destructive and avenging energies, which elevate her to almost legendary proportions. Her woman's wrath as the sharecropper's illicit violation of "my chile!" spirals, inflating Kate to the metaphorical stature of an implacable executioner: "Then I sees her right up on me, big. She's swingin' her arms like a man swingin' a ten-pound sledge and I sees the knuckles of her hand is bruised and bleedin. . . and I sees her swing and I smells her sweat and. . . I sees that ax" (*IM,* 63). Trueblood tries to forestall Kate's punishing blow but, he says, he "might as well been pleadin' with a switch engine" (*IM,* 63). The ax falls, and the farmer receives the wound whose blood spills on Matty Lou. The wound becomes the "raw and moist" scar the protagonist notices when he first moves "up close" on the sharecropper (*IM,* 50).

Kate becomes not only an awesome agent of vengeance in the sharecropper's account but also the prime mover of the parodic ritual drama enacted in the chilly southern cabin.

It is Kate's secular rage that results in the substitute castration-crucifixion represented by Trueblood's wound. She is the priestess who bestows the scarifying lines of passage, of initiation--the marks that forever brand the farmer as a "dirty lowdown wicked dog" (*IM,* 66). At her most severe, she is the moral, or socioreligious, agent of both Trueblood's "marking" and his exile. She banishes him from the community that rallies to support her in her sorrow. In keeping with her role as purifier--as supervisor of the wash--she cleans up the pollution, and dirt and danger, represented by Trueblood's taboo act.

It is important to bear in mind, however, that while Kate is a figure of moral outrage, she is also a fertile woman who, like her husband, provides "cultural gifts" in the form of new life. In her family manifestation, she is less a secular agent of moral justice than a sensitive, practical parent who turns away in sick disgust at the wound she inflicts on Trueblood. And though she first banishes the farmer, she also accepts his return, obeys his interdiction against abortions for herself and Matty Lou, and welcomes the material gains of that ironically accrue after Trueblood's fall from grace. The sharecropper says, " Except that my wife an' daughter won't speak to me, I'm better off than I ever been before. And even if Kate won't speak to me she took the new clothes I brought her from up in town and now she's gettin' some eyeglasses made what she been needin' for so long" (*IM,* 67).

As a woman possessed of a practical (one might say a "blues") sensibility, Kate knows than men are, indeed, sometimes "dirty lowdown wicked" dogs who can perceive a whore in a pigtailed girl. She is scarcely resigned to such a state of affairs where her own daughter is concerned but like the black mother so aptly described in Carolyn Rodger's poem "It Is Deep," Kate knows that being "religiously girdled in her god"[7] will not pay the bills. She thus brings together the sacred and the secular, the moral and the practical, in a manner that makes her both a complement for Trueblood and (again in the words of Rodgers) a woman who "having waded through a storm, is very obviously, a sturdy Black bridge" (12).

To freight Trueblood's sexual manifestation and its complement in Kate with more significance than they can legitimately bear would be as much a critical disservice as were previous failures, or refusals, even to acknowledge these aspects. For while it is true that sexuality burdens the content of his narrative, it is also true that Trueblood himself metaphorically transforms his incestuous act into a single, symbolic instance of his total life situation:

> There I was [atop Matty Lou] trying to git away with all my might, yet having to move *without* movin'. I flew in but I had to walk out. I had to move without movin'. I done thought 'bout it since a heap, and when you think right hard you see that that's the way things is always been with me. That's just about been my life. (*IM,* 59)

Like the formidable task of the Invisible man's grandfather, who gave up his gun during the Reconstruction but still had to fight a war, Trueblood's problem is that of getting out of a tight spot ,without undue motion--without perceivable moving. The grandfather adopted a strategy of extrication by indirection, pretending to affirm the designs of the dominant white society around him. Having relinquished his gun, he became "a spy in the enemy's country," a man overcoming his adversaries with yeses. He represents the trickster as subtle deceiver. Trueblood, in contrast, claims that to "move without movin' " means to take a refractory situation uncompromisingly in hand: "You got holt to it," he says, "and you caint let go even though you want to" (*IM,* 60). He conceives of himself in the throes of his incestuous ecstasies as "like that fellow . . . down in Birmingham. That one what locked hisself in his house and shot [with a gun that he had *refused to give up*] at them police until they set fire to the house and burned him up. I was lost" (*IM,* 60). An energetic, compulsive, even ecstatically expressive response is required:

> Like that fellow [in Birmingham], I stayed. . . . He mighta died, but I suspects now that he got a heapa satisfaction before he went. I *know* there ain't nothin' like what I went through, I caint tell how it was. It's like when a real drinkin' man gets drunk, or like a real sanctified religious woman gits so worked up she jumps outta her clothes, or when a real gamblin' man keeps on gamblin' when he's losing. (*IM,* 60)

In his energetic response, Trueblood says a resounding no to all the castratingly tight spots of his existence as a poor black farmer in the undemocratic South.[8]

The most discursively developed *expressive* form of this no is, of course, the narrative that Trueblood relates. But he has come to this narrative by way of music. He has fasted and reflected on his guilt or innocence until he thinks his "brains go'n bust," and then, he recalls, "one night, way early in the morning', I looks up and sees the stars and starts singin'. I don't know what it was, some kinda church song, I guess. All I know is I *ends up* singin' the blues. I sings me some blues that night ain't never been sang before"(*IM,* 65-66). The first unpremeditated expression that Trueblood summons is a religious song. But the religious system that gives birth to the song is, presumably, one in which the term "incest" carries pejorative force. Hence, the sharecropper moves on, spontaneously, to the blues.

* * *

In *The Legacy of the Blues,* Samuel Charters writes:

> Whatever else the blues was it was a language; a rich, vital, expressive language that stripped away the misconception that the black society in the United States was simply a poor, discouraged version of the white. It was impossible not to hear the differences. No one could listen to the blues without realizing that there are two Americas. (22)

On the origins of this blues language, Giles Oakley quotes the blues singer Booker White: "You want to know where did the blues come from. The blues come from behind the mule. Well now, you can have the blues sitting at the table eating. But the foundation of the blues is walking behind the mule way back in slavery time" (*Devil's Music,* 7). The language that Trueblood summons to contain his act grows out of the soil he works, a soil that has witnessed the unrecompensed labor of many thousand blacks walking "behind the mule," realizing, as they negotiated the long furrows, the absurdity of working from "can to caint" for the profit of others.

Born on a farm in Alabama and working, at the time of his incestuous act, as an impoverished, cold, poorly provisioned sharecropper, Trueblood has the inherent blues capacity of a songster like Lightnin' Hopkins, who asserts, "I had the one thing you need to be a blues singer. I was born with the blues" (Charters, 183). Originating in the field hollers and work songs of the agrarian South and becoming codified as stable forms by the second decade of the twentieth century, the blues offer a language that connotes a world of transience, instability, hard luck, brutalizing work, lost love, minimal security, and enduring human wit and resourcefulness in the face of disaster. The blues enjoin one to accept hard luck because, without it, there is "no luck at all." The lyrics are often charged with a surreal humor that wonders if "a match box will hold my clothes." In short, the "other America" that they signal is a world of common labor, spare circumstances, and grimly lusty lyrical challenges to a bleak fate.

In the system of the blues Trueblood finds the meet symbolic code for expressing the negativity of his own act. Since he is both a magical storyteller and a blues singer par excellence, he can incorporate the lean economics and fateful intranscience of the blues world into his autobiographical narrative. His metaphorical talent, which transforms a steamboat's musicians into a boss quail's whistle and then likens the actions of the quail to those of a good man who "do" what he "got to do," reflects a basic understanding of the earthy resonances of blues. He says of his evenings listening to boats in Mobile:

> They used to have musicianers on them boats, and sometimes I used to wake her [Margaret] up to hear the music when they come up the river. I'd be layin' there and it would be quiet and I could hear it comin' from way, way off. Like when you quail huntin' and it's getting dark and you can hear the boss bird whistlin' tryin' to get the covey together again, and he's coming toward you slow and whistlin' soft, 'cause he knows you somewhere around with your gun. Still he got to round them up, so he keeps on comin'. Them boss quails is like a good man, what he got to do he *do*. (*IM*, 55).

Further, the farmer begins his story by describing his desperate economic straits, like those frequently recorded in blues--that is, no wood for fuel and no work or aid to be found (*IM*, 53)--and then traces the outcome of his plight. Matty Lou is in bed with her mother and father because it is freezing: "It was so cold all of us had to sleep together; me, the ole lady and the gal. That's how it started" (*IM*, 53). It seems appropriate--even natural--that blues should expressively frame the act resulting from such bitter black agrarian circumstances. And it is, in fact, blues affirmation of human identity in the face of dehumanizing circumstance that resonates throughout the sharecropper's triumphant penultimate utterance: "I make up my mind that I ain't nobody but myself and ain't nothin' I can so but let whatever is gonna happen, happen" (*IM*, 66).

The farmer's statement is not an expression of transcendence. It is, instead, an affirmation of a still recognizable humanity by a singer who has incorporated his personal disaster into a code of blues meanings emanating from an unpredictably chaotic world. In translating his tragedy into the vocabulary and semantics of the blues and, subsequently, into the electrifying expression of his narrative, Trueblood realizes that he is not so changed by catastrophe that he must condemn, mortify, or redefine his essential self. This self, as the preceding, discussion indicates, is in many ways the obverse of the stable, predictable, puritanical, productive, law-abiding ideal self of the American industrialist-capitalist society.

The words the sharecropper issues for "behind the mule" provide a moral opposition (if not a moral corrective) to the confident expressions of control emanating from Mr. Norton's technological world. From a pluralistic perspective, the counteractive patterns represented by the sharecropper and the millionaire point to a positive homeostasis in American life. In the southern regions represented by Trueblood, an oppositional model might suggest, the duty-bound but enfeebled rationalist of northern industry can always achieve renewal and a kind of shamanistic cure for the ills of civilization. But the millionaire in the narrative episode hardly appears to represent a rejuvenated Fisher King. At the close of the sharecropper's story, in fact, he seems paralyzed by the ghostly torpor of a stunned Benito Cereno or a horrified Mr. Kurtz. Thus a pluralistic model that projects revivifying opposition as the relation between sharecropper and millionaire does not adequately explain the Norton-Trueblood interaction. Some of the more significant implications of the episode, in fact, seem to reside not in the opposition between industrial technocrat and agrarian farmer, but in the two sectors' commercial consensus on Afro-American expressive culture. Eshu and Hermes are not only figures of powerful creative instinct. They are also gods of the marketplace. Two analytical reflections on the study of literature and ideology, one by Fredric Jameson and the other by Hayden White, elucidate the commercial consensus achieved by Trueblood and his millionaire auditor.

Fredric Jameson writes:

> The term "ideology" stands as the sign for a problem yet to be solved, a mental operation which remains to be executed. It does not presuppose cut-and-dried sociological stereotypes like the notion of the "bourgeois" or the "petty bourgeois" but is rather a mediatory concept: that is, it is an imperative to re-invent a relationship between the linguistic or aesthetic or conceptual fact in question and its social ground. . . .Ideological analysis may . . . be described as the rewriting of a particular narrative trait or seme as a function of its social, historical, or political context. (Jameson, 510-11)

Jameson's interest in a reinvented relation between linguistic fact and social ground is a function of his conviction that all acts of narration inscribe social ideologies. In other words, there is always a historical, or ideological, subtext in a literary work of art. For, since history is accessible to us only through texts, the literary work of art either has to "rewrite" the historical texts of its time or "textualize" the uninscribed events of its day in order to "contextualize" itself. What Jameson calls the "ideology of form" White calls "reflection theory." If literary art can indeed be said to reflect, through inscription, the social ground from which it originates, at what level of a specifically social domain, asks White, does such reflection occur? How can we most appropriately view literary works of art as distinctively "social" entities?

White's answer is that ideological analysis must begin with a society's exchange system and must regard the literary work as "merely one commodity among others and moreover as a commodity that has to be considered as not different in kind from any other." To adopt such an analytical strategy, according to White, is to comprehend "not only the alienation of the artist which the representation of the value of his product in terms of money alone might foster, but also the tendency of the artist to fetishize his own produce as being itself the universal sign and incarnation of value in a given social system" (White, 378). White could justifiably summon Ellison's previously quoted remarks on the transformative powers of art to illustrate the "fetishizing" of art as the incarnation of value. In Ellison's view, however, artistic value is not a sign or incarnation in a given social system but, rather, a sign of humane value in toto. What is pertinent about White's remarks for the present discussion, however, is that the relation Jameson would reinvent is for White an economic one involving challenging questions of axiology.

To apply Jameson's and White's reflections in analyzing the Trueblood episode, one can begin by recognizing that the sharecropper's achievement of expressive narrative form is immediately bracketed by the exchange system of Anglo-American society. Recalling his first narration of his story to a group of whites, the sharecropper remembers that Sheriff Barbour asked him to tell what happened:

> . . . and I tole him and he called in some more men and they made me tell it again. They wanted to hear about the gal lots of times and they gimme somethin' to eat and drink and some tobacco. Surprised me, 'cause I was scared and spectin' somethin' different. Why, I guess there ain't a colored man in the county who ever got to take so much of the white folkses' time as I did. (*IM,* 52).

Food, drink, tobacco, and audience time are commodities the sharecropper receives in barter for the commodity he delivers--his story. The narrative of incest, after its first telling, accrues an ever-spiraling exchange value. The Truebloods receive all the items enumerated earlier, as well as a one-hundred-dollar bill from Mr. Norton's Moroccan-leather wallet. The exchange value of the story thus moves from a system of barter to a money economy overseen by northern industrialists. The status of the farmer's story as a commodity cannot be ignored.

As an artistic form incorporating the historical and ideological subtext of American industrial society, the sharecropper's tale represents a supreme capitalist fantasy. The family, as the fundamental social unit of middle-class society, is governed by the property concept. A man marries--takes a wife as his exclusive "property"--to produce legitimate heirs who will keep their father's wealth (i.e., his property in the family. Among royalty of the aristocracy such marriages may describe an exclusive circle of exchange. Only certain women are eligible as royal or aristocratic wives. And in the tightest of all circumstances, incest may be justified as the sole available means of preserving intact the family heritage--the nobleman's or aristocrat's property. An unfettered, incestuous procreativity that results not only in new and legitimate heirs but also in a marked increase in property (e.g., Trueblood's situation) can be viewed as a capitalist dream. And if such results can be achieved without fear of holy sanction, then procreation becomes a secular feat of human engineering.

Mr. Norton reflects that his "real life's work" has been, not his banking or his researches, but his "first-hand organizing of human life" (*IM.* 42). What more exacting control could this millionaire New Englander have exercised than the incestuous domination of his own human family as a productive unit, eternally giving birth to new profits? Only terror of dreadful heavenly retribution (i.e., of punishment for "impropriety") had prevented him from attempting such a construction of life with his pathetically idealized only child, now deceased. Part of his stupefaction at the conclusion of the sharecropper's narrative results from his realization that he might have safely effected such a productive arrangement of life. One need not belabor the capitalist-fantasy aspect of Trueblood's narrative, however, to comprehend his story's commodity status in an industrial-capitalist system of exchange. What the farmer is ultimately merchandising is an image of himself that is itself a product--a bizarre product--of the slave trade that made industrial America possible.

Africans became slaves through what the West Indian novelist George Lamming describes as an act of "commercial deportation" overseen by the white West (Lamming, 93). In America, Africans were classified as "chattel personal" and turned into commodities. To forestall the moral guilt associated with this aberrant, mercantile transformation, white Americans conceptualized a degraded, subhuman animal as a substitute for the actual African. This categorical parody found its public, physical embodiment in the mask of the minstrel theatrical. As Ellison writes in "Change the Joke and Slip the Yoke," the African in America was thus reduced to a "negative sign" (*S&A,* 63): "the [minstrel] mask was the thing (the 'thing' in more ways than one) and its function was to veil the humanity of Negroes thus reduced to a sign, and to repress the white audience's awareness of its moral identification with its own acts and with the human ambiguities pushed behind the mask." Following the lead of Constance Rourke, Ellison asserts that the minstrel show is, in fact, a "ritual of exorcism" (*S&A,* 64). But what of the minstrel performance given by the Afro-American who dons the mask? In such performances, writes Ellison:

> Motives of race, status, economics and guilt are always clustered. . . . The comic point is inseparable from the racial identity of the performer . . . who by assuming the group-debasing role for gain not only substantiates the audience's belief in the "blackness" of things black, but relieves it, with dreamlike efficiency, of its guilt by accepting the very profit motive that was involved in the designation of the Negro as a national scapegoat in the first place. There are all kinds of comedy; here one is reminded of the tribesman in *Green Hills of Africa* who hid his laughing face in shame at the sight of a gut-shot hyena jerking out its own intestines and eating them, in Hemingway's words, "with relish." (*S&A,* 64-65)

Trueblood, who assumes the minstrel mask to the utter chagrin of the Invisible man ("How can he tell this to white men, I thought, when he knows they'll say that all Negroes do such things?"), has indeed accepted the profit motive that gave birth to that mask in the first place. He tells his tale with relish: "He talked willingly now, with a kind of satisfaction and no trace of hesitancy or shame" (*IM,* 53). The firm lines of capitalist economics are, therefore, not the only ideological inscriptions in the sharecropper's narrative. The story also contains the distorting contours of that mask constructed by the directors of the economic system to subsume their guilt. The rambunctiously sexual, lyrical, and sin-adoring "darky" is an image dear to the hearts of white America.

Ideologically, then, there is every reason to regard the sharecropper's story as a commodity in harmony with its social ground--with the system of exchange sanctioned by the dominant Anglo-American society. For though Trueblood has been denied "book learning" by the nearby black college, he has not failed to garner some knowledge of marketing. Just as the college officials peddle the sharecropper's "primitive spirituals" to the white millionaires who descend every spring, so Trueblood sells his own expressive product--a carefully constructed narrative, framed to fit market demands. His actions as a merchant seem to compromise his status as a blues artist, as a character of undeniable folk authenticity. And his delineation as an untrammeled and energetic prime mover singing a deep blues no to social constraints appears to collapse under the impress of ideological analysis. The complexities of American culture, however, enable him to reconcile a merchandising role as oral storyteller with his position as an antinomian trickster. For the Afro-American blues manifest an effective, expressive duality that Samuel Charters captures as follows:

> The blues has always had a duality to it. One of its sides is its personal creativity--the consciousness of a creative individual using it as a form of expression. The other side is the blues as entertainment. But the blues is a style of music that emphasizes integrity--so how does a singer change his style without losing his credibility as a blues artist? (Charters, 168)

As entertainment, the blues, whether classic or country, were sung professionally in theaters.[9] And their public theatricality is analogous to the Afro-American's donning of the minstrel mask. There is, perhaps, something obscenely--though profitably--gut-wrenching about Afro-Americans delivering up carefully modified versions of their essential expressive selves for the entertainment of their Anglo-American oppressors. And, as Charters implies, the question of integrity looms large. But the most appropriate inquiry in the wake of his comment is, Integrity, *as what?*

To deliver the blues as entertainment--if one is an entertainer--is to maintain a fidelity to one's role. Again, if the performance required is that of a minstrel and one is a genuine performer, then donning the mask is an act consistent with one's stature. There are always fundamental economic questions involved in such uneasy Afro-American public postures. As Ellison suggests, Afro-Americans, in their guise as entertainers, season the possum of black expressive culture to the taste of their Anglo-American audience, maintaining, in the process, their integrity as performers. But in private sessions--in the closed circle of their own community--everybody knows that the punch line to the recipe (and the proper response to the performer's constrictive dilemma) is, "Damn the possum! That sho' is some good gravy!" It is just possible that the "gravy" is the inimitable technique of the Afro-American artist, a technique (derived from lived blues experience) as capable of "playing possum" as of presenting one.

A further question, however, has to do with the artist's affective response to being treated as a commodity. And with this query, White's and Jameson's global formulations prove less valuable than a closer inspection of the self-reflexive expressivity of Afro-American spokespersons in general. Ellison's Trueblood episode, for example, suggests that the angst assumed to accompany commodity status is greatly alleviated when that status constitutes a sole means of securing power in a hegemonic system.

In the Trueblood episode, blacks who inhabit the southern college's terrain assume that they have transcended the peasant rank of sharecroppers and their cohorts. In fact, both the college's inhabitants and Trueblood's agrarian fellows are but constituencies of a single underclass. When the college authorities threaten the farmer with exile or arrest, he has only to turn to the white Mr. Buchanan, "the boss man," to secure immunity and a favorable audience before Sheriff Barbour, "the white law" (*IM,* 52). The imperious fiats of whites relegate all blacks to an underclass. In Trueblood's words, "no matter how biggity a nigguh gits, the white folks can always cut him down" (*IM,* 53). For those in this underclass, Ellison's episode implies, expressive representation is the only means of prevailing.

Dr. Bledsoe, for example, endorses lying as an effective strategy in interacting with Mr. Norton and the other college trustees. And Trueblood himself adopts tale telling (which is often conflated with lying in black oral tradition) as a mode of expression that allows him a degree of dignity and freedom within the confines of a severe white hegemony. The expressive "mask," one might say, is as indispensable for college blacks as it is for those beyond the school's boundaries. Describing the initial meeting between Mr. Norton and the sharecropper, the protagonist says, " I hurried behind him [Mr. Norton], seeing him stop when he reached the man and the children. They became silent, their faces clouding over, their features becoming soft and negative, their eyes bland and deceptive. They were crouching behind their eyes waiting for him to speak--just as I recognized that I was trembling behind my own" (*IM,* 50). The evasive silence of these blacks is as expressive of power relations in the South as the mendacious strategy advocated by Dr. Bledsoe.

When the protagonist returns from his ill-fated encounters with Trueblood and the crew at the Golden Day, the school's principal asks him is he is unaware that blacks have "lied enough decent homes and drives [got enough material advantage by lying] for you to show him [Mr. Norton]" (*IM,* 136). When the protagonist responds that he was obeying Mr. Norton's orders by showing the millionaire the "slum" regions of Trueblood rather than "decent homes and drives," Bledsoe exclaims, "He *ordered* you. Dammit, white folk are always giving orders, it's a habit with them. . . . My God, boy! You're black and living in the South--did you forget how to lie?" (*IM,* 136).

Artful evasion and expressive illusion are equally traditional black expressive modes in interracial exchange in America. Such modes, the Trueblood episode implies, are the only resources that blacks at any level can barter for a semblance of decency and control in their lives. Making black expressiveness a commodity, therefore, is not simply a gesture in a bourgeois economics of art. Rather, it is a crucial move in a repertoire of black survival motions in the United States. To examine the status of Afro-American expressiveness as a commodity, then, is to do more than observe, within the constraints of an institutional theory of art, that the art world is a function of economics. In a very real sense, Afro-America's exchange power has always been coextensive with its stock of expressive resources. What is implicit in an analysis of black expressiveness as a commodity is not a limited history of the "clerks" but a total history of Afro-American cultural interaction in America.

In *When Harlem Was in Vogue*--a brilliant study that treats the black artistic awakening of the 1920s known as the "Harlem Renaissance"--David Levering Lewis captures the essential juxtaposition between white hegemony and black creativity as a negotiable power of exchange. Writing of Charles Johnson, the energetic black editor of *Opportunity* magazine during this period, Lewis says:

> [Johnson] gauged more accurately than perhaps any other Afro-American intellectual the scope and depth of the national drive to "put the nigger in his place" after the war, to keep him out of the officer corps, out of labor unions and skilled job, out of the North and quaking for his very existence in the South--and out of politics everywhere. Johnson found that one area alone--probably because of its very implausibility--had not been proscribed. No exclusionary rules had been laid down regarding a place in the arts. Here was a small crack in the wall of racism, a fissure that was worth trying to widen. (48)

"Exclusionary rules" were certainly implicit in the arts during the 1920s, but what Lewis suggests is that they were far less rigid and explicit than they were in other domains. Blacks thus sought to widen the "fissure," to gain what power they could to determine their own lives, through a renaissance of black expressiveness.

An ideological analysis of expressiveness as a commodity should take adequate account of the defining variables in the culture where this commercialization occurs. In Afro-American culture, exchanging words for safety and profit is scarcely an alienating act. It is, instead, a defining act in aesthetics. Further, it is an act that lies at the heart of Afro-American politics conceived in terms of who gets what and when and how. Making a commodity of black expressiveness, as I try to make clear in my concluding section, does entail inscription of an identifying economics. But aggressively positive manifestations of this process (despite the dualism it presupposes) result from a self-reflexive acknowledgment that only the "economics of slavery" gives valuable and specifically black resonance to Afro-American works of art.

* * *

The critic George Kent observes a "mathematical consistency between Ellison's pronouncements and his creative performance" (Kent, 161). Insofar as Ellison provides insightful critical interpretations of his own novel and its characters, Kent's judgment is correct. But the "critical pronouncements" in Ellison's canon that suggests a devaluing of Afro-American folklore hardly seem consistent with the implications of his Trueblood episode. Such statements are properly regarded, I believe, as public remarks by Ellison the merchant rather than as incisive, affective comments by Ellison the creative genius.

Trueblood's duality is, finally, also that of his creator. For Ellison knows that his work as an Afro-American artist derives from those "economics of slavery" that provided conditions of existence for Afro-American folklore. Black folk expression is a product of the impoverishment of blacks in American. The blues, as a case in point, are unthinkable for those happy with their lot.

Yet, if folk artists are to turn a profit from their monumental creative energies (which are often counteractive, or inversive, vis-à-vis Anglo-American culture), they must take a lesson from the boss quail and "move without moving." They must, in essence, sufficiently modify their folk forms (and amply advertise themselves) to merchandise such forms as commodities in the artistic market. To make their products commensurate with a capitalistic marketplace, folk artists may even have to don masks that distort their genuine selves. Ralph Ellison is a master of such strategies.

Ellison reconciles the trickster's manifestations as untrammeled creator and as god of the marketplace by providing critical advertisements for himself as a novelist that carefully bracket the impoverishing economics of Afro-America. For example, in "Change the Joke and Slip the Yoke" he writes, "I use folklore in my work not because I am a Negro, but because writers like Eliot and Joyce made me conscious of the literary value of my folk inheritance. My cultural background, like that of most Americans, is dual (my middle name, sadly enough, is Waldo)" (*S&A*, 72).[10] What is designed in this quotation as "literary value" is in reality market value. Joyce and Eliot taught Ellison that if he was a skillful enough strategist and spokesman he could market his own folklore. What is bracketed, of course, is the economics that required Ellison, if he wished to be an Afro-American artist, to turn to Afro-American folklore as a traditional, authenticating source for his art. Like his sharecropper, Ellison is wont to make literary value out of socioeconomic necessity. But he is also an artist who recognizes that Afro-American folk forms have value *in themselves*; they "have named human situations so well," he suggests in "The Art of Fiction," that a whole corps of writers could not exhaust their universality" (*S&A*, 173). What Ellison achieves in the Trueblood episode is a dizzying hall of mirrors, a redundancy of structure, that enables him to extend the value of Afro-American folk forms by combining them with an array of Western narrative forms and tropes. Written novel and sung blues, polysyllabic autobiography and vernacular personal narrative, a Christian Fall and an inversive triumph of the black trickster--all are conjoined in a magnificently embedded manner.

The foregoing analysis suggests that it is in such creative instances that one discovers Ellison's artistic genius, a genius that links him inextricably and positively to his invented sharecropper. For in the Trueblood episode conceived as a chapter in a novel, one finds not only the same kind of metaexpressive commentary that marks the character's narration to Norton but also the same type of self-reflexive artist that the sharecropper's recitation implies--an artist who is fully aware of the contours and limitations, the rewards and dilemmas, of the Afro-American's uniquely expressive craft.

In the expository, critical moment, by contrast, one often finds a quite different Ralph Ellison. Instead of the *reflexive* artist, one finds the *reflective* spokesman. Paraphrasing Babcock-Abrahams, who uses a "failed" Narcissus to illustrate the difference between the "reflective" and the "reflexive," one might say that in his criticism Ralph Ellison is not narcissistic enough ("Reflexivity," 4). His reflections in *Shadow and Act* seem to define

Afro-American folk expressiveness in art as a sign of identity, a sign that marked the creator as unequivocally Afro-American and, hence, other. I have sought to demonstrate, however, that Ellison's folk expressiveness is, in fact, "identity within difference." While critics experience alienation, artists can detach themselves from, survive, and even laugh at their initial experiences of otherness. Like Velazquez in his *Las Meninas* or the Van Eyck of *Giovanni Arnolfini and His Bride,* the creator of Trueblood is "conscious of being self-conscious of himself" as artist.[11] Instead of solacing himself with critical distinctions, he employs reflexivity mirroring narratives to multiply distinctions and move playfully across categorical boundaries. Like his sharecropper, he knows indisputably that his most meaningful identity is his Afro-American self image in acts of expressive creativity.

Ralph Ellison's bracketings as a public critic, therefore, do not forestall his private artistic recognition that he "ain't nobody but himself." And it is out of this realization that a magnificent folk creation such as Trueblood emerges. Both the creator and his agrarian folk storyteller have the wisdom to know that they are resourceful "whistlers" for the tribe. They know that their primary matrix as artists is coextensive not with a capitalistic society but with material circumstances like those implied by the blues singer Howard Wolf:

> Well I'm a po' boy, long way from home.
> Well, I'm a po' boy, long was from home.
> No spendin' money in my pocket, no spare meat on my bone. (Nicholas, 85).

One might say that in the brilliant reflexivity of the Trueblood encounter, we hear the blues whistle among the high-comic thickets. We glimpse Ellison's creative genius beneath his Western critical mask. And while we stand awaiting the next high-cultural pronouncement from the critic, we are startled by a captivating sound of flattened thirds and sevenths--the private artist's blues-filled flight.

NOTES

1. Ralph Ellison *Shadow and Act,* 82-83. This work comprises the bulk of Ellison's critical canon. All subsequent references to this work are cited in text as *S&A*.

2. Ellison, *Invisible Man,* 55. All subsequent references to this work are cited in text as *IM.*

3. One of the general questions provoking Freud's inquiry into totemism is "What is the ultimate source of the horror of incest which must be recognized as the root of exogamy?" Sigmund Freud, *Totem and Taboo,* 122, 141-46.

4. Paul Radin, *The Trickster,* Tale 16. Originally published in 1955 in London by Routledge & Kegan Paul, it has been reprinted several times, the most recent by Schocken Books, Inc. in 1972.

5. For a stimulating discussion of the trickster in his various literary and nonliterary guises, consult Barbara Babcock-Abraham's provocative essay, "'A Tolerated Margin of Mess': The Trickster and His Tales Reconsidered," *Journal of the Folklore Institute* 11 (1974): 147-86. She writes, "In contrast to the scapegoat or tragic victim, trickster belongs to the comic modality or marginality where violation is generally the precondition for laughter and communitas, and there tends to be an incorporation of the outsider, a leveling of hierarchy, a reversal of statues" (153).

6. I had enlightening conversations with Kimberly Benston on the Trueblood episode's parodic representation of the Fall, a subject that he explores as some length in a critical work in progress. I am grateful for his generous help.

7. See Carolyn Rodgers, *How I Got Ovah: New and Selected Poems,* 11.

8. The significance of the sharecropper's incestuous progeny may be analogous to that of the broken link of leg chain given to the Invisible Man during his early days in the Brotherhood. Presenting the link, Brother Tarp says, "I don't think of it in terms of but two words, *yes* and *no,* but it signifies a heap more" (*IM,* 379).

9. Ellison introduces this claim, which contradicts LeRoi Jones's assertions on blues, in a review of Jones's book *Blues People* in *Shadow and Act*, 249.

10. The implicit "trickiness" of Ellison's claim--its use of words to "signify" quite other than what they seem to intend on the surface--is an aspect of the Afro-American "critic as trickster." In "The Blackness of Blackness': A Critique of the Sign and the Signifying Monkey," a paper presented at the Modern Language Association Convention, New York, December 30, 1981, Henry Louis Gates, Jr., began an analysis--in quite suggestive terms--of the trickster's "semiotic" manifestation. For Gates, the Afro-American folk figure of the "signifying monkey" is an archetype of the Afro-American critic. In the essays " Change the Joke and Slip the Yoke" and "The World and the Jug," Ellison demonstrates, one can certainly conclude, an elegant mastery of what might be termed the "exacerbating strategies" of the monkey. Perhaps one also hears his low Afro-American voice directing a sotto voce "Yo' Mamma!" at heavyweights of the Anglo-American critical establishment.

11."Reflexivity," 4. One of the most intriguing recent discussions of the Velazquez painting is Michel Foucault's in *The Order of Things*, 3-16. Jay Ruby briefly discusses the Van Eyck in the introduction to his anthology, *A Crack in the Mirror*, 12-13.

WORKS CITED

Babcock-Abrahams, Barbara. "The Novel and the Carnival World." *Modern Language Notes* 89 (1974): 912.

______. "Reflexivity: Definitions and Discriminations." *Semiotica* 30 (1980): 4.

Charters, Samuel. *The Legacy of the Blues: Lives of Twelve Great Bluesmen.* New York: DaCapo 1977.

Ellison, Ralph. *Invisible Man.* New York: Vintage-Random House, 1974.

______. *Shadow and Act.* New York: Signet-NAL, 1966.

Foucault, Michel. *The Order of Things.* New York: Random House, 1973.

Freud, Sigmund. *Totem and Taboo.* Trans. James Strachey. New York: Norton, 1950.

Geertz, Clifford. "Deep Play: Notes on the Balinese Cockfight," *Interpretation of Cultures.* New York: Basic, 1973.

Jameson, Fredric. "The Symbolic Inference; or, Kenneth Burke and Ideological Analysis." *Critical Inquiry* 4 (1978): 510-11.

Kent, George. *Blackness and the Adventure of Western Culture.* Chicago: Third World, 1972.

Lamming, George. *Season of Adventure.* London: Allison and Busby, 1979.

Lewis, David Levering. *When Harlem Was in Vogue*. New York: Knopf, 1981.

Nicholas, A.S., ed. *Woke Up This Mornin': Poetry of the Blues.* New York: Bantam,1973.

Oakley, Giles. *The Devil's Music: A History of the Blues.* New York: Harvest, 1976.

Radin, Paul. *The Trickster: A Study in American Indian Mythology.* London: Routledge Kegan Paul, 1955.

Rodgers, Carolyn. *How I Got Ovah: New and Selected Poems.* New York: Doubleday, 1975.

Ruby, Jay ed. *A Crack in the Mirror: Reflexive Perspectives in Anthropology.* Philadelphia: University of Pennsylvania Press, 1982.

Turner, Victor. *The Forest of Symbols: Aspects of Ndembu Ritual.* Ithaca: Cornell University Press, 1967.

_____. "Myth and Symbol." *International Encyclopedia of the Social Sciences*, Vol. 10. New York: Free Press, 1986.

White, Hayden. "Literature and Social Action: Reflections on the Reflection Theory of Literary Art." *New Literary History* 12 (1980): 378.

From *PMLA* 98 (October 1983), 828-845.

Dante's *Inferno* and Ellison's *Invisible Man*: A Study in Literary Continuity

Robert J. Butler

It has often been observed that much of the power and complexity of Ralph Ellison's *Invisible Man* is due to its being so deeply rooted in many literary and folk traditions. Drawing skillfully upon black, American, and Western cultures, the novel embodies the particular society from which it springs and also achieves a universality enabling it to "splice into the deeper currents of life."[1] There has been much investigation into the special ways Ellison employed black folk materials, and many critical studies have also explored his sophisticated uses of literary masterworks such as *The Odyssey, Huckleberry Finn,* "Benito Cereno," and *A Portrait of the Artist as a Young Man.* But surprisingly little attention has been given to the remarkable affinities which exist between Dante's *Inferno* and *Invisible Man,* even though the two works echo each other significantly.[2]

In the Prologue to *Invisible Man* Ellison's hero mentions that in listening to jazz he "not only entered the music but descended, like Dante, into its depths."[3] The entire novel can be seen as this kind of complicated interplay of cultures, at once a Dantean journey into a nether world and also a jazz symphony. It is my purpose here to analyze how the *Inferno* functions for Ellison as a literary model in order to reveal some previously unnoticed aspects of *Invisible Man's* structure and vision. For although Ellison is not an essentially religious writer, he was profoundly influenced by Dante both as an artist and as a thinker.

As I have argued elsewhere, the overall narrative structure of Ellison's novel consists of a series of episodes which are intricately circular in nature.[4] In fact, the novel is made up of an overture, the Battle Royal, which telescopes all of the book's important motifs, and nine major episodes which then serve as variations. This narrative design, therefore, is strikingly similar to that found in the *Inferno.* Each work takes the form of massive inverted cones, ten concentric circles arranged in an exact progression to dramatize its central themes.

This narrative structure is reinforced by important images of circularity which are used in nearly every major scene to dramatize the hero's psychological disorientation. As he boxes during the Battle Royal, the room seems to spin around in "a swirl of lights" (p. 19). After his conference with Bledsoe, his thoughts are "a mad surreal swirl" (p. 112) and the meeting with Emerson concludes with his mind flying "in circles" (p. 147). As he smarts from Kimbro's criticisms at the Liberty Paint Factory, his emotions are described as "whirling" (p. 155). Arguing bitterly with Jack about his function in the Brotherhood, he feels his head spinning as though he were on "a supersonic merry-go-round" (p. 357). The final result of his liaison with Sybil is to cut him loose from any center of gravity and to put his head "awhirl" (p. 401). And the terror and confusion inspired by the Harlem Riot are vividly depicted by the hero stumbling "in circles" (p. 424) as he searches for Mary Rambo's apartment.

These patterns define the hero's inward and outward life prior to moving underground as circles of necessity which trap him in his own compulsions and the rigid expectations which his social environment imposes upon him. His "hell," therefore, consists of incoherent movement in a world whose circumference he can not transcend and whose center he can not reach. This is underscored in a powerful, nearly Dantean, allegorical moment toward the end of the novel when he falls into a manhole and then looks up at the cover which the police use to seal him in a kind of tomb. Examining this "circle of holes in steel," he thinks, "This is the way it's always been, only now I know it" (p. 428). The circular cover, dotted with holes arranged in a circle, is an allegorical emblem of his entire life up to this point--mindless repetitions embedded in the hard metallic mold of forces beyond his control.

Invisible Man, therefore, provides a compelling illustration of what George Poulet has described as a crisis in modern intellectual life--bringing the wild "centrifugality" of modern experience under human control. Whereas Medieval poets such as Dante could imagine the universe harmoniously, as a set of concentric circles firmly fixed in God's will, our writers find that such order has been dissolved, thus condemning man to either "demented vertigo" or "the disappearance of the self through vaporization."[5] Ellison's hero is threatened throughout the novel by madly disorienting experiences such as those found in the Liberty Paint episode and the death of Tod Clifton--scenes where fast-spinning events threaten to destroy the self. He is also endangered while underground by the slow "vaporization" of the self, sliding into a deadly lassitude resulting in nonbeing. His way of overcoming these two dangers is to center his life in consciousness and then move out to progressively larger circles of experience. Although such a strategy will never give him the ultimate harmonies and securities of the Dantean universe, they nevertheless provide him with a rough secular equivalent of "salvation," the existential creation of his true identity.

* * * * *

When asked in an interview if *Invisible Man* followed a preconceived plan, Ellison observed that he began his novel with a highly calculated three-part structural framework:

> The symbols and their connection were known to me. It began with a chart of the three-part division. It was a conceptual frame with most of the ideas and some incidents indicated. The three parts represent the narrator's movement from, using Kenneth Burke's terms, purpose to passion to perception. These three major sections are built up of smaller units of three which mark the course of the action and which depend for their development upon what I hoped was a consistent and developing motivation. However, you'll note that the maximum insight on the hero's part isn't reached until the final section. After all, it's a novel about innocence and human error, a struggle through illusion to reality.[6]

This suggests several important parallels with the *Inferno.* Dante's poem is also divided into three basic parts which are then carefully subdivided. And in both works the hero's journey through these parts is an intricate movement from "illusion to reality," culminating in a "maximum insight" contained in the final episode. Moreover, the various sections of each journey form a scale of value where different forms of evil are gradated, getting progressively more serious as we move more and more deeply into the respective journeys.

Ellison's vision, like Dante's is consciously schematic. A listing of the major parts of *Invisible Man* clearly illustrates this:

a. Introduction: The Battle Royal

b. Part One ("Purpose"): (1) The Jim Trueblood episode, (2) The Golden Day episode, and (3) The expulsion from college

c. Part Two ("Passion"): (1) The Liberty Paint sequence, (2) The eviction, and (3) Tod Clifton's death

d. Part Three ("Perception"): (1) Disaffection with the Brotherhood, (2) The imitation of Rhinehart, and (3) The Harlem riot

Using this breakdown, it is easy to see some striking thematic parallels between *Invisible Man* and the *Inferno*. For both books trace a very similar progression of "sins" which their respective heroes must understand and transcend on their way to achieving their "salvation." Just as Dante's upper hell is filled with sins of "incontinence," the first part of Ellison's novel pictures people who are primarily in search of creature comforts--the money, status, and power, which comprise the major "purposes" of the American dream. As the middle sections of Dante's hell provide a terrifying panorama of the sins of violence, so do the interior parts of Ellison's novel show scenes of "passion" where various types of violence occur. And if the lower reaches of the *Inferno* depict sins of fraud, the final episodes of *Invisible Man* portray the hero's perception that his world is at its deepest levels corrupted by certain varieties of radical dishonesty and manipulation.

A brief comparison of Dante's vestibule with Ellison's Battle Royal clearly demonstrates many important similarities. Dante fills his vestibule with opportunists who race forever in circles chasing banners which will always elude them. Likewise, the Battle Royal pictures the hero and his nine cohorts boxing blindfoldedly in circles as they seek the "opportunities" with which their society deludes them. Ellison describes his characters as having succumbed to "blind terror" (p. 17), and Dante portrays his sinners as being in "a blind and unattainable state."[7] Both scenes also employ many images of chaotic movement and frenzied noise--the Battle Royal is "complete anarchy" (p. 19), and the vestibule is a "confusion of tongues," pure "pandemonium" (p. 42). A "black haze" (p. 42) permeates Dante's setting and Ellison's scene is acted out in a "smoky-blue atmosphere" (p. 19). Wasps and hornets sting Dante's characters, producing a horrible flow of blood and pus. So, too, do Ellison's boxers sting each other with punches which draw blood and spittle. Moreover, the electric rug which entices Ellison's opportunists with fake coins further jolts them with electric shocks. At the end of his ordeal, Dante swoons and Ellison's hero is knocked unconscious by Tatlock.

Ellison's scene concludes with an important ironic inversion of what appears in the *Inferno*. Whereas Dante can be reoriented by Virgil, who can help him to understand and thus put into perspective what he has just witnessed, Invisible Man is further befuddled by his "guides"--the white townspeople who explain "reality" to him. Virgil explains the vestibule as containing the root cause of all sin--a selfishness which turns the soul away from God. He therefore warns Dante to reject this sin in himself as a necessary first step in his quest for salvation. But the white townspeople encourage the divisive egoism in Ellison's hero by rewarding his efforts with a scholarship and a briefcase, "prizes" which only make him forget what the whole incident should have taught him. The net effect is to make him more of an opportunist than ever as he pursues the "proper paths" (p. 25) toward "success" which they lay out for him.

The next three major episodes in *Invisible Man* can be clearly organized under Ellison's rubric of "purpose." For they show the hero acting in terms of the false values imposed upon him at the end of the Battle Royal. In the Trueblood and Golden Day sequences he functions as the college's guide for Norton, operating mechanically in support of the school's values, which are in fact an extension of the standards endorsed by the southern whites who gave him the scholarship. Even after Bledsoe expels him from school, he remains a staunch believer in its purposes. His chief goal in all of these scenes remains the same, to get ahead in American life.

Each of these three scenes strongly parallels certain early sections of the *Inferno.* The madmen of the Golden Day occupy a limbo very similar to the one depicted in Dante's poem. Limbo--for all its "many people gathered in the light" (p. 53), and despite its "luminous and open height" (p. 53)--is essentially a "blind world" (p. 50) because it is a place of darkness separated from the reality which was central to Dante, God's grace. In the same way, the Golden Day is named ironically because it is a place of darkness separated from the reality central to Ellison, true consciousness, Except for the Vet, all of the people at the Golden Day are indeed blind people who have lost control of their lives, even though many have, like Dante's pagans, achieved some distinction in the world. Just as Dante's virtuous pagans live "without hope" and "in desire" (p. 51), Ellison's pathetic characters live only for the satisfaction of their animal desires by drinking and whoring. This, however, is a measure of their hopelessness since they are allowed to indulge in these pleasures only because white society wishes to pacify them by depleting their energies. Even though they "whirled about like maniacs" (p. 65), they are, paradoxically, like Dante's people, in a "passive state" (p. 50) because they can do nothing to change their situation.

Although Ellison mainly inverts Dante's Citadel of Human Reason by populating it with madmen, he does place one genuine philosopher in the Golden Day. The Vet, for all his apparent irrationality, does give the hero sound advice and in this respect resembles "the great souls of philosophy" (p. 53) who make up Dante's Limbo. Like Aristotle, Socrates, and Plato, he warns the hero to cultivate his own mind and to look beneath the surface of things. He tells Invisible Man and Norton essentially what Virgil told Dante about Limbo's blindness:

> "You cannot see or hear or smell the truth of what you see. . . . Poor stumblers, neither of you can see the other. To you he is a mark on a score-card of your achievement, a thing and not a man; a child, or even less--a black amorphous thing. And you, for all your power, are not a man to him, but a God, a force." (p. 73)

Ellison's hero had made the same mistake as Dante's virtuous pagans, for each has been blinded by a false "god."

Trueblood's story, similarly, bears close resemblance to Circle Two, where Dante depicts the carnal. Now we are in "hell proper": Trueblood's intense suffering is relieved neither by drink nor sex, and his uneducated but sensitive mind is not blunted by madness. As Dante's sinners are punished by "a great whirlwind" (p. 56) which pushes them in eternal circles, Jim has been driven into incest by the whirlwind of his passions. His dream of running into a clock parallels in certain ways the image of Dante's sinners buffeted about in darkness by hot winds:

> "I git loose from the woman now and I'm runnin' for the clock. At first I couldn't get the door open . . . . But I gets it open and gets inside and it's hot and dark in

> there. I goes up a dark tunnel . . . . It's burnin' hot as iffen the house was on fire, and I starts to runnin', tryin' to get out. I runs and runs. . . . (p. 46)

Dante and Ellison respond to the carnal in comparable ways. Both writers view the sins of the flesh as relatively easy to forgive since they are closely tied in with man's drive toward love. Accordingly, Paolo and Francesca are given very sympathetic treatment, and Jim Trueblood becomes a sort of folk-hero, whose story is one of the most poignant in the novel. Significantly, both scenes culminate with similar gestures. Dante swoons because he is overcome with the "pity and confusion" (p. 60) which Paolo's and Francesca's tale aroused in him. Likewise, Norton passes out after hearing Trueblood's tale because he is overwhelmed by his own confused and incestuous feelings toward his daughter.

The episodes with Bledsoe have subtle but important links with Circle Three, where Dante portrays the gluttons. Here Cerberus watches over those who wallow in filth for all eternity, just as Bledsoe presides over the college which is aptly epitomized by the "stagnant" (p. 28), algae-filled river which runs by it. Like Cerberus, who has three heads, Bledsoe, who can compose his face "like a sculptor" (p. 19), has three faces, one he shows to important whites, another he officially shows to students, and a third he privately reveals to the hero. Also like Cerberus, who "flays and mangles" (p. 66) souls with his claws, Bledsoe is, as his name suggests, a bleeder of souls. He surely tries to tear apart the hero by shouting at him, "You're nobody, son" (p. 110). Appropriately, Invisible Man feels himself the victim of almost "a total disembowelment" (p. 112) after his session with Bledsoe. Reeling from the knowledge that he has been expelled from school, which he had earlier imagined as a kind of Eden, he thinks, "The very idea stabbed my insides again" (p. 113).

The second part of the novel deals with the hero's early experiences in the North and fits nicely under Ellison's category of "passion." As such, it corresponds exactly to the second part of the *Inferno,* where sins of violence are punished. The Liberty Paint episode, the eviction of Primus Provo, and Tod Clifton's death each define a period in the hero's life where he becomes actively involved with forms of physical, economic, and moral violence. Like Dante, he must first understand and then purge himself of such tendencies.

The entire Liberty Paint sequence has very strong affinities with Circle Five, where Dante envisions the wrathful and the sullen. Everything about the paint factory bespeaks these two qualities, from Lucius Brockway, who views the hero "sullenly" (p. 157), to the wrathful union members, whose every member "looked upon (the hero) with hostility" (p. 169). Appropriately, the company's trademark is "a screaming eagle" (p. 150). As Dante pictures his sinners attacking each other in foul slime, Ellison allegorically imagines the American industrial system as a fierce struggle between union and management which ultimately produces a slime of sorts, white paint described as a "sticky goo" (p. 154). If Dante entombs his sinners under layers of muck, Ellison presents Lucius working "three levels underground" (p. 157) in a dirty room where the sticky vehicle of the paint is made. The hero's dealings with Lucius culminate in a strangely allegorical fight where he is actually bitten, a striking parallel to Dante's sinners savagely biting one another. And Ellison's scene ends appropriately with the boiler exploding, covering the hero with a foul-smelling resin. Like Dante's characters who are "fixed in slime" (p. 76), he is immobilized by the angry, filthy world around him.

In the hospital scene which follows, Invisible Man is subjected to more violence, this time of a psychological nature. This scene contains a number of interesting analogues to Circle Six, where Dante portrays the heretics entombed in fiery chests, corresponding to the iron lung which Invisible Man describes as "fiery" (p. 176). Virgil and Dante become immobilized by the terrifying environment surrounding them and must wait for the Heavenly Messenger to lead them through this part of hell. In a similar way, Ellison's hero passes out in the streets after he is released from the hospital, and his heavenly messenger takes the form of Mary Rambo, a Madonna figure who nurses him back to health again. Likewise, the three Furies who address Dante and Virgil from a tower resemble the three nurses who attend to Invisible Man in such a cold, remote way. One nurse is described as "a panel arrayed with coils and dials" (p. 177), perhaps suggestive of the Fury who tries to call the coil-haired Medusa so that she can turn Dante and Virgil into stone.

The eviction episode confronts Invisible Man with economic violence which nearly results in a race riot. This scene, which Dante would see as violence against neighbors, clearly resembles Round One of the *Inferno's* Seventh Circle. Ellison consciously uses Dantean images of circularity, for example, when the hero feels "a rising, whirlpool of emotion" (p. 205) and later seems "to totter on the edge of a great dark hole" (p. 208) as he begins his speech. And the hellish lives of the evicted couple are portrayed as "junk whirled eighty-seven years in a cyclone" (p. 210). The trusties who try to keep order resemble the centaurs who patrol Dante's river of boiling blood. Ellison internalizes such a river, making it a parallel to the turbulent feelings which "boiled up" (p. 208) inside the hero as he prepares to give the speech which will melt the "emotion-freezing ice" (p. 197) of his prior life.

Tod Clifton's death concludes the second phase of Ellison's hero's journey through hell. Although Clifton has been able to see through the "heresies" of the Brotherhood, he fails to discover a meaningful alternative to them. As a result, he "falls out of history" (p. 328) into a hell of physical and moral violence. Literally reduced to hawking Sambo dolls, which represent everything he hates in himself, he commits a kind of suicide, deliberately provoking an armed policeman into a violent confrontation. He is likened to Dante's suicides who in the Seventh Circle are deprived of human form, turned into "unnatural" (p. 119) trees and devoured by harpies. For after being stripped of his Brotherhood identity, Clifton has become like the grotesque cardboard dolls which he sells. Both are seen as "performing a degrading act in public" (p. 326) which involves the use of a "black mask-like face" (p. 326). Dante's suicides are destroyed by harpies, "defilers of all they touch" (p. 118), and Clifton is ruined by the Brotherhood, which perversely manipulates everyone for its own selfish ends.

The episode contains several other images which suggest the second division of Dante's hell. For example, the hero becomes depressed soon after he hears of Clifton dropping out of the Brotherhood and compares New York to "a city of the dead" (p. 324), a sort of Dis. As he walks toward the place where he will observe Clifton's sales pitch, he complains of the "blazing summer heat" where everything is starting "to boil" (p. 325). And the "circling" (p. 329) pigeons which whirl in the air as Clifton fights the policeman underscore the futility of his act. Ultimately, his death is seen as a descent into Dante's world of absolute nullity, a "plunge into nothingness, into the void of faceless faces, of soundless voices" (p. 331).

This is a pivotal experience for the hero, and his subsequent adventures form the final section of the book in what Ellison has called "perception." For he discovers at this point that he, like Clifton, has been betrayed by all that he has previously trusted. The Brotherhood, in forcing him to deny his culture and forget his past, has indeed done violence to his true human "form." But, unlike Clifton, he can go into a mental underground, thus recovering his humanity by developing genuine consciousness, the "light" which "confirms [his] reality, gives birth to [his] form" (p. 5). He thus avoids the moral suicide offered him by radical politics, whose cold abstractions are at odds with his true identity.

The world the hero perceives in the final section of the novel has at its outer layers the selfishness and violence that Dante deplored in his first two parts of hell. But at its core is the sort of fraud which is found in Circles Eight and Nine of the *Inferno*. For Rhinehart, Ras, and Jack--three figures against whom the hero consciously struggles in the novel's final three major episodes--are primarily associated with forms of treachery which weaken the foundations of the world that Ellison imagines in the novel. Invisible Man, therefore, must fully understand and transcend each of these characters in order to "save" himself.

Rhinehart, labeled by the hero as a "fraud" (p. 375), is identified with every type of deceit shown in the ten *malebolges* which comprise the Eighth Circle of Dante's poem. As "Daddy" Rhinehart, he is a pimp and a womanizer who thrives on pandering, seduction, flattery, and the selling of countless sexual "favors"--a kinky modern counterpart to simony. As Bliss P. Rhinehart, the revivalist preacher, he is guilty of hypocrisy, divining, and what Dante may call "evil counsel." As "Rhine" the numbers runner, he makes his living on graft, theft, and a kind of "alchemy"--turning plain numbers into money. In each of these three roles he is a sower of discord, one who exploits people for his own advantage by playing upon their dreams of money, sex, and transcendence. The result of such activity is a lack of fulfillment in the community, the smouldering *angst* which later erupts in the form of the Harlem riot.

Ras is clearly a more sympathetic figure but is nevertheless an almost allegorical personification of the effects of fraud. Although his politics are sincere, they are tragically naive because they delude people with a phoney Pan-African ideology resulting in insane violence and discord. The nearly Dantean punishment given to him when the hero impales him on his own spear, locking his jaws in mid-speech, recalls the punishment depicted in the Eighth Bolgia. Here the sowers of discord are guarded by a demon who uses a long sword to inflict pain on them. In particular, Ras resembles Curio, whose reckless tongue has been cut in punishment for giving false counsel to Caesar.

Jack, who in the middle of the novel was associated with "heresy," party ideology which grossly oversimplifies experience, is ultimately seen in a more damning light as a fraud. Whereas Rhinehart had been identified largely with what Dante would call "simple fraud" consisting of self-serving schemes, and whereas Ras is depicted as a demented victim of a bogus ideology which he has uncritically accepted from others, Jack is guilty of what Dante would call compound fraud. Not only does he personally betray the hero by secretly undermining his position in the Brotherhood, he is also consciously treacherous against kin and country by engineering the Harlem riot for the advancement of his political goals. These aims are clearly at odds with the welfare of both the black community and American society. Jack's cold intellectuality, his utter disregard for people, and his willingness to use violence to advance his aims align him with those whom Dante punishes in the deepest pit of hell--Judas, Brutus, and Cassius.

The riot, which is the book's last major scene, becomes a horrifying epiphany of the most disturbing aspects of the hero's world, the hell with which he must ultimately come to terms. It is indeed Ellison's Ninth Circle, and his hero is pulled toward it with as much force as Dante is impelled toward the central pit of the *Inferno*. Just as Cocytus is "the center of all weight" (p. 269), Harlem becomes an immense magnet pulling Invisible man after he hears of the riot:

> I walked with eyes closed, seeming to float. . . . High above, the cars sailed round and round the drive, their headlights stabbing. All the taxis were hired, all going downtown. *Center of gravity.* I plodded on, my heard awhirl. (p. 401; italics added)

Spinning in psychological circles and also caught in a vortex of equally mad outward activity, he spirals down to the riot, an experience which powerfully gathers up the meaning of all his prior life. Like Cocytus, which sums up everything which Dante has seen in the *Inferno,* the riot is a spectacular revelation of the dark, elemental forces which have been operation in every major episode of *Invisible Man.*

While never doing violence to the realistic texture of the scene, Ellison artfully provides Harlem with a powerful allegorical significance. From the very beginning, his protagonist has a strong sense of being in an all-too-real world, which in fact was modelled upon the 1943 Harlem Riot. But he also feels caught in a strange universe that transcends both time and space. Speeding down the road, he thinks: "Time ran fluid" (p. 402) and upon entering Harlem, he feels "a sudden and brilliant suspension of time" (p. 404). Inhabiting this surrealistic landscape, he thinks "the rioting seemed in another world" (p. 418) and consistently likens his experiences to those of a dream. Furthermore, he has a persistent sense of gravitating toward an underworld, even though he consciously tries at several points to move upwards and forward. For example, he initially compares the rioters to "moles deep in the earth" (p. 413) and feels "sucked under" (p. 419) by the force of events when he later tries to run away. After his encounter with Ras, he attempts to move uptown to Mary Rambo's apartment but is forced to "go downtown through dripping streets rather than up" (p. 423). Finally, as he escapes into the underground from the policemen, who are intent upon killing him, he "plunge[s] down, down, a long drop" (p. 427) into apparently empty "black space" (p. 428).

The settings in the *Inferno* and *Invisible Man,* therefore, are timeless places suggesting both Apocalypse and the innermost reaches of the dark side of the human mind. In each case, the hero is saved by consciously rejecting such a hell. Dante's contempt for the Inferno is epitomized by his savagely abusing Bocca in the Ninth Circle, and Invisible Man emphatically rejects the riot which earlier had such a fascination for him. He comes to see it as pure madness, a perverse scheme planned by insane ideologues in the Brotherhood and executed by equally crazy people such as Ras. Like Dante, who is described as "blind" (p. 46) at the beginning of the *Inferno* but who is saved by his ability to later see what hell is, Ellison's hero is shocked by the riot into a clear view of things:

> I could see it now, see it clearly and in growing magnitude. It was not suicide but murder. The committee had planned it. And I had helped, had been a tool. A tool just at the moment I had thought myself free. (p. 418)

Although the riot does not make him visible, it puts an end to his blindness. Because it results in this "stripping away of illusions" (p. 422), his underground is only a stage in the hero's quest for salvation, not his final damnation. When he hurls the spear at Ras, in effect rejecting everything the riot embodies, he feels that he has "surrendered [his] life and begun to live again" (p. 423). The same hell which consumes Ras provides "a new sense of self" (p. 420) for him. Even as he stumbles about in circles while trying to escape Ras' men, he undergoes a sort of baptism from the "full naked force of water" (p. 424) spraying from a burst hydrant.

As the hero develops a growing awareness of the selfishness, violence, and fraud which have made his world such a hell, he comes increasingly to value the sort of Christian love which Dante speaks of in the *Commedia.* The episode with Sybil reveals him to be incapable of coldly manipulating her for her own purposes--he strongly feels that "Such games were for Rhinehart, no not for me" (p. 395). Being careful to put her in a cab which will send her away from Harlem, he continues to worry about her at several points during the riot. He also adopts a basically compassionate view of nearly everyone caught up in the violence at the end of the novel. Even Ras is treated with tragicomic sympathy rather than hatred after the hero realizes that "I was no worse than he, nor any better" (p. 421). When Ras' men pursue him for revenge, therefore, he wants to tell them, "let's stop running and respect and love one another" (p. 423). Likewise, he sees the rioters sympathetically, viewing them as tragic victims rather than criminals. And the initial purpose of his escape is to return to Mary Rambo, a character always associated with generosity and love, whom one might be tempted to compare in certain ways with Dante's Beatrice. His statement underground, that "in spite of all, I find that I love" (p. 437), is therefore solid proof that he has not been destroyed by his experiences.

His loss of innocence and his subsequent movement underground become a "fortunate fall" which prompts him to take genuine responsibility for his own life. Admitting that at least half of his problems lay within himself, he concludes that he has two possibilities: "You can either make passive love to your sickness or burn it out and go on to the next conflicting phase" (p. 435). Clearly this next phase is purgatorial in nature, and to suggest this, Ellison draws several strong parallels between the *Purgatorio* and his hero's subterranean world. On the most obvious level, the purification through fire which Invisible Man undergoes while burning the contents of his briefcase recalls the purifying flame which Dante experiences on the final level of purgatory. Incinerating his high school diploma, Clifton's doll, Jack's letter, and his Brotherhood identification card, he is able to transcend his past errors. Although the process is painful, producing much screaming and a nightmare where he imagines himself as castrated, he does in fact emerge from these agonies "whole" (p. 431) with the awareness that he has "run enough," that he is "through with them at last" (p. 429).

Both purgatories are also defined by image patterns of light and sight. They are essentially mid-worlds which combine the darkness of hell with the radiance of heaven. Each hero must therefore develop the extraordinary vision which can cope with such extremes. While Dante is first blinded by Beatrice's radiance, he is eventually able to behold her without flinching. Likewise, Invisible Man must accommodate his vision to the darkness of his cellar and the brightness of the 1,369 light bulbs he uses to illuminate it. In this way, both narratives are educative journeys of intensified, expanded perception. Beatrice prods Dante "to break the grip of fear and shame" so that he will no longer be "like one half-awake."[8] Invisible Man must also overcome his fear of the outside world and his shame of what it has made him so that he can become more than the "sleepwalkers" (p. 12) whom he has met above ground.

Ellison ultimately gives us "a complex double vision,"[9] where his hero, like Dante, can "condemn and affirm, say no and say yes" (p. 437). For although he realizes that life is "ornery, vile," he also deeply believes that it can be "sublimely wonderful" because it contains "infinite possibilities" (p. 435). Those who interpret *Invisible Man* as nihilistic, therefore, grossly oversimplify the novel.[10] Unlike Sartre's *No Exit* and Baraka's *The System of Dante's Hell,* both of which reduce all human experience to infernal emptiness, Ellison's book is finally concerned with its hero's emergence from hell. This is not to say, though, that Invisible Man is supplied with a transcendent vision of faith distilled from suffering. Indeed, one of his main problems has always been an excessive "faith" in the "gods" who have ruled his world--Norton, Bledsoe, and Jack. But Ellison, operating in an existential context, can provide his hero with a modern version of salvation. As he observed in a 1974 interview:

> Perhaps the antidote to *hybris,* overweening pride, is irony, that capacity to discover and systemize ideas. Or as Emerson insisted, the development of consciousness, consciousness, *consciousness.* And with consciousness, more refined conscientiousness, and most of all, that tolerance which takes the form of humor.[11]

Although this outlook is clearly secular in nature, it is not so very different in several key respects from what Dante offers in the *Commedia.* Dante and Ellison view *hybris,* an egoism which blinds one to reality, as destructive of the self. And they also provide visions which are finally "comic" in nature. Even though Ellison can not subscribe to the metaphysical certainties which are the basis of Dante's faith, does possess the refined, balanced consciousness which produces a true comic vision.

Put another way, Invisible Man's story, like Dante's, ultimately takes the form of a transfigured circle. Dante imagined purgatory as a mountain ringed with seven terraces and heaven as a rose consisting of petals arranged in concentric circles, thus transforming the symbol as it appeared in the *Inferno.* Whereas the circularity of hell is a trap, the circularity of Paradise suggests God, whom Dante classically imagines as a circle whose center is everywhere and whose circumference is nowhere. So too does Ellison redefine his hero's journey, endowing it with dramatically new positive meanings. For Invisible Man is finally able to see life as a series of vital circles which radiate outward from a coherent center, the self. Unlike Norton, who on the last pages of the novel is looking for a Centre Street which will betray him because it is merely the focal point for New York City politics, Ellison's narrator is no longer trapped by the outward "power" that has earlier controlled him. He is now moving toward dynamic inward centers of strength, rejecting the public masks he has worn throughout the novel. As he tells Norton, all outward trains lead only to the Golden Day. But in going underground, he has gotten off the hard rails of other people's expectations and is able to penetrate the circle of his life. By falling *into* a manhole, he moves into the self, symbolized by the underground, and by later *lifting* the manhole cover, he will be able to emerge from his "hibernation." His claims that life moves in the form of a boomerang and that "the end was in the beginning" (p. 431), therefore, are not cries of despair. Rather, they are proof that he has discovered the primal stuff of the self which can now center his experiences and is thus able to move toward larger areas of involvement. His mind is now a circle whose center is everywhere and whose circumference is nowhere.

* * * * *

Critics have long speculated on the reasons why Ellison has never published another novel since the appearance of *Invisible Man* in 1952. O'Meally recently pointed out that Ellison has been unable to combine his Hickman stories into a novel because he failed to discover a suitable "structural principle"[12] which would fully integrate them. McPherson observed in 1970 that Ellison had "enough typed manuscripts to publish three novels" but lacked a way of giving "total structure "[13] to these materials. In an interview, Ellison himself admitted that his chief problem as a writer has been "an anxiety over transitions"[14] which would help to unify his fiction. Admiring both Eliot's *The Waste Land* and Joyce's *Ulysses* for the ways they used "ancient myth and ritual . . . to give form and significance"[15] to their materials, he strongly suggests that in writing *Invisible Man* he was able to make his vision coherent by using myths from Western literature and rituals from his own experience as an American black man.

Seen in this way, Dante's *Inferno* was important to Ellison because it provided him with a literary model which helped to endow *Invisible Man* with the structural framework which is unfortunately missing in his subsequent work. The *Inferno* furthermore was to Ellison what the *Odyssey* was to Joyce--a source of irony and a touchstone of value. Thus drinking from a rich variety of cultural streams, all of which flow in a deep and complex harmony, *Invisible Man* is a major achievement in modern literature. Dante's poem, along with many other masterworks from Western, American, and Afro-American traditions, was one of the many sources of inspiration for Ellison's richly pluralistic vision. It must be stressed, however, that Dante's influence, so little discussed by the critics, was crucial in the development of *Invisible Man*, for it gave that novel a unity, depth, and resonance it otherwise might not have had.

NOTES

1.John Hersey, ed., *Ralph Ellison: A Collection of Critical Essays* (Englewood Cliffs, N.J.: Prentice Hall, 1974), p. 19. In numerous interviews and articles Ellison has observed that Western writers such as Homer, Dostoevski, and Malraux were crucial to the shaping of his fiction. He also has stressed on several occasions that his fiction makes extensive use of black folk tales and music. Moreover, he has often cited as strong influences American novelists such as Melville, Twain, and Hemingway.

Recently Susan Blake has taken exception to Ellison's use of so many traditions, arguing that he employed Western myths as a way of cancelling out the special meanings of the black folk experience. See her essay, "Ritual and Rationalization: Black Folklore in the Works of Ralph Ellison," *PMLA*, 94 (Fall 1978), 121-36. As this paper will demonstrate, I sharply disagree with this reductive view of Ellison's work.

2.When mentioned at all, the connections between Dante and Ellison are discussed very briefly. Esther Merle Jackson makes a passing comparison between the heroes of *Invisible Man* and the *Inferno*. See her article "The American Negro and the Image of the Absurd," *Phylon*, 13 (Winter 1962), 359-71. Michael Cooke's excellent study of the underground in black fiction does not mention Dante's impact on Ellison, even though he does analyze the affinities between the *Inferno* and other black writers in his essay "The Descent into the Underworld and Modern Black Fiction," *The Iowa Review*, 5 (1974), 72-90.

3.Ralph Ellison, *Invisible Man* (New York: Random House, 1952), p. 7. All subsequent references to the text are to this edition. Page numbers appear in parentheses after the quote.

4.Robert James Butler, "Patterns of Movement in Ellison's *Invisible Man*," *American Studies*, Spring, 1980, pp. 5-21.

5.Georges Poulet, *The Metamorphoses of the Circle* (Baltimore: Johns Hopkins Univ. Press, 1966), p. 109.

6.Ralph Ellison, *Shadow and Act* (New York: New American Library, 1966), p. 177.

7.John Ciardi, *The Inferno* (New York: New American Library, 1954), p. 5. All subsequent references are to this edition. Page numbers appear in parentheses.

8.John Ciardi, *The Paradiso* (New York: New American Library, 1961), p. 330.

9.*Shadow and Act*, p. 137.

10.Roger Rosenblatt, for example, argues that the novel is a parody of quest fiction and finally ends up as a journey to "nothing" (*Black Fiction* [Cambridge, Mass.: Harvard Univ. Press, 1974], p. 185). Likewise, Floyd Horowitz insists that the hero's movements lead him "nowhere" and that "his self-imposed basement is therefore an escape from responsibility" ("Ellison's Modern Invisible Man," *Mid-Continent American Studies Journal*, 4 [1963], 221).

11.Quoted in Robert O'Meally's "Ralph Ellison's Invisible Novel," *The New Republic*, Jan. 1981, p. 29.

12.Robert O'Meally, *The Craft of Ralph Ellison* (Cambridge, Mass.: Harvard Univ. Press, 1980), p. 118.

13.James Alan McPherson, "Indivisible Man," *The Atlantic* 226, No. 6 (Dec. 1970), 58.

14.*Shadow and Act*, p. 180.

15.Ibid., p. 174.

From *CLA Journal* XXVIII (September 1984), 57-77.

Frequencies of Eloquence: The Performance and Composition of *Invisible Man*

John F. Callahan

In *Their Eyes Were Watching God* Zora Neale Hurston is her own narrator in collaboration with Janie Crawford. But Janie remains a storyteller and a participant solely in the oral tradition; it is Hurston who brings that tradition to bear on the written word and the literary form of the novel. For the sake of rhetorical intimacy, Hurston adapts the call-and-response between Janie and Pheoby (and potentially the community) to her relationship with the individual reader and perhaps a constituency of readers. But in Ralph Ellison's *Invisible Man*, the narrator is a failed orator. Because he is unable to communicate directly with those he meets in American society, Invisible Man abandons the oral tradition in favor of a "compulsion to put invisibility down in black and white."[1] Yet Invisible Man moves back and forth over frequencies of both the spoken and the written word. After giving up as a speechmaker, he writes an improvisatory, vernacular narrative of utterance. Both the prologue and epilogue with which he frames his tale reveal a continuing, obsessive pursuit of an audience. In the prologue he is too hurt and vulnerable to risk intimate address even with readers he cannot see. So he puts on a defiant, sometimes hostile mask of invisibility impenetrable to readers except on his terms. Then, as he writes down his story, he does the tough psychological rhetorical work of creating a resilient, genuine voice. After he has told his story, he feels liberated enough to write an epilogue. There he converses with readers in an intimate, ironic voice whose democratic eloquence calls us to respond with our own dangerous, courageous, socially responsible verbal acts.

Three decades after the 1952 publication of *Invisible Man*, Ellison explores the fluctuating, often ambiguous, sometimes contentious relation between his novel and the oral tradition in an introduction that is both a meditation and a tall tale about the birth of *Invisible Man*. In the beginning, there were only Ellison and his protean character's voice. And they faced each other not in friendship but opposition, not in intimacy but confrontation. Ellison reveals that Invisible Man's passage from the spoken to the written word involved an initial struggle between his voice and Invisible Man's until, in a sustained act of "antagonistic co-operation,"[2] Invisible Man performed and he composed the novel. Earlier, Ellison observed that "although *Invisible Man* is *my* novel, it is really *his* memoir."[3] Now, still the trickster, he writes his introduction as a factual and fictional interpretive response to Invisible Man's last call: "Who knows but that, on the lower frequencies, *I* speak for *you*?" (*IM*, p. 439, my italics).

Thirty-seven years after Invisible Man announced his presence, Ellison identifies the improvisational beginnings of his form. As he tells it, Invisible Man intruded on him in a barn in Vermont during the summer of 1945 while he was "on sick leave from service in the merchant marine" (*IM*, p. ix). Looking to identify the interloper, Ellison found "nothing more substantial than a taunting disembodied voice" (*IM*, p. xiv) who cried out without preliminaries: "I am an invisible man." The upstart voice compelled Ellison to stop writing and listen. "Therefore," he recalls, "I was most annoyed to have my efforts interrupted by an ironic, down-home voice that struck me as being as irreverent as a honky-tonk trumpet blasting through a performance, say, of Britten's *War Requiem*" (*IM*, p. xv). Ellison, who came to New York in 1936 as an aspiring symphonic composer, knows what he is talking about. Nevertheless, as riffs from the honky-tonk trumpet invaded his imagination, they challenged him to seize the fire and energy of Invisible Man's jazz voice.

Like Dostoevski's narrator in *Notes from the Underground*,[4] Invisible Man spoke up, univited and unannounced. His was the last voice Ellison wanted to hear. So he jammed Ellison's frequency because it was the only way he could be heard. For although Ellison quickly sensed "that the voice of invisibility issued from deep within our complex American underground," he held back, "still inclined to close my ears and get on with my interrupted novel" (*IM*, p. xvii). Ellison tried not to hear because, in his tradition, hearing carries with it a responsibility to respond to what has been said, however marginal the speaker, however discordant and threatening his voice and message. But the jazz voice spoke in an insistent, syncopated rhythm that lured Ellison to imagine "what kind of individual would speak in such accents" (*IM*, p. xvii). Consequently, for Ellison as a "fledgling novelist," the problem of voice became the problem of character and form. To *write* a novel, he needed to *hear* this disturbingly familiar voice. And for Invisible Man to exhibit his skill in performance, Ellison needed to create an identity for the "taunting disembodied voice." "I decided, he writes, "that it would be one who had been forged in the underground of American experience and yet managed to emerge less angry than ironic" (*IM*, p. xvii).

Ellison is no longer a resisting or reluctant listener. He becomes a responsive audience and a potentially collaborative author. He openly coaxes Invisible Man to tell the story behind his riff. Soon Ellison sees as well as hears the spokesman for invisibility. He imagines him as "young, powerless (reflecting the difficulties of Negro leaders of the period) and ambitious for a role of leadership; a role at which he was doomed to fail" (*IM*, p. xviii) because, among other reasons, he is so slow to grasp what Ellison elsewhere calls "the ambiguity of Negro leadership in the United States" (*SA*, p. 18).[5] Retrospectively, even as he performs, Ellison distinguishes the task of composition from performance. He tells of his effort to tease out the character and story behind the solo voice: "*I* began to structure the movement of my plot while *he* began to merge with my more specialized concerns with fictional form and with certain problems arising out of the pluralistic literary tradition from which I spring" (*IM*, p. xviii). Slowly, Ellison arrives at a form resilient enough to advance both Invisible Man's distinct, uncategorical voice and identity and the novel's craft.

Ellison is explicit about the new ground he wanted to break with the unsought, unexpected, unwanted, unexpurgated voice of Invisible Man. Meditating on the state of the novel in the 1940's, he wondered "why most protagonists of Afro-American fiction (not to mention the black characters in fiction written by whites) were without intellectual depth" (*IM*, p. xviii), which for him was bound up with a democratic idea of eloquence. "One of the ever present challenges facing the American novelist," he writes, "was that of endowing his inarticulate characters, scenes and social processes with eloquence. For it is by such attempts that he fulfills his social responsibility as an American artist" (*IM*, p. xviii). From his first "taunting, disembodied" utterance, Invisible Man challenges Ellison to write in an urgent vernacular voice and in a form simultaneously novelistic and autobiographical.

Ellison's quest is for eloquence. So is Invisible Man's. Because of the unfinished business of self and American democracy, the act of eloquence is not simple; at times the pursuit of eloquence calls Invisible Man to think while he is acting and, at others, to act while he is thinking. Eloquence is bound up with persuasion, and therefore, Invisible Man's eloquence turns on his ability to improvise in genuine response to a situation and an actual audience. In a *tour de force* near the end of his introduction, Ellison identifies the improvisatory forms and forces urging him to experiment with the novel: "Having worked in barbershops where that form of oral art flourished, I knew that I could draw upon the rich culture of the folk tale as well as that of the novel, and that being uncertain of my skill I would have to improvise upon my materials in the manner of a jazz musician putting a musical theme through a wild starburst of metamorphosis" (*IM*, p. xxi). Who in America is not "uncertain of his skill"? And as a test of creative poise and energy, is not improvisation a potential act of eloquence? Ellison's reliance on improvisation reinforces his (and Invisible Man's) theme of identity, and their urgent appearance of an invisible voice in protean form calls for techniques of performance. Furthermore, as a novelist whose sense of improvisatory eloquence is informed by jazz as well as speech, Ellison looks to the jam session for confirmation of his collaboration with Invisible Man.[6]

Ellison's writing on jazz provides a provocative clue to his intentions and highlights the significance of performance in his novel. "In improvised jazz," he said a few years ago, as if to describe *Invisible Man*, "performance and creation can consist of a single, complex act."[7] And in a piece on Charlie Christian, Ellison calls jazz a form of combat: "true jazz is an art of individual assertion *within and against* the group" (*SA*, p. 234, my italics). A jazz group achieves its full effect only if the musicians test each other's skills and, through improvisation explore the full range of each member's untapped potentialities. "Each true jazz moment (as distinct from the uninspired commercial performance) springs from a contest in which each artist challenges all the rest; each solo flight, or improvisation, represents (like the successive canvasses of a painter) a definition of his identity: as individual, as member of the collectivity and as a link in the chain of tradition" (*SA*, p. 234). Likewise, in the context of the novel, Invisible Man's "taunting, disembodied voice" challenges Ellison to try his skill to the utmost. So, too, Ellison prods Invisible Man to tell of his efforts to be eloquent simultaneously within and against the grain of his different audiences: black and white, southern and northern, Americans all, optimistic and often confused about the workings of individual and institutional power.

Through his experience as orator and rabble-rouser, Invisible Man discovers the combination of luck, will, and skill ("shit, grit, and mother wit") and the coincidence of self and other required in order for "performance and creation" to merge in a "single, complex act." He is so thoroughly a performer that he defines and tests his identity on those occasions when he becomes a public voice. In his speeches, Invisible Man's voice evolves into an instrument more and more keyed to the necessities, limits, and possibilities of call-and-response. To persuade others and move them to action, he relies mostly on techniques of improvisation. Sometimes after the jolt of reversal he learns that his words have consequences dramatically and drastically opposed to his intentions. Several times his speeches lead to unintended actions. For a long time he underestimates the dynamic mutual awareness required between performer and audience for an improvisation to become eloquent. But gradually--too late for a career as an orator, in time for his vocation as a writer--he learns to challenge his audience's skills as well as his own.

Despite his failure to be eloquent with the spoken word, Invisible Man ends up committed to self-reliance as an optimist as well as an ironist. In the novel's paradox, he learns how and why the power of speech can be the power of action only when his potential eloquence falls on closed ears during the chaos of a race riot. In time he comes to see eloquence in much the same way as Ellison's literary ancestor and namesake, Ralph Waldo Emerson, understood it. "There is no orator who is not a hero," Emerson declared. "He is challenged and must answer all comers," and his words evoke Invisible Man's struggle for identity through improvisatory oratory. But the comparison also breaks down because Invisible Man has been too obsessed with advancing "to the top" to embody Emerson's heroic conception of eloquence. "The orator's speech," wrote Emerson in the 1840s when he and others believed in the power of the word to persuade Americans to live out their democratic ideals and free the slaves, "is not to be distinguished from action. *It is the electricity of action.*"[8] Nonetheless, Invisible Man attempts to make Emerson's metaphor work for him. He sends out words like so many charges intended to flow through his audience in a current of action. He misjudges the explosiveness of language and fails as an orator. But later, underground, solitary and silent, he taps into a literal power line and drains off enough electricity from Monopolated Light and Power to provide light and heat while he generates the energy and symbolic action of his autobiography. He tells us this in a voice at once brooding and insulting, peremptory and inquiring, in a prologue that is the self-conscious "portrait of the artist as rabble-rouser" (*SA*, p, 179). In his prologue, Invisible man does not seek conversation; responsive voices might talk back to him, disagree with him, belittle his point of view, question his motives, undermine his vulnerable, evolving self. Only in the epilogue, having made ironic peace with his identity and his voice, is he ready for response, for conversation, ready to risk verbal acts of intimacy, ready, in short, for eloquence.

In between, eloquence has a range of Emersonian meanings for Invisible Man. He sets out to be a leader whose speech is action, and not just symbolic action. Later, when he discovers the tricks of false eloquence and the conditions of genuine eloquence, he descends, and aspires, during the interim it takes to write his memoirs, to the symbolic action possible through literary form.[9] His transformation from "an orator, a rabble-rouser," who succeeds or fails, lives or dies through eloquence, to a writer learning his craft in underground hibernation involves a reversal of form and identity. As an orator, first free-lance and later an employee of the Brotherhood committee, Invisible Man misses the subtle connections between speech and action, performer and audience. In the world, he fails at eloquence and political leadership because he is out of touch, too much an isolated, solitary traveler, too much in the grip of illusion (his own and that of others), and because he does not yet understand that he and his words are variables in the American equation of power. Afterward, in the epilogue, he approaches the question of language and action as a writer able to affirm the very contradictions he resists during his quest for heroic political eloquence. Becoming a writer, he transforms the power of the spoken word into the ironic, self-conscious, symbolic potential action of his improvisatory autobiography and Ellison's novel...

* * *

...In his essays, Ralph Ellison proposes a reading of American fiction rooted in the idea and practice of democracy. What Invisible Man calls division is, in Ellison's view, essential if one is to understand and participate fully in American life, socially and culturally as well as politically. In "Twentieth Century Fiction and the Black Mask of Humanity," an essay written in 1946 when he was struggling with *Invisible Man*, Ellison asks why contemporary American fiction had failed to create "characters possessing the emotional, psychological and intellectual complexity which would allow them to possess and articulate a truly democratic world view?" (*SA*, p. 37). This is less a question than an assertion of the task Ellison sets for characters and narrators alike. Invisible Man's arduous self-reconstruction forces him to recognize the ambiguity and contradiction as well as the possibilities inherent in the "principle on which the country was built" (*IM*, p. 433), its many violations, and in his own contrary and complementary impulses toward love and politics. In the epilogue the pursuit of narrative becomes the Declaration's pursuit of happiness as Invisible Man calls eloquently for reconsideration of the rights and responsibilities of democratic citizenship.

Formally, too, Ellison's commitment to an American improvisatory vernacular rescues Invisible Man: namely, the epilogue's embodiment of an open, responsive, literary text. Call-and-response turns the dialectic of words into Invisible Man's resolve to act, to emerge from his underground solitary confinement to play "a socially responsible role." Together, his experience and narrative confirm the concept of eloquence. Invisible Man's failure as an orator and would-be African-American leader and his slow, painfully, self-critical comprehension of that failure have "taught [him] something of the cost of being an individual who aspires to conscious eloquence" (*SA*, p. 117). And so he enacts a favorite Ellison proposition: that a work of art "is a social action in itself" (*SA*, p. 137). This in no way exalts the word over the world. Rather, it declares allegiance to both language and action, and calls for collaboration between writer, narrator, and reader, between oral and literary techniques and traditions, between performance and composition.

For Ralph Ellison, the struggle with form is bound up with America. He is fascinated by his country and affirms its principles and possibilities in complicated, mysterious, tender, satiric, vulnerable, and multifaceted ways. Then and now, he refuses to leave definition of the nation to those who misunderstand or underestimate the richness, complexity, and possibility inherent in its vernacular culture. Therefore, Ellison chooses to write a patriotic novel, but on his terms. "My problem," he has written, "is to affirm while resisting."[10] And he condemns and renounces many of his country's practices; this, too, is the essence of the patriot's role. As an American novelist and a Negro, he strives to influence the novel in somewhat the same way that the civil rights movement of the 1950s and 1960s set out to change the social and political character of American society. Who knows, to paraphrase Invisible Man's last lingering question, but on the "lower frequencies," Ellison's articulate, intellectual passion informed the struggles of the 1950s and 1960s? Who knows but that *Invisible Man* was a cultural catalyst for some of the energy and achievement of the civil rights movement?

Certainly, few values were more unfashionable among American intellectuals during the late 1940s and early 1950s than patriotism. For expressions of that attitude and tone, Ellison looked to the nineteenth century and discovered a sense of national complexity and responsibility, an experimental attitude appropriate to the metamorphoses taking place in *Invisible Man*. There, he declares, "the moral imperatives of American life that are implicit in the Declaration of Independence, the Constitution, and the Bill of Rights were a part of both the individual consciousness and the conscience of those writers who created what we consider our classic novels--Hawthorne, Melville, James, and Twain" (*GT*, p. 248).[11] Yet Ellison could not simply return to the aesthetic terms of the nineteenth-century novel when for him "every serious novel is, beyond its immediate thematic preoccupations, *a discussion of the craft*," and when "more than any other literary form of the novel is obsessed with the impact of change upon personality" (*GT*, pp. 240-241, 244, my italics)--and with the impact of social change upon literary form. Nor could he merely innovate because for him form for form's sake renounces the novelist's responsibilities to society. "The novel," he insists throughout the 1950s, "is bound up with the notion of nationhood" (*GT*, p. 242).

When Ellison contends that "the interests of art and democracy converge" and when he connects "the development of conscious, articulate citizens" to "the creation of conscious, articulate characters," he makes inextricable the evolving twin experiments of democracy and the novel. In his view "resonant compositional centers" of fiction express the complexity of both the novel and American democratic society (*IM*, pp. xviii, xix). For him the novelist's individual imagination responds to the flux of American life. According to Ellison's 1982 introduction, Invisible Man already existed as a very real, as yet unimagined version of the "conscious, articulate citizen." Ellison did not so much invent him as fill in his character from the grain of his voice. And this is exactly Ellison's point about American society: there are countless articulate but invisible men and women in the nation's complex underground who profess "a certain necessary faith in human possibility before the next unknown" (*GT*, p. 319). Similar voices, yet to be identified and given palpable form in American fiction, excite Ellison's faith in the possibility of expressing that special American fluidity of class, culture, and personality. These variations on a volatile, seething, largely unheard and ignored eloquence spur Invisible Man's call for collaboration with Ellison and with us, his kin at his narrative's end.

Finally, because of his symbolic performance in the epilogue, Invisible Man merges social and personal impulses in "a single complex act" of narrative. When he writes *you*, he refers to Ellison as well as to potential and actual readers--after all, Ellison was his initial audience. In some sense each sets the other free. What began as an act of "antagonistic cooperation" (*SA*, 0. 143) ends as a sympathetic, continuing dialectical act. Like the reader, Ellison is enjoined to talk back to Invisible Man. And he does. Moreover, his author's act of response builds on an earlier idea about the protean nature of fiction. Back in 1946, Ellison argued for the novel's potential as a social action and form catalytic to the continuing experiment of American democracy. "Once introduced into society," he wrote, "the work of art begins to pulsate with those meanings, emotions, ideas *brought to it by its audience* and over which the artist has but limited control" (*SA*, p. 38, my italics). Now, more than three decades later, Ellison strengthens his novelist's bill of rights with an amendment: the writer, before and after his act of composition, is audience to his work and has the same rights and responsibilities as the rest of us--equally and individually, in the name of eloquence and action, in the name of citizenship.

NOTES

1. Ralph Ellison, *Invisible Man* (1952; rpt., with author's introduction, New York: Random House, 1982), p. 439. This volume will be cited hereafter as *IM*.

2. Ralph Ellison, *Shadow and Act* (New York: Random House, 1964), p. 143. This volume will be cited hereafter as *SA*.

3. Ralph Ellison. *Going to the Territory* (New York: Random House, 1986), p. 59.

4. Invisible Man refers to *Notes from the Underground* at the beginning of his prologue and revises and revoices Dostoevski's narrator's perspective to express his African-American voice and condition. Unlike Dostoevski, Ellison does not intervene and write an ironic footnote as apologia for his character/narrator. Invisible Man consciously plays off Dostoevski and his underground man to imply that he will go to both traditions of the vernacular, literary and folk, to become a writer in what Ellison repeatedly calls this "crazy country."

5. For Ellison's further comment on his view of Negro leadership at the time of writing *Invisible Man*, see *Going to the Territory*, pp. 44, 45, 59, 60, 62, 63, 125-33, 144, 317, 318.

6. Both Larry Neal and Albert Murray have found evidence of musical form in *Invisible Man*. In "Ellison's Zoot Suit," *Ralph Ellison: A Collection of Critical Essays*, ed. John Hersey (Englewooa Cliffs: Prentice-Hall, 1974), Neal argues that from the entrance of Louis Armstrong's "Black and Blue" in the prologue, "the subsequent narrative and all of the action which follows can be read as one long blues solo" (p. 71). And in *The Onmi-American* (New York: Outerbridge, 1970), Murray claims that "Ellison had taken an everyday twelve-bar blues tune ... and scored it for full orchestra" (p. 167). Likewise, in his biography, *The Craft of Ralph Ellison* (Cambridge, Mass.: Harvard University Press, 1980) ch. 5, pp. 78-104, Robert G. O'Meally discusses jazz and folk songs in *Invisible Man*.

7. Ishmael Reed, Quincy Troupe, and Steve Cannon, "The Essential Ellison: An Interview," *Y'Bird* no. 1 (1978), 132.

8. *The Journals and Miscellaneous Notebooks of Ralph Waldo Emerson*, Vol. IX, 1843-1847, ed. Ralph H. Orth and Alfred Ferguson (Cambridge, Mass.: Belknap Press, 1971), pp. 425-26, my italics.

9. Ellison discusses the impact of Kenneth Burke's "The Rhetoric of Hitler's Battle" and his own notion of "symbolic action" in the *Y'Bird* interview, "The Essential Ellison," pp. 148, 156.

10. Letter from Ralph Ellison to the author, Aug. 12, 1983. For further discussion of the importance of history and the pursuit of democratic fiction in Ellison's work, see my "Chaos, Complexity, and Possibility: The Historical Frequencies of Ralph Waldo Ellison," *Black American Literature Forum* 11, no. 4 (Winter, 1977) rpt. with revisions in *Chant of Saints*, ed. Michael S. Harper and Robert B. Stepto (Urbana: University of Illinois Press, 1979), pp. 33-52, and in *Speaking for You: Ralph Ellison's Cultural Vision*, ed. Kimberly Benston, in press, and also see my "Democracy and the Pursuit of Narrative," *Carleton Miscellany* 18, no. 3 (Winter 1980), 51-68.

11. Ellison was reading Henry James's fiction extensively when he began to write *Invisible Man*, and acknowledges a debt to the aesthetic and moral complexity with which James pursued the "American" theme. Yet Ellison found James largely deaf to the democratic commitment to "make the illiterate and inarticulate eloquent enough so that the educated and more favorably situated will recognize wisdom and honor and charity, heroism and capacity for love when found in humble speech and dress" (*GT*, p. 273). For Ellison's discussion of James, see also *GT*, pp. 249-54, 262-73, 313-16. Daniel Duke made a number of helpful comments on the importance of the relationship between speaker and audience to democratic eloquence.

From *In the African-American Grain: Call-and-Response in Twentieth-Century Black Fiction, Second Edition*. Wesleyan University Press, 1990.

He Speaks for Whom? Inscription and Reinscription of Women in *Invisible Man* and *The Salt Eaters*

Anne Folwell Stanford

1

What happens to "the second sex" in a novel as powerful as Ellison's *Invisible Man* where the trope of invisibility functions as a critique of racist American society? When the text itself perpetuates the invisibility it seeks to undo, it seems inevitable that it will invite response and revision. In Toni Cade Bambara's *The Salt Eaters* we can discern an argument, not with Ellison's manifest text of invisibility and "the blackness of blackness," but with the subtext of gender erasure.

African American feminist critics have, especially in the last fifteen or twenty years, articulated the problematic of double invisibility, the double jeopardy that results from being both black and female. They have sought to add gender to DuBois's well known analysis of the sense of "double-consciousness" with which many African Americans live (3). Bell Hooks claims that "no other group in America has so had their identity socialized out of existence as have black women" (7). It is not simply that race, gender and class compound oppression arithmetically, to cite Valerie Smith (who borrows from Barbara Smith), but that "issues of class and race alter one's experience of gender, just as gender alters one's experience of class and race" ("Loopholes" 225). Much work in black feminist theory and criticism has taken as its subject the construction and/or erasure of African American women, and especially how the combined categories of race, class, and gender intensify and illuminate in important ways both reading and writing, believing "that the meaning of blackness in this country shapes profoundly the experience of gender, just as the conditions of womanhood affect ineluctably the experience of race" (Smith, "Black Feminist Theory" 47).

Many novels written by black women since the publication of Ralph Ellison's *Invisible Man* have (among other things) filled in gaps or given voice to the silences that have kept black women invisible. Toni Cade Bambara's *The Salt Eaters* is one such novel. Published in 1980, twenty-eight years after Ellison's *Invisible Man*, after the turbulent sixties and some gains had been made by the Civil Rights Movement, *The Salt Eaters* moves beyond its own created world, engaging other texts like *Invisible Man* in a dialogic relationship. Henry Louis Gates explains the phenomenon thus:

> Literary works are in dialogue not because of some mystical collective unconscious determined by the biology of race or gender, but because writers read other writers and ground their representations of experience in models of language provided largely by other writers to whom they feel akin. (7)

Gates is speaking here of the construction of a tradition of black women writers, but this phenomenon/strategy is similar even when the writers do not, perhaps, feel such kinship.

Invisible Man itself is peopled with the discourse of Anglo-American male writers from Jefferson and Whitman to Faulkner and Hemingway, providing a "twentieth-century Western gloss in the use of Freudian, Marxist, and existentialist notions of self" (Byerman 11). Ellison brings the language, imagery, and symbols of these writers and works into his text, and by placing them in an entirely new context, he "changes the joke and slips the yoke," or rather reverses, revises, or augments the writing and thinking of these men in ways that Russian Formalists would have called "defamiliarization." Viktor Shklovsky's 1917 essay, "Art as Technique," explains:

> After we see an object several times, we begin to recognize it. The object is in front of us and we know about it, but we do not see it—hence we cannot say anything significant about it. Art removes objects from the automatism of perception in several ways. (13)

If the object in question happens to be another work of art, a literary text, for example—a Whitman poem or the Declaration of Independence—the "estrangement" or defamiliarization occurs when that work is pulled into an unfamiliar context, such as a novel about the impossibility of freedom and "the body electric" for a man who is socially and culturally invisible. The shifted discursive ground makes possible fresh patterns of thought and action, and (among other things) provides readers with a different lens through which to read well-known cultural documents. In much the same way, *The Salt Eaters* takes on *Invisible Man*.

One of the primary projects of black women's writing has been, according to Deborah McDowell, "a revisionist mission aimed at substituting reality for stereotype" (284) and correcting a record of invisibility. This project is not unlike Ellison's dialogue with and revision of Anglo-American white writers, but for African American women, it necessarily takes into account and foregrounds gender. In addition, Mary Helen Washington says that it is a move that "takes the trouble to record the thoughts, words, feelings, and deeds of black women, experiences that make the realities of being black in America look very different from what white men have written" (xxi). For Bambara, that project has included a specific dialogue with Ralph Ellison's text, a move that, to borrow from Mae Henderson speaking about black women writers in general, is "a deliberate intervention…into the canonic tradition of sacred/literary texts" (124).

> Through this interventionalist, intertextual, and reversionary activity, black women writers enter into dialogue with the discourses of the other(s). Disruption—the initial response to hegemonic and ambiguously (non)hegemonic discourse—and revision (rewriting or rereading) together suggest a model for reading black and female literary expression. (Henderson 131)

By inscribing in her main character, Velma Henry, the consequences of double invisibility and silencing, and by constructing a female healer who bears similarities with Ellison's major female character, but who stands in stark contrast to her, Bambara's text functions not only as a critique of and an argument with, but as a corrective to, Ellison's text.

Particular signals, patterns of imagery, and thematic similarities suggest strong links between *The Salt Eaters* and *Invisible Man*, making an inquiry into the intertextual relationship between the two especially appropriate.[1] Many as yet unexplored suggestions of links between *Invisible Man* and *The Salt Eaters* exist. Bambara's use of bird imagery recalls Ellison's, where birds function as signals, warnings, or emblems within both texts, often signifying a character's shift of understanding or perception, or (in *The Salt Eaters*) a shift in space/time relationships. Patterns of circles and cycles appear in both novels; indeed, the structure of *The Salt Eaters*, while a plot exists, is more circular than linear. This is much the same for *Invisible Man*, about which Kimberly Benston says, the "plot—the soul of (hi)story, as Aristotle would have it—is circular yet inconclusive, ordered yet open" (90).[2] Explorations of the role of memory are crucial to both; both novels make brilliant use of dream-fantasy narratives. Another striking resemblance to Ellison's text, as Eleanor Traylor points out, is Bambara's use of the jazz mode as a form. Both novels ultimately seek to map out a terrain in which, among other things, American myths of self-reliance and integrity are probed and challenged, and where "the liberating epiphany...can occur...only when the 'telos' of discovery is seen truly as a point of departure" (Benston 89).

2

Ellison's novel begins, "I am an Invisible Man," thus voicing the narrator's hard-won realization that his search for identity begins and ends in the paradox of invisibility. Indeed, invisibility becomes the trope Ellison uses to critique and explore what it means to be a black man in American. The narrator of the novel, rendered invisible "because people refuse to see" him, searches for the answer to the questions, who am I, where did I come from, and "what did I do to be so black and blue?"

Written prior to the civil rights movement and the second wave of the women's movement, Ellison's novel predictably foregrounds race—"the blackness of blackness"—in his character's search for identity, meaning, and place in American history. The novel insists, however, that this problem of origins and identity is not, of course, limited to blacks, but permeates the fabric of American society, and is shared by all Americans (albeit in quantitatively and qualitatively different ways). Critics have accordingly drawn attention to the novel's "universality," noting that Ellison's story reaches far beyond racial boundaries. Gene Bluestein argues that the protagonist of *Invisible Man* moves through various stages of acceptance and identity as a black man, as an American, and finally, to the stage "which expresses the universal values of humanity" (604). While the impulse to come to terms with one's personal history (ethnic identity, folk heritage, family tradition) and to claim a national identity is no doubt shared by many, the very notion of "universal humanity," erases or at least blurs more political considerations about how a text is produced as well as about how is it received. J. Lee Greene notes that critics often had "strained to make the definition of 'universality' in *Invisible Man* synonymous with 'white'" (154).

I would add that "universal" is not only synonymous with "white," but with "male" also. The very premise of the novel's universality ignores the problematic of gender, and thus perpetuates the invisibility it seeks to undo. Both black and white female characters throughout the novel are constructed along a spectrum that replicates the classic duality embodied in representations of women—madonna or whore, mother or seductress—reinforcing and adding to the bulk of literature that produces women's characters according to this bifurcated vision. (These dichotomies show up curiously at several points in *Invisible Man* through milk/beer or milk/wine imagery associated with some female characters.)

The mother/mammy/madonna figures in *Invisible Man* include Mary Rambo, Mrs. Provo, Lottie (the pregnant wife of the kerosene wielding Dupre), the nameless women and children who inhabit the soon to be burned tenement, and the duped "sisters" of Rev. Rinehart's church. Even in the narrator's dream vision at the beginning of the novel, he encounters "the old singer of spirituals" and her sons (9-10). The women in sharecropper Jim Trueblood's chaotic household represent both sides of the duality: Trueblood's pregnant wife, Kate, and pregnant daughter Mattie Lou (both of whom are impregnated by him), are mother figures, but Mattie Lou functions as a seductress as well ("maybe sometimes a man can look at a little ole pigtail gal and see him a whore" [59]). Other seducers include college student Jack Maston's girlfriend (who sends a message for a secret meeting by way of the narrator), the whores in the Golden Day (who also display maternal characteristics), and Rinehart's seductive, exotic, and nameless "girl," to name a few. Even Harlem's female "brotherhood" members are commandeered as majorettes, "the best-looking girls we could find, who pranced and twirled and just plain girled in the enthusiastic interest of the Brotherhood" (371). Finally unifying in two images (milk/beer) both mother and what might loosely be termed seductress is the "huge woman in a gingham pinafore" who careens through Harlem on a Borden's milk wagon, "drinking beer from a barrel which sat before her."

> We stepped aside, amazed, as she bowed graciously from side to side like a tipsy fat lady in a circus parade, the dipper like a gravy spoon in her enormous hand. Then she laughed and drank deeply while reaching over nonchalantly with her free hand to send quart after quart of fresh milk crashing into the street. (532)

Even while the fat woman rejects the milk of human (read maternal) kindness for what might be seen as the beer of loose living, she holds the dipper like a "gravy spoon," locked into a gender-marked system that "pens" her between two polarities. Because *Invisible Man* is indeed frequently assumed to be universal, we need to ask for *whom* it is "universal," a question that in the asking undoes the term's very premise.

It is, ultimately, a mother figure, Mary Rambo, who stands out as the only positively memorable woman character in the novel (out of a cast of almost twenty black women characters), and it is precisely with the construction of Mary that Bambara takes issue most forcefully. Mary, the mother/healer of *Invisible Man*, enters the text immediately preceding the narrator's harrowing stay at the Liberty Paints factory hospital where, after perceived intransigence at work, he is confined and forced into shock treatment. He is pronounced "well" when he cannot remember his name, his mother's name, nor who Brer Rabbit is. (The politics of diagnosis alone provides an important lens through which to examine this section.) Stripped of his cultural and familial memory, the narrator is finally released—weak, hungry, and disoriented.

Enter Mary Rambo, a comfortingly nonsexual "big dark woman," who offers the narrator help when she sees him stagger and faint on a sidewalk in Harlem. Taking charge, she directs the crowd to "stand back and let the man breathe." Once the narrator is back on his feet, Mary convinces him to come home with her ("you weak and caint hardly walk...and you look what's more like you hungry"). Mary, who apparently has time on her hands, pleads, "let me do something for you" (246). A nearby man chimes in like a Greek chorus, "You in good hands, daddy. Miss Mary always helping somebody" (247). My point here is not to diminish the significance of black women's traditional importance to their communities as networkers and caregivers, but to look at how this particular stereotype functions to erase the nonessential diversity of black women by slotting them into two extreme and essentialist characterizations. Mary Rambo joins a long line of textual representations of women as "helpers," "caretakers," and "nurturers," women who occupy the moral high ground of the madonna/whore duality.

Although Mary is locked into her representation as a self-effacing, maternal caretaker, Ellison's text has a momentary rupture in which Mary emerges demonstrating considerable sagacity and wit. In this section, Mary delivers a riddling passage to the narrator as he is readying himself to leave her for the last time. He listens, but fails to understand fully when Mary tells him,

> And you have to take care of yourself, son. Don't let this Harlem git you. I'm in New York, but New York ain't in me, understand what I mean? Don't git corrupted. (249)

This uncharacteristically wise and direct discourse can be traced to an earlier version of the "Mary Rambo" section of *Invisible Man*, a version Ellison excised because of "space constraints." In this version Mary figures as a fully described, spunky, physically strong and self-reliant healer. A paid employee at the Liberty Paints hospital, she is also connected through her 104-year-old mother to the traditional healing arts of rootwork and conjure. This Mary was quite nearly buried until 1963 when Herbert Hill's collection, *Soon, One Morning*, appeared, including the excised chapter from *Invisible Man*.

Introducing the segment, Ellison explains that this longer narrative

> marked an attempt to get the hero...out of the hospital into the world of Harlem. It was Mary's world, the world of the urbanized (or partially urbanized) Negro folk, and I found it quite pleasurable to discover, during those expansive days of composition before the necessities of publication became a reality, that it was Mary, a woman of the folk, who helped release the hero from the machine. ("Out" 243)

Ellison adds that he is "pleased to see this version in print" because Mary "deserved more space in the novel and would, I think, have made it a better book" ("Out" 243).

In this segment, titled "Out of the Hospital and Under the Bar," the action begins after an explosion (and not coincidentally, after the narrator has aroused suspicion of being a union sympathizer) at the Liberty Paints factory. The narrator has been held inside a glass box, figuring much like a jail or coffin, for extended electric-shock treatments designed to "cure" him into forgetting his blackness. Mary appears to the narrator while he is still strapped inside the box. Weak from lack of food, disoriented and exhausted, the narrator notices her grinning down at him. The differences in physical description between this Mary and *Invisible Man*'s shapeless, sexless, "big dark woman" is striking:

> When I awakened she stood looking down. Her newly straightened hair gleamed glossily in the intense light, her blue uniform freshly ironed and stiffly starched. Seeing me awake she shook her head and grinned. I tensed, expecting a trick. But not this time. Instead, she tried seriously to communicate with me. (244)

Mary's communication consists of attempts to find out the reasons for the narrator's confinement in the hospital. Once satisfied that he has committed no crime, she sets about the dangerous business of freeing him. Not only her courage, but Mary's physical strength, becomes evident as she pries the lid of the box, so heavy that "an expression of pain gripped her features" as she does so (246).

Mary encourages the enervated man not to come *home* with her (as in the later, published version), but to remember why he was put in the hospital in the first place, to talk, to eat, and to become strong enough to escape the hospital. She challenges him to "stop being such a sissy" (262) and later returns with something "green like balled grape leaves that had dried without fading," obtained from her rootworking mother, a woman who

> useta sing alto, grow the best crops in the country, and right now...knows more about roots and herbs and midwifery and things than anybody you ever seen. (261)

Two remarkable women—strong, subversive, and not only willing to assist the narrator in his escape but practically demanding it of him. The "stuff" works its intended magic, and soon the narrator gains the strength of "Jack-the-Bear," making a hair-raising escape from the hospital, running completely naked in an underground ritual of rebirth. It is only through Mary's fearless and determined preparation, as well as her competent engineering, that the narrator makes his escape at all.

Leaving aside debates over Ellison's artistic judgement in rewriting this episode for his novel, it is interesting to look at the textual regression of a Mary who, with her mother, functions as healer/rescuer/conjure woman to the narrator, in contrast to the shapeless Mary Rambo of *Invisible Man*, whose function as a healer is implied but only briefly evident, and in addition, is diminished by sexual stereotype. This is not to argue that Ellison should have written a different novel. It is, however, to explore the terrain of absence, silence, or invisibility that inheres in the novel's gender bias, and to consider how another text, *The Salt Eaters*, pulls from *Invisible Man* the "not said" in order to construct a more expansive discourse of the female self.

3

One is struck, reading *The Salt Eaters*, by the presence of two unusually strong women characters: Minne Ranson, the healer, and her patient, Velma Henry. Velma, much like the Invisible Man of Ellison's novel, has failed to make sense of the world in which she lives—a world where her blackness is not as apparently erased as the Invisible Man's, but where social forces, such as sexism and racism, endanger her functioning as well as her spiritual, mental and physical health. A politically correct superwoman, Velma Henry ends up in her own version of the underground—the cave of her gas stove as she attempts suicide. And, as is the case for Ellison's narrator, an important aspect of Velma's moving beyond her nightmarish trajectory toward suicide will be her willingness to travel the dark inroads of memory and recover lost or forgotten wisdom within herself. For Velma, however, the search is doubly vexed: she must come to terms with herself as an African American and as a woman. "What has brought Velma to that stool and her confrontation/interaction with Minnie is in many ways the history of black women characters in contemporary Afro-American fiction" (Harris 152). Velma's illness is, in part, a result of the gender erasure exemplified in *Invisible Man*. However, while both *Invisible Man* and *The Salt Eaters* chronicle (in different ways) the search for an identity and integrity of self in a world that would deny, denigrate, or exploit that self, the novels differ sharply in the contrast between the two healers, Mary Rambo and Minnie Ransom (and indeed, in the differences that inhere in each character's understanding of caregiving and/or healing processes).

Both Mary Rambo and Minnie Ransom (who incidentally share the same initials) are single, older women who play special roles in their respective communities. Where Minnie is the "celebrated healer" of 1980s Claybourne, Georgia, Mary is the well-known helper of Harlem in the 1940s. Both women are important to their communities in bringing people together and in providing spiritual and physical sustenance, nurture and healing. But here the similarities end, Bambara has drawn Minnie with sharper, more complex lines, making her much less predictable than Ellison's Mary, who not only fulfills a classic stereotype of black women, but also undergoes a progressive erasure within the textual system of *Invisible Man*, becoming finally a mere abstraction in the mind of the narrator.

Language sharply delineates the two characters. Dramatically different from Mary's initial utterances ("Let me help you."), Minnie Ransom's first words (and indeed the first words of the novel) arrive by way of high challenge: "Are you sure, sweetheart, that you want to be well?" (3). Minnie is no self-effacing stranger eager to "fix" Velma. She offers a question fraught with risks, one that shifts the location of healing from external sources to Velma herself. Instead of the yoked and potentially entrapping me-help-you proposition of Mary's offer, Minnie's words establish clear boundaries between herself and Velma, paradoxically clearing a space between them in which the two women connect at deeply intimate levels throughout the healing process. Under the surface of Mary's words, on the other hand, the image of mother as a (s)mothering womb/tomb floats uneasily.

Making sure mother is safely asexual, the narrator describes Mary Rambo as a "heavy composed figure" (249) with "worn brown fingers" (247). She is also ultimately invisible as a "big dark woman" (245). Minnie Ranson, on the other hand, presents something of a sensation, described in *The Salt Eaters* as "Minnie Ransom herself,"

> the fabled healer of the district, her bright-red flouncy dress drawn in at the waist with two different strips of kenti cloth, up to her elbows in a minor fortune of gold, brass and silver bangles, the silken fringe of the shawl shimmying at her armpits. Her head, wrapped in some juicy hot-pink gelee.... (3)

Bringing together both sexuality and nurture, Minnie's appearance suggests a celebration of her own womanhood, history and culture, embodying the implied "yes" in the title (borrowed from Sojourner Truth) of Bell Hooks's study of African American women and feminism, *Ain't I A Woman?* Where Mary Rambo appears as asexual, Minnie thinks about (and is reproached by her spirit guide for doing so) a sexual liaison later that night with the younger Doctor Meadows. Where Mary sings "Back Water Blues," Minnie Ransom plays "some sassy twenties singer... 'Wiiiild women doan worrreeee, wild women doan have no bluuuzzzzzz'" (262). Furthermore, where Mary only briefly shows evidence of seeing beyond surface realities—or at least does so in terms of traditional religion, Minnie freely negotiates the spiritual world.[3] Functioning at the threshold between physical and spiritual realms, Minnie communes with her patient, Velma, while at the same time "travelling" and conversing with her spirit guide, Old Wife. She remains both separate from and yet integrally a part of Velma's healing.

As I mentioned earlier, Mary has a moment in *Invisible Man* where she shares a portion of Minnie's spiritual acuity when she delivers her New York riddle ("I'm in New York, but New York ain't in me"). Mary urges the narrator to embrace his past, to learn from and draw upon it, and to use it as necessary equipment for functioning in an alien and deracinating culture. And in fact, shortly after this conversation, the narrator meets a man selling hot yams and has an epiphany of sorts as he gulps down the soul food he long ago repudiated. Mary's words prompt a series of questions about identity for the narrator, to which the yams give a partial answer. "I yam what I yam," the narrator puns, embracing momentarily, significant aspects of the Southern upbringing he has previously lost.

Bambara's Minnie develops Mary's "New York idea" more fully as she encourages Velma to go deep within herself, to track the muddy backroads of memory and face the ghosts of her past. She must learn to live in a corrupt world (for *The Salt Eaters* never once loses sight of imminent global peril), but she must not let that corrupt world become or define her. Minnie knows that Velma

> thought she knew how to build resistance, make the journey to the center of the circle, stay poised and centered in the work and not fly off, stay centered in the

> best of her people's traditions and not be available to madness, not become intoxicated by the heady brews of degrees and career and congratulations for nothing done, not become anesthetized by dazzling performances with somebody else's aesthetic, not go under. (258)

Read "college" and "philanthropists" and "brotherhood," for "degrees" and "career" and we have a nicely developed version of the Invisible Man's dilemma both Mary and Minnie wisely perceive.

Much like many women before her, Mary functions as a community networker. Even as Mary tends to the narrator's needs at their initial encounter on the street, she established links with those members of the community standing near her:

> "...my name's Mary Rambo, everybody knows me round this part of Harlem, you heard of me, ain't you?" And the fellow saying, "Sure, I'm Jenny Jackson's boy, you know I know you, Miss Mary." And her saying, "Jenny Jackson, why I should say you do know me and I know you, Ralston, and your mama got two more children, boy named Flint and gal named Laura-jean, I should say I know you—me and your mama and your papa useta—..." (246)

Mary's character, however, is constructed upon the assumption that women who are not sexually promiscuous *naturally* function as the emotional and spiritual ligaments of a community. This plus the fact that Mary's depiction focuses on the naturalness of her role rather than on the very real such a function holds. *The Salt Eaters* seeks to correct the record, demonstrating first the cost of such connection without corresponding internal strength (Velma's frightening move toward suicide being one such cost). Velma, who had tried to be a bridge, has no internal, spiritual bridges for the many pieces of herself that drift no further and further apart within her. In addition, she lives and works in a community that ,although politically progressive, continues to operate as though its men were the prime, indeed only, movers.[4] The image of Velma having organized and marched with numbers of other women in a large-scale protest, camping in a soggy tent, covered in mud, exhausted, and searching through her purse frantically for a ragged tampax to stanch in the flow of blood from her menstrual period is juxtaposed with the image of the sleek, polished black political candidate emerging from an expensive hotel with the requisite woman in silk on his arm. Velma's attempts to provide bridges and to work for social change in her community are consistently undercut by a social system that upholds male superiority, as well as by her lack of internal resources to deal with such a system by establishing and maintaining her own personal boundaries.

However, *The Salt Eaters* also thematizes the extraordinary power behind the kinds of connections both Mary and Velma make in their communities. Reflecting on Velma's gift for bringing together disparate elements, her husband recalls that:

> ...things had seemed more pulled together when Velma had been there, in the house and at the Academy. Not that her talents ran in the peace-making vein. But there'd been fewer opportunities for splinterings with her around. (92)

On the surface, Velma has simply done a more sophisticated kind of connecting than Mary, but Bambara's text insists upon a new understanding of community and connecting—the necessity "to be whole" before you can "see whole" (92). Sara Hoagland's notion of "autokoenony" captures much of The Salt Eater's construction of community. Hoagland explains,

> An autokoenonous being is one who is aware of her self as one among others within a community that forms her ground of being, one who makes her decisions in consideration of her limitations as well as in consideration of the agendas and perceptions of others. (145)

Being autokoenonous and seeing whole, however, is no small task, as Velma's godmother knows:

> A deep rift had been developing for centuries...beginning with the move toward the material world and away from nature. Now there was a Babel of paths, of plans. "There is a world to be redeemed...and it'll take the cooperation of all righteous folks." (92)

What is, in Ellison's text, a commonplace about women's roles as community networkers and caretakers takes on new dimensions in the dynamic of *The Salt Eaters*: dimensions having implications for the survival of the human race.

In *Invisible Man*, on her way from being a networker to becoming a virtual abstraction, Mary enacts another stereotype, a permutation of woman-as-mother. She is finally inscribed as the entrapper implied in "let me help you," which by now in the novel has become a version of "let me own you." Her language changes from an initial concern to a controlling, domineering and even carping invasiveness:

> Boy, when you come home?....ain't you going to eat supper?...What kind of business you got in a cold night like this?....hurry back here and get something hot in your stomach. (290-91)

> Take some of that water in the kettle and go wash your face. Though sleepy as you look, maybe you ought to just use cold water.... You didn't come back for supper.... Boy, you better start eating again. (314-315)

Thus the focus of Mary's interest in the narrator changes from redemptive to restrictive, from mother to (s)mother. The Invisible Man becomes restive and guilty under her watchful (and anxious) care. Here, Mary has shifted from one cliché to another, becoming the tar baby from whom the Invisible Man must escape in order to continue his search for identity.

In contrast, Minnie Ransom's relationship with Velma remains detached yet enabling. Her touch, the music she plays, and her reliance upon the other, spirit, world, give Minnie the necessary power to help set Velma free. Bambara's text insists, after all, that healing is a release from bondage (a "ransom" of captives), and that caring constitutes both detachment and connection at the same time. Velma, sitting on a stool next to Minnie, feels "the warm breath of Minnie Ransom on her, lending her something to work the bellows of her lungs with. To keep on dancing, like the sassy singer said (263-264). Minnie loans her breath to Velma; she does not attempt to breathe for her, nor to surround or entrap her. In fact, at the end of the novel (and of the healing session), Minnie knows when there is "no need of [her] hands...withdraws them, drops them in her lap just as Velma [rises] on steady legs," the "burst cocoon" of her shawl left behind on the stool (295). Minnie's detached intimacy becomes the counter to Ellison's construction of smothering female "care." Mary, however, is finally written out of *Invisible Man* entirely as the narrator flees from her help. The "big dark woman" regains her helpfulness only when the narrator is physically distant from her, and she ultimately becomes an abstraction—a lodestar and symbol that the invisible man both embraces and resists:

> Nor did I think of Mary as a "friend"; she was something more—a force, a stable familiar force like something out of my past which kept me from whirling off into some unknown which I dared not face...at the same time, Mary reminded me constantly that something was expected of me, some act of leadership, some newsworthy achievement; and I was torn between resenting her for it and loving her for the nebulous hope she kept alive. (252-53)

It is no accident that Mary's force becomes most intense after she is erased from the text altogether. For the final three hundred pages of the novel, Mary remains an abstraction, reappearing only in the consciousness of the narrator when he is in danger and in need of motherly guidance.

To point out the ways Bambara draws on and remakes Ellison's text is not to posit a simple Ellison-as-oppressor, Bambara-as-liberator opposition. Ellison's *Invisible Man* is a brilliant novel. Bambara's textual intervention and record-correcting is also only *one* part of a story as multiple and complex as any must be that attempts to construct gendered characters. Indeed, Minnie Ransom, by breaking one stereotype, may herself be constituting or upholding another.[5] But in the references and signals that call *Invisible Man* into the text of *The Salt Eaters*, Bambara's novel interrogates a pervasive treatment of black women characters, rewriting the tradition, and in so doing, infusing it with a new vitality and angle of vision. Here, she demonstrates a strategy used by many other women writers to critique and correct textual records that perpetuate destructive and essentialized sexual stereotypes.

When Bambara's text draws directly on Ellison's trope of invisibility, the ground shifts enough to break up the terrain of the unsaid, and "invisibility" takes on new significance. A minor character in *The Salt Eaters*, Porter, explains that

> They call the Black Man The Invisible Man. And that becomes a double joke and then a double cross then a triple funny all around. Our natures are unknowable, unseeable to them. They haven't got the eyes for us. Course, when we look at us with their eyes, we disappear. (158-59)

The question, in Bambara's terms, becomes one of who hasn't got the eyes for whom? *The Salt Eaters* consistently raises the possibility that those "unknowable, unseeable" natures of which Porter speaks are not those of all African Americans, but inscribed in the terms of Ellison's text, those of black women, rendered invisible under a system of essentially androcentric seeing.

The author would like to thank J. Lee Greene for extensive comments on an earlier draft of this paper.

NOTES

1. Critics have noted similarities in the two novels. Gloria Hull, for example argues that *The Salt Eaters* "accomplishes even better for the 1980s what...*Invisible Man* [did] for the 1950s" (124). In addition, Eleanor Traylor suggests that Bambara was quite familiar with *Invisible Man*, and points out in great detail her debt to Ellison in her uses of the jazz mode in *The Salt Eaters*.
2. This is underscored in a slightly different way in Byerman's comment that "disintegration is the primary concern of Bambara's only novel, as the black community, the main character, and the book's structure are all decentered" (123).

3. See Trudier Harris, "From Exile to Asylum," for an incisive examination of the role of religious experience in black women writers. Harris points out that writers like Bambara, Toni Morrison, Ntozake Shange, Alice Walker, and Gloria Naylor "redefine religion as a means of showing devotion toward and communing with the self, with other women, with nature, and with the expansive forces of the universe" (153).

4. This is somewhat confusing, since the community set forth in *The Salt Eaters* is politically progressive and collectively committed to social justice. It does, however, suggest sixties Civil Rights activism where women began to see that their position to the movement replicated the oppression they had experienced in their lives prior to Civil Rights. See, for example, in *The Salt Eaters*, where Velma furiously recounts incidents of the near past:

> Like work and no let up and tears in the night. Like being rolled to the edge of the bed, to extremes, clutching a stingy share of the covers and about to droop over the side, like getting up and walking, bare feet on cold floor, round to the other side and climbing in and too mad to snuggled for warmth, freeze. Like going to jail and being forgotten, forgotten, or at least deprioritized cause bail was not as pressing as the printer's bill. Like raising funds and selling some fool to the community with his heart set on running for public office. Like being called in on five-minute notice after all the interesting decisions had been made, called in out of personal loyalty and expected to break her hump pulling off what the men had decided was crucial for the community good. (25)

5. Although Minnie Ransom is drawn from a tradition of African American female healers and "spiritual adepts" (as Bambara would put it), I think the character type may be in danger of being over-used in contemporary African American women's fiction, and appropriated as a stereotype by readers looking for simple, untroubling niches into which these characters might be placed.

WORKS CITED

Bambara, Toni Cade. *The Salt Eaters*. New York: Vintage-Random House, 1981.

Benston, Kimberly. "Controlling the Dialectical Deacon: The Critique of Historicism in Invisible Man." *Delta* (April 1984): 89-103.

Bluestein, Gene. "The Blues as a Literary Theme." *Massachusetts Review* (Fall 1967): 593-617.

Byerman, Keith. *Fingering the Jagged Grain: Tradition and Form in Recent Black Fiction*. Athens: U Georgia P, 1985.

DuBois, W.E.B. *The Souls of Black Folk: Essays and Sketches*. 1903 Rpt. Millwood, NY: Draus-Thomson, 1973.

Ellison, Ralph. *Invisible Man*. 1952. NY: Vintage-Random House, 1972.

_____. "Out of the Hospital and Under the Bar." *Soon, One Morning: New Writing by American Negroes 1940-1962*. Ed. Herbert Hill. NY: Knopf, 1963, 242-90.

Gates, Henry Louis, Jr. "Introduction." *Reading Black, Reading Feminist: A Critical Anthology*. Ed. Henry Louis Gates, Jr. New York: Penguin/Meridian, 1990. 1-20.

Greene, J. Lee. "Ralph Ellison." *Fifty Southern Writers after 1900*. Ed. Robert Bain and Joseph Flora. Westport, Connecticut: Greenwood P, 1985.

Harris, Trudier. "From Exile to Asylum: Religion and Community in the Writing of Contemporary Black Women." *Women's Writing in Exile*. Ed. Mary Lynn Broe and Angela Ingram. Chapel Hill: U North Carolina P, 1989. 151-169.

Henderson, Mae. "Speaking in Tongues: Dialogues, Dialectics, and the Black Woman Writer's Literary Tradition." Gates, *Reading Black, Reading Feminist*. 116-142.

Hoagland, Sarah Lucia. *Lesbian Ethics: Toward New Value*. Palo Alto, CA: Institute of Lesbian Studies, 1988.

Hooks, Bell. *Ain't I A Woman? Black Women and Feminism*. Boston: South End, 1981.

Hull, Gloria. "What I Think It Is She's Doing Anyhow: A Reading of Toni Cade Bambara's *The Salt Eaters*." *Home Girls: A Black Feminist Anthology*. Ed. Barbara Smith. New York: Kitchen Table P, 1983.

McDowell, Deborah. "The Changing Same': Generational Connections and Black Women Novelists." *New Literary History* 18.2 (1987): 281-302.

Shklovsky, Viktor. "Art as Technique." *Russian Formalist Criticism: Four Essays*. Trans. Lee T. Lemon and Marion J. Reis. Omaha: U Nebraska P, 1965. 5-24.

Smith, Valerie. "Black Feminist Theory and the Representation of the 'Other.'" *Changing Our Own Words: Essays on Criticism, Theory and Writing by Black Women*. Ed. Cheryl Wall. New Brunswick, NJ: Rutgers UP, 1989. 38-57.

____. "'Loopholes of Retreat': Architecture and Ideology in Harriet Jacobs's *Incidents in the Life of a Slave Girl*." Gates, *Reading Black, Reading Feminist*. 212-226.

Traylor, Eleanor W. "Music as Theme: The Jazz Mode in the Works of Toni Cade Bambara." *Black Women Writers (1950-1980): A Critical Evaluation*. Ed. Mari Evans. Garden City, NY: Anchor/Doubleday, 1984, 58-70.

Washington, Mary Helen. *Invented Lives: Narratives of Black Women 1860-1960*. New York: Anchor/Doubleday, 1987.

From *MELUS* 18 (Summer 1993), 17-31.

Ellison's Short Fiction

Ralph Ellison's "Flying Home"

Joseph F. Trimmer

Ralph Ellison is known chiefly for his single novel, *Invisible Man*, for which he won the National Book Award for Fiction in 1952, and for his collection of essays, *Shadow and Act*, published in 1964. It is not widely acknowledged, however, that Ellison is also a master of the short story. This ignorance or neglect of Ellison's short fiction is due mainly to two facts—his stories have appeared in relatively obscure journals, and to date they have remained uncollected.[1] Recently, anthology editors have discovered this wealth of material, and slowly but surely Ellison's short stories are being reprinted.[2] But despite this increased exposure, the stories remain neglected by critics. Marcus Klein, in *After Alienation: American Novels in Mid-Century* (New York: World, 1964), pp. 71-147, discusses some of the stories in his chapter on Ellison; but since his purpose was to trace the thematic concerns that eventually surfaced in *Invisible Man*, his treatment of individual stories was necessarily abbreviated. Yet his brief treatment of Ellison's stories is still the only one in print. What is needed is a detailed and systematic evaluation of all of Ellison's stories. I intend to begin that evaluation by examining a story that is readily available for inspection, "Flying Home."[3]

As Klein has pointed out, "Flying Home" has its beginnings in a political issue: "A Negro air school had been established at Tuskegee during the war, apparently as a sap to civil libertarians. Its pilots never got out of training. The school became a sufficient issue for Judge Hostie to resign from the War Department in protest over it..."[4] Ellison commented on this issue in "Editorial Comment," *Negro Quarterly*, 1 (Winter-Spring 1943), 298. He also indicated to Rochelle Girson in their interview in "Sidelights on Invisibility," *Saturday Review*, March 14, 1953, p. 49, that "he had intended after the war to write a novel about a flyer. This story would seem to be its beginning."[5]

The plot of the story is relatively simple: Todd, a young black pilot on a training mission, crashes his plane on an Alabama farm where he is saved from the white racist owner, Dabney Graves, by a black "peasant" named Jefferson. What is not so simple is the symbolic patterns that permeate the story. As with all vintage Ellison, these patterns proceed simultaneously on at least two levels, racial and mythic. On the racial level, the story gives us a parable of the complex interrelationship between the individual black man and his racial community; on the mythic level, the story refashions the Daedalus myth. The two levels are connected symbolically by implied parallels to three other related sources—the myth of the Phoenix, the Christian doctrine of *felix culpa*, or fortunate fall, and the story of the prodigal son.

Todd's basic problem is what W.E.B. DuBois called the problem of "double-consciousness": "It is a particular sensation, this double-consciousness, this sense of always looking at one's self through the eyes of others, of measuring one's soul by the tape of a world that looks on in amused contempt and pity. One ever feels his twoness,—an American, a Negro; two souls, two thoughts, two unreconciled strivings; two warring ideals in one dark body, whose dogged strength alone keeps it from being torn asunder."[6] Todd aspires to be a flyer, but everyone tells him that planes and flying are for white men. Thus Todd's desire to fly seems to be a desire to fly away from his Black identity and supposed inferiority and toward white acceptance and supposed fulfillment. The problem is that Todd is ambivalent. He wants to please the old black men who come to see him train at the air field, but they do not really understand his skill: "He felt cut off from them by age, by understanding, by sensibility, by technology and by his need to measure himself against the mirror of other men's appreciation" (p. 257). Yet he could never be certain what his white officers really thought of him. So, "between ignorant black men and condescending whites, his course of flight seemed mapped by the nature of things away from all needed and natural landmarks." (*ibid.*)

Todd's relationship to the black community is communicated more enigmatically in a series of allusions relating to buzzards and horses. Todd's girl friend has written to him that he should not be bothered by the old allegation of intellectual inferiority: "they keep beating that dead horse because they don't want to say why you boys are not yet fighting" (p. 255). It is to escape that "dead horse" that Todd flies. But as he manipulates his "advanced trainer" he spots a kite below him, like the ones he flew as a boy. In an attempt to "find the boy at the end of the invisible cord...[he flies]...too high and too fast.... And one of the first rules you learn is that if the angle of thrust is too steep the plane goes into a spin. And then, instead of pulling out of it and going into a dive you let a buzzard panic you. A lousy buzzard" (p. 259). The plane then falls out of the sky "like a pitchin' hoss" (p. 258), onto a field. When Todd recovers consciousness he discovers that he has broken his ankle. While a Negro boy, Teddy, goes for help, Todd is attended by an "old buzzard" named Jefferson. When he is asked about the blood on the plane, Todd tells Jefferson about the buzzard. Jefferson acknowledges that buzzards are "bad luck," and that they are only after "dead things." In fact, "Teddy's got a name for 'em, calls 'em jimcrows" (p. 259). Jefferson then offers the following cryptic fable: "Once I seen a hoss all stretched out like he was sick, you know. So I hollers, 'Gid up from there, suh! Just to make sho! An' doggone, son, if I don't see two ole jimcrows come flying right up outa that hoss's insides! Yessuh! The sun was shinin' on 'em and they couldn't a been no greasier if they'd been eating barbecue." (*ibid.*) Todd's stomach convulses at this picture and he protests that Jefferson "made that up." But Jefferson says "Nawsuh! Saw him just like I see you." (*ibid.*)

The changing identities of horse and buzzard become delightfully confusing as "Todd-plane-bird-hoss" is seen as being knocked out of the sky by "Jefferson-buzzard-dead-horse-jimcrow." But what is clear in Jefferson's parable is that the dead horse of Negro inferiority provides the nourishment for the white society that enforces Jim Crow ethics, and for those "talented tenth buzzards" like Todd who wish to fly away from a sense of identification with "dead horse buzzards" like old Jefferson. Todd complains that he can never be simply himself but 'most always be seen by whites as being "part of this old black ignorant man" (p. 256). It is this prideful aspiration away from "home," which precipitates his fall, his "flying home."[7]

While Todd speculates on the meaning of his fall, he sees a black spot in the sky. He expects to see a plane from the airbase coming to pick him up, but sees instead a buzzard glide into the woods: "Why did they make them so disgusting and yet teach them to fly so well?" (p. 260). Jefferson's second fable, his experiences as an angel in heaven, follows this question, and reinforces the meaning of Todd's experience from a different perspective. Jefferson says that when he was in heaven he wanted to "let eve'ybody know that old Jefferson could fly as good as anybody else" (p. 261). But the "colored angels" had to "wear a special kin' a harness when we flew" (*ibid.*). Jefferson, like Todd, was not bothered by the harness, the second class status of advanced trainee, and tried to fly like everybody else. He flew so well that he was warned by Saint Peter that his "speedin' is a danger to the heavenly community" (p. 262). When Jefferson continues to speed, despite these warnings, Saint Peter must punish him: "If I was to let you keep on flyin', heaven wouldn't be nothin' but uproar. Jeff, you got to go!" (*ibid.*). The white angels rush Jefferson to the pearly gates, give him a parachute and a map of Alabama. But before he falls, Jefferson is allowed to say a few words: "Well, you done took my wings. And you puttin' me out. You got charge of things so's I can't do nothin' about it. But you got to admit just this: While I was up here I was the flyinest sonofabitch what ever hit heaven!" (*ibid.*)

While Jefferson's first fable seemed to say that those who aspired to fly did so at the expense of others and were therefore ultimately to be properly humbled, this second fable suggests that aspirations of flight are not bad but are simply limited by the existing power structure. Todd responds to Jefferson's second fable in much the same way that he responded to the first: he senses that Jefferson is mocking him. Todd then connects the two stories by protesting against what each seems to be implying about his desire to fly: "Maybe we are a bunch of buzzards feeding on a dead horse, but we can hope to be eagles can't we?" (p. 263). This question leads Todd to a series of reminiscences about his boyhood—he traces the invisible line from the kite back to the boy who desired to fly.

Todd remembers that he became fascinated with flight when he saw a model airplane "suspended from the ceiling of the automobile exhibit at the State Fair" (p. 264). But his mother tells him that it is a white boy's toy and that he should not only not expect to ever have one but that to even circulate the desire for one would only lead to frustration: "Airplane. Boy, is you crazy? How many times I have to tell you to stop that foolishness.... I bet I'm gon' wham the living daylight out of you if you don't quit worrying me 'bout them things!" (p. 265). But Todd does not listen; and when he sees a real airplane flying in the sky, he thinks a "little white boy's plane's done flew and all I got to do is stretch out my hands and it'll be mine!" (*ibid.*). He climbs over the screen and reaches for the plane and feels "the world grow warm with promise." But the plane flies on and as he reaches after it he falls. Todd's mother asks the doctor if her son is crazy, and Ellison has Todd's grandmother quote the opening lines of James Weldon Johnson's "Prodigal Son":[8]

> Young man, young man
> Yo' arms too short
> To box with God. (p. 266)

Todd's third childhood experience with a plane came when he and his mother were walking through the Negro slum. A plane flies over the neighborhood, showering the streets with white cards. In expectation, Todd grabs one only to see on the card a picture of a Klansman's white hood, resembling the face of death, and the caption: "Niggers Stay From Polls." (p. 268)

Todd's childhood experiences certainly *seem* to reinforce the sense of Jefferson's fables. He is wrong to want to fly because it makes him aspire toward something that is an illusion and which will ultimately occasion his fall. He is also wrong to want to fly because it makes him desire to participate in an activity that is ultimately designed to cause death and destruction to his people: the godlike white man seems to have charge of things, and Todd's arms are too short to box with him.

That the white man is an agent of death and destruction is indicated in Jefferson's characterization of the man who owns the farm, Dabney Graves: "Everybody knows 'bout Dabney Graves, especially the colored. He done killed enough of us" (p. 267). When Todd asks what the "colored" had done to cause their murder, Jefferson says "thought they was men" (*ibid.*). Todd is appalled and asks why, if this is the condition under which Jefferson is forced to live, he remains. Jefferson says simply that all black men, including Todd, "have to come by white folks" (*ibid.*) because Dabney Graves owns "this land." Todd continues to protest mainly because he still aspires to fly away from the stigma of blackness and the apparent limits that the identity places on his destiny. But "the closer I spin toward the earth the blacker I become." (p. 268)

At this point Todd spots three men moving across the field. The men are dressed in white, and sensing that they are doctors come to save him, Todd feels immense relief. But Todd's "vision" is again significantly in error. The men are the attendants from the "crazy house;" they have been looking for an escaped patient, Dabney's nephew, but at Dabney's insistence they settled instead for Todd. They put him in a "white straight jacket" because as Graves says, "You all know you cain't let the nigguh git up that high without his going crazy. The nigguh brain ain't built right for high altitudes..." (p. 269). The men put Todd on a stretcher; but when they begin to carry him away, Todd protests: "Don't put your hands on me!" (*ibid.*) What follows is a predictable act of repression: Graves stomps on Todd's chest. Todd, in the midst of horrible pain, responds with laughter which for some reason reminds him of Jefferson's laughter. He looks toward Jefferson "as though somehow he [Jefferson] had become his sole salvation in an insane world of outrage and humiliation" (p. 270). Jefferson does come to Todd's rescue by diverting Graves's attention to the problem of the airplane. Graves is willing to let the airplane stay in his field but "you take this here black eagle over to the nigguh airfield and leave him." (*ibid.*)

The story ends as Teddy and Jefferson lift the stretcher and carry Todd across the field. Todd feels a "new current of communication...between the man and boy and himself" (*ibid.*). He feels that he has been "lifted out of his isolation, back into the world of men" (*ibid.*). As they continue to move across the field, Todd hears a mockingbird. He looks up only to see a buzzard. The whole afternoon then "seemed suspended and he waited for the horror to seize him again" (*ibid.*). Instead, Teddy begins to hum a song, in symbolic counterpoint to the mockingbird, and Todd "saw the dark bird glide into the sun and glow like a bird of flaming gold." (*ibid.*)

This transformation of the buzzard into the "bird of flaming gold" ties together the various symbolic patterns which have been at work in the story. Todd, like Icarus, has tried to fly too close to the sun, and his fall has taught him his conceit.[9] But like Adam's, Todd's fall can be seen as fortunate for it eventually occasions his salvation. The Daedalus figure, Jefferson, has taught his "son" the error of his ways. That error is not so much in aspiration—the story certainly does not counsel acceptance of jimcrow—but in the method and motive of aspiration. Todd cannot box with God alone, and, like the Prodigal Son, he cannot expect to find salvation in Babylon. To expect fulfillment from the white world is an illusion since that world is designed to make "Niggers Stay From Polls." The tragic consequence of such an illusion is that it makes Todd deny not only Jefferson but himself: to fly for white approval is not a way to fulfillment but a way to psychic suicide.

Todd's ambivalent position as a black flyer, straight-jacketed and harnessed by white officers and by his own desire for white approval, has placed him in a world of isolation, His fall has brought him back home from Babylon, back to a sense of who he is. Once he accepts that identity, once he accepts the fact that he and Jefferson are part of each other, then he is resurrected, "lifted out of his isolation, back into the world of men" (*ibid.*). The myth of the Phoenix suggests a similar pattern: the fabulous bird lives from five hundred to a thousand years; then at the close of this period, he sings a melodious dirge, flaps his wings to set fire to his nest and is consumed only to come forth with a new life. Todd has crashed, but in the process he has destroyed the harness of his white aspiration, the plane, and has been resurrected by a song of communal acceptance. Once he accepts this community identity, Todd, the buzzard-jimcrow, is transformed into the bird of flaming gold. Like the Prodigal Son, Todd was dead and is now alive again and is ready to begin his flight home.

NOTES

1. Because Ellison's stories are uncollected there is some confusion as to how many stories he has written. One of the most inclusive lists, published in the bibliography of James A. Emanuel and Theodore L. Gross, eds. *Dark Symphony: Negro Literature in America* (New York: Free Press, 1968), cites the following ten stories:

   "Slick Gonna Learn," *Direction* (September 1939), pp. 10-16.
   "Afternoon," *American Writing*, ed. Hans Otto Storm et al., pp. 28-37. .
   "Mister Toussan," *The New Masses*, 41 (November 4, 1941), 19, 20.
   "That I Had the Wings," *Common Ground*, 3 (Summer 1943), 30-37.
   "Flying Home," *Cross Section*, ed. Edwin Seaver (New York: L.B. Fischer, 1944), pp.469-85.
   "In a Strange Country," *Tomorrow*, 3 (July 1944), 41-44.
   "King of the Bingo Game," *Tomorrow*, 4 (November 1944), 29-33.
   "Did You Ever Dream Lucky?" *New World Writing No. 5* (New York: The New American Library of World Literature, Inc., 1954), pp. 134-145.
   "A Coupla Scalped Indians," *New World Writing No. 9* (New York: The New American Library of World Literature, Inc., 1956), pp. 225-36.
   "And Hickman Arrives," *The Noble Savage I*, 1956.

2. Again, Emanuel and Gross seem to lead the way with the printing of both "Flying Home" and "King of the Bingo Game." These two stories are the only ones reprinted consistently; however, most anthology editors, even those who edit anthologies of Black Literature, still seem to prefer excerpts from *Invisible Man* presented as short stories—for example, "The Battle Royal" sequence of Chapter I. One recent exception is *Black Literature in America: A Casebook*, ed. Roman K. Singh and Peter Fellowes (New York: Thomas Y. Crowell, 1970) in which the hilarious "Did You Ever Dream Lucky?" is reprinted.

3. "Flying Home" has been reprinted in several places—most notably in *The Best Short Stories by Negro Writers*, ed. Langston Hughes (Boston: Little, Brown and Co., 1967); *Black American Literature: Fiction*, ed. Darwin T. Turner (Columbus, Ohio: Charles E. Merrill, 1969); *Afro-American Literature: Fiction*, ed. William Adams, Peter Conn, Barry Slepian (Boston: Houghton-Mifflin Co., 1970). References to "Flying Home" in this essay will be documented by page numbers referring to the text as found reprinted in Emanuel and Gross, pp. 254-270.

4. Klein, pp. 102-103.

5. *Ibid.*, p. 103n.

6. W.E.B. DuBois, *Souls of Black Folk* (Chicago: A.C. McClurg & Co., 1903), p.3.

7. Klein identifies "Flying Home" as the title of a jazz piece written by Benny Goodman and Lionel Hampton, p. 103.

8. James Weldon Johnson, "Prodigal Son," *God 's Trombones* (New York: Viking Press, 1927), p.21.

9. Klein, p. 103.

From *Studies in Short Fiction* 9 (Spring 1972), 175-82.

In Need of Folk: The Alienated Protagonists of Ralph Ellison's Short Fiction

Mary Ellen Doyle, S.C.N.

In an interview, Ralph Ellison stated that a man must both find and create his identity, starting with those given elements he did not pick: "His problem is to recognize himself through recognizing where he comes from, recognizing his parents and his inherited values. . . . The way to create a false identity is to think that you can ignore what went before."[1] Though these words refer to Ellison's Invisible Man, they could easily be applied to most of the protagonists of his short stories. Excluding from consideration only a very few stories and the excerpts of the unpublished novels and *Invisible Man*,[2] one can generalize that the typical protagonist of an Ellison short story is a boy or a young man who is alienated in some degree from himself, his own race, and white-controlled society; he either does not really know or cannot accept who he is. Hope of reconciliation and self-identification exists, if at all, in his first establishing or restoring a sense of cohesion with his own race through some symbolic folk member or custom.

The boy protagonists reveal present confusion and the seeds of future alienation in a lack of adequate racial awareness and pride, in rejection of some Negro person or cultural practice, and in compulsion to follow the way of whites. Alienation has blossomed in the adults, but all except one achieves at least a partial reconciliation.

Ellison has a favorite boy figure, Riley, who, with his friend Buster confronts life in three stories. In all three Riley is somehow confused by the values and demands of whites and adult blacks and is powerless to decide his own values and direct his own free action. In "Mr. Toussan"[3] he and Buster are situated between old white man Rogan, who refuses them the fruits of his cherry tree, and Riley's mother who commands them to please the whites by playing quietly out back. The boys can adjust without damaged egos because they have identified in vigorous and noisy drama with a "good clean mean" (102) black hero, Toussaint l'Ouverture, conqueror of Napoleon and his "peckerwood soldiers" (99). Neither boy is developed in this brief sketch, but Riley is more sensitive to the ambiguities of their situation and more dampened by their final need to submit than is Buster, who hopes for the practical victory of stealing the cherries.

"A Coupla Scalped Indians"[4] is essentially an initiation-to-manhood story, but the recently circumcised Riley is also floundering among identities as respectable white Boy Scout, "real stud Indian" living in the woods (226) and emerging black man repeatedly called by the music of carnival horns, which seems to be joyously playing the dozens. His tension is heightened, then resolved, through a confrontation with Aunt Mackie, the local conjure woman, young of body and old of face, spell caster and church member, who functions symbolically as the total black folk woman, embracing all ages and cultures and values in the black community, rejected by it yet its respected and feared central figure.

She is to be seen naked in a ritual dance, which is not degrading but rather "like praying without kneeling down" (236), and she is to be accepted beyond fear and guilt and "kissed" by the black man, newly man and newly black. This secret initiation is not for Buster, already attuned to his race's ways, but for Riley, still the more thoughtful, more sensitive for fear and love, and more in need of special help to embrace his people and culture.

In these two stories, an early experience of accepting and identifying promises to prevent serious future damage to Riley. But alienation is much more severe and unresolved in "That I Had Wings."[5] Here restriction, fear and punishment are embodied for Riley in Aunt Kate, a relic of "slavery times" who insists on the need and adequacy of the "wings of the spirit to help yuh through this worl'" (31) and to fly away to Jesus and be at rest. In practice, this means fearing, pleasing and managing God and white folks, and Aunt Kate tries by scolding or cajolery to instill in the boys a safe social and gospel behaviour.

But Riley wants none of Aunt Kate's kind of flying; she is "too ole to understand a man" (32). He is ashamed of older folks' shouting and crying in church, mocks their gospel songs, and has one desperate desire: to fly or make something else do so. He admires a baby robin which begins to fly as soon as the old bird leaves him alone; he envies pigeons and kites that can fly away freely and beautifully, and he insists that falling off the church roof felt good, like "white guys" parachuting. He attempts unsuccessfully to capture Ole Bill the rooster and make him fly; finally, he fits rag parachutes to some chicks and has Buster drop them from the chicken house. But, paralyzed by Aunt Kate's angry call, he fails to catch the chicks in time, turns on her with wounding words of hatred and while thus off-guard, is attacked and cut by Ole Bill's spurs.

Buster, who has all along raised the objections to Riley's "sins" and schemes, can adjust to Aunt Kate's ways; to Riley she is the destroyer of all who could fly and must be essentially rejected. But absorption in this feeling leaves him vulnerable to Ole Bill's attack. The rooster is finally a symbol of the mixed forces in Riley's life. He has "evil yellow eyes, old like Aunt Kate's" (34) and he punishes Riley for the death of the chicks. Yet he is also male, indomitable, the "fightin'est, crowin'est rooster in the whole wide world" (33), proud, powerful, able to "whip anything whut wears feathers" (33). He can't be captured, but neither can he fly, and the story leaves the impression that eventually the chicks—and boys—must learn to. And to fly they must have not only the white guy's right to parachutes but also the wings of Aunt Kate's culture. Riley must "come by" Aunt Kate and find her courage as well as her cruelty reflected in Ole Bill, must accept her into his identity as well as pass her limitations. He won't find it easy.

The Riley stories employ three of Ellison's most consistent symbols: the older black folk person, music and flying. Together they signify freedom and inner wholeness achieved through integration of old and new, racial and universal values. They appear again in the working out of the adult protagonists' alienation conflicts.

Mr. Parker, the black sailor protagonist of "In a Strange Country"[6] is attacked by white Yanks just after landing in Wales, is rescued by a Welshman and taken to a singing concert at his club. The attack, his need of rescue and his blackened eye have roused in him "anger and resentment," a "smoldering sense of self-hate and ineffectiveness" (41) and "the familiar and hateful emotion of alienation" (42). "Massa's in de Old Cold Masochism!" he thinks to himself. His experience has also, in the familiar Ellison symbol, blinded him. The whites rendered him defenseless by a flashlight, and now white spots dance before his closing eye. He will not be able to see Wales as planned, "with fresh eyes, like those with which the Pilgrims had seen the New World" (41).

But if he cannot see well, he can hear. At the club, he becomes progressively more involved with the music and the emotions of the singers. He knows both black and Russian folk songs, mentally links them to Welsh songs, and recognizes that black songs do not reflect "love of the soil or of country." He feels "a growing poverty of spirit" and "a surge of deep longing to know the anguish and exultation of such love" (43).

But then he also becomes aware that the mixture of economic classes in the Welsh chorus is analogous to the union of races through jazz which he had experienced at, and only at, an American jam session. If black folk music is not nation-oriented, it is still one thing that generates in blacks a strong enough sense of personal and equal identity that they can share it proudly with whites and thus create a society, a nation, for all: "When we sing, we are Welshmen" and "When we jam, sir, we're Jamocrats!" (43). Thus, the "unity of music, a 'gut language,' the 'food of love'" (43) prepares him emotionally for the final songs, the Welsh national anthem, God Save the King, the Internationale (which reminds him of his Southern marching band music), and, in his honor, the Star-Spangled Banner. The last he experiences momentarily as a lure into "an unwilled and degrading act," then as "charged with some vast new meaning" for "that part of him that wanted to sing." He does sing, feeling a "wave of guilt," then a "burst of relief"; and for the first time in his life, "the words [are] not ironic" (44).

In the end, he will see by his Welsh friend's torch to return to his ship. More, he can return to his homeland in renewed self-love, racial love and pride, and human sympathy, to deal as necessary with the "family quarrel" (41) and strive for a nation of "Jamocrats."

Todd, the injured aviator of "Flying Home,"[7] might be Riley grown up and still struggling to fly. In boyhood he craved an airplane and fell from a window because he thought he could seize one flying over his house; in young manhood he craves acceptance as a World War II pilot. But the Army has withheld combat wings from blacks, and now a buzzard has knocked him into a tailspin and crash landing. He is succored by the very symbol of all he wants to escape, an old black sharecropper, who irritates him by a lie-tale of how he had died and gained wings with which he raced all over heaven until expelled by the frightened whites. Only when the vicious redneck landowner has Todd straitjacketed as a crazy "nigguh flyer" (269) does he hear old "Jefferson's voice with gratitude" and recognizes that only Jeff—and his type—can relieve his isolation in "an insane world of outrage and humiliation" (270).

"Flying Home," perhaps Ellison's finest short story, is complex and fruitful in its themes and the symbols that carry them. Todd has made a grave error in linking his sense of personal worth, dignity and freedom to that successful control of technology which his white officers have and respect. He craves their recognition of his ability but expects to receive it only from the enemy, and despises himself for caring. Still worse, he fails to recognize dignity and power in old, down-home black folks, and their wondering praise of black aviators humiliates him because it suggests his blood bond to their peasant ignorance. Powerless before whites, ashamed of blacks and contemptuous of himself for his inability to find his value in his own person, Todd is a deeply disorientated man.

The chief symbols of all this are the airplane and the buzzard. The former concretizes for Todd all the desirable pleasures, powers and possessions of whites. In his childhood it was their toy, but also their weapon for dropping threats on the black community. Now his training plane is "the only dignity I have," "not a machine, [but] a suit of clothes you wear"; without it he is naked (256). Flying, he thinks, is the "most meaningful act in the world" because it makes him less like old Jefferson (258).

But it doesn't. For to Jeff also, flying is a symbol of dignity and freedom, and he has invented his own experience of it; their difference is in their reactions to the loss of wings; Todd's burning humiliation, rage and self-hatred v. Jeff's humor and self-assertion ("you puttin' me out. . . . But you got to admit just this: While I was up here I was the flyinest sonofabitch what ever hit heaven!" [262]).

The buzzard, feeder on dead animals and men, is called a "jimcrow" by Jeff and thus linked to the whites who would like to "bother" the black flyers. Todd approves that label, but her also calls the flyers, "a bunch of buzzards feeding on a dead horse" (263) while vainly longing to be eagles. He was knocked out of the heavens by hitting a "storm of blood and blackness" (259), a symbol of his own self-rejection. Until he reconciles his "loathing and admiration" (260) for the buzzards as his own people, he is symbolically dead, prey to the buzzard as "jimcrow" white people.

Ironically, it is jimcrow Dabney Graves who calls Todd what he wants to be, a "black eagle" (270). And it is Graves, incarnation of "all the unnamed horror and obscenities that he had ever imagined" (269) who causes Todd to feel new communication with Jeff, his "sole salvation" (270), to be simultaneously thrust off the plantation and "lifted out of his isolation, back into the world of men" (270). Then Todd sees "the dark bird glide into the sun and glow. . . ." (270).

This final line may be overdrawn; the symbolism is extremely obvious, and all the black-white world will not glow for Todd hereafter.[8] He still has to find a way to fly, has to "come by the white folks" (267) just as Jeff does; but his restored bond to his own folk has given him some peace with reality and may enable him, like Jeff, to retain true perception and self-respect and also to survive.

Ellison has one protagonist who cannot survive reality, the nameless "King of the Bingo Game,"[9] who attends a northern city theater where the movie is followed by bingo and the winner spins for a jackpot. In a frantic effort to win enough money to get a doctor for his wife, he plays five cards at once, does win, and then madly refuses to let go of the button that controls the wheel that controls the jackpot. Fantasies and desperation take possession of his mind, in it he is forever trying to race ahead of death and destruction, trying to control a game of chance, always trapped and always losing until this moment when he thinks he controls the life-wheel. But when the button is seized from him and he is knocked out, this is not, I think, a sign that Ellison has reached a vision of the human condition as essentially and universally irrational.[10] The "King's" powerlessness to control the wheel of life is explicitly associated with his powerlessness to get a job, to relieve his hunger, and to save his sick wife. Most of all, he is frantic from isolation. In all the city he has no one but Laura (277); in this theater, he cannot ask anyone for a share of peanuts or wine as he would down home. "Folks down South stuck together. . . . But up here it was different" (271). When he spins the jackpot wheel, it is chiefly the catcalls of the audience which enrage, embitter and confuse him and drive him into madness. The King's luck runs out on the stage, and the curtain descends, not so much because of the cosmic white "man with the microphone" (275) as because he is a lost loner from down South without folks in an uncomprehending and unsympathetic urban crowd.

Ellison has said that folklore preserves and projects the Negroes' wisdom, sustaining values and efforts to humanize the world.[11] It makes sense, then, that his protagonists find human connection with the world primarily and inevitably through the folk. He offers no easy solution to alienation, no facile access to happiness, but he does offer hope if humans will but seize whom they are born. This is, I submit, universal wisdom, and in the artistic incarnation of its lies much of Ralph Ellison's greatness.

NOTES

1. John O'Brien, *Interview with Black Writers* (New York: Liveright, 1975), p. 76.

2. "Did You Ever Dream Lucky?" and "It Always Breaks Out" have different thrusts, and I have been unable to obtain a copy of "Afternoon." The collection of Ellison's short fiction would greatly facilitate the criticism which it richly deserves and has received scarcely at all. "Slick Gonna Learn" (*Direction*, September, 1939) is labeled "From an Unpublished First Novel." If the novel is never to be published, "Slick" could be included, for historical completeness, in the collection; in any case, it does not fit this paper's theme.

3. Ralph Ellison, "Mister Toussan," in *Black American Literature: Fiction*, ed. Darwin T. Turner (Columbus: Charles E. Merrill Publishing Company, 1969), pp. 96-102. For all the stories, a full reference will be given, and subsequent page references will be contained in the text.

4. Ralph Ellison, "A Coupla Scalped Indians," in *New World Writing: Ninth Mentor Selection* (New York: New American Library of World Literature, Inc., 1956), pp. 225-236.

5. Ralph Ellison, "That I Had Wings," *Common Ground*, III (Summer 1943), 30-37.

6. Ralph Ellison, "In a Strange Country," *Tomorrow*, III (July 1944), 41-44.

7. Ralph Ellison, "Flying Home," in *Dark Symphony: Negro Literature in America*, ed. James A. Emanuel and Theodore L. Gross (New York: Macmillan Company, the Free Press, 1968), pp. 254-270.

8. Marcus Klein, *After Alienation: American Novels in Mid-Century* (Cleveland: The World Publishing Company, 1962), p. 104. I disagree with much of Klein's analysis of this story and with his general evaluation of Ellison's short fiction, but I am grateful to him for the only critique I have yet found of the body of the short stories. Joseph Trimmer has done a fine analysis of "Flying Home" in *Studies in Short Fiction*, 9 (1972), 175-182.

9. Ralph Ellison, "King of the Bingo Game," in *Dark Symphony*, pp. 271-279.

10. See Klein, pp. 105-7 for exposition of this view of the story.

11. Ralph Ellison, *Shadow and Act* (New York: Random House, Vintage Books, 1972), p.171.

From *CLA Journal* 19:2, December 1975, 165-172.

Ellison's "Black Eye": Transforming Pain into Vision

Robert J. Butler

Scholars and teachers have eagerly awaited the publication of Ellison's collected short fiction for many years. For a variety of reasons which are still difficult to understand fully, Ralph Ellison's short stories have never been collected during his lifetime, making many of them all but impossible to use in the classroom and extremely difficult to use for scholarly purposes since many of his stories were published in obscure journals which have been defunct for quite some time. The Buster/Riley stories, despite their intrinsically high quality and the considerable light they shed on Ellison's development, are virtually unknown to all but a small group of Ellison specialists. "Flying Home" and "King of the Bingo," two extraordinary stories which rank with the very best American short fiction written since the end of WWII, have appeared in a variety of anthologies but most are now out of print and some have become too expensive or too specialized for many courses. Ellison's unpublished stories, like his much-awaited second novel, have been rumored for years to be very high in quality, but could only tantalize several generations of critics, scholars, and teachers, who have hoped for their eventual publication.

Flying Home and Other Stories, superbly edited by John F. Callahan, therefore is an important event in American and African American literary life since it collects for the first time what Callahan considers to be "Ellison's best published and unpublished freestanding fiction" (xxi). Designed as "a reader's edition" and not intended to be a "variorum or scholarly edition" (xxiv), it consists of thirteen short stories, six of which were unpublished in Ellison's lifetime. (Two were recently published in 1996 issues of *The New Yorker*.) They are of enormous value since they now make possible a careful study of Ellison's considerable achievements as a short story writer and also enable us to see in a much clearer way Ellison's development as an artist in the crucial period when he emerged as a writer in the late 1930s and early 1940s. Moreover, this book finally makes it possible to bring Ellison's short fiction productively into the classroom where it can be studied for its own merits and for the ways in which it illuminates his great novel, *Invisible Man*.

Certainly the most eye-opening part of this book in its cluster of six new stories, what Callahan aptly describes as "stories that had never been published, never-mentioned, stories no one knew about" (xxi). Most of them are initiation stories of one kind or another in which young protagonists are abruptly awakened into a painful awareness of the harsh realities of adult experience. "A Party Down at the Square," for example, is narrated by a nameless white boy who describes a lynching which he is forced to watch while making a summer visit to his uncle in Alabama. "Boy on a Train" focuses on a young black protagonist who is suddenly thrust into the early stages of adulthood after the death of his father as he, his mother, and brother are forced to take a train to a strange new place where they hope to begin a new life. "Hymie's Bull" and "I Did Not Learn Their Names" deal with anonymous black *picaros* riding the rails during the darkest years of the Great Depression, all the while encountering shocking moments of violence and surprising experiences of human tenderness and solidarity. "The Black Ball," which Callahan describes as "perhaps the most subtly crafted of the unpublished stories" (xxxiv), brilliantly dramatizes the psychic wounds of a single father and his son as they try to establish a decent life for themselves in a racist society intent on "blackballing" them. The only bit of comic relief in this group of previously unpublished fiction appears in "A Hard Time Keeping Up," which culminates in an amusing episode of mock-violence.

Of these six stories, only "Hymie's Bull" can be precisely dated, since it was scheduled to appear in a 1937 issue of *New Challenge* but the journal folded before the story could be published. "A Hard Time Keeping Up" and "The Black Ball," judging from convincing external evidence, were completed during the period from late 1937 when Ellison was in Dayton, Ohio after his mother's death there until April 1938 when he returned to New York to work for the New York Writers Project of the WPA. Callahan speculates that the other three stories were completed before 1940 since they were found in an envelope labeled by Ellison as "Early Stories" and containing his 1940 address of 25 Hamilton Terrace in New York City. All six stories, therefore, are a rich source of information about Ellison's early development as a writer when he was strongly influenced by leftist politics in general and Richard Wright's example in particular. (The lynching described in the collection's opening story, for example, clearly reflects Wright's commitment to depicting racial violence in an uncompromisingly frank and graphic manner and the proletarian sympathies implicit in "I Did Not Learn Their Names" and "The Black Ball" demonstrate with equal clarity that Ellison was strongly influenced by leftist thought, even though he never became a member of the Communist Party.)

Other literary influences are also clearly in evidence in these unpublished stories, particularly Ellison's conscious use of themes and techniques from Joyce, Hemingway, and Twain. Each story culminates in a Joycean epiphany and employs a very spare and ironic form of hard-boiled realism which Hemingway used in his fiction, particularly in the Nick Adams stories. (At the end of "A Party Down at the Square," for example, we are told that the wind "blew for three days steady" (11), a tip of the hat to Hemingway's "Three Day Blow." And "I Did Not Learn Their Names" signifies in a fascinating way on the "The Battler," down to the point where the elderly white man, like Hemingway's Bugs, gives Ellison's protagonist a "wrapped sandwich" which he sticks in his pocket as he is about to leave.) For those used to the highly rhetorical and richly layered symbolic style which Ellison would later make his trademark, these six stories seem a bit strange, their "voice" a complete reversal of what we have come to expect from Ellison's writing. But as Ellison went out of his way to remind us in *Shadow and Act* and *Going to the Territory*, Hemingway's understanding of ritual and concern for style made him a valued literary "ancestor," who had an important but subtle influence on the crafting of *Invisible Man*.

Twain's influence, particularly in the crucial matter of point of view, is also clearly evident in these stories. The boy who narrates "A Party Down at the Square" is surely a literary descendent of Huckleberry Finn, a "naive" narrator who makes the reader experience racism in its starkest, most troubling form by revealing how it corrupts the mind of a young boy whose social conditioning prompts him to mouth the racist ideas of his culture, all the while being sickened by it on the more fundamental, instinctive levels of his being. Like Huck, the boy has a "deformed conscience" which forces him to see the lynched man as a "nigger" (9), but, also like Huck, he is secretly and inwardly appalled by what his conscious mind approves of—he becomes "sick" (11) as he observes the flames consuming the lynched man just as Huck becomes "sick" when he visualizes the damage that will be inflicted on Jim by returning him to slavery. Caught between these two conflicting impulses, he experiences the same kind of paralysis which overcomes Huck when he observes innocent young boys being slaughtered in the Grangerford-Shepherdson feud:

> . . . And the nigger looked up with his great white eyes, looking like they was about to pop out of his head, and I had enough. I didn't want to see anymore. I wanted to run somewhere and puke, but I stayed. I stayed right there in front of the crown and looked (8).

Those who have unfairly charged Ellison throughout his career of lacking sufficient anger and militance will find very little evidence in these six unpublished stories to support their claims. Most of the stories smoulder with anger and repulsion which often match that found in typical Wright stories of the period. Just as the white boy in "A Party" is finally sickened by the lynching which he wants to run away from but is forced to watch, the young protagonist is so outraged by the sudden loss of his father and the segregated conditions which he and his family must endure that he finds himself "smouldering inside" (19) and finally acknowledges a fierce, nearly Ahabian, desire "to kill God and not be sorry" (20). The nameless central character in "Hymie's Bull" takes a perverse pleasure in observing a fellow hobo coldly slit the throat of a railroad "dick." And his counterpart in "I Did Not Learn Their Names" perhaps speaks for most of the central characters in these stories when he frankly reveals "I was having a hard time not to hate in those days" (9).

One crucially important thematic pattern informing these six unpublished stories, which becomes even more pronounced in Ellison's later fiction, is Ellison's unwillingness merely to express this rage—throughout the stories he searches for ways to enable his characters to transcend raw anger and resentment which will either paralyze or destroy them and to develop human resources which enable them to deal productively with such feelings. As Callahan has arranged the stories, one can see the outlines of an overall narrative portraying the central character's growth from an alienated and impotent observer to a more mature person who can master his feelings and deal with the world in existentially productive ways. Although the first two stories end with characters emotionally and psychologically blocked by traumatic experiences, later stories describe ways of overcoming this condition. The narrator of "I Did Not Learn Their Names" thus balances his suspicion of people and his resentment over his marginalized position in American society with the fact that a crippled white man has saved his life and an elderly white couple not only share their food with him but also reveal to him some of the intimate details of their lives. He is finally able to go beyond his own suffering by identifying with the pain of others and sensing a common bond between them, realizing that on the most fundamental levels "you were all the same" (93). In a similar way, the single father in "The Black Ball" is able to contain and transcend his frustrations with a racist society by identifying with and joining the cause of a white union organizer who has also been wounded by a society which ostracizes him for defending a black man who was wrongfully accused of rape. In each case, Ellison's protagonists are able to repair the damage done to the self by moving beyond their personal grief to a larger vision of solidarity with others. In this way, they are able to overcome "a smouldering sense of self-hate and ineffectiveness" (139).

The four Buster-Riley stories in this collection provide Ellison with another resource for mastering and transcending pain, a comic tradition rooted in American and African American folklore. The humor which sparkles throughout these pieces is closely tied to the blues which Ellison has described in *Shadow and Act* as "a near-tragic, near-comic lyricism" (90) which enables one to triumph over pain by developing a "sheer toughness of spirit" (104) characterized by deepened consciousness and emotional resilience. Both Buster and Riley, although acutely aware of themselves as outsiders, reject the status as victims and instead affirm themselves as individuals who are smart enough and tough enough to secure for themselves the promises of American life. (Their heroes are trickster figures like Mr. Rabbit or black rebels such as Jack Johnson and Toussaint L'Overture.) The "word play" (33) which they delight in as they imagine themselves in the role of President of the United States or Joe Louis, is therefore much more than mere child's play. It is instead an exercise in imaginative rebellion and self-creation of the kind which the hero of *Invisible Man* will later use to triumph over a social world intent on making him a naturalistic victim. The wisdom they acquire from their folk traditions give them the power, to use Ellison's later statements in *Shadow and Act*, to "slip the yoke" by changing "the joke" (61); that is, developing the kind of supple and ironic consciousness one needs to escape socially constructed traps and build new space for themselves.

The collection's other stories, "King of the Bingo Game," "In a Strange Country," and "Flying Home" were each published in 1944, only one year before Ellison began writing *Invisible Man*. Taken as a group, they powerfully express the book's central theme, an overcoming of alienation and powerlessness through a process of self-actualization rooted in deepened consciousness and comic reintegration with the world. "The King of the Bingo Game" is a classic study of *anomie*—its main character has no satisfactory answer to the question of "Who am I?" (133) because he puts all of his "faith" (126) in an absurd outward world, symbolized in the story as a bingo game which he can not win. Placing himself at the mercy of a "ritual" (128) driven by the self-interest of others who use the "blind wheel" (123) of bingo to tantalize him with rewards of money he may never win, he ends up predictably defeated, knocked unconscious by a deterministic system which can only conceive of him as a "jerk" (133) whose lack of identity is aptly symbolized by "double zero" (136) which his turn at the wheel has resulted in.

Parker, the central character of "In a Strange Country" confronts the same absurd system but is neither "blind" nor "fated" because he develops the inward resources to assert himself as a human being. A black soldier stationed in Wales during WWII who hopes to see this new land "with fresh eyes" (138), he is attacked and nearly blinded in one eye by "fellow" American soldiers who beat him because they can only see him as "a goddamn nigger" (138). Ironically, he is saved from the "blind rage" (139) which threatens to consume him by the unexpected kindness of the Welsh men who first take him to a pub where he is revived physically with a few beers and later to a "private club" (139) where he is revived psychologically by listening to their Welsh folk songs and, strangely enough, singing the American national anthem for them in return. He overcomes "the familiar and hateful emotion of alienation" (142) by achieving a "unity of music" (143) with the Welshmen which affirms their common bonds as human beings. Experiencing their "deeper humanity" (144), they become "Jamocrats" (143). In the story's extraordinary epiphany, Parker becomes fully aware of the bluesy humor of his experiences, stepping out of a familiar world where he is beaten by his fellow countrymen and entering the "strange country" of deepened perception and broadened empathy where he is revived by strangers. His "black eye" (146) mentioned in the story's final sentence, therefore, is no longer a sign of pain and blindness; rather, it is an eye that can clearly see the off-beat ironies and complexities of his American identity, endowing his life with "a vast new meaning" (146).

Todd, the central character of "Flying Home," likewise experiences a life-saving comic reversal which rejuvenates him by enabling him to also see vast new meanings as his consciousness is purified in the crucible of his pain. The plane crash that initially threatens his life and envelops him in physical pain, which is likened to "a ball of fire" (133), ironically results in his rising to a new and truer life. Like Parker, he experiences this process of spiritual purgation and moral growth by developing a "black eye"; that is, viewing reality from an enriched perspective as an outsider who can see well beyond the outwardly powerful but inwardly blind people who control his world. Just as Parker is assisted in this process by "strangers" who awaken him to a fuller understanding of his human possibilities, Todd's growth is triggered by an elderly black sharecropper whom he first perceives as a stranger in a "foreign" country but finally comes to see as a kinsman and mentor. And the experience of art is a crucial part of the growth dramatized in both stories as the songs which Parker sings with the Welsh men play the same function as the folk tale which Jefferson relates to Todd in "Flying Home." In both cases, artistic performance transfigures pain into vision and vision supplies the central character with the tools he needs to fashion a true identity rooted in the fertile soil of his cultural past and human community.

As the story begins, Todd (whose name in German means death) is shown as psychologically crippled long before the plane crash physically immobilizes him because he has perceived a career in aviation in precisely the same terms as the protagonist of "King of the Bingo Game" has perceived bingo, as a quick and mechanical means of resolving his human problems. Sensing that becoming an aviator will result in his leaping beyond the limitations of his black skin and then achieving the possibilities of American life, he undergoes a deep "humiliation" (150) when his plane crashes and he fears that he will be found wanting by his white superiors. But Jefferson, who has developed a truer identity by keeping his distance from whites and developing the blues-like consciousness he needs to master circumstances with a richly ironic comic vision, becomes Todd's "salvation" (172) by the end of the story. Not only does this kindness and empathy release Todd from "his overpowering sense of isolation" (172), but his folk wisdom has provided Todd with a new vision which allows him to see both the real nature of his segregated society and to transcend it by changing the joke and thus slipping the yoke. By the end of the story he is no longer a buzzard feeding of the carcass of his dead illusions but has become "like a bird of flaming gold" (173). Due to Jefferson's intervention, he is finally taken to a hospital where he can recover and return to the world strengthened and ready for new forms of action rather than being consigned to a madhouse which the white system and his own illusions have constructed. As Jefferson's tall tale artfully reveals, he has been expelled from a phony white heaven, but he is now "free at last" (158) to become "the flyin'est son of a bitch that ever hit heaven" (160).

* * *

What these thirteen stories emphatically demonstrate is that Ellison's *Invisible Man* did not spring like Topsy out of nowhere but were the product of a long period of artistic and philosophical growth dating back to 1937 when Ellison emerged as a writer. For all of his career Ellison was fascinated by stories of initiation and was able to endow these narratives with richer, more nuanced meanings as he was able to conceive of more complicated central characters and bring them to life with techniques which became increasingly more expressive, and complex. His existential heroes can finally turn the "black eye" of pain into a very different "black eye" of deepened consciousness and broadened sympathies. As Ellison developed this remarkable blues vision, he was forced to experiment with and master a great variety of styles. Starting with a very disciplined and understated realism which he learned from Hemingway, he learned to see the small details of real life in fresh ways. He combined this with a lucid naturalism picked up from Wright which gave him a deepened understanding of how social environment impacts upon the lives of individuals. He then developed an ability to alternate these styles with a finely textured, many-layered symbolism which he learned from Joyce and Malraux. Going one step further, he was able to judiciously blend these styles with comic techniques from American and African American folk tradition, developing a distinctive voice which can only be called "Ellisonian." *Flying Home and Other Stories* is an important book because it documents more fully than any other primary source this remarkable literary development, in addition to adding six stories of high quality to the Ellison canon.

This book should not be seen as merely filling in lacunae in Ellison's *oeuvre* in order to bring certain aspects of Ellison studies to a closure. Rather, it should whet our appetite for new work which needs to be done so that we can finally have an adequate view of Ellison's entire career and his achievement as a writer. Not only do the previously unpublished stories need to be critically analyzed and assessed but Ellison's long-awaited second novel should finally be put together and published. Ellison's superb non-fiction prose, which has only been fitfully explored by scholars and critics, deserves much closer scrutiny. And, of course, biographies of Ellison are desperately needed, especially to provide us with a better understanding of his early years in Oklahoma, his formative years as a writer in New York, and his later years after he had achieved fame as a major novelist. Ellison studies, therefore, are about to enter an exciting new phase, thanks in no small measure to the publication of *Flying Home and Other Stories*.

WORKS CITED

Callahan, John F. *Flying Home and Other Stories*. New York: Random House, 1996.
Ellison, Ralph. *Shadow and Act*. New York: Signet Books, 1966.

From *African American Review* 32 (Spring 1998), 164-167.

Ellison's Non-Fiction

The Wright Interpretation: Ralph Ellison and the Anxiety of Influence

Joseph T. Skerrett, Jr.

> *That which we do is what we are. That which we remember is, more often than not, that which we would like to have been; or that which we hope to be. Thus our memory and our identity are ever at odds; our history ever a tall tale told by inattentive idealists.*
>
> Quoted by Ralph Ellison in *Shadow and Act,* author unidentified

In *The Anxiety of Influence,* Harold Bloom argues that the feeling of major writers regarding their imaginative predecessors can be as powerful, as primary, as the psychodynamics of the family which Freud described. The literary relationship between the influencer and the influencee is a kind of father-son relationship, and the history of the relationship across the centuries is essentially "the story of how poets as poets have suffered other poets, just as any true biography is the story of how anyone suffered his family—or his own displacement of family into lovers and friends" (*Anxiety,* 94).

The new writer, contemplating the work of some beloved predecessor, conceives an anguishing anxiety, a dread that he will not be able to achieve a significant, immortalizing, and freedom-granting sense of originality, because, in the course of nature, the predecessor has, like a father, not only authority, but also priority; he got there first. The influencee must resent and reject his authority *and* this priority if he is to avoid the debilitating feeling of being an addendum or qualification to the predecessor's work. The strategy by which the writer meets the challenge of his influences Bloom calls "poetic misprision": the new writer misreads his powerful predecessor "so as to clear imaginative space for himself " (*Anxiety,* 5). Bloom puts this central point of his general theory most forcefully:

> Poetic Influence—when it involves two strong, authentic poets—always proceeds by a misreading of the prior poet, an act of creative correction that is actually and necessarily a misinterpretation. The history of fruitful poetic influence, which is to say that the main tradition of Western poetry since the Renaissance, is a history of anxiety and self-saving caricature, of distortion, of perverse, willful revisionism without which modern poetry as such could not exist. (30)

The writer's creative misreading of his predecessor goes beyond intellectual revisionism. It takes on a much more personal cast. Rethinkers are not essentially disturbed by the priority of those they revise. Like children with their fathers, the influenced artist-son is involved in a complex, necessary, and compulsive emotional and imaginative as well as intellectual relationship with his influencing artist-father. As Bloom describes the operation of the poetic tradition, the acts of misreading are embodied in poems themselves, acts of the imagination which publicly imitate, reject, transform, subsume, or transcend the predecessor's style, stance, or thought.

Bloom is at pains to demonstrate that this theory is relevant to the great tradition of English poets from Milton to Yeats. He does not apply the theory to the imaginative relationships between prose writers, but nowhere does he suggest that poetic misprision is a strategy unavailable to the prose writer in his efforts to deal with artistic anxiety regarding a predecessor. Indeed, Bloom uses a prose writer as example in noting "the frantic dances of Norman Mailer," in *Advertisements for Myself,* "as he strives to evade his own anxiety that it is, after all, Hemingway all the way" (*Anxiety,* 28). Other authors come readily to mind. Angus Wilson's fascination with his predecessor Dickens is revealed not only in his characterization—the sweetly malevolent Mrs. Curry in *Hemlock and After,* the grotesque Ingeborg Middleton in *Anglo-Saxon Attitudes*—and scenes like the disastrous opening of Vardon Hall in *Hemlock and After,* but also in scholarly readings of Dickens, acts of criticism. In speaking of the personal crisis that led him, at the age of thirty-six, to begin writing fiction, Wilson reports that he used his reading to protect his ignorance of life and self:

> I had always been, and still am, addicted to the great Victorian novelists, especially to Charles Dickens. The conflicts of the novels of Dickens or Balzac, for example, so frequently clearer on the symbolic under-level than on the surface story level, seem to me to have not only remarkable social and moral insight but also a cosmic significance that is often denied to them by critics. (*Wild Garden,* 22).

The novelist's personal burden and sense of life in Wilson's case is inextricably tied up with a sense of the emotional power and deep significance that lies beneath the narrative surface of Dickens's work. In his confusion, he relished the Victorian sentimentality "attaching to childish or childlike innocence," and "battled strongly on behalf of the value of this Victorian sentimentality . . . rather than making allowance for it as an inadequacy" (*Wild Garden,* 23). The recovery of mental health was for Wilson the loss of a false and sentimentally childish self-ignorance, a loss which has become a major theme in his work and which is his personal twist on the themes of his predecessor.

In American literature, the example of William Faulkner has been the dragon by the roadside for many a young writer. Flannery O'Connor voiced the case for a whole generation of southern writers faced with the priority of Faulkner:

> I think the writer is initially set going by literature more than by life. When there are many writers all employing the same idiom, all looking out on more or less the same social scene, the individual writer will have to be more than ever careful that he isn't just doing badly what has already been done to completion. The presence alone of Faulkner in our midst makes a great difference in what the writer can and cannot permit himself to do. Nobody wants his mule and wagon stalled on the same track the Dixie Limited is roaring down.[1]

This anxiety about the Dixie Limited, this dread of the priority of Faulkner has, moreover, an element that is not so much related to the psychodynamics of interacting imaginations as to the economics of literary culture. Writers "employing the same idiom" and "looking out on the same social scene" must contend for critical and popular attention in the same market place. So that it is not Faulkner's imaginative priority alone that engages the anxiety of the young writer, but his contemporaneity, prestige, acceptance—his proximity—as well. The fame and prestige of a near contemporary can profoundly influence the development of a new writer whose work is, for reasons intrinsic or extrinsic to that work itself, inescapably related to that of a more established figure.

Which is exactly the situation in which Ralph Ellison found himself as he began his career. For Ellison, Richard Wright was more than a mere contemporary. Although Wright was only ten years older than Ellison, he was a presence, an image as well as a person, a reality that had to be dealt with both in the imagination and the marketplace. Whatever place a young black writer might make for himself in the critical public attention would be a place won, to some degree and in some fashion, from Richard Wright.

Ralph Ellison grew up in Oklahoma, at some distance, both geographically and psychologically, from the violently charged racial atmosphere experienced by Richard Wright in Mississippi. Ellison was from an early age deeply interested in music, and when he came East to college it was to study under William Levi Dawson, the black symphonist whose "Negro Folk Symphony" was premiered by the Philadelphia Orchestra during Ellison's first semester at Tuskegee. But Ellison's father had intended him to be a poet, had named him Ralph Waldo for that very reason, and though his father died when Ralph was only three, Ellison's mother fostered and supported his interest in language, literature, the human imagination, and human relations.[2]

Stimulated by an impressive young teacher with an idealistic vision of the potential Negro contribution to American letters, this literary curiosity developed rapidly. Ellison dabbled in poetry after careful reading in Millay, Jeffers, Eliot, and Pound, and read heavily in classic British fiction, from Defoe to Hardy. He applied himself with great discipline to understanding artistic expression generally, and slowly lost his exclusive focus on music. After his junior year, he went up to New York, in part to earn money for his last year of music study, in part to continue experimenting with sculpture, in part to experience what he could of the New York literary scene that he had glimpsed in the journals recommended by his professor friend.[3] Someone arranged for an introduction to Langston Hughes, and, through Hughes (and during Ellison's first week in Harlem in the summer of 1937), he met Richard Wright.

Wright was then just about to come into success. The appearance of "Big Boy Leaves Home" in 1936 had brought Wright considerable status among his peers. He was now editing a journal, *New Challenge,* with Marian Minus and Dorothy West, and he was therefore eager to meet and promote new black talent. Ellison had read some of Wright's poems and liked them. Wright was impressed with Ellison's broad reading and critical acumen, and quickly gave him a new book to review for *New Challenge.* When the review was accepted for publication, Wright persuaded Ellison to try writing fiction.[4] Ellison read Wright's unpublished manuscripts and discussed modern literature and Wright's work in progress, *Native Son,* with his new friend, thus broadening and deepening their relationship. When Wright moved from the defunct *New Challenge* to the Federal Writers Project, Ellison went with him; in off-hours "they would get together at someone's house to attend the theater, a party, or a political meeting" (*Unfinished Quest,* 168). In August 1939, Wright got married and chose Ellison for his best man (*Unfinished Quest,* 200).

A personal relationship was thus established between the two men that lasted over ten years, until Wright sailed for France in the late 1940s. By that time, Wright no longer fully trusted Ellison and did not confide in him, and Ellison had already made significant progress on the work that would, ultimately, dethrone his old friend and mentor.

During those two or three palmy years at the beginning of their friendship, Ellison was an eager and apt pupil in Richard Wright's informal school of writing. Wright guided

Ellison to James's and Conrad's prefaces and other useful criticism, and pointed out how the great writers had achieved their effects. Though Ellison was grateful to Wright for showing him how Joyce and Dostoevski attained their artistic ends, it was Wright himself that Ellison first honored by imitation.

"Birthmark," Ellison's earliest story (published in *New Masses* in 1940), reveals the undeniable presence of Wright in Ellison's literary imagination. The story reads like an addendum to *Uncle Tom's Children.* It has the dramatic immediacy of Wright's rural southern setting. Moreover, the story imitates Wright's dialectal style in dialogue; when Ellison came through to an independent sense of self as a writer, he would avoid this orthographic approach to black speech and adopt an idiomatic style for black dialogue.

Ellison's aborted novel of this period, *Slick Gonna Learn,* also reveals the influence of the manuscripts on Wright's desk. His model here was Wright's then unpublished novel, *Lawd Today.* Ellison's Slick Williams, like Wright's Jake Jackson, is a poor, uneducated urban black who is frustrated by difficulties arising from the responsibilities of marriage. In the brief excerpt from the book that appeared in *Direction* in September 1939, Slick is more mature emotionally than Jake Jackson. He loves his wife and children; his desperation is motivated by that love. But Ellison is incapable of bringing the story to life because he has no understanding of what such a person might seem to think about his predicament. Slick's psychology eluded his creator. He felt helpless before the chaos of psychological reality—"the images, symbols and emotional configurations" that seethed under the veneer of "apparently rational human relationships."[5]

Ellison's next stories marked a steady progress away from the specific and almost singular influence of Wright toward a more diverse and individualized style and manner. "Afternoon" (*American Writing,* 1940), "Mister Toussan" (*New Masses,* 1941) and "That I Had the Wings" (*Common Ground,* 1943), owe as much to Twain as to the Wright of "Big Boy Leaves Home"—and perhaps more. Further, Ellison here draws together literary models and personal experience in ways that his more direct imitations of Wright had not done. He pulls back from the public themes and typical black protagonists and situations to deal with a limited but familiar universe, the world of young boys. In these stories Ellison overcame Wright's social analysis and the resultant aesthetic imperatives insofar as they directly shaped Ellison's efforts to write fiction. But also, perhaps more significantly, he achieved the mastery of narrative structure and point of view that had blocked his first attempt at a novel. In his next stories, he moved into greater artistic maturity; "Flying Home" and "King of the Bingo Game," both published in 1944, marked Ellison's graduation from his apprenticeship.

But the apprentice achieved his journeyman's status, as it were, just as his mentor became a master. Wright, who respected Ellison's critical talents enough to discuss the structural problems of Book 3 of *Native Son* with him before sending it off to the publishers in the fall of 1939, came into fame and fortune with the novel's publication in March of 1940. The critical reception was excellent, and popular interest was high. "In many bookstores stock was depleted in a matter of hours. The novel sold 200,000 copies in under three weeks, breaking a twenty-year record at Harper's." Wright gave interviews, appeared at luncheons, visited universities, received fan mail, even had his name engraved on a wall at the New York World's Fair, "next to those of Phyllis Wheatley, Paul Laurence Dunbar, James Weldon Johnson, W.E.B. DuBois, Marian Anderson and Ethel Waters" (*Unfinished Quest,* 180). Now Wright became a seemingly permanent and formidable presence, not only a private teacher to be admired and imitated while one learned the techniques of the art of writing, but rather, now, a public eminence which any writer working in the same tradition and looking out on the same social scene would have to deal with.

Ellison's recognition of this fact was explicit. In his critical articles of the early forties, he uses Wright and *Native Son* as touchstones of excellence for black writers. In "Recent Negro Fiction," Ellison dismisses the Harlem Renaissance writers, for the most part because their work was not firmly grounded in reality. He praises Hughes and Wright as the only mature black writers because their work expressed both "an awareness of the working class and socially dispossessed Negro and his connection with the international order of things" and the ability to draw upon folklore with advanced literary techniques. Wright is singled out for portraying, in *Uncle Tom's Children,* Negro men and women at bay in the oppressive southern environment and for delineating "the universals embodied in Negro Experience."[6] In Ellison's estimation, Wright's contrasting sharecroppers and rebel youths and revolutionary ministers possessed "an emotional complexity never before achieved in American Negro writing." And this achievement, he thought, was only a preface to the greatness of Wright's novel.

> In Wright's *Native Son* we have the first philosophical novel by an American Negro. This work possesses an artistry, penetration of thought, and sheer emotional power that places it in the front ranks of American fiction. Indeed, except for its characters and subject matter, it seems hardly identifiable with previous Negro fiction; but this however, only in a superficial sense concealing factors of vital importance to the understanding of Negro writing. ("Recent," 22)

Ellison saw Wright's exposure to the great prose writers of the European tradition and to his contemporaries in America as a freedom-granting experience that made Wright a mature writer in ways never achieved by his Negro predecessors of the Harlem Renaissance. This intellectual and artistic maturity, manifested in thought and technique, and coupled with "the tensions and disciplines" built up in Wright as the result of his social activism, had made of Wright a new kind of black writer, one possessed of "a new sensibility." As a result, Wright's novel was a monumental cultural achievement:

> *Native Son,* examined against past Negro fiction, represents the take-off in a leap which promises to carry over a whole tradition, and marks the merging of the imaginative depiction of American Negro life into the broad stream of American literature. For the Negro writer it has suggested a path which he might follow to reach maturity, clarifying and increasing his social responsibility. The writer is faced with the problem of mastering the culture of American civilization through the techniques and disciplines provided by his art. ("Recent," 25)

These high claims for the impact of Wright's work are capped by Ellison's insistence that for the aspiring black writer "there must be no stepping away from the artistic and social achievements of *Native Son*" if the writer seeks, through his work in art, to help black Americans "to possess the conscious meaning of their lives" ("Recent," 26).

But, of course, it was necessary for Ellison—and for other black American writers in the forties and fifties—to get past Wright, to "step away from" *Native Son* in some freedom-granting direction of their own. The danger was twofold: they might either be swallowed up in the priority of Wright's imaginative manner, or suffer for lack of audience and critical attention because their work was "irrelevant." Ellison's own aim in writing, presented here as a prescription for all his contemporaries and fellow successors, veers away from Wright's powerful but essentially apocalyptic address to current social conditions and out toward more prophetic expressions of what Ellison calls, here and elsewhere "unlimited intellectual and imaginative possibilities" ("Recent," 22).

Ellison's movement away from Wright during the forties was accompanied by changes in the nature of their personal relationship as well. Langston Hughes has noted that during the last years of the thirties Ellison was very close to Wright; in a letter to Michel Fabre, Hughes, who had introduced Ellison to Wright, said that for the young man "Wright became a sort of literary god for a time."[7] As the relationship deepened, Ellison became involved in Wright's personal matters. He was the best man at Wright's first marriage to Dhima Rose Meadman, in August of 1939. But the warm friendship cooled slightly as Ellison became entangled in the dissolution of the marriage as well. In the late spring of 1940, when the hullabaloo over *Native Son* had somewhat abated, Wright and his bride honeymooned in Mexico for three months, quarreled, and returned to New York separately. Dhima moved into an apartment with the Ellisons (who gave up a comfortable place to accommodate her plans), in hope that "Richard's friendship with them would give them more chances to see each other and become reconciled" (*Unfinished Quest,* 206). But Wright wanted nothing more to do with Dhima, and, despite Ellison's encouragements to the contrary, he divorced her. Meanwhile, Wright resented the apartment expenses that he felt he was paying for, and when he married Ellen Poplar in 1941, he did not invite Ellison and his wife to the wedding, though Ellison knew and liked Ellen. Ellison reports that it was only through "stray remarks" that he deduced they had wed. Ellison did not long stand in the shadow of Wright's disapproval—Wright deeply involved himself in Ellison's efforts to avoid conscription into a Jim Crow army during 1944 and 1945—but the intensity of their relationship lessened permanently.[8] And as Ellison had less and less personal contact with Wright, his own literary career found sustenance outside the circle of Wright's contacts. He never became a member of the Party, and even publications like *New Masses* paid him for his contributions.

Such essentially circumstantial differentiations, of course, make little difference in the kind of battle with a predecessor's priority and proximity that I mean to trace here. Ellison's "situation," in Kenneth Burke's terms, was a complex one—partly biographical (i.e., personal and circumstantial), partly intellectual and ideological, partly aesthetic. Toward the resolution of this complex of relationships with Wright and what Wright stood for, Ralph Ellison would have to bring to bear "strategies" of symbolic action in his imaginative and in his personal life that would deal not only with the literal proximity of Wright, but with his threatening imaginative priority as well.

* * *

In *The Anxiety of Influence* Bloom speaks of one of the possible relationships between writers and their predecessors as an antithetical one. Like the initiate in one of the ancient mystery religions, the artist must, to be recognized, supply a completing fragment or *tessera* which, taken in conjunction with his predecessor's work, makes a satisfactory whole, redeeming the incompleteness of the predecessor's vision (*Anxiety,* 67). By thus laboring to "complete" his predecessor, the new writer establishes his absolute necessity—his real priority—for his is by implication the larger vision. To make this "strategy" work for him, the influenced writer must impose an interpretation on his predecessor's work so that he can see it as requiring fulfillment or completion.

Now Ralph Ellison's career as a writer, begun and fostered by the influence of Richard Wright, has been maintained upon Ellison's efforts to supply *tessera* to Richard Wright's *Black Boy.* Both his critical and imaginative writing turn around Wright's posture in this now famous passage in *Black Boy:*

> (After I had outlived the shocks of childhood, after the habit of reflection had been born in me, I used to mull over the strange absence of real kindness in Negroes, how unstable was our tenderness, how lacking in genuine passion we were, how

> void of great hope, how timid our joy, how bare our traditions, how hollow our memories, how lacking we were in those intangible sentiments that bind man to man, and how shallow was even our despair. After I had learned other ways of life I used to brood upon the unconscious irony of those who felt that Negroes led so passional an existence! I saw that what had been taken for our emotional strength was our negative confusions, our flights, our fears, our frenzy under pressure. Whenever I thought of the essential bleakness of the black life in America I knew that Negroes had never been allowed to catch the full spirit of Western Civilization, that they lived somehow in it but not of it. And when I brooded upon the cultural barrenness of black life, I wondered if clean, positive tenderness, love, honor, loyalty and the capacity to remember were native with man. I asked myself if these human qualities were not fostered, won, struggled and suffered for, preserved in ritual from one generation to another.) (33)

Ellison's works provide contrast to Wright's expression here of the spiritual limitations of black American experience. *Invisible Man* asserts again and again the crucial role of both folk personalities (Trueblood and Mary, for example) and folk culture (the blues, the yams) in the development of a spiritually acute black leader. The hero is not, however —as Rufus Scott in Baldwin's *Another Country* is—a negation of Wright's Bigger; rather, he is *tessera* to Wright's "representative" image of his self, the "Richard" of *Black Boy.*

Ellison's opportunity to interpret his predecessor came timely to him. In the summer of 1945, very shortly after *Black Boy* appeared, Ellison published a long essay called "Richard Wright's Blues" in the *Antioch Review.* The essay is a brilliant review piece and an excellent and useful exploration of aspects of Wright's book. But I am not concerned with that here. In considering "Richard Wright's Blues" as part of Ellison's strategy for escaping Wright's priority, I am concerned with what the essay is doing for its author, and not with what it is doing for its subject. If anything, what it is doing *to* its subject must be brought into focus.

In the essay Ellison argues Wright over into his own territory. Attempting to place *Black Boy* among associated art forms and works, he asserts that the cultural form which most significantly shapes the narrative is the blues, which he defines as "an impulse to keep the painful details and episodes of a brutal experience alive in one's aching consciousness, to finger its jagged grain, and to transcend it, not by the consolation of philosophy, but by squeezing from it a near-tragic, near-comic lyricism" (*S&A,* 90). *Black Boy* is then to be interpreted as a blues, "an autobiographical chronicle of personal catastrophe" that represents the flowering of the folk form into full artistic potential (*S&A,* 91).

The question is not whether Wright's book is or is not an elaboration of the blues, but why Ralph Ellison says so. Wright nowhere expressed such an understanding of the potential usefulness of lyric forms for prose compositions. And in another context Ellison has only scorn for Wright's imaginative relationship to the blues tradition. Almost twenty years later, defending himself against Irving Howe's charge that he had stepped too far away for the protest tradition and the challenge of Wright's work, Ellison quite specifically denied Wright's influence in defining the emotional or blues tone of his work. Here he names Hemingway his father-as-artist, praising him for "a spirit beyond the tragic with which [he] could feel at home, for it was very close to the feeling of the blues," while denying Wright any communication with that spirit: "And if you think Wright knew anything about the blues, listen to a 'blues' he composed with Paul Robeson singing, a *most* unfortunate collaboration!; and read his introduction to Paul Oliver's *Blues Fell This Morning*" (*S&A,* 145).[9]

This is, of course, having your cake and eating it, too. Ellison's interpretation of Wright's life-story begins with a palpable misreading, a displacement of Ellison's own literary/cultural concerns into his predecessor's work, the better to antithetically "develop" and "complete" and "fulfill" them. Ellison constructs, for his own purposes, a version of Wright's psychology as artist that he can use to explain the limited version of the passage from *Black Boy* quoted earlier. He argues that whatever positive values, supportive of poetic sensibility and nurturing artistic interest, Wright's Mississippi environment may have contained, they "had as little chance of prevailing against the overwhelming weight of the child's unpleasant experiences as Beethoven's Quartets would have of destroying the stench of a Nazi prison" (*S&A*, 94). Such values and elements were rightly omitted from the image of the black community in *Black Boy* on the grounds of the selectivity of art. The core of Wright's experience was violence; violence was "inflicted upon him by both family and community," and his response as artist had been to shape and thus give significance to that violence (*S&A*, 94). Wright was thus not able to express in his work moral and cultural attitudes that had played no significant roles in his development, though they may have existed in the community. Here Ellison is willing to grant Wright his given that they did not, and forms his generalization around that given.

> Man cannot express that which does not exist—either in the form of dreams, ideas or realities—in his environment. Neither his feelings, his sensibility nor his intellect are fixed, innate qualities. They are processes which arise out of the interpenetration of human instinct with environment, through the process called experience, each changing and being changed by the other. (*S&A*, 98)

But Ellison's use of this idea is ambivalent. On the one hand, it explains Wright's image of himself struggling for identity without contact with personal models or artifacts to inspirit his poetic sensibility as an historical/cultural peculiarity of Wright's experience, beyond which he would himself be carried by reading and, later, ideology. On the other hand, it seems also to account for Wright's weakness as an artist. He uses it to explain why Wright's major fictional creation, Bigger Thomas, is, as far as Ellison is concerned, inadequately achieved. The *lacunae* of Wright's biography are reflected in his image of Bigger struggling to express thoughts essentially philosophical in nature with a vocabulary limited to sensual counters:

> Here lies the source of the basic ambiguity of *Native Son*, wherein in order to translate Bigger's complicated feeling into universal ideas, Wright had to force into Bigger's consciousness concepts and ideas which his intellect could not formulate. Between Wright's skill and knowledge of Bigger's mute feeling lay a thousand years of conscious culture. (*S&A*, 100)

This "conscious culture," denied Wright by his Southern environment, was what Wright looked for and could not see in his black community. In asking whether qualities like love, honor, loyalty and remembrance were not "fostered, won, struggled for and suffered for," he is affirming the black American's capacity for culture, knowing that "Western culture," in Ellison's terms, "must be won, confronted like the animal in a Spanish bullfight, dominated by the red shawl of codified experience and brought heaving to its knees" (*S&A*, 103).

But Ellison's idea of the black American's relationship with Western culture is in fact very different from Wright's precisely because his sense of personal, biographical history in relation to Afro-American culture and North American culture generally was far more complex than Wright's. If Wright conceptualizes Afro-American culture in terms of its absence for his life, its non-supportiveness, Ellison's images of the Afro-American community in his essays show it in a more positive light, as available to a youth inspired to attempt its codification. By reading Wright's autobiography as a "blues," Ellison imputes to Wright a dim, uncertain, and inadequate vision of the black American's necessarily complex relationship with his community and culture, and accepts—in Wright's name, as it were—the limitations of Wright's environment as an explanation of his vision. Wright is thus encompassed, encapsulated by his own life-story, which Ellison need not feel representative of his own. "Richard Wright's Blues" is an act of definition, a misreading of the father-as-artist that clears the way for antithetical assertion of the ways in which Afro-American experience, Ralph Ellison's experience in particular, functions in the shaping of an artist.

The projection of an encompassing vision of that experience in Ellison's autobiographical writing is closely tied to Ellison's alternative version of his birth into art. In "Hidden Name and Complex Fate," Ellison invents for himself a literary paternity that excludes Richard Wright and holds the origins of his authorship within his family circle. As I have already noted, Ellison's biological father died when Ellison was a three-year-old. In the essay, and elsewhere, Ellison grants his father a gift of prophecy which the normal course of events in his Oklahoma youth, so different from Wright's Mississippi youth and early manhood, allowed to come to fruition.

Attempting to explain his experience as an American writer, Ellison pointedly sidesteps "the details of racial hardship" which have, he insists, too often been evoked when writers of his "cultural background" have "essayed their experience in public." Without denying their validity, he means to suggest that they are, "at least in a discussion of a writer's experience as *writer,* as artist, somewhat beside the point" (*S&A,* 148). Again, there is here an implicit rejection of the connection Wright draws between his environment and his artistic expression. Ellison sees Wright's ideas as inadequate, "beside the point," and thus in need of completion.

But when Ellison stands *on* the point, it is with a view in an entirely different direction. He projects his father's action in naming him after Ralph Waldo Emerson a conferral of a destiny. The first step in achieving a sense of control in relation to the world, Ellison argues, is coming to terms with the destiny implied by one's own name. The enigmatic world, he says, is like Tar Baby in the folktale, who is "utterly noncommittal under our scrutiny" and once we have begun to struggle with him demands that we "perceive the necessity of calling him by his true name as the price of our freedom." Coming to grips with the Tar Baby requires more than will; it requires composition, technique, self-consciousness:

> It is unfortunate that he had so many "true names"—all spelling chaos; and in order to discover even one of these we must first come into possession of our names. For it is through our names that we first place ourselves in the world. Our names, being the gift of others, must be made our own. (*S&A,* 151)

Charging our names with meaning—"hopes, hates, loves aspirations"—so that they become "our masks and our shields and the containers of all those values and traditions which we learn and/or imagine as being the meaning of the familial past" is the way the individual completes the destiny set for him by his ancestors. For Ellison, coming to terms with "Waldo" involved a long process of learning something of his dead father's love for literature and for Emerson in particular, a process which only began during his adolescence. Later in his life—"much later, after [he] began to write and work with words"—he came to suspect that his father had been aware of "the suggestive powers of names and of the magic involved in naming" (*S&A,* 154).

In suggesting, however metaphorically, the efficacy of his father's naming him after a writer, Ellison is realigning his artistic paternity, denying the central agency of Wright that I have herein attempted to demonstrate. Ellison's artistic sensibility is not approached by him with the idea that it "just grew," unsupported and even opposed by familial and communal forces, as in Wright's version of *his* development in *Black Boy*. Ellison carefully accounts for familial, environmental and artistic elements that entered his consciousness through his experience of the black community in frontier Oklahoma. His catalogues of these cultural stimulants stand in strong contrast to Wright's very Whitmanesque catalogue in *Black Boy*. In Wright's version of his childhood sensibility, nature is the dominant stimulus; it is nature that inspires him to feeling—"nostalgia" in a string of southward-bound geese, "melancholy" in the odor of burning hickory, "alarm" in the glaring redness of the sun mirrored in windowpanes. When Wright catalogues his responses to human culture it is to note irrelevancies, superstitions *that* he used as a child to redeem through imagination his "bare and bleak" environment, but *which* played no role in his recomposition of the world's image in his art.[10]

In contrast, Ellison's memories of his Oklahoma environment are rich with images of human culture. While nature—"all kinds of weather . . . catalpa worms and jack rabbits . . . sunflowers and hollyhocks"—is not ignored, the greater part of the storehouse of imagery that Ellison claims for his own is filled with human stock—all manner of language, ceremony, manners, and music. Things which in Wright's childhood world were threatening are in Ellison's only a rich freight of potent value:

> I was impressed by expert players of the "dozens" and certain notorious bootleggers of corn whiskey. By jazz musicians and fortunetellers and by men who did anything well; by strange sicknesses and by interesting brick or razor scars; by expert cussing vocabularies as well as exalted praying and terrified shouting, and by transcendent playing or singing of the blues. (*S&A*, 160)

All of this, of course, went into Ellison's writing, but only after he had succumbed to the "fatal suggestions" of Richard Wright that he try his hand at it. Perhaps, as Ellison asserts, the more literature and criticism he read, under Wright's guidance and beyond it, the more the details of his background were transformed in his thinking, revealing the profound extent of their value and thus fulfilling his father's intention and his communal experience. But none of that was possible, it seems to me, until after Ellison had composed, in "Richard Wright's Blues," a theory of his mentor that enabled him to assert his own imaginative priority. If Wright had caught a sense of freedom and "glimpses of life's possibilities" only as an adolescent and though the agency of literature, Ellison's relationship is more primary—fated by family, nurtured by community, enriched by culture. And in projecting, after Wright's death, the image of his own father as his most necessary literary progenitor, Ellison closes the loop; in making that gift of his name his own, in asserting the activity of living up to the potential destiny foisted upon him by tradition and culture, Ellison reduces the importance of his apprenticeship under Wright and becomes his own major influence, his own father-as-artist.

NOTES

1. See Flannery O'Connor, *Mystery and Manners*, 45.
2. Ellison discusses in some detail the influence of his mother in an interview with John Hersey that serves as Introduction to Hersey's *Ralph Ellison: A Collection of Critical Essays*, 2-5 in particular.
3. Albert Murray, a friend of Ellison's from the Tuskegee days, notes the impact of Professor Morteza Drexel Sprague on both of them in his *South to a Very Old Place*, 112-13. Ellison dedicated *Shadow and Act* to Professor Sprague.

4. See Michel Fabre, *The Unfinished Quest of Richard Wright,* 146.

5. Ralph Ellison, *Shadow and Act,* 175. This work is subsequently cited in text as *S&A.*

6. See Ellison, "Recent Negro Fiction," 22. This work is subsequently cited in text as "Recent."

7. Quoted in Keneth Kinnamon, *The Emergence of Richard Wright,* 72.

8. See Constance Webb, *Richard Wright: A Biography,* 408 (n.22) and 227-30.

9. Judging by Ellison's sources, he is right. Fabre gives the text of the blues collaboration with Robeson in his biography, and it is more Red than Blue. Wright seems never to have understood or accepted the deep-down personal funkiness of blues, their raucous, sensual, ornery and celebratory qualities.

10. Richard Wright, *Black Boy,* 7. Ellison quotes this same passage in "Richard Wright's Blues."

WORKS CITED

Bloom, Harold. *The Anxiety of Influence: A Theory of Poetry.* New York: Oxford University Press, 1973.

Ellison, Ralph. "Recent Negro Fiction." *New Masses* 40:6 (August 5, 1941).

______. *Shadow and Act.* New York: New American Library, 1966.

Fabre, Michel. *The Unfinished Quest of Richard Wright.* New York: William Morrow & Company, 1973.

Hersey, John. *Ralph Ellison: A Collection of Critical Essays.* Englewood Cliffs, N.J.: Prentice Hall, 1974.

Kinnamon, Keneth. *The Emergence of Richard Wright.* Urbana: University of Illinois Press, 1972.

Murray, Albert. *South to a Very Old Place.* New York: McGraw-Hill, 1971.

O'Connor, Flannery. *Mystery and Manners: Occasional Prose,* ed. Sally and Robert Fitzgerald. New York: Farrar, Straus and Giroux, 1969.

Webb, Constance. *Richard Wright: A Biography.* New York: G.P. Putnam's Sons, 1968.

Wilson, Angus. *The Wild Garden, or Speaking of Writing.* Berkeley and Los Angeles: University of California Press, 1963.

Wright, Richard. *Black Boy: A Record of Childhood and Youth.* New York: Harper & Brothers, 1945.

From *The Massachusetts Review* 21:1 (Spring 1980), 196-212.

The Testament of Ralph Ellison

John M. Reilly

Suppose we take Ralph Ellison at his word when he tells us that the basic significance of the essays and occasional pieces collected in *Shadow and Act* is autobiographical.[1] Then, despite the omission from this version of a life writing of dates and particularized events that would mark it as an objective chronicle of the passage from youth to maturity and obscurity to fame, the reader's expectation that the autobiography will depict a destiny is met by Ellison's repeated mention of the essential experience that forms the condition for his life's project.

The dominant feature emerging from his reflective viewpoint is the good fortune he had being brought up in Oklahoma, whose settlement by black and white Americans hardly more than a generation before his birth exempted its society, for a time, from the equilibrium of rigid caste relationships prevalent in the Old South and the fixed systems of power characteristic of the capitalist industrial sectors of the United States. It was a newer America where he was born, and, though soon enough it fastened upon itself the rites of racial segregation and the forms of a class society, during the early years of its statehood and Ellison's life, Oklahoma recapitulated in the minds of its citizens, if not entirely in the circumstances of their material lives, the situation of the American frontier. Exhilarated by the sense of possibility in a loosely structured community, the young Ellison and his confréres could imaginatively transcend the categories of race, thinking of themselves as the "Renaissance men" of an American comedy rather than as victims in a racist melodrama.

Through the selections of memory and the emphasis of rhetoric, Ellison invests the musicians who created the vernacular idiom of the region's native music—Southwestern jazz—with the authority of practical philosophers on his latter-day frontier. In the outlaw status earned by their exclusion and willed separation from the company of respectable judges, ministers, and politicians who were the agents of repressive "civilization," the jazzmen embodied in the art for which they lived the attributes of popular archetype. Their versatility and improvisational style evinced the idealized individualism of American legend and evoked the witty triumphs of Afro-American folk heroes, while in the processions of their art they performed a kind of democratic enactment, singing the self in musical phrases that combined in an utterance en masse. True jazz, Ellison writes

> Is an art of individual assertion within and against the group. Each true jazz moment...springs from a contest in which each artist challenges all the rest; each solo flight, or improvisation, represents (like the successive canvases of a painter) a definition of his identity; as individual, as member of the collectivity and as a link in the chain of tradition. (*S&A*, 234)

The climax of Ellison's projection of the importance of the frontier in his life is, of course, his won emergence as an artist. Exuberance and ambition allied with incontestable talent impelled him, as it did the jazzmen, to creative expression as a means of self-definition. It diminishes his accomplishment not at all to say that this was a result of personality more than of conviction that he possessed prodigious abilities. Taking up writing, he says, depended upon the chance of Richard Wright's asking him to do a review and then a short story for *New Challenge* magazine. Even so, writing "was a reflex of reading, an extension of a source of pleasure, escape and instruction" (*S&A*, xii). And before that, the composition of music for which he originally hoped to prepare himself appears to have signified less an immersion in a process than the hope of achieving a state of being, as in *being* another Richard Wagner by composing a great symphony before the age of twenty-six. Furthermore, there was a good deal of serendipity and scarcely any sense of determinism bringing him to New York and within the reach of Wright's literary suggestions before he completed the prescribed course of formal study at Tuskegee Institute. A problem about his scholarship and the lure of he city he knew from Alain Locke's *The New Negro* as the setting of a contemporary "Renaissance" led him to yet another frontier.

Ellison's mention in *Shadow and Act*, and elsewhere, of writers from whose friendship and example he learned something of craft—Eliot, Hemingway, Malraux, Wright—has unquestionable interest, but not because they constitute a list of influences to be discerned in his writing. Rather, these references complete the imaginative paradigm of the inceptive autobiography by introducing his companions in the free republic of letters, an environment whose inhabitants define themselves through works undertaken individually, as members of the collectivity, and as links in the chains of tradition. A life of literature can be a difficult, combative one, but it is lived, Ellison tells us, in a zone of undiscovered possibilities that is the natural home and destiny of a man formed and conditioned by the historical and cultural environment of America's last physical frontier.

Intriguing as the factual details Ellison provides us of his life may be, they are insufficient to satisfy fully our curiosity. In "The World and the Jug" (*S&A*, 141), he asks Irving Howe to remember that an act of Chekhov's "was significant only because Chekhov was Chekhov, the great writer." So, because Ralph Ellison is Ralph Ellison, we should like to know all manners of things about his life in the hope that they could "explain" him, and if not that, at least give us the fullest possible description of the man. But *Shadow and Act* offers a truncated autobiography. Even with the addition of writings not collected in that volume, we have only the framework of a life, and a subjectively rendered framework, at that. Ellison has situated his life for us within a broadly outlined episode of history resonant of the schemes of Frederick Jackson Turner and the images of popular culture. It is a generalized, a priori picture that will not reveal how the unique Ralph Ellison, equipped with certain predispositions, actually became the particular man. "Negroness" is nothing like a metaphysical condition, he says.

> It is not skin color which makes a Negro American but cultural heritage as shaped by the American experience, the social and political predicament, a sharing of that "concord of sensibilities" which the group expresses through historical circumstances...(*S&A*, 131)

What, then, are the features of person, the experiences in family and intimate relationships that particularized Ellison's assumption of the Afro-American cultural heritage and, thus, individualizes him within the group? He does not say.

It might be objected that this is a querulous response to the casual remark Ellison makes about the autobiographical significance of *Shadow and Act*. Perhaps. But to note that the plot of a life we glimpse only in fragments dispersed throughout his essays is an abstract representation of the self establishes two crucial points for understanding his nonfiction. The first point is that Ellison presents himself as a symbolic figure in whose portrayal the absence of particularized data encourages us to see a typical product of the American frontier. Moreover, in delineating his experience among a people who intentionally left the realm of slavery to make a new way, he indicates that the frontier effects the necessary rupture in the repetitive order of social oppression that gives birth to history. Like the protagonist of *Invisible Man*, who claims to speak for all of us on one frequency or another, Ellison the essayist stands at the beginning of self-determining Afro-American history. The second crucial point to observe about the generalized autobiography is that its broad frontiersman scheme is obviously a fiction, not in the sense that it bears no relationship to a reality that can be documented from other sources, but rather it is like fiction in the selectivity it uses to enforce the compelling significance of a single, unqualified feature of Ellison's life: his certain and intuitive resolve to achieve the birthright of a free citizen of a democracy.

So the apparent autobiography in *Shadow and Act* is an exemplum; yet, in its purpose it is more than that. It provides the authenticating image for a volume of writing devoted to exploration of classical issues in American social philosophy. As it discusses democracy from the unusual vantage point of an aesthetic concept of self-realization, Ellison's fragmentary autobiography certifies that the source of discussion is a representative Afro-American.

The Afro-American, as citizen and artist, engages in a continual struggle against reductive stereotype, not merely the Negrophobic characterizations of vicious racists, but also the interpretations of black life advanced by a social science that describes its object almost entirely by reference to the dominant white majority. Nineteenth-century students of the "Negro problem" applied their supposed science to a demonstration of the black's comparative inferiority, thereby creating a justification for continued exploitation. More "progressive" thought in the twentieth century has redefined the condition once perceived as subhuman as a situation wherein blacks are the victims of whites. In either interpretation Afro-Americans are conceived as existing in dependency. Even the corrective work of Gunnar Myrdal, whose influential study *An American Dilemma* earns Ellison's praise for discrediting the "non-scientific nonsense that has cluttered our sociological literature" (*S&A*, 305), must be eventually disqualified as a truthful or useful tool for understanding, because despite its microscopic empirical analyses it retains in conclusion the reductive idea that "the Negro's entire life and, consequently, also his opinions on the Negro problem are, in the main, to be considered as secondary reactions to more primary pressures from the side of the dominant white majority" (*S&A*, 315). Ellison's displeasure with this conclusion would seem to be phrased moderately enough to suit the decorum of an academic journal, but in 1944, when the review failed to be published in the *Antioch Review*, maybe it was a different story. Nevertheless, it took twenty years before Ellison could explain the point of difference between that famous study of the Negro and the perspective of the critic whose source of knowledge is the living of a Negro life. "Can a people," Ellison asks,

> Live and develop for over three hundred years simply by reacting? Are American Negroes simply the creation of white men, or have they at least helped to create themselves out of what they found around them? Men have made a way of life in caves and upon cliffs, why cannot Negroes have made a life upon the horns of the white man's dilemma? (*S&A*, 316)

Ellison could easily be bringing ethical proof to his commentary on Myrdal and the traditions of American social science. Common sense dictates that he ought to be qualified by "Negroness" to evaluate discussions of Afro-American social reality. The common-sense assumption will not pertain, however, in the face of the closed systems erected on the premises of stereotypes. These systems hold that opinions of Negroes are products of dependency, too, and Ellison has no inclination to counter with an invocation of racial mysticism. The counterattack would be as irrational as the view it meant to rebut is absurd. In any case, the contest with stereotypes is not a simple matter of posing truth, even the truth of personal testimony, against falsity. The "struggle over the nature of reality" (*S&A*, 26) does not concern data. Nor does it involve contrary perceptions. What the struggle is about is conceptions, the patterns and forms men and women construct from their observations and by their actions to give life a shape.

The function of stereotypes is instrumental. Arising "from an internal psychological state...from an inner need to believe" (*S&A*, 28), bigotry seizes upon the stock ideas current in social exchange to sanction irrational needs with the plausible appearance of overgeneralized evidence. To complicate the matter, other intellectual structures spring from personal needs by a similar process. Ellison's explicit example is art, which psychologically

> represents the socializations of some profoundly personal problem involving guilt (often symbolic murder—parricide, fratricide—incest, homosexuality, all problems at the base of personality) from which by expressing them along with other elements (images, memories, emotions, ideas) he [the artist] seeks transcendence. To be effective as personal fulfillment, if it is to be more than dream, the work of art must simultaneously evoke images of reality and give them formal organization. And it must, since the individual's emotions are formed in society, shape them into socially meaningful patterns. (*S&A*, 39)

Somewhere between the pathology of bigotry and the sublimation of profound art occurs the use of stereotype that amounts to a linguistic redundancy, the repetition of customary formulas without examination of their implications. The continuum of conceptions interests Ellison much less for its genesis hidden in the fog of singular psyches than for its significance in fostering or obstructing the progress of democracy. The instrumentality of concepts working in relation to democracy he images as a dialectic of texts.

During his literary apprenticeship among left-wing American writers, Ralph Ellison was familiar with the plan of the Communist party of the United States to establish a black republic in the South ("Study," 421). Although the plan had been criticized by anti-Communists as an alien notion, it attracted the interest of Richard Wright and other blacks who viewed it as a synthesis of nationalism and socialism. The program for the autonomous republic was built upon an analysis of the lower South, where blacks had been historically a majority in certain contiguous countries, had shared a common life in agricultural production, and had evolved distinctive institutions;[2] thus, the Black Belt, by this analysis, met Stalin's definition of a nation as "a historically evolved, stable community of language, territory, economic life and psychological make-up manifested in a community of culture."[3] Apart from the political campaign in which it was used, Stalin's description of a nation is hardly remarkable. It is in fact consistent with a current of American thought beginning in Crevecoeur's *Letters from an American Farmer* and continuing to the present to define American character by association with a unique social and physical environment. Yet the truly remarkable thing is that Ellison offers his conception of the origin of the American nation without regard to material and social history or to a current in American writing with which in other contexts he shows unquestionable sympathy:

> We began as a nation not through the accidents of race or religion or geography...but when a group of men, some of them political philosophers, put down, upon what we now recognize as quite sacred papers, their conception of the nation which they intended to establish on these shores. They described, as we know, the obligations of the state to the citizen, of the citizen to the state; they committed themselves to certain ideas of justice, just as they committed us to a system which would guarantee all of its citizens equality of opportunity. (*S&A*, 163-64)

Again, when he speaks in a later essay, "The Little Man at Chehaw Station," of the struggle to define the corporate American identity, he established the site of conflict as intellectual:

> The terrain upon which we struggle is itself abstract, a terrain of ideas that, although man-made, exert the compelling force of the ideal, of the sublime; ideals that draw their power from the Declaration of Independence, the Constitution, and the Bill of Rights. We stand, as we say, united in the name of these sacred principles. But indeed, it is in the name of these same principles that we ceaselessly contend, affirming our ideals even as we do them violence. ("Little Man," 34)

According to these definitions, America, and especially the American character, are voluntarist creations, the dialectic of their development abstracted from the circumstances of material processes to the level of the word.

In its search for an essence, Ellison's image of etiology endows America with the characteristics of intentional documents. Assuming the aura of philosophical principles, the history of America, which is to say a history of texts, is all consequential to their appearance. For documents of universal significance there can be no point to an inquiry into the recesses of the authors' psychology or even the particular circumstances that made up their original context. Instead, what is pertinent is a history from the point of view of efforts to realize, or evade, the meaning of those sacred documents, a history that is a record of intended effects and that is apprehensible through the symbolic actions and cross references of succeeding texts. Such a history becomes the primary theme of Ralph Ellison's nonfiction.

Among the most important works succeeding upon the axiomatic democratic documents are novels, instances of a literary genre that in America has always been tied up with the idea of nationhood, because it is "a form which deals with change in human personality and human society," that is, with individual and social life that has broken the cake of custom. In treating its inevitable subject the American novel brings "to the surface those values, those patterns of conduct, those dilemmas, psychological and technological, which abide within the human predicament," thereby proposing answers to the questions: What are we? Who are we? ("Novel," 1023). The tentative and open form of the novel associates with democratic philosophy; its morality confirms an identity between democracy and fiction. "The novel," Ellison explains in an interview, "is a complex agency for the symbolic depiction of experience, and it demands that the writer be willing to look at both sides of characters and issues....You might say that the form of the novel imposes its morality upon the novelist by demanding a complexity of vision and an openness to the variety and depth of experience" ("Study," 428).

Ellison sees the discussion of the nature of democratic life taking place in texts but this is not to say he believes reality is exclusively linguistic, or that the texts embodying the varied concepts of democratic life exist autonomously. Using his exemplary autobiography to illustrate the origins of an outlook, he offers an ample listing in "Hidden Name and Complex Fate" of the materials he gathered for art in his formative years. In addition to weather, the sounds of black people's voices, and experiences of the physical world reminiscent of the catalogued responses of Richard Wright's sensibility that impressed him when he reviewed *Black Boy* (*S&A*, 81), Ellison cites the characters of players of the "dozens," fortunetellers, bootleggers, "men who did anything well," blind blues singers, "Negroes who were part Indian...and Indians who had children who lived in towns as Negroes, ...certain Jews, Mexicans, Chinese cooks. A German orchestra conductor and an English grocer who owned a Franklin touring car. And certain Negro mechanics ... who had so assimilated the automobile that they seemed to be behind a steering wheel even as they walked the streets or danced with girls. And there were the whites who despised us and the others who shared our hardships and our joys" (*S&A*, 158-59). Each figure independently suggests an anecdote that might develop as a story of uniqueness; collectively they defy the expectations of categorization by race, class, or type. Like the legendary jazzmen, they imply a transcendence of the limits upon the self. Their lives, too, might be art, and, in telling of their diversity, the writer like Ellison would appropriate from life the sense of human potentiality and plasticity that links the values of fiction with the principles of democracy.

"The novel," Ellison declares, "is a way of possessing life, of slowing it down, and giving it the writer's own sense of values in a deliberately and subtly structured way" ("Novel," 1023), which is another way of saying that art objectifies the subjective experiences, making available to the audience the substance of a consciousness that through the discipline of art—its morality and techniques—has acquired a way of seeing and feeling, summoning and directing the imagination (*S&A*, 162).

Ellison's faith in the novel depends upon a further point that is implicit in his adoption of a speaking voice in some of his writings, his evident interest in readings of the classic American novels, and the metaphor for audience he presents as the little man at Chehaw Station. Fiction is social communication. It exists only as it is read. The reader's subjectivity is equally important as the writer's consciousness objectified in the text. The novel is a product of the self and, at the same time, becomes something different from the self, namely, an object in the world. The reader who discerns and participates in the writer's intention by recovering the transmuted world in art freely chooses to enter a contract with the writer by the terms of which art becomes a collective enterprise. Thus, writer and reader form a community of free equals offering by their relationship a prevision of a fuller democracy. In the works of Mark Twain, Herman Melville, Stephen Crane, and Ralph Ellison, the prevision gains added sanction from the direct attention given to democracy by writers with an abiding faith in it, but even writers who ignore democratic obligations altogether participate in the community of freedom that distinguishes the aesthetic dimension of life. They can not choose to do otherwise. Nothing could be more important, then, than creating structures of reality that are consistent with their artistic medium, and no recognition could be more significant to the artist than that he or she engages in the democratic culture.

Ellison's dislike of hard-boiled individualistic writers grows out of a belief that their techniques and outlook contradict the quality of aesthetic community, but criticism of hard-boiled mannerism is comparatively easy. Much more difficult is developing a criterion to distinguish the stereotype on a philosophical level from the profound structures of democratically enhancing art that arise, we recall, in similarly subjective ways. Complexity of reference is one measure but not a sufficient one, because Ellison's own concepts often display a simplified eloquence echoing the "self-evident" declarations of eighteenth-century political writing. The inadequacy of stereotypes, starkly asserted or embedded in complex writing, is to be discerned in their employment of false resolutions to the basic contradictions of American experience.

America's "founders asserted the noble idea of creating a free, open society while retaining slavery, a system in direct contradiction to their rhetorically inclusive concept of freedom. Thus, from the beginning, racism has mocked the futuristic dream of democracy" ("Essential," 137). Stereotypes confront this contradiction with "symbolic magic" by which "the white American seeks to resolve the dilemma arising between his democratic beliefs and certain antidemocratic practices, between his acceptance of the sacred democratic belief that all men are created equal and his treatment of every tenth man as though he were not" (*S&A*, 28). Patently ridiculous representations of blacks as biologically unfit to participate in democratic fraternity resolve the contradiction between practice and belief with racist myth, Yet, even among those made queasy by overt racism, a racial segregation persists within the mind, as though the reconciliation of North and South that provided the denouement to the Civil War and Reconstruction by effectively excluding blacks from the national economic and political life also erased them from white public memory.

According to Ellison's reading, the black once served as the inevitable symbol of humanity in literature written by the generation that spanned the time of the Civil War, and the rebelliousness of authors repulsed by the conventional evil of "civilization" projected fraternal association of blacks and whites as their social ideal (*S&A*, 32-33). Alas, by the mid-twentieth century it was no longer true. The Negro remained resident in the American consciousness to the extent that "it is practically impossible for the white Americans to think of sex, of economics, his children or womenfolk, or of sweeping socio-political changes, without summoning . . . fear-flecked images of black men." But now the white American, even the literary artist, rejects his own consciousness "discarding an ambiguous substance which the artists of other cultures would confront boldly and humanize into the stuff of tragic art" (*S&A*, 100). Legalized racism of the past was an outrageous denial of human community, but the evasion of the significance of the black in contemporary public discourse is equally outrageous, for it is an act of bad faith, positing a separation of white and black that cannot, and did not, in fact, ever exist. Failing to confront the existence of black Americans even for the purpose of constructing a myth to resolve the contradiction between pragmatic morality and the creed that supposedly informs our institutional life, the new segregationists of the intellect invalidate their own conceptions of reality and can produce only more stereotypes.

Finally, in addition to exposing the stereotypes of racists and the segregationists of the intellect, there is the more subtle problem of judging and describing the inadequacy of the social science Ellison deplores. This sort of writing on the Afro-American does not conspicuously evade the contradiction between professions of Americanism and its practices; still, as his review of Myrdal and his response to Irving Howe indicate, Ellison sees in the sociological habit of thought no chance of texts that will be worthy of the democratic literary tradition. Melville or Twain could employ their fictions as tragedy because of their conceptions of the black men in society, but no tragedy can pertain when the actors are defined as objects of history disabled by their exterior circumstances from imitating the legendary figures of the Oklahoma frontier and leaping the boundaries of the enclosing circle that enforcers of practical order think they can draw about the alien blacks. Ellison is probably convinced that most of the new "friends of the Negro" mean well, but in their own way, he might say, the concepts embodying and expressing their concern for blacks are still little better than segregationist, because they do not acknowledge human kinship beneath outward circumstances.

Those who struggle over the definition of American reality are united in a dialectic that replicates the reciprocal relationships that characterize America. Particularly on the level of culture there is an irrepressible movement toward integration illustrated, among other ways, by the three examples of cultural pluralism in "The Little Man at Chehaw Station": (1) a recollection of the Tuskegee teacher who taught Ellison never to substitute mere technique for artful structure of emotion—that teacher, Hazel Harrison, had been a successful concert performer, a student of Ferruccio Busoni, and a friend of world-renowned figures in music, including Sergei Prokofiev, who presented her with a signed manuscript; (2) his observations of "a light-skinned, blue-eyed, Afro-American-featured young man" clad in dashiki and English riding clothes who set up a reflex camera on Riverside Drive to photograph himself in histrionic poses beside a customized Volkswagen Beetle; and (3) his anecdote of a startling encounter in a basement of the formerly black section of New York City called San Juan Hill, with local coal heavers who carried on an expert discussion of operatic technique they had learned by years of appearances as extras at the Metropolitan Opera in the southern idiomatic vernacular of formally uneducated Afro-American workingmen. The latter occurrence especially seemed a great "American joke ... centered on the incongruities of race, economic status, and culture" that vastly extended his "appreciation of the arcane ways of American cultural possibility" ("Little Man," 48).

Any comprehensive study of American music, dance, language, costume, cuisine, or, for that matter, mating practices might provide the evidence to substantiate Ellison's impressionistic anecdotes and put the lie to the notion that the races are separate. Useful as such proof of syncretism might be as further illustration of democratic exchange, Ellison's main interest in culture remains disclosure of the motive for creation. "Who wills to be a Negro?" he asks at one point in *Shadow and Act*. "I do!" (*S&A*, 132). And so do the musicians who play black music and the storytellers whose tales project their Afro-American identity in an improvised vernacular that is the equivalent of jazz. Again and again he proclaims that cultural expression comes from the urge to control reality. The blues, he says in explanation, is "an assertion of the irrepressibly human over all circumstances whether created by others or by one's own human failings" (*S&A*, 246). The voice of his long-time friend Jimmy Rushing carries a "rock-bottom sense of reality, coupled with our sense of the possibility of rising above it" (*S&A*, 242). And although the blues is not obvious political protest, it is "an art form and thus a transcendence of those conditions created within the Negro community by the denial of social justice" (*S&A*, 257). No wonder Jimmy Rushing, Charlie Christian, and Mahalia Jackson appear in the essays as leaders of ritual in the community. Their performance draws the audience into a sacred rite celebrating the musician-hero and affirming the presence within their ceremony of the central principle of collective Afro-American life—the control of destiny by aesthetic will that was once the slaves' means of humanizing their servitude.

Ellison has been criticized for weighing the material circumstances of oppression too lightly in the balance with his convictions about this power of Afro-American cultural initiative. Apart from his sympathetic exposition of Richard Wright's "almost unrelieved picture of a personality corrupted by brutal environment" (*S&A*, 81), Ellison writes only twice at length about the bleakness of oppression. Once is the essay "The Way It Is," originally printed in *New Masses*. In this reconstructed interview, a Harlem woman voices the bitterness she feels about sacrificing for the war effort of a country that evidently intends to do nothing about "all the little Hitlers over here" (*S&A*, 289). This is the closest Ellison may have ever come to the familiar mode of protest writing. Just as unique in the

Ellison canon is the piece titled "Harlem is Nowhere," unprinted before *Shadow and Act*. In a discussion of the Lafargue Clinic's psychiatric treatment of patients without defense against the chaos that threatens their personalities, he comes nearer than anywhere else to attempting a total analysis of the Afro-American condition. The report mentions that "talented youths . . . leap through the development of decades in a brief twenty years" (*S&A*, 296), but its burden is description of the people who stumble through anxiety and alienation because their abrupt arrival in the modern world has stripped them of the supports of traditional folk culture, while for the old reasons of racial discrimination they are denied a place in a new institutional life that might nurture them through change. In a rare combination of the approach of historical anthropology and the philosophy of democratic idealism, Ellison limns *this* Harlem as an area of perverse freedom, the home base, perhaps, of Bliss Proteus Rinehart.

These exceptional departures of Ellison's from his usual stance in nonfiction point up the genuine need for a defense of his work against the charge that it takes too sanguine a view of Afro-American life, because it ordinarily minimizes the effects of material reality. For all his concern with combating the vicious and dehumanizing stereotypes, his struggled over the nature of reality takes place on the level of concept; and despite the undoubted attraction of the frontiersman's autobiography and the celebratory characterizations of black artists, these portrayals may be said to be just momentary pauses between the beats of day-to-day living.

There is no possibility of converting the criticism into a depiction of Ellison as an ingenious optimist. On the contrary, he has no doubt that evil will always define the plot of the American story and some form of victimization will always be with us, although he aims to see that racial prejudice will not determine the designation of evil or scapegoat (*Interviews*, 69-70). Whether we call that conservatism or realism, Ellison's nonfiction still must be seen as conducting its campaign on a site that even by analogy cannot be identified with the location of the socioeconomic conflict that necessarily preoccupies the mass of black people.

Nevertheless there is a ready defense to be made, and it is not sophistically tricky, equivocal, or dependent upon establishing culture as a superior reality. Ralph Ellison is not evasive or casuistic. In a paraphrase of Kenneth Burke, his favorite theorist, he says that the words evoking democratic principles are

> charismatic terms for transcendent order....Being forms of symbolic action, they tend, through their nature as language, to sweep us in tow as they move by a process of linguistic negation toward the ideal. As a form of symbolic action, they operate by negating nature as a given and amoral condition, creating endless series of man-made or man-imagined positives....In this way...man uses language to moralize both nature and himself. ("Little Man," 35)

So, of course, these words are involved in a search for a system of aesthetics and they influence our expositions in the area of artistic form, but precisely how do they actually become active influences in the realm of sociopolitical life? Here the argument needs a development that must be inferred from the tone and total effect of Ellison's nonfiction.

The subsystem of language in art is social as well as symbolic action, social for the reasons explained in the discussion of the community of writer and reader as a prevision of democracy, active because the qualitative difference of aesthetic language from the immediate physical world generates new behavior. Detaching themselves from the empirical world in order to apprehend the recreated world of art, writers, performers, and their audiences experience reality with its shape and underlying principles laid open by virtue of art's conceptual structures. The world in art presents a more complete entity than the empirical world; thus, it becomes an engaging totality without mystification, yet at the same time a totality possessing the power to enhance life through appropriation of the significance of reality to consciousness. The processes of art, its creation and reception, found a zone of freedom, even for the oppressed. The audience recognizes human intention, a piece of deliberate work, in the creation of the aesthetic artifact. Collaborating in the tasks of completing the work or artifact, the reader or listener finds immanent his or her own freedom and possibility of intentional action. Moreover, the substance of art induces reflection, perhaps through recognition of plausibility in the story, admiration of technique, or identification with a character to accompany identification with the artist. That reflection experienced as discovery redresses the sense of powerlessness and alienation previously felt amid the welter of routine events. Set free, however briefly, by the aid of art, the audience is prepared to abandon spontaneous or reflexive behavior and to act with the same deliberate intention as the artists toward the world. For example, in the communion of the blues the audience joins with the singer to supplant suffering with the splendid control of tragicomic lyricism, or readers of *Invisible Man* who join the protagonist in his quest realize that because their own identity, like his, entails no obligation to the expectations of others, they have achieved a decisive moment of self-knowledge and are free to make themselves in action.

Shadow and Act has much further use, too, as a guide to Ellison's fiction. As he points out in his *Paris Review* interview, each section of *Invisible Man* "begins with a sheet of paper; each piece of paper is exchanged for another and contains a definition of his identity, or the social role he is to play as defined by others" (*S&A*, 177). In other words, a contest of concepts regarding American reality conducted through textual relations and interrelations forms an armature for the novel's plot, and not only in the representation of literal texts, but also through the associations of simulated speeches and metaphoric descriptions that read as texts of commentary about approximations and departures from the intent of the principal documents that founded the ideal of American democracy. Together this intertextuality within the complex enveloping form of the novel constitutes Ellison's assessment of the contradictions in which the possibility of making history is born.

The making of history—Ellison's ultimate subject—has subjective significance, for the freedom to act intentionally and humanize the world arises in consciousness. One becomes an historical actor by coming to know one can transcend the conditions made by others. The anecdotes and selective memories we receive as Ellison's inchoate autobiography in the nonfiction take their tone and form from the need to represent the first emergence of what philosophers would call his project. We feel the episodes are fragmentary, because doubtless the sense of the possibility of becoming one's own product could only have been seen in glimpses, at first. Acquaintance with purposive life awaited his meeting with musicians in the black community whose witness he celebrates in the essays grouped under the rubric "Sound and Mainstream." The discipline enabling Ellison to initiate his own transcendent project he discovered through literature, the art whose semantic and referential nature can synthesize the entire range of human experience. Finally, through the happy accident of living in the culture of a nation preoccupied with its social novelty, Ellison located in the founding texts of America the words that addressed his emergence as a writer as well as a citizen. Thus, the subtext of *Shadow and Act* charts the evolution of its author's conscious motive. Here are the particulars that will be overlooked if the reader looks for a conventionally drawn autobiography, particulars that explain the necessity to counter stereotypes that would deny his capacity, because of his race, to enter history as a conscious player. As a self-determining figure, then, he writes his primary text—the evidently topical discussions—out of devotion to confronting the

American contradiction of race and democracy with a theory meant to surpass the contradiction, a theory explaining the appearance of a synthetic democratic culture that acquires its requisite vigor from the Afro-American arts.

Let us, therefore, take Ralph Ellison at his word when he tells us that the significance of *Shadow and Act* is basically autobiographical, not because he tells us things that can interest us only because he is a famous writer, but because this autobiographer addresses the fundamental literary question: Why write? In the answer he gives, we find both the essential Ralph Ellison and his compelling democratic testament.

NOTES

1. Ralph Ellison, in the Introduction to *Shadow and Act*, xviii. All subsequent citations of this source appear in the text as *S&A*.
2. The position was developed most fully in James S. Allen, *The Negro Question in America*.
3. Joseph Stalin, *Marxism and the National and Colonial Question* (London: n.d.). 8. [A paperback edition of this work was printed in the U.S.]

WORKS CITED

Allen, James S. *The Negro Question in America*. New York: International, 1936.

Ellison, Ralph. "The Essential Ellison." Interview by Ishmael Reed, Quincy Troupe, Steve Canon. *Y'Bird Reader* 1 (Autumn 1977): 126-59.

______. "The Little Man at Chehaw Station: The American Artist and His Audience." *American Scholar* 47 (Winter 1977-78): 25-48.

______. "The Novel as a Function of American Democracy." *Wilson Library Bulletin* (June 1967): 1022-27.

______. *Shadow and Act*. New York: Random House, 1964.

______. "Study and Experience: An Interview with Ralph Ellison." With Michael S. Harper and Robert B. Stepto. *Massachusetts Review* 18 (Autumn 1977): 417-435.

O'Brien, John, ed. *Interviews with Ten Black Writers*. New York: Liveright, 1973.

Stalin, Joseph. *Marxism and the National and Colonial Question*. London: n.d. Also: San Francisco: Proletarian Pubs., 1975.

From *Speaking for You: The Vision of Ralph Ellison*, edited by Kimberly W. Benston. Howard University Press, 1987.

Ellison's Racial Variations on American Themes

Kun Jong Lee

Ralph Ellison's *Invisible Man* has been a happy hunting ground for scholars looking for literary allusions. Indeed, the search for echoes of and references to antecedent writers and works in the novel has been one of the most flourishing areas in Ellison criticism. Of the seven books on Ellison, Valerie Bonita Gray's *Invisible Man's Literary Heritage: Benito Cereno and Moby Dick*, Robert List's *Dadelus in Harlem: The Joyce-Ellison Connection*, and Alan Nadel's *Invisible Criticism: Ralph Ellison and the American Canon* concentrate exclusively on Ellison and his literary ancestors. Moreover, Mark Busby's *Ralph Ellison* recognizes the significance of the area and devotes Chapter 4, entitled, "The Actor's Shadows: Ellison's Literary Antecedents," to a survey of the topic. On the other hand, African American scholars such as Robert B. Stepto, Robert G. O'Meally, Houston A. Baker, Jr., Valerie Smith, and Henry Louis Gates, Jr., put Ellison firmly at the heart of African American cultural/literary tradition in their books.[1] The fertility of the topic can be demonstrated also in the collections of essays and special issues of journals on Ellison: While Joseph F. Trimmer's *A Casebook on Ralph Ellison's Invisible Man*, Kimberly W. Benston's *Speaking for You*, and Susan Resneck Parr's and Pancho Savery's *Approaches to Teaching Ellison's Invisible Man* devote a considerable portion of their selections to the novelist's literary heritage, other collections contain at least one article situating Ellison in the African American, American, or European literary tradition.[2] More intimidating than the number of these books and journal articles is the incredible range of Ellison's allusions. Scholars have noted or demonstrated Ellison's allusions to almost every major writer in the European, American, or African American literary traditions: As Rudolf F. Dietze writes rather hyperbolically, "The more thoroughly familiar one becomes with the work of Ralph Waldo Ellison the fewer are the chances of finding a major literary work published before 1950 that does not have some bearing on *Invisible Man*" (25).

Yet, despite Ellison scholars' all-out search for his literary ancestors, there is still one "invisible" influence on Ellison that has not been studied satisfactorily in Ellison criticism: his indebtedness to early nineteenth-century American literary nationalism. Ellison locates the African American in the typical position of an early nineteenth-century American artist vis-à-vis exclusive European traditions: "The white American has charged the Negro American with being without past or tradition..., just as he himself has been so charged by European and American critics with a nostalgia for the stability once typical of European cultures" (*Shadow* 54). Naturally enough, the African American in Ellison is preoccupied with major themes in the early nineteenth-century nationalist campaign. In other words, Ellison reads race into early nineteenth-century literary nationalism and "African Americanizes" its conspicuous ideologies in his critical writings. No less significant, his strategy of African Americanizing American literary nationalism constitutes the basis of his revisionist aesthetic and informs his complex engagements with the major writers of the American literary tradition.

Although vestiges of the early nineteenth-century nationalist palimpsest are pervasive in Ellison's essays and interviews, only Barbara Fass and John S. Wright have noted Ellison's intertextuality with the nationalist movement. In 1971, Fass observed a "clear" analogy between nineteenth-century American culture's struggling to free itself from European imperialism and the twentieth-century African American's endeavoring to free himself from American paternalism. She also found it "particularly ironic" that "the latter struggle is going on in the land where the former to[o]k place" (321). Ten years later, Wright pointed out that Ellison and "American literary nationalists from Emerson onward" share "the 'organic' theory [of national culture], Herderian in origin," and he went on to find Ellison's uniqueness in the nationalist tradition in his extension of inherited "cultural pluralism and ...egalitarian 'folk ideology,'" with emphasis on "the radical heterogeneity" of the American population (165). Fass's and Wright's perceptive observations hint at Ellison's complex relationship to American literary nationalism, but their insights have not been developed. And since there has, to date, been no article-length study of Ellison's simultaneous dependence on and independence from American literary nationalism, the need exists to investigate thoroughly Ellison's appropriation of early nineteenth-century American literary nationalism and its centrality in his critical vision.

American literary nationalism commenced with the American Revolution, gained its momentum after the War of 1812, and culminated in the 1830s and 1840s. It was propagated by those cultural nationalists of the early republic who, in order to make America's independence from England complete culturally as well as politically, called for native romances, national dramas, or American epics to represent American realities and appeal to Americans' feelings.[3] Since the nationalists' basic orientation was the same, most of their arguments were "repetitive and cumulative" (Ruland xv) and might be subsumed, at the risk of being reductive, under four coterminous rubrics: denunciation of domestic lamentations over America's aesthetic barrenness, criticism of the colonist mentality, differentiation of British literature's belletristic greatness from its ideological implications, and the search for American materials and themes. Nationalists denounced those who lamented the lack of a native literary tradition, a remote antiquity, and literary associations on the American continent. They ascribed the meagerness of American literature not to America's aesthetic barrenness but to the colonist mentality seeking British models and materials in America, and they warned that, unless the colonist mentality were overcome, American writes would remain literary vassals of England. Although they could denounce the depressing influences of British literature, however, nativists could not deny the greatness of the British literary tradition and its masterpieces. This dilemma they resolved by differentiating British works' belletristic greatness from their extraliterary implications, and contending that the monarchic and aristocratic values reflected in British literature were inimical to America's democratic and republican principles. While rejecting such anti-American ideologies, most continued to maintain that an American writer should assimilate the aesthetic and intellectual greatness of British literature. Some proponents of literary nationalism held, on the other hand, that an American writer should study the literatures of ancient Greece, France, and Germany together with British literature in order to negate or neutralize the undemocratic ideologies of the British. After thus defining an American writer's proper relationship to the British literary tradition, nationalist campaigners ransacked America's past and present, and found rich materials for literary exploitation, such as wars against Native Americans, careers of the Revolutionary heroes, and customs and manners of its diverse peoples. With these various raw materials for epics, romances, and fiction of manners, nativists envisioned that American literature would embody distinctively American ideals such as individual liberty, natural rights, democracy, and republicanism.[4]

Although this oversimplified summary does not do justice to the complexity and diversity of the nationalist arguments, it contains most of the prominent issues of the campaign that Ellison repeats and revises in his critical writings. In "Society, Morality, and the Novel," Ellison traces the American "obsession with defining the American experience" back to America's "consciously experimental and revolutionary origins," and explicates the thrust of the nationalists' campaign to differentiate American from European experience and to determine the uniqueness of American civilization. Among the still pertinent issues of cultural nationalism, he argues, the issue of "dealing with the explicitness of the omnipresent American ideal" has been more important and problematic than that of "guarding against superstitious overevaluation of Europe" (*Going* 249). He similarly highlights the significance of American ideals while mentioning early nineteenth-century literary nationalism in his address at West Point, "On Initiation Rites and Power": "By the 1830s, or the late 1820s, several things were being demanded. One, that we have a literature which would be specifically American, which would tell us who we are and how we varied, and how we had grown, and where we are going—and most importantly, how the ideals...were being made manifest within the society" (46-47). Although Ellison thus valorizes American ideals in his explication of American cultural/literary nationalism, the nineteenth-century nationalists and Ellison express a crucial difference in the meaning of American ideals. Whereas the Anglo-Saxon nationalists had in mind such ideals as individual liberty, natural rights, democracy, and republicanism, the African American writer reads race into America's motto "e pluribus unum" and accentuates America's racial diversity, usually phrased "unity-in-diversity" or "oneness-in-manyness." By thus reading the American motto into nationalist arguments, Ellison in fact pits white American discourses against each other, and ultimately redefines American ideals with his unique African American viewpoint. Ellison's problematization and redefinition of American ideals derive mainly from his African American identity, which necessitates "a special perspective" and a "complex double vision" on America's national ideals and conduct (*Shadow* 131-32).

In "What America Would Be Like Without Blacks," Ellison argues that from the beginning of the republic white Americans have used African Americans "as a marker, a symbol of limits, a metaphor for the 'outsider'" in order to define their identity (*Going* 110-11). Ellison might have defined the role of Native Americans in white Americans' self-identification in his *Time* essay, since he sees African Americans as the "surrogates" for Native Americans in a 1976 interview with Robert B. Stepto and Michael S. Harper (434). By identifying the centrality of race in white Americans' self-identification, Ellison ultimately criticizes the racial limitations of American cultural nationalism and discloses its un-Americanness. In fact, early nineteenth-century American cultural nationalism was propagated with an explicit agenda to use Native Americans as disposable literary materials and to deny the existence of African Americans.[5] Hence Jane Tompkins is correct when she notes that white Americans tried to define their identity most strenuously during the period that saw two crucial events in the history of America's race relations: "the founding of the American Colonization Society in 1816 and Monroe's policy of Indian removal formulated in 1824" (110).

But white Americans' tendency to disregard Native Americans and African Americans in their definition of the American started earlier than American cultural nationalism did. Probably the most famous formulation of the American identity at the expense of the Native American and the African American can be found in J. Hector St. John de Crevecoeur's *Letters from an American Farmer*. In "Letter III: What Is an American?" Crevecoeur defines the American by a kind of double dissociation from the European. The American is different from the European in his political privileges: "We have no princes for whom we toil, starve, and bleed....Here man is free as he ought to be, nor is this pleasing equality so transitory as many others are" (67). The American is different from the European in his ethnic diversity as well: The American is "a mixture of English, Scotch, Irish, French, Dutch, Germans, and Swedes" (68). Crevecoeurs's fundamentally Eurocentric definition of the American as a transplanted European banishes from the American community the authentically autochthonous Native American and the pre-Mayflower African American. His definition of the American might be paradigmatic of white Americans' manner of self-identification with what Ellison calls "symbolic acts of disaffiliation" from non-white Americans (*Going* 19).

In a 1958 interview, Ellison would define the African American in terms that curiously remind one of Crevecoeur's definition of the American: African Americans are "a people whose origin began with the introduction of African slaves to the American colonies in 1619, and which today represent the fusing with the original African strains of many racial blood lines—among them English, Irish, Scotch, French, Spanish and American Indian" (*Shadow* 262). As is usual with Ellison, the passage is double-voiced: While defining the African American, Ellison questions and revises Crevecoeur's definition of the American. Ellison's focus on the slave origin and racial heterogeneity of the African American not only discloses the inhuman slavery behind the façade of the eighteenth-century writer's American freedom and equality but also expands the exclusive membership of the French immigrant's American to include the African American and the Native American. Ellison's critique, revision, and expansion of Crevecoeur's American is a prototype of his signifying on the major themes of early nineteenth-century American cultural nationalism.

Like the early nineteenth-century nationalists, Ellison first addresses himself to the tradition of domestic lamentations over America's aesthetic barrenness. The tradition, started as early as 1728 in Richard Lewis's "Dedication to Musipula" (Ruland 29), found its most eloquent expression in Nathaniel Hawthorne's famous enumeration of America's missing materials in his preface to *The Marble Faun*: "No author, without a trial, can conceive of the difficulty of writing a romance about a country where there is no shadow, no antiquity, no mystery, no picturesque and gloomy wrong, nor anything but a commonplace prosperity, in broad and simple daylight, as is happily the case with my dear native land" (5). As Donald M. Kariganer and Malcolm A. Griffith note, Hawthorne's passage, while expressing the skepticism of a writer in a land without cultural and literary traditions, "barely conceals a pride that in this most recalcitrant locale [Americans] have indeed created a literature" (2). Understandably enough however, Ellison, after quoting the passage in full in "Society, Morality, and the Novel," deliberately disregards its ambiguities and rather single-mindedly takes issue with almost every item on Hawthorne's list:

> This is Mr. Hawthorne, and while admiring what he made of his position, one must observe that in this world one finds that which one has the eyes to see. Certainly there was gloomy wrong enough both in the crime against the Indians and in the Peculiar Institution which was shortly to throw the country into conflict; there was enough mystery in Abraham Lincoln's emergence, then in process, still to excite us with wonder; and in that prosperity and "broad and simple daylight" enough evil was brewing to confound us even today. (*Going* 263)

The passage is Ellison's most direct critique of a canonical American writer. Although *Invisible Man* echoes Hawthorne's themes of appearance-and-reality, identity, invisibility, isolation, moral death-and-rebirth, and revolt against authority, the passage criticizes the nineteenth-century writer for his blindness to America's racial realities and explains why Hawthorne rarely figures in Ellison's pantheon of American moral/democratic writers. Ellison situates Hawthorne's list in the context of antebellum race relations and argues that Hawthorne's barren America was in fact a field rich in literary materials with far-reaching resonance. In doing so, Ellison locates race at the core of his predecessor's aesthetic vision and ultimately criticizes the canonical writer's racial limitations, which failed to notice the literary and moral significance of the crimes against Native Americans and African Americans committed "in broad and simple daylight."

Henry James seems to have had in mind what Kartiganer and Griffith call Crevecoeur's "exuberant negativism" (1) when he extended "the items of high civilization" missing from Hawthorne's America to the extent of making them "almost ludicrous" in his Hawthorne (34). Ellison quotes James's famous catalogue right after his critique of Hawthorne, but, contrary to his reading of Hawthorne's passage, he draws the reader's attention to the context of the catalogue and reads there not American despair but an American joke. In other words, he takes his cue from James's ironic reading of Hawthorne and stresses the point that James addressed his remarks to Europeans with his tongue in his cheek (*Going* 263-66).

Unlike his reading of Hawthorne and James, Ellison's interpretation of Richard Wright in the tradition is complex. Wright discards James's ironic tone in translating James's version of the aesthetic barrenness of Hawthorne's America into the cultural bleakness of the African American community in *Black Boy*:

> (After I had outlived the shocks of childhood, after the habit of reflection had been born in me, I used to mull over the strange absence of real kindness in Negroes, how unstable our tenderness, how lacking in genuine passion we were, how void of great hope, how timid our joy, how bare our traditions, how hollow our memories, how lacking we were in those intangible sentiments that bind man to man, and how shallow was even our despair. After I had learned other ways of life I used to brood upon the unconscious irony of those who felt that Negroes led so passional an existence! I saw that what has been taken for our emotional strength was our negative confusions, our flights, our fears, our frenzy under pressure.
> (Whenever I thought of the essential bleakness of black life in America, I knew that Negroes had never been allowed to catch the full spirit of Western civilization, that they lived somehow in it but not of it. And when I brooded upon the cultural barrenness of black life, I wondered if clean, positive tenderness, love, honor, loyalty and the capacity to remember were native with man. I asked myself if these human qualities were not fostered, won, struggled and suffered for, preserved in ritual from one generation to another.) (45)

This is arguably the most negative description of African American life that has come out of the African American community. But Ellison's initial response to Wright's lamentation over the "essential bleakness" and "cultural barrenness" of African American life was far more optimistic. In "Richard Wright's Blues," Ellison first notes Wright's compulsion toward "a profound spiritual vomiting," which is to reject not only the white South but also "that part of the South which lay within" (*Shadow* 92). He goes on to characterize Wright as a rebel who "formulated that rejection negatively, because it was the negative face of the Negro community upon which he looked most often as a child" (92-93). Ellison's portrayal of Wright as rebelling against the South is his creative reading of

Wright's first paragraph. After thus paraphrasing the first paragraph, Ellison quotes only that part of the second paragraph that could support his sympathetic interpretation. He rejects "one critic['s]" negative interpretation of the second paragraph and reads it as "the strongest affirmation" of the African American's capacity for culture. Far from bemoaning the essential bleakness of African American life, Ellison argues, the paragraph in fact denounces the social and historical forces that have "conditioned" African American sensibility and calls upon the African American to struggle for and win Western culture as a Spanish bullfighter confronts and subdues a bull. After representing the African American as a Hemingwayesque hero with discipline and experience, Ellison concludes confidently that Wright had no question about the African American's possession of "all those impulses, tendencies, life, and cultural forms" of Western society (93).

But Ellison's sympathetic reading of Wright's passage in this 1945 essay changed into a diametrically opposed one 20 years later. In "The World and the Jug," Ellison first distinguishes Wright's memories of Mississippi from Ellison's memories of his native Oklahoma. For a good illustration of the difference, Ellison quotes his predecessor's two-paragraph passage in full and observes that Wright's "manner of keeping faith with the Negroes who remained in the depths is quite interesting" (118). The phrase "quite interesting" is his typical understatement, since, in a series of rhetorical questions, he contends that his sense of African American life is "quite different" from Wright's, and he condemns Wright's manner of keeping faith as raising a fundamental question about African American humanity. He denounces Wright as being, in Irving Howe's phrase, "literary to a fault," which means that Wright relied on an inappropriate literary model to describe the African American community (119). More concretely, he traces the genealogy of Wright's passage back to James's items of high civilization absent from Hawthorne's America, and interprets Wright's racial variation on James's ironic catalogue as "his list of those items of high humanity which he found missing among Negroes" (120). In passing his negative verdict on Wright's passage, Ellison understandably reads the first paragraph only and disregards the second paragraph completely. His rebuttal of Wright based on a literal reading of the first paragraph might seem unfair, for Wright in his passage lamented not the absence of African American humanity but "the essential bleakness" and "the cultural barrenness" of African American life. But Ellison does not see any real difference between the two, since to deny possibilities of human fullness and richness to African Americans, even in Mississippi, is, at least, to Ellison, to negate the significance of their "human life" maintained despite harsh realities—and ultimately to deny their humanity. In short, Ellison's point is that African American life in Mississippi was much more varied than that which Wright depicted. Ellison drives his point home most powerfully when he states that "Wright, for all of his indictments, was no less its product than that other talented Mississippian, Leontyne Price" (112).

For Ellison, the example of Wright and Price is the best argument to refute Wright's bleak characterization of African American cultural life. Ellison regards Wright as an interesting "enigma" in that he could not "for ideological reasons depict a Negro as intelligent, as creative, or as dedicated as himself" (120, my emphasis). According to Ellison, the main problem with Wright is that he relied on Marxist ideology rather than on the validity of his own experience in his portrayal of African American life. Ellison's criticism of Wright's reliance on foreign ideologies closely echoes the early nineteenth-century critique of domestic lamenters' dependence on Anglophile orientations: As the nationalists found at the heart of domestic lamentations a colonial mentality, so does Ellison find at the core of Wright's lamentation what W.E.B. Du Bois called the "double-consciousness, [the] sense of always looking at one's self through the eyes of others, of measuring one's soul by the tape of a world that looks on is amused contempt and pity"

(8). Ellison's criticism of *Native Son* turns also on his critique of Wright's double consciousness:

> In *Native Son* Wright began with the ideological proposition that what whites think of the Negro's reality is more important than what Negroes themselves know it to be. Hence, Bigger Thomas was presented as a near-subhuman indictment of white oppression. He was designed to shock whites out of their apathy and end the circumstances out of which Wright insisted Bigger emerged. Here environment is all—and interestingly enough, environment conceived solely in terms of the physical, the non-conscious. (114)

Ellison's denunciation of Wright's reliance on environmentalism is not to deny the harshness of African American life but to argue that the African American is more than the passive product of her or his physical environment. Ellison states that African Americans have dealt with their dehumanizing environment consciously enough to create themselves, "in a limited way," because their lives were after all "no mere abstraction in someone's head" (112-13). For Ellison, Wright's environmentalism, Marxism, and belief in the notion of literature as weapon are in the final analysis the very "abstractions" in non-African American scholars' heads (114, 120). Since Wright bought foreign ideology at the expense of the validity of African American experience, maintains Ellison, Wright distorted the complexity of African American life and emphasized African Americans' "hatred, fear and vindictiveness," while disregarding equally significant characteristics, such as "their resistance to provocation, their coolness under pressure, their sense of timing and their tenacious hold on the ideal of their ultimate freedom" (114).

For Ellison, African American cultural manifestations are true to the African American spirit, since they affirm African American experience and reject white American values. A case in point is African American choreography. Ellison traces the origin of African American choreography back to the dancing of those slaves who imitated at the yard of a plantation manor house their masters' grave European steps and then "added to them their own special flair, burlesquing the white folks and then going on to force the steps into a choreography uniquely their own" (*Going* 223). He continues to elaborate on the slaves' appropriation of a European cultural form and its mocking element:

> The whites, looking out at the activity in the yard thought that they were being flattered by imitation and were amused the incongruity of tattered blacks dancing courtly steps, while missing completely the fact that before their eyes a European cultural form was becoming Americanized, undergoing a metamorphosis through the mocking activity of a people partially sprung from Africa. So, blissfully unaware, the whites laughed while the blacks danced out their mocking reply. (223-24)[6]

The dancing slaves are the supreme personifications of what Ellison calls "the vernacular process"; that is, the eclectic "amalgamation" of traditional cultures with "native folk and popular" viewpoints, a dynamic process of appropriation which Ellison regards as the gist of American culture (Reed et al. 143). He also calls the process "Americanization" and finds its examples in a wide range of American cultural manifestations, such as architecture, costume, cuisine, dance, language, literature, music, tools, and technology. He sees the vernacular process as "a gesture toward perfection" in that "the styles and techniques of the past are adjusted to the needs of the present," and, more specifically, the aristocratic styles and techniques of the past are "democratized," as is tellingly demonstrated by the slaves' appropriation of European courtly steps (*Going*

139-40). Hence the vernacular process is almost synonymous with "the democratic process" in Ellison (141).

Ellison dates the origin of American cultural nationalism from early colonial times when, he argues, the vernacular process, the gist of the American way to establish and discover "national identity," started with interaction among Europeans, Africans, and American geography (140, 142). Most significantly, he situates the African slaves at the origin of the nationalist movement: The slaves' combination of their masters' European music and religion with their African heritage set the definitive pattern of Americanizing foreign cultures with native perspectives (143). He makes this point clearly in his interview with Stepto and Harper: African Americans have contributed to "the evolution of a specifically American culture" from the very beginning of the nation and have often provided white American artists with "a clue for their own improvisations. " He maintains that the slaves were placed in the prestigious position of originating specifically American cultural idioms, ironically by circumstance of their enslavement: They could be "culturally daring and innovative" simply because they were, unlike their Eurocentric masters, free from "the strictures of 'good taste' and 'thou shall-nots' of tradition" (Stepto and Harper 431).

Thus Ellison's explication of the vernacular process praises the slaves' cultural freedom and criticizes their masters' cultural enslavement. Ellison highlights the fact that the vernacular process operated in defiance of "the social, aesthetic, and political assumptions of [American] political leaders and tastemakers." He denounces their duplicity by disclosing their Anglo and Europhilic propensities when he points out that they "boasted" new spirit and outlook but "still looked to England and the Continent for their standards of taste." Consequently, he asserts, the slaves were more American and dedicated, since they, in their own unobserved fashion, gave expression to the uniquely American experience with whatever cultural elements they could find from their surroundings (*Going* 141-142). As the slaves burlesqued their masters' colonial mentality that prized European models and styles at the expense of American ones, Ellison argues, Duke Ellington would mock white Americans' "double standards, hypocrisies, and pretensions" with his remark that Fate did not intend him "to be to famous too young" when a Pulitzer Prize committee, too concerned with European musical standards, declined to give him a special award for music (223). Significantly enough, Ellison criticizes white Americans' colonial mentality that has failed to recognize or appreciate quintessentially American composers and musical forms by evoking the very spirit of American literary nationalism:

> In a country which began demanding the projection of its own unique experience in literature as early as the 1820s, it was ironic that American composers were expected to master the traditions, conventions, and sub[t]leties of European music and to force their own American musical sense of life into the forms created by Europe's greatest composers. Thus the history of American classical music has been marked by a struggle to force American experience into European forms. (224)

Here Ellison criticizes the American classical musical tradition for having failed to live up to the spirit of American cultural nationalism. More precisely, by portraying Ellington as the representative American composer, he denounces the tradition's racial exclusivity that denies Ellington due recognition simply because of his race and African American musical form. Fittingly enough, then, Ellison reads in the musician's works and manners a mockery of the "inadequacies" of American myths, legends, conduct, and standards (225).

Ellison's emphasis on African Americans' mockery and rejection of white Americans' colonial mentality and racial limitations reminds one of earlier American cultural nationalists' strategies to negate or neutralize exclusionist and imperialistic dimensions of British literature. One strategy, suggested by Orestes A. Brownson in "Specimens of Foreign Literature," was to maintain a distinctly American perspective by playing British literature off against other European literatures (437-39). Ellison echoes Brownson's tactic in the Introduction to *Shadow and Act*, where he reveals that he wanted to "find [his] own voice" through the main tradition of American literature with the aid of "what [he] could learn from the literatures of Europe" (xix). Indeed, he situates himself in the tradition of American democratic and moral writers, a tradition which he constructs partly with the help of the insights and visions of such European writers as Fyodor Dostoevsky, James Joyce, and André Malraux, to name a few. But his usual manner of engagement with the American literary tradition is to accept transcendent elements of the tradition while rejecting its allegedly immoral, racist, and undemocratic undertones—the very strategy of many nineteenth-century nationalists, who differentiated the aesthetic greatness of British literature from its aristocratic ideologies.

In a 1973 interview with Hollie West, Ellison recalls the American strategy:

> Americans had to create themselves. We had to be conscious of language in a way that English people did not have to be. It was their mother tongue. It was our mother tongue but we were in rebellion against it—against the values on which it was based, which were those of kin[g]ship. We didn't reject the great traditions of British literature, the King James version of the Bible, Shakespeare or the great poets, but we rejected the values which enspirited that language and we began to try to discover how to create an American literature. This was consciously stated over and over by many people. (37)

Ellison summarizes succinctly the American strategy of appropriation while arguing for the African American influence on American literature. In a sense, he suggests an African American origin of American cultural/literary nationalism in the same way that he locates slave-dancers at the origin of American cultural manifestations. From the same perspective, Ellison asserts that African Americans have "a highly developed ability to abstract desirable qualities from those around them, even from their enemies" (*Shadow* xx), and that African American folklore "took what it needed to express its sense of life and rejected what it couldn't use" (*Going* 283).

In his 1964 review of LeRoi Jones's *Blues People*, Ellison ascribes the African American strategy to the peculiar situation of African slaves in colonial times: The slaves, "with the ruthlessness of those without articulate investments in cultural styles, [took] whatever they could of European music, making of it that which would, when blended with the cultural tendencies inherited from Africa, express their own sense of life—while rejecting the rest" (*Shadow* 255). He also maintains that the tactic of simultaneous acceptance and rejection was one of the "survival strategies" encoded in African American folklore that warns against "embrac[ing] uncritically" white values in rejection of "the validity, even the sacredness" of the African American experience (*Going* 179; *Shadow* 166). But Ellison perfectly knows that the strategy of acceptance and rejection, which he calls "identification and rejection," is not an (African) American monopoly, since he finds it in Jawaharlal Nehru's *Toward Freedom* as well as in Wright's *Black Boy* (78).

In a 1965 interview with James Thompson, Lennox Raphael, and Steve Cannon, Ellison defines "identification and rejection" as a pattern to "identify with what a writer has written, with its form, its manners, techniques, while rejecting the writer's beliefs, his prejudices, philosophy, [and] values." He finds its best examples in Jewish American writers' appropriations of T.S. Eliot, James Joyce, and Ernest Hemingway. According to Ellison, Jewish American writers identified with the canonical figures "as writers" while rejecting their racial, religious, and political views in order to express their own sense of reality and definition of the American experience (*Going* 278). Ellison, then, appropriates the very position of the Jewish American writer when he defines his relationship to American literary tradition: "...my sense of reality could reject bias while appreciating the truth revealed by achieved art" (*Shadow* xx).

The strategy of "identification and rejection"—variously termed "embracing and distancing" (Lyne 323) or "engagement and revision" (Benston, "Introduction" 4)—lies at the heart of Ellison's critical vision.[7] In fact, the complex tactic has become his second nature, probably because he started his literary career with book reviews, combining praise and criticism. Even in his first publication, "Creative and Cultural Lag," he approves Waters Edward Turpin's exploration of "the rich deep materials of the Negro" in *These Low Grounds* but denounces the characters' "lack of historical and political consciousness" (90-91). Ellison's pattern continues in his reviews of Gunnar Myrdal's *An American Tragedy* and LeRoi Jones's *Blues People*: He joins "in the chorus of 'Yeas'" while "utter[ing] a lusty and simultaneous 'Nay'" to Myrdal's book; he approves of Jones's attempts to see the blues in a larger context but questions some of his assumptions (*Shadow* 303, 248). This duality also informs Ellison's reading of his literary "ancestors" and "relatives": He admires Hawthorne's belletristic achievements but criticizes his blindness to America's racial realities; he agrees with Hemingway regarding the importance of *Huckleberry Finn* in the tradition of the American novel but takes issue with "his dismissal of its ethical intention"; he recognizes *Native Son* as Wright's achievement to "define the human condition" as seen from a specific African American perspective "at a given time in a given place" but refuses to see Bigger Thomas as "any final image" of an African American personality (*Going* 263, 268; *Shadow* 118). Similarly, Ellison praises the Founding Fathers' democratic and egalitarian ideals as revealed in what he calls America's "sacred documents" but denounces their "mystification," "blatant hypocrisy," "racial pride," or "failure of nerve" motivated by their hierarchical status and economic interests (*Going* 332-35). His customary tribute to Abraham Lincoln is also qualified by his hint at the President's "vacillation, procrastination, and rescissions" prior to the Emancipation Proclamation (80). Even his theories of the novel are colored by the conflicting pattern: Ellison recognizes the "artistic perfection" of "the tight well-made Jamesian novel" but denounces its concern as too belletristic and parochial to contain the diversity of American life; he regards the language of the hard-boiled novel as a supreme achievement of twentieth-century American writing but finds it still "embarrassingly austere" when compared with African American idiomatic expression, full of "imagery and gesture and rhetorical canniness" (*Shadow* 103). He also maintains, paradoxically, that true novels "would preserve as they destroy, affirm as they reject" (114). Lastly, the pattern of identification and rejection is the very vision at which Ellison's nameless protagonist arrives in the Epilogue of *Invisible Man*: "So it is that now I denounce and defend, or feel prepared to defend. I condemn and affirm, say no and say yes, say yes and say no" (566).

The invisible narrator acquires this vision after he has interpreted his grandfather's deathbed riddle as advice to affirm the principle of America's sacred documents but to denounce its manipulators and corrupters (561). His decoding of the grandfather's cryptic message is in fact Ellison's own stance toward the political documents, the stance which he first learned while working in an Oklahoma barbershop. In "Perspective of Literature," Ellison recalls listening to barbershop conversations of the affair of a Mr. Harrison, an African American lawyer, who, Ellison states, was expelled from Oklahoma because of his excellent legal skill. What he found interesting in the conversations was that the African Americans taking part in the conversations "directed their disapproval not so much against law in general, but against those persons and forces that imposed the law undemocratically" (*Going* 323). As if to echo those African Americans, Ellison repeatedly expresses his belief in the spirit of America's democratic documents, but not in their application. But this does not mean that he finds no problem in the documents per se. He judges them to be self-contradictory and problematic since they both affirm and negate equality and freedom: "In the beginning," writes he, "was not only the word, but the contradiction of the word" (243). He understands that all great democratic documents "contain a strong charge of anti-democratic elements." In the face of the contradiction, he suggests the strategy of identification and rejection:

> Perhaps the wisest attitude for democrats is not to deplore the ambiguous elements of democratic writings but to seek to understand them. For it is by making use of the positive contributions of such documents and rejecting their negative elements that democracy can be kept dynamic. (*Shadow* 304)

Since he believes that "the interests of art and democracy converge" (*Invisible* xvi), Ellison in this passage expresses the clearest reason that he uses the tactic of identification and rejection in his engagements with democratic and literary traditions. In short, he identifies with the positive qualities of a tradition and rejects its negative qualities in order to affirm and expand its fundamental and redeeming principles.

Identification and rejection, then, lead ultimately to what Ellison calls "antagonistic cooperation," which means simultaneously to cooperate and resist in the spirit of "an it-takes-two-to-tango binary response" (*Going* 7). Ellison hints at the spirit of antagonistic cooperation in his open debate with Stanley Edgar Hyman, whom he characterizes as "an intellectual sparring partner," and he first used the term at the end of "The World and the Jug" when he asked Irving Howe to regard their open debate as "an act of...'antagonistic co-operation'" (*Shadow* 45, 143). Although he discovers the process of antagonistic cooperation also in the relationship between an artist and her or his audience, Ellison finds the supreme example of antagonistic cooperation in jazz musicians' jam sessions (*Going* 7, 29). Ellison's much-quoted definition of jazz is probably the best explanation of antagonistic cooperation: "true jazz is an art of individual assertion within and against the group. Each true jazz moment...springs from a contest in which each artist challenges all the rest; each solo flight, or improvisation, represents...a definition of his identity: as individual, as member of the collectivity and as a link in the chain of tradition" (*Shadow* 234). The Ellisonian jazz artist must express his uniqueness through his antagonistic engagements with his musical tradition. More concretely, the jazz musician should demonstrate his individuality in tone while maintaining the musical harmony between his own voice and other musicians' voices during group improvisation.

The harmonious balance between a jazzman and his group during a jam session is Ellison's metaphor for the ideal relationship between an artist and his tradition. For Ellison, jazzmen are more than artists; they personify the Renaissance Man. Just as the Renaissance Man represented "an idea of human versatility and possibility," so jazz musicians were "artistically free and exuberantly creative adventurers" who had made the maximum use of the little freedom lying within their musical restrictions and social limitations (xiv, xiii). Thus the "delicate balance" between a jazzman and his group has extramusical implications for Ellison, who regards this balance as a "marvel of social organization" reflecting the spirit of antagonistic cooperation (189). In other words, Ellison argues, "the lyrical ritual elements of folk jazz" embody "a supreme democracy in which each individual cultivate[s] his uniqueness and yet d[oes] not clash with his neighbors" (300).

Naturally enough, then, Ellison reads the spirit of antagonistic cooperation in the sociohistorical context of America's race relations, and maintains that Americans of various backgrounds have used their experiences and values "as sources of morale" in the "continuing process of antagonistic cooperation," the process of "adjusting the past to the present in the interest of the future" (*Going* 26). In all these instances, Ellison argues, antagonistic cooperation has enhanced "the original theme" (129). Indeed, Ellison himself has enhanced the original theme of American cultural nationalism by participating in the American debate on national culture in the spirit of antagonistic cooperation and revising the monologic cultural ideologies of the early nineteenth century to the needs of the dialogic social context of the twentieth century.

In his last effort to revise the nineteenth-century nationalists, Ellison takes issue with their representations of the Native American. Nationalists did not portray the Native American realistically in his own terms but delineated him fictively according to the Homeric, Ossianic, Gothic, or Roussauistic models, for they incorporated him with a specific role into their master plan of American literature. Whether depicted as a noble hero or a diabolic antihero, the Native American was, in the final analysis, no better than a foil to an Anglo-Saxon American hero in the nationalist imagination. He was ultimately the personification of dissolution, death, and disappearance, and, even in symbolic roles, was associated only with the dark side of human imagination, such as the somber, the terrible, and the pathetic. Hence he was rarely endowed with such quintessential Americanism as American ideals and manners in the nationalist agenda.[8] Ellison questions and refutes the nationalists' characterization of the Native American obliquely with his representation of the African American because African Americans are the "surrogates" for Native Americans in Ellison (Stepto and Harper 434).[9] Indeed, he inverts the racial dichotomy of the nationalist imagination when he sees "the mixture of the marvelous and the terrible" as "a basic condition of human life" and finds "the essence of the terrible" in the white American community while endowing the African American community with a sense of the marvelous (*Shadow* 20-21). He also challenges the nationalists' profession of American ideals indirectly when he contends that African American slaves took the essence of the aristocratic and Christian ideals more seriously than did their masters (xviii). Thus, finding "sources of strength" in the African American slave past, he affirms those things which are "warm and meaningful" in African American life and the African American community: courage, faith, humor, independence, optimism, patience, and sense of life (269, 7, 21). He celebrates African Americans' democratic, human, and moral qualities, partly because they are quintessentially American attitudes and values. For instance, he finds the main significance of the Civil Rights Movement in the fact that the best of the American tradition—"the moral and physical courage"—found its most eloquent expression through African Americans (Geller 18). In a similar vein, he argues that "the most dramatic fight for American ideals" has been sparked by African Americans in accordance with "American Constitutionalism" (*Shadow* 270). Even in discussing African Americans' concern with names and naming, he contends that African Americans, not their white "relatives" across the color line, are the true inheritors of the admirable qualities possessed by the original bearers of their common family names (149). His argument is an indirect attack on the hypocrisy or duplicity of the American cultural nationalism that was first propagated with a divided agenda to affirm a democratic and free society while retaining slavery (Reed et al. 137). In conclusion, after denouncing the racial limitations of the nationalist campaign, he portrays African Americans as the true inheritors of American ideals and makes them "a source of moral strength to America"

(*Shadow* 17), thereby ultimately contesting nineteenth-century nationalists' assumption of the representative American.

Ellison regards American civilization not as an independent thing in itself but as "a continuation of a European civilization" and finds its uniqueness in Americans' "variations upon...[and] amplification of" European themes (*Going* 312). One can similarly characterize Ellison's African American cultural nationalism as a continuation of American cultural nationalism and find his uniqueness in his "racial" variations on and amplifications of American themes, since he repeats, challenges, reinterprets, and expands major themes of American cultural nationalism by substituting "race" for "nation" and translating the American/British dichotomy into an African American/Anglo-Saxon American one. In other words, as his most famous protagonist situates himself in "the great American tradition of tinkers" and taps a power line from Monolpolated Light & Power to illuminate "the blackness of [his] invisibility" (7, 13), so Ellison aligns himself with the tradition of early nineteenth-century American cultural/literary nationalism and appropriates its power ultimately to affirm his African American identity.

Of course, Ellison is not the only African American writer to use this strategy of appropriation in African American literature. The strategy was first used by the writers of antebellum slave narratives in African American literary history. Zora Neale Hurston, in "Characteristics of Negro Expression," calls the strategy "modification" and states that the African American, while living in the midst of a white civilization, has reinterpreted "everything...he touche[d]...for his own use" (230). Wright anticipates Ellison's "identification and rejection" perfectly when he recalls in *Black Boy* that he and his childhood friends "always twisted [Bible stories], secularized them to the level of [their] street life, rejecting all meanings that did not fit into [their] environment" (92-93). Moreover, he makes the classic statement of the tactic in "How 'Bigger' Was Born": "I took these [white writers'] techniques, these ways of seeing and feeling and twisted them, bent them, adapted them, until they became my way of apprehending the locked-in life of the Black Belt areas" (*Native* xvi).

But Ellison uses and theorizes the African American tactic throughout his works more arduously and persistently than any other writer. He quotes Wright's classic statement on the African American strategy, significantly enough, in his first important literary essay, "Recent Negro Fiction" (24-25). He echoes the strategy in characterizing his and his boyhood friends' self-projection as "Renaissance Men": Their activity "expressed a yearning to make any – and everything of quality Negro American; to appropriate it, possess it, re-create it in [their] own group and individual images" (*Shadow* xvii). He has the tactic in mind even when he defines his fiction as "the agency" of his efforts to answer one of his perennial questions: "What does American society mean when regarded out of my own eyes, when informed by my own sense of the past and viewed by my own complex sense of the present?" (xxii). It is also the strategy of appropriation through identification and rejection that lies at the core of his life-long negotiations with the canonical writers in the American literary tradition.

Ellison's negotiation with T.S. Eliot provides a case in point. Ellison acknowledges his indebtedness to Eliot on several occasions and even confesses that his reading of *The Waste Land* was his "real transition into writing" (159). Ellison also reveals that the neoclassicist poet made him conscious of the elements and "traditions" that went into the creation of literature (*Going* 40). Indeed, Eliot's essay "Tradition and the Individual's Talent," which contends that a new artist alters the tradition while he is directed by it, has had an indelible influence on Ellison's revisionist aesthetic. Suffice it to note that jazz, the quintessential art form in Ellison, is explained in Eliotic terms: The jazz tradition "insist[s] that each artist achieve his creativity within its frame"; the jazz musician, therefore, "must learn the best of the past, and add to it his personal vision" (*Shadow* 189).

More often that not, however, Ellison makes a subtle change of Eliot when he alludes to his literary ancestor. In the "Preface" to *For Lancelot Andrews*, Eliot describes the general viewpoint of the collected essays, published partly to "refute any accusation of playing 'possum,'" as "classicist in literature, royalist in politics, and anglo-catholic in religion" (ix). As if intrigued by the incongruity between the Americanism of "playing possum" and the un-American viewpoints, Ellison characterizes African American culture in terms that curiously echo Eliot in a 1958 interview: "Its spiritual outlook is basically Protestant, its system of kinship is Western, its time and historical sense are American (United States), and its secular views are those professed, ideally at least, by all the people of the United States" (*Shadow* 262-63). In his emphasis on America, Ellison indirectly criticizes his predecessor's fundamentally Eurocentric viewpoint and questions the "ideal" and "complete" order of the Eliotic tradition. Ellison signifies on *The Waste Land* from a similar perspective. What initially interested him in the poem was its jazz-like rhythms and range of allusion, "as mixed and as varied as that of Louis Armstrong" (159-60).

In a 1965 interview with Richard Kostelanetz for the BBC, Ellison elaborated on this point and stated that he found in the poem "overtones of a sort of religious pattern" that could be identified with the African American religious community and "a style of improvisation" that was very close to jazz. The similarity of *The Waste Land* and jazz was inevitable, Ellison continues, since both grew out of "a similar and quite American approach to the classics"; that is, to "take a theme and start improvising." Ellison identifies the poem with jazz by interpreting the poet's "ruthless assault" on and "irreverent reverence" for the literature of the past as literary translations of jazz musicians' almost iconoclastic appropriation of classical and religious music (4). For instance, Eliot's eclecticism—his "snatching of phrases from the German, from the French, from the Sanskrit, and so on"—is in harmony with jazz musicians' eclectic appropriation of musical traditions—sacred, classical, and secular (*Going* 40). It comes as no surprise to Ellison, then,"that at least as early as T.S. Eliot's creation of a new aesthetic for poetry through the artful juxtapositioning of earlier styles, Louis Armstrong, way down the river in New Orleans, was working out a similar technique for jazz" (*Shadow* 225). In identifying Eliot with Armstrong, Ellison resituates the Eurocentric poet/critic in the American context and reconceives him in African American cultural terms. In so doing, he suggests the African American influence on the poet and reinterprets the Eliotic tradition as meaning not only the classical tradition but also the various cultural/racial traditions of America (Kostelanetz 4-5). Thus Ellison ultimately claims the Eliotic tradition by reading jazz into the poet.

Relatedly, Ellison praises and claims Stephen Crane and Hemingway as his literary ancestors by filling in the understated backgrounds of their works: He reads Crane's critique of America's "tendency toward moral evasion" in *The Red Badge of Courage*, a book that has only one African American character (68), and paradoxically he finds Hemingway's affirmation of American values and morality in his explicit denial of them (*Going* 255). Ellison deliberately misreads or overreads Crane's and Hemingway's understatements. Kimberly W. Benston finds "this strategy of 'misprision'" at the heart of Ellison's confrontation with tradition generally: Ellison "claims for Wright's *Black Boy* a 'ritual' and 'blues' thrust which [are]...actually repudiated by that book" and "overreads the blues into Hemingway's fiction," thereby including "two essentially non-blues writers" into his blues tradition ("Ellison" 343). Robert G. O'Meally also notes the misprision in Ellison's debates with Hyman and Howe: "In fact, in his attempts to correct what he saw as these critics' distortions of the Afro-American image, he scatters the form and substance of certain of their literary theories, twisting them, sometimes unfairly, to serve his own purposes" (Craft 164).

As he reads jazz into Eliot, morality into Crane and Hemingway, and the blues into Wright and Hemingway to claim them, so Ellison reads blackness, race, slavery, democracy, and morality into the American Renaissance to claim its tradition. He argues that, from 1776 to 1876, there was a conception of democracy "that allowed the writer to identify himself with the Negro." According to Ellison, "Whitman, Emerson, Thoreau, Hawthorne, Melville and Mark Twain" could identify themselves with the African American slave, since slavery "was a vital issue in the American consciousness, symbolic of the condition of Man, and a valid aspect of the writer's reality" (*Shadow* 98). His 1945 reading of these canonical writers is original and interesting, but far from being convincing since even his own critique of Hawthorne's racial limitations, as I have demonstrated earlier, undoes his praise of the romancer's democratic vision. Therefore, although most scholars have tended to accept Ellison's interpretation of nineteenth-century writers uncritically, R.W.B. Lewis was right when he questioned Ellison's assertion that the slave and slavery were central to the canonical writers' imaginations. Lewis identifies Ellison's reading of the canonical writers with "Eliot's Protestant American reading of Donne and Dante": Both are "the critical paraphrase by which every authentic writer creates a new literary tradition for himself, to suit his artistic needs and abilities" (10).

Ellison has never been blind to the canonical writers' racism, as his acceptance speech for National Book Award amply demonstrates. While locating himself in their tradition, he reinterprets the image of the African American in their writings only after understanding their racial ideas: "Whatever they thought of my people per se, in their imaginative economy the Negro symbolized both the man lowest down and the mysterious, underground aspect of human personality" (*Shadow* 104; my emphasis). Ellison's passage clearly differentiates the image of the African American in the canonical writers' "imaginative economy" from their conceptions of the African American in real life. He similarly reveals the fictionality of his construct of the democratic themes in American literature when he confesses that, while writing *Invisible Man*, he wanted to "relate [him]self to certain important and abiding themes which were present—or which [he] thought were present—in the best of American literature" (*Going* 45).

Ellison's reading blues, jazz, morality, democracy, blackness, race, or slavery into the canonical writers, then, evidences his covert allusion to the racial limitations that complicate and undo their liberating visions. We can find a case in point also in Ellison's negotiations with Eliot. Ellison's racial variations on the Eliotic tradition ultimately make one reread Eliot's theory of the artistic tradition. Indeed, "Tradition and the Individual Talent" contains problematic implications that do not allow an easy appropriation by an African American writer. The problem of Eliot's neoclassical paradigm is best demonstrated when one reads race into it, for race, while not a category in Eliot's essay, was of some concern to Eliot, whose search for the tradition embodying "the Mind of Europe" made the concept of race implicit. If the tradition was understood to be comprised of exclusively European literatures, literatures of other cultures and races were handicapped from the start. Eliot's construct of the tradition was a sophisticated Eurocentric fiction that effectively disqualified literary works of other races with "aesthetic" criteria that valorized only European standards. His construct of the tradition evinced the critical apotheosis of the long-held Eurocentric assumption that literature as the quintessence of human culture was a European monopoly.

Eliot's racial idea, bracketed skillfully in "Tradition and the Individual Talent," showed itself in his reformation of the tradition in the context of the American scene in his 1933 lectures at the University of Virginia. There he argued that "the chances for the re-establishment of a native culture" in America were better in the South than in the North, partly because the South had been "less invaded by foreign races" than the North, in which "the influx of foreign populations ha[d] almost effaced" a tradition (*After* 15-17). He continued to maintain that tradition involved human activities that "represent[ed] the blood kinship of 'the same people living in the same place'" (18). For Eliot, race was thus a significant condition congenial to the establishment of a tradition. He betrayed his racism in the notorious passage "...reasons of race and religion combine to make any large number of free-thinking Jews undesirable" (20). Even though Eliot does not mention the African American or the Native American specifically, his elitist and aristocratic view on literature, emphasis on racial homogeneity, and anti-Semitism do not make it difficult to guess his opinion on American racial minorities.[10] From the viewpoint of the American racial minorities, then, Eliot's Eurocentric construct of the tradition is, as Henry Louis Gates, Jr., has interpreted it, a literary equivalent of the "grandfather clause" ("Writing" 4). Hence, Ellison claims the Eliotic tradition through his identification with Eliot's revisionist frame and rejection of the poet's racial limitations.

As in the case if his negotiation with Eliot, Ellison upholds and undermines his literary ancestors at the same time. To use his own rhetoric, he has enjoyed the comic and almost hilarious game of wearing his traditionalist mask, hiding his revisionist face in his incongruous and fluid America. After all, his struggle as a writer has been "a desperate battle" usually fought "in silence"—"a guerilla action in a larger war" (*Shadow* 122). He seems merely to follow his white American literary ancestors when he recalls the canonical writers through direct references to their names, oblique echoes of their passages and scenes, comic paraphrases of their key concepts, and ironic repetitions of their characterization, symbolism, imagery, and narrative structure. As befits a man who shows a healthy distrust of all "trustee[s] of consciousness," however, his repetitions of the canonical writers are "never quite on the beat" (*Invisible* 88, 8). The off-beat allusions to the canonical writers defamiliarize their most prominent ideas, rhetoric, symbols, and visions, thereby baring the incongruities of their ideas, rhetoric, and symbols, disclosing their racial limitations, and ultimately reformulating their abstract visions in the context of America's race relations. As in the case of his signifying allusions to early nineteenth-century literary nationalism, Ellison's responses to the canonical writers' (unintended) calls are in the final analysis antiphonal and dialogic, since they contain his ironic comments, comic satires, devastating critiques, ruthless rejections, and creative reformulations, as well as the ultimate expansion of his literary ancestors. His racial variations on American themes are, then, his way "to make some small contribution" and "offer some necessary modifications" to American literature with his unique African American perspective (*Shadow* xix).

NOTES

1. See Baker, *Journey* and *Blues*; Gates *Figures* and *Signifying*, O'Meally; Smith; and Stepto.

2. See *Black World* 20.2; Bloom; *CLA Journal* 13; *Delta* 18; Gottesman; Harper and Wright; Hersey; O'Meally, *New*; and Reilly.

3. Although most contemporary writers and journalists joined in the nationalist campaign, its major proponents were Orestes A. Brownson, Edward Tyrell Channing, William Ellery Channing, Timothy Dwight, Ralph Waldo Emerson, Philip Freneau, David Humphreys, Grenville Mellen, John Gortham Palfrey, Theophilus Parsons, William Gimore Simms, Jared Sparks, William Tudor, Royall Tyler, Robert Walsh, and G.M.

Wharton. See Ruland and Spiller for comprehensive selections of nationalist writings during the period, and Spencer for a good study of the nationalist campaign.

4. See Brownson, "American" and "Specimens"; Edward Tyrell Channing; Emerson, "The American Scholar" and "The Poet"; Humphreys; Parsons; and Walsh.

5. See Brownson, "Literature"; Mellen, Palfrey; Simms; Sparks; Tudor; and Wharton.

6. Ellison, in his 1964 review of LeRoi Jones's *Blues People*, first highlights the elements of burlesque or satire in the slaves' music and dance and criticizes the "social and cultural snobbery" of white Americans that led to their failing to notice these elements: "The effectiveness of Negro music and dance is first recorded in the journals and letters of travelers but it is important to remember that they saw and understood only that which they were prepared to accept. Thus a Negro dancing a courtly dance appeared comic from the outside simply because the dancer was a slave. But to the Negro dancing it...burlesque or satire might have been the point, which might have been difficult for a white observer to even imagine" (*Shadow* 255-56).

Ellison's statement of white travelers' blindness to the satiric element, however, is not correct and can be easily refuted by, among other things, Nicholas Cresswell's journal entry written sometime between 1774 and 1777: "In [the black slaves'] songs they generally relate the usage they have received from their Masters or Mistresses in a very satirical stile [sic] and manner" (qtd. In Gates, *Signifying* 66).

7. African American scholars have found the strategy in most areas of African American cultures and literature and, echoing Ellison consciously or unconsciously called it "'differentiation' within repetition" (Snead 65), "productive misunderstanding" (Ostendorf vii), or "repetition with a difference, a signifying black difference" (Gates, "Criticism" 3).

8. See Brownson, "Literature"; Mellen; Palfrey; Simms; Sparks; Tudor; and Wharton.

9. This is not to suggest that Ellison identifies the African American with the Native American in every respect. He differentiates them clearly in their destinies (*Going* 299), but identifies their symbolic roles in the white American imagination. His identification seems to have derived partly from the African American-Native American "confusion" in the African American community of Oklahoma City during his childhood (*Shadow* 158). See also *Going* 132-33 and *Shadow* 156-57 for Ellison's understanding of African American-Native American relationships.

10. Eliot understands that the repository of culture is the dominant élite class of a society. Though he recognizes the role of the lower classes as producers of culture, Eliot minimizes their role as conscious consumers, preservers, and transmitters of culture. His élitist view of culture in a society can easily be expanded into a worldwide scene: While other societies may produce cultures, these can be transmitted as significant cultures to posterity only after being endorsed by the élitist European societies. See Soldo on Eliot's élitism and its American background.

WORKS CITED

Baker, Houston A., Jr. *Blues, Ideology, and Afro-American Literature: A Vernacular Theory*. Chicago: U of Chicago P, 1984.

_____. *The Journey Back: Issues in Black Literature and Criticism*. Chicago: U of Chicago P, 1980.

Benston, Kimberly W. "Ellison, Baraka, and the Faces of Tradition." *Boundary* 2 6 (1978): 333-54.

______. "Introduction: The Masks of Ralph Ellison." Benston, *Speaking* 3-8.

______. ed. *Speaking for You: The Vision of Ralph Ellison*. Washington: Howard UP, 1987.

Black World 20.2 (1970): 1-125.

Bloom, Harold, ed. *Ralph Ellison*. New York: Chelsea House, 1986.

Brownson, Orestes A. "American Literature." *The Works of Orestes A. Brownson*. Ed. Henry F. Brownson. 20 vols. Detroit: Thorndike Nourse, 1885. 19: 22-39.

______. "Literature, Love, and Marriage." *Brownson's Quarterly Review* ns 1 (1864): 315-39.

______. "Specimens of Foreign Literature." *Boston Quarterly Review* 1 (1838): 433-44.

Busby, Mark. *Ralph Ellison*. Boston: Twayne, 1991.

Channing, Edward Tyrell. "On Models in Literature." *North American Review* 3 (1816): 202-09.

Channing, William Ellery. "National Literature." *Christian Examiner* 36 (1830): 269-95.

CLA Journal 13 (1970). 217-320.

Crevecoeur, J. Hector St. John de. *Letters from an American Farmer and Sketches of Eighteenth-Century America*. Ed. Albert E. Stone. New York: Penguin, 1986.

Delta 18 (1984): 1-131.

Dietze, Rudolf F. "Crainway and Son: Ralph Ellison's *Invisible Man* as Seen Through the Perspective of Twain, Crane, and Hemingway." *Delta* 18 (1984): 25-46.

Du Bois, W.E.B. *The Souls of Black Folk*. 1903 New York: Vintage, 1990.

Eliot, T.S. *After Strange Gods*. New York: Harcourt, 1934.

_____. *For Lancelot Andrews: Essays on Style and Order*. London: Faber & Gwyer, 1928.

_____. "Tradition and the Individual Talent." 1917 *Selected Essays*. London: Faber and Faber, 1980. 13-22.

Ellison, Ralph. "Creative and Cultural Lag." *New Challenge* 2 (1937): 90-91.

_____. *Going to the Territory*. New York: Random, 1986.

_____. *Invisible Man*. 30th anniv. ed. New York: Vintage, 1982.

_____. "Recent Negro Fiction." *New Masses* 40 (5 Aug. 1941): 22-26.

_____. *Shadow and Act*. 1964. New York: Vintage, 1972.

Emerson, Ralph Waldo. "The American Scholar." Emerson, *Complete* 1: 81-115.

_____. *The Complete Works of Ralph Waldo Emerson*. Ed. Edward Waldo Emerson, 12 vols. Boston: Houghton, 1903-04.

_____. "The Poet." *Emerson, Complete* 3: 3-42.

Fass, Barbara. "Rejection of Paternalism: Hawthorne's 'My Kinsman Major Molineux' and Ellison's *Invisible Man*." *CLA Journal* 14 (1971): 317-23.

Gates, Henry Louis, Jr., Ed. *Black Literature & Literary Theory*. New York: Methuen, 1987.

_____. "Criticism in the Jungle." Gates, *Black* 1-24.

_____. *Figures in Black: Words, Signs, and the "Racial" Self*. New York: Oxford UP, 1989.

_____. *The Signifying Monkey: A Theory of Afro-American Literary Criticism*. New York: Oxford UP, 1988.

_____. "Writing 'Race' and the Difference It Makes." *Writing and Difference*. Ed. Gates. Chicago: U of Chicago P, 1986. 1-20.

Geller, Allen. "An Interview with Ralph Ellison." *Tamarack Review* Summer 1964: 3-24.

Gottesman, Ronald, ed. *The Merrill Studies in Invisible Man*. Columbus: Merrill, 1971.

Gray, Valerie Bonita. *Invisible Man's Literary Heritage: Benito Cereno and Moby Dick*. Amsterdam: Rodopi, 1978.

Harper, Michael S., and John Wright, eds. *Carleton Miscellany* 18.3 (1980): 1-237.

Hawthorne, Nathaniel. *The Marble Faun: or, The Romance of Monte Beni*. Ed. Richard H. Rupp. Indianapolis: Bobbs, 1971.

Hersey, John. *Ralph Ellison: A Collection of Critical Essays*. Englewood Cliffs: Prentice, 1974.

Humphreys, David. "On the Happiness of America." *The Miscellaneous Works of David Humphreys*. New York: n.p., 1804. 19-43.

James, Henry. *Hawthorne*. Ithaca: Cornell UP, 1956.

Kartiganer, Donald M, and Malcolm A. Griffith. *Introduction. Theories of American Literature*. Ed. Kartiganer and Griffith. New York: Macmillan, 1972. 1-9.

Kostelanetz, Richard. "An Interview with Ralph Ellison." *Iowa Review* 19.3 (1989): 1-10.

Lewis, R.W.B. "Ellison's Essays." *Bloom* 7-11.

List, Robert. *Dedalus in Harlem: The Joyce-Ellison Connection*. Washington: UP of America, 1982.

Lyne, William. "The Signifying Modernist: Ralph Ellison and the Limits of the Double Consciousness." *PMLA* 107 (1992): 319-30.

Mellen, Grenville. "The Red Rover." *North American Review* 27 (1828): 139-54.

Nadel, Alan. *Invisible Criticism: Ralph Ellison and the American Canon*. Iowa City: U of Iowa P, 1988.

O'Meally, Robert G. *The Craft of Ralph Ellison*. Cambridge: Harvard UP, 1980.

______., ed. *New Essays on Invisible Man*. Cambridge: Cambridge UP, 1988.

Ostendorf, Berndt. *Black Literature in White America*. Brighton: Harvester P, 1982.

Palfrey, John Gorham. "Yamoyden." *North American Review* 12 (1821): 466-88.

Parr, Susan Resneck, and Pancho Savery, Ed. *Approaches to Teaching Ellison's Invisible Man*. New York: MLA, 1989.

Parsons, Theophilus. "Earlier and Later English Writers." *North American Review* 10 (1820): 19-33.

Reed, Ishmael, Quincy Troupe, and Steve Cannon. "The Essential Ellison." *Y'Bird Reader* 1 (1977) 126-59.

Reilly, John M., Ed. *Twentieth Century Interpretations of Invisible Man*. Englewood Cliffs: Prentice, 1970.

Ruland, Richard, Ed. *The Native Muse*. New York: Dutton, 1976.

Simms, William Gilmore. *Views and Reviews in American Literature, History and Fiction: First Series*. Cambridge: Belknap P, 1962.

Smith, Valerie. *Self-Discovery and Authority in Afro-American Narrative*. Cambridge: Harvard UP, 1987.

Snead, James A. "Repetition as a Figure of Black Culture." Gates, *Black* 59-79.

Soldo, John J. "The American Foreground of T.S. Eliot." *New England Quarterly* 45 (1972): 355-72.

Sparks, Jared. "Escalala, an American Tale." *North American Review* 20 (1825): 210-14.

Spencer, Benjamin T. *The Quest for Nationality: An American Literary Campaign*. Syracuse: Syracuse UP, 1957.

Spiller, Robert E., ed. *The American Literary Revolution: 1783-1837*. New York: New York UP, 1967.

Stepto, Robert B. *From Behind the Veil: A Study of Afro-American Narrative*. Urbana: U of Illinois P, 1979.

_____, and Michael S. Harper. "Study & Experience: An Interview with Ralph Ellison." *Massachusetts Review* 18 (1977): 417-35.

Tompkins, Jane. *Sensational Designs: The Cultural Work of American Fiction, 1790-1860*. New York: Oxford UP, 1986.

Trimmer, Joseph F. *A Casebook on Ralph Ellison's Invisible Man*. New York: Crowell, 1972.

Tudor, William. "An Address Delivered to the Phi Beta Kappa Society." *North American Review* 2 (1815): 13-32.

Walsh, Robert. "American Drama." *American Quarterly Review* 1 (1827): 331-57.

West, Hollie. "Travels with Ralph Ellison through Time and Thought" (interview). Benston, *Speaking* 37-44.

Wharton, G.M. "Literary Property." *North American Review* 52 (1841): 385-404.

Wright, John S. "Dedicated Dreamer, Consecrated Acts: Shadowing Ellison." Harper and Wright 142-99.

Wright, Richard. *Black Boy*. 1945. New York: Harper, 1966.

_____. *Native Son*. 1940. New York: Harper, 1987.

From *African American Review* 30 (Fall 1996) 421-440.

Posthumous Assessments

The Oklahoma Kid

Stanley Crouch

When Ralph Ellison saddled up the pony of death and took that long, lonesome ride into eternity on Saturday morning, April 16, the quality of American civilization was markedly diminished. He had always traveled on a ridge above the most petty definitions of race and has given us a much richer image of ourselves as Americans, no matter how we arrived here, what we looked like or how we were made. Alone of the internationally famous Negro writers of the last half-century, Ellison had maintained his position as a citizen of this nation. His deservedly celebrated 1952 novel, *Invisible Man*, his two collections of essays—*Shadow and Act* and *Going to the Territory*—the public addresses he gave and what he read and published from the most-awaited second novel in this country's literary history spoke always of the styles, the intrigues, the ideas, the lamentations and the desires that bewitchingly reached across race, religion, class and sex to make us all Americans. This champion of democratic narrative wasn't taken in by any of the professional distortions of identity that have now produced not the astonishing orchestra of individuals our country always promises, but a new Babel of opportunism and naïveté, one we will inevitably defeat with a vital, homemade counterpoint.

Ellison had been trained as a musician, intending to become a concert composer. But the books got him and he boldly took on the job of ordering the dissonance and the consonance of our culture into the orchestrated onomatopoeia that is the possibility of the novel at its highest level of success. At every point, he was definitely the Oklahoma Kid—part Negro, part white, part Indian and full of the international lore a man of his ambition had to know. I sometimes thought of him as riding tall into the expanses of the American experience, able to drink the tart water of the cactus, smooth his way through the Indian nations, gamble all night long, lie before the fire with a book, distinguish the calls of the birds and the animals from the signals of the enemy, gallop wild and woolly into the big city with a new swing the way the Count Basie band had, then bring order to the pages of his work with an electrified magic pen that was both a warrior's lance and a conductor's wand.

In our time, there is a burden to straight shooting, and Ellison accepted it. Those troubles snake all the way back to the '30s, when the Marxist influence began to reduce the intricacies of American problems to a set of stock accusations and dull but romantic ideas about dictatorial paradises rising from the will of the workers. Because Ellison had come through all of that and, like Richard Wright, had rejected it, he was prepared for the political bedlam of the '60s. He refused to forgo his vision of democracy as an expression of high-minded but realistic courage, one that demanded faith and vigilant engagement. His tutoring by blues musicians and the world of blues music had given him a philosophical ease in face of the perpetual dilemmas of human existence. What he wrote of Afro-Americans at their best expressed his own sensibility as surely as the tar of that deceptively silent baby stuck to Br'er Rabbit:

> There is no point in complaining over the past or apologizing for one's fate. But for blacks, there are no hiding places down here, neither in country or city. They are an American people who are geared to what is and who yet are driven by a sense of what is possible for human life to be in this society. The nation could not survive being deprived of their presence because, by the irony implicit in the dynamics of American democracy, they symbolize both its most stringent testing and the possibility of its greatest human freedom.

The most stringent testing that Ellison himself had to face was the rejection of his stance and his work by the intellectual zip coons of black nationalism. The Oklahoma Kid took every emotional and psychological blow thrown at him; he didn't submit to the barbarian gate-rattlers who intimidated so many into accepting a new segregation as a form of self-expression and ethnic authenticity. He knew that segregation was never less than an instrument of cowardice and rejected it. Those sufficiently misled tried to drum Ellison all the way out of the Afro-American experience and were not beyond calling him names to his face. They didn't know they were messing with the wrong man. The writer had the same kind of leathery hide possessed by those dusky Western demons who broke horses, drove cattle and wore the scars left by arrowheads and desperado bullets. Fanny Ellison, his wife of forty-eight years, recalled a luncheon where the embattled novelist sat next to one of the black power literary stooges so anxious to bring him down. Ellison said to him, "I'm a street boy; I'm mean, and I have a dirty mouth." It was an announcement of his essence and a declaration of war.

Ellison wasn't a street boy like the ones who sell pornographic novelties under the banner of rap, their nihilism made superficially complex by the editing and overlaying processes of the recording studio. He was from the same spiritual corner as Louis Armstrong, who knew of cutting and shooting but had danced in the gutter while doggedly staring at the stars. He was also of Duke Ellington's persuasion, an artist bent on the democratic eloquence that speaks most indelibly through the tragicomic resolution of the primitive and the sophisticated. Citing the peerless bandleading composer and the great trumpeter in "Homage to Duke Ellington on His Birthday," Ellison clarified once more his aesthetic vision of how artistic quality both added to the social promise and helped to protect it against vernacular demons:

> Even though few recognized it, such artists as Ellington and Louis Armstrong were the stewards of our vaunted American optimism and guardians against the creeping irrationality which ever plagues our form of society. They created great entertainment, but for them (ironically) and for us (unconsciously) their music was a rejection of that chaos and license which characterized the so-called jazz age associated with F. Scott Fitzgerald, and which has returned once more to haunt the nation. Place Ellington with Hemingway, they are both larger than life, both masters of that which is most enduring in the human enterprise: the power of man to define himself against the ravages of time through artistic style.

Sneering at the tedious political pulp that would shrink Negro experience to no more than a social soap opera, the Oklahoma Kid, cigar in his teeth and fingers at his keyboard, strove to make his knowledge of race in conflict and confluence a wildly orchestrated metaphor for all of human life. He sought combinations of the concrete and the mythic, the excitement of intricate ideas and the boisterous flare-ups of fantasy.

Ellison was too sophisticated to stumble into the dungeon of "magic realism," feeding on surreal hardtack and water. Like the Alejo Carpentier of *Reasons of State*, Ellison knew that the fusions and frissons of race and culture in the Western Hemisphere supply all that is needed for an unforced way out of convention. The miscegenated multiplications of human meaning and effort allow shocking syncopations of fictional narrative and endless variations on hilarity, horror and inspiration.

The Oklahoma Kid told one writer that craft was an aspect of morality and that is perhaps why his unfinished novel took so long, even given the incineration of a manuscript near completion in the middle '60s. His ambition might have gotten the best of him. Ellison refused to say when he thought he would finish the book. This led some to assert that he was some sort of a coward who couldn't face the possibility that the novel might not be up to snuff, that critics with sharpened teeth might gnaw at it like wild dogs, that a second novel might prove the first no more than a fluke. Those who heard him read from the manuscript during the early and middle '80s doubted the skeptics. What Saul Bellow wrote of *Invisible Man* in 1952 was still quite true:

> I was keenly aware, as I read this book, of a very significant kind of independence in writing. For there is a "way" for Negro novelists to go at their problems, just as there are Jewish or Italian "ways." Mr. Ellison has not adopted a minority tone. If he had done so, he would have failed to establish a true middle-of-consciousness for everyone.

At Baruch College in 1983 he delivered a lecture titled "On Becoming a Writer," stressing the freedom from the limitations of segregation that reading granted. Around 1924 books from the downtown library were jammed into a pool hall in the Negro section of Oklahoma City. As older men told tales, laughed and gambled, the young Ellison investigated the unalphabetized books, which meant that a volume of fairy tales might be right next to a volume of Freud. While the books took him into worlds much broader than those he then knew, they also made it possible for him to better appreciate the contrasting humanity of a state in which a large number of whites and Negroes had facial features and skin tones affected to greater or lesser degrees by Indian blood. Ellison's Oklahoma City was informed as much by those formally educated as by jazz musicians like Lester Young and Charlie Christian, who took innovative positions in the band battles and jam sessions of the era. Local aspirations were extended by the precedents of college-educated Negroes from the Eastern Seaboard who took on the missionary goal of traveling and educating their less fortunate brethren after the smoke of the Civil War cleared and the spiritual lion of freedom was roaring at the social limitations imposed by racism. The message of the lecture was that the shaping of language and the comprehension of it amplified that roar in the soul of the young Oklahoma Kid, allowing him to do battle with the riddles of human life and affirm the victories evident in the verve of Negro culture.

In later readings given at the Library of Congress, The New School and the Sixty-Third Street YMCA in Manhattan, Ellison made it clear who he was. Whether or not the novel ever reached publication, each time he gave public voice to his words, those writers in attendance had an opportunity to witness just how big a lariat the old master was twirling. With *Invisible Man*, he brought the resonance of genius to his variations on the Southern themes of racial misunderstandings and the disillusionment with Northern radicalism found in the full text of Richard Wright's *American Hunger*. The later work made it clear that he had advanced upon his initial ambitions and raised what was already a richly ironic style to a level of Melvillian complexity.

Taken by his readings, this writer looked up everything Ellison had published from the work-in-progress, some of it dating back to 1960. One of the themes was corruption and its charisma. A prominent character was a Southern senator named Sunraider. His tale was perfectly Ellisonian. A very light-skinned Negro or a white child who somehow found himself part of a traveling revival unit of Negroes, Sunraider, then known as Bliss, was "brought back from the dead" before various tent congregations. Leaving his background and misusing the lessons of his mentor, the Negro preacher Hickman, Bliss went into politics, changed his name and became famous for the public speaking he had learned at the knees of black people.

In "Hickman Arrives," the wounded Sunraider lies in the hospital after an assassination attempt, dreaming about his past, recalling himself nervously sucking air through a rubber tube inside a coffin as Hickman whipped up the congregation in the tent. But caught by the spirit, Hickman goes on longer than usual. Bliss is awestruck by the spontaneous eloquence as he trembles inside the wooden cigar. Chaos takes over the counterfeit Lazarus routine when a white woman claiming to be Bliss's mother bursts into the act. The hypnotic corruption at the center of the revival meeting, the fooling people for their own good and to prove the greatness of God, is a tool Bliss uses quite differently when he becomes a pro-segregation senator. Nothing is ever simple in Ellison, nor is his vision naïve. In essence, Ellison was saying that Negroes, because of their charismatic relationship to American culture, have the moral responsibility to use their gifts with as much integrity as possible. Otherwise, they might unintentionally contribute to the disorder that always pushes at our culture's borders.

If the novel ever appears, good; if it doesn't, Ellison's contribution to the higher possibilities of our society won't be diminished. He outlasted two generations of attackers, the white and black writers and critics who hated *Invisible Man* and those from the black power era who found him too "white," too "European," too "middle-class." With each passing year his already published rendition of American life grew stronger and his work spoke even more accurately of what came to pass—the fluid shifts of social position, the tragedies of corruption, the unpredictable turns that pivot on our technology and on how we interpret our heritage as improvising Americans, people whose roots stretch into Africa, Europe, Asia and both directions in this hemisphere; people who remake sometimes perfectly and sometimes too swiftly; people who will never realize their potential unless we take on the challenge of democratic recognition, of understanding that both good and evil, folly and corruption, excellence and mediocrity can come from any place in the society. Ralph Ellison, the Oklahoma Kid, knew that we can never count on closed theories, on limiting explanations of our history—or any history. The only thing we can count on is the chaos that ever threatens our humanity and the willingness the best of us have to stand up to it. When we get lucky, as we Americans have so often, people like Ralph Ellison rear the hooves of their horses up toward the sky, then charge, taking every risk necessary to sustain the vitality of our civilization.

From *The New Republic* (May 9, 1994): 23-25.

Frequencies of Memory: A Eulogy for Ralph Waldo Ellison

John F. Callahan

I

Mrs. Ellison, Mr. Ellison, friends and neighbors of Ralph's. Michael, you're taking advantage. I can hear Ralph saying, "For God's sake, Harper," with that long melodious round a of his, "don't set John up like that." And if he were here, he'd chuckle over being the excuse for a little banter between old friends. He'd be glad there was kidding and laughter giving some relief to our grief. Remember Ralph on the comic in American life. "If we laugh at each other, we won't kill each other," he said. Remember Ralph on the blues as a lyrical way to embrace and transcend pain. And remember Ralph on form.

"The characters are good and the stories are good," he'd say once in a while about his novel-in-progress. "But Ah don't know about the damn form, he'd add, both his formal pronunciation and the hint of a drawl he slipped in every so often, impeccable and complimentary in that complex American vernacular he loved so.

Listening to what the other speakers have said and remembering we're gathered at Trinity Cemetery on Riverside Drive above the Hudson in sight of the George Washington Bridge, a landscape Ralph loved and put into his writing in so many clear and camouflaged ways, I feel his presence intensely and palpably, as if, passing on, he's turned into a seabird now swooping in from the bridges out beyond the Statue of Liberty to explore the river. Here and now the memories and images flood in as if borne toward the Hudson on a heroic tide rushing through the harbor from the Atlantic where Ralph made so many voyages ferrying arms to Murmansk and other ports in Allied Europe in his Merchant Marine days during World War II. I hear and feel the touch of his voice, his gestures. Mostly, I hear the rhythms and refrains of his voice:

"Ai-yi-yi."

"For God's sake."

"For God's sake, Fanny."

("For God's sake" was to Ralph what "mother-fucker" was to a later generation, an all purpose phrase: Expletive, term of scorn or endearment, it did duty as noun or verb, conjunction or interjection, though his fidelity to the parts of speech was such that, unlike a later generation, he rarely used his signature phrase to perform the proper functions of adverb or adjective.)

"So it goes," he'd say so often to mark a transition, signal the end of a telephone conversation or give cover to a sudden dreamy mood he sought to conceal from his companions.

"Well John," he'd find some reason to say almost every time we saw each other, "it's a crazy country." He spoke those words, another of his signature phrases, with the wonder and mischievousness of a schoolboy as well as a man and a writer of immense gifts and very American ambition. In conversation as well as on the page, Ralph Ellison made certain words his own. Chaos was one, complexity another, not to mention fluidity or possibility, his touchstones for American democratic promise, usually used in relation to what he called the "social hierarchy." Calling the country—his country—crazy was Ralph's pledge of allegiance to complexity, his artist's declaration of independence from the tyranny of ideology, and perhaps his Negro American's anti-stereotypical Amendment to the Bill of Rights. Like his Invisible Man, Ralph affirmed "the principle" on the page and in conversation, while he resisted the reduction of art, personality or, for that matter, politics, to categories or formulas. With everything he had, Ralph fought any diminishment of personality or the novel, that democratic literary form to which he was so fiercely dedicated that in the last years of his life he sacrificed almost everything to a work-in-progress which, like the crazy country he loved and struggled with, wouldn't be quite finished.

There will be time, all too much time, I fear, just beginning to sense the timeless quality Dick Lewis talked about and the magnitude of Ralph's loss to his friends, most terribly to Fanny, and, yes, to American literature, to reflect on the legacy of his work—not a little of it, I suspect, to come. But now it is still possible to imagine him slipping in to stand at one side of this room, unnoticed for a while but, again, as Dick Lewis reminded us, terrifically alert to every nuance of the occasion and the individuals who comprise it. And so this afternoon I'd like to build upon three memories I have of Ralph, three among many, and the first is the beginning of our friendship. Well it's more than that...

Ralph Ellison was a hard man to surprise but in 1987 I surprised him with an advance copy of my book, In the African-American Grain. *He had read some of it in manuscript and commented helpfully in a couple of letters. But he did not know that I had dedicated it to him and did not know that his wife, Fanny, and I had been in cahoots for months on the inscription and its placement on the page.*

Late on a December afternoon, the sky's pale light streaking the Hudson below the Ellisons' Riverside Drive apartment, I handed Ralph the first copy of my book. He took his time, admired the heft, the Oliver Jackson painting on the cover, the clean, vernacular typeface. Then he started to leaf through it, pleased with the object, pleased for me. But he went right by the dedication page.

"Ralph," I said. "You're missing something."

He looked puzzled and, as if to indulge me on my occasion, thumbed back, did a double take, then another, and grinned.

"Fanny," he cried, looking instinctively in his wife's direction. "Fanny, look. He dedicated it to me." After a minute his expression changed, and a wonderful, boyish look came over his face as he realized she'd been in on it and had helped play something of a joke on him, indeed a version of the American joke. "Ai-yi-yi," he said as he regained his composure. "You two," he shook his head. And then: "Fanny Mae, how about a martini? John wants one, and I need one."

"To Ralph Ellison," my dedication read, "on the higher frequencies." In acknowledgement of the origins of our friendship, at the bottom of the page I had quoted his inscription to me in February 1978: "that vision of fraternity expressed by Danny O'C. and Frederick D." Ralph wrote these playful, sneaky, rhyming words before we knew each other, except as writers. He wrote them in a copy of the Winter 1977-78 American Scholar *he sent to me containing "The Little Man at Chehaw Station," a wonderful autobiographical essay on the mystery, risk and possibility inherent in the complexity of American culture and personality. Ellison's riff of an inscription*

celebrated the "higher frequencies" of that shared human condition invoked by Invisible Man's last haunting, taunting words of ambiguous kinship with his readers: "And it is this which frightens me: Who knows but that, on the lower frequencies, I speak for you?"

So my dedication was homage to Ralph Ellison and the inscription a camouflaged tribute to Ralph, to our friendship, and to the mysteries and wonders of American kinship. And that friendship, as I reflect on it now, still hard-pressed to accept the fact that Ralph is gone, reveals facets of his personality and humanity not often appreciated or understood. For it was Ralph who took the initiative—took it, it's true—in response to what I'd written and to the self I put into what I wrote in a 1977 essay called "Chaos, Complexity, and Possibility: The Historical Frequencies of Ralph Waldo Ellison." After it came out, I sent it to Ralph with a circumspect little note: "Dear Mr. Ellison: Enclosed...Sincerely,..." And that, I thought, was that.

I was wrong. About a month later, I received a two-page, single-spaced letter. "Dear Mr. Callahan," the letter began, and in it Ellison responded warmly, wittily, concretely, generously to what I'd written, and he went on to express doubt and delight over a couple of his uncollected essays that he said my essay had "restored to a place in [his] working memory." At the end, he wrote: "If you're ever in New York, give us a call. Mrs. Ellison and I would love to see you." A couple of months later, I was and did, though my cavalier words do not convey the formal care with which the meeting was arranged by Mrs. Ellison.

"Come at four, Mr. Callahan," she said when I called from New York on the appointed day. "Ralph will see you, and then we'll feed you," the tone and words less formal than her notes. Still, it was daunting. I remember being inspired to bring a bunch of lilacs, for it was the kind of spring afternoon when New York and especially the Ellison's neighborhood—Broadway between 145th and 150th streets—explodes with color.

Lilacs were an Ellison favorite, and there was a warmth about the greetings, which seemed all the more felt and real because of the formality of "Mr. Callahan" and "Mr. Ellison" and "Mrs. Ellison"—"Mrs. and Mrs. of Ellison," my 3-year-old daughter, Sasha, was to giggle as my wife, and two daughters and I drove toward the Ellisons' home in the Berkshires a couple of summers later, and when I corrected her, she shouted her line, "Mrs. and Mrs. of Ellison," more uproariously as if she and this couple she'd never met were in on a secret I didn't know.

Back in the apartment at our first meeting, Ralph showed me to a seat on a tan leather couch in front of a square, glass-topped coffee table across from his proprietary brown leather couch. It was "Mr. Callahan" and "Mr. Ellison" as we talked back and forth about many things: the foibles of students and colleagues; the pain and pleasure of teaching (he was Schweitzer Professor at NYU then) and writing; politics and the 1960s (Lyndon Johnson, Robert Kennedy, Eugene McCarthy, Hubert Humphrey, mostly Lyndon Johnson by whom Ralph was fascinated perhaps because as a Negro Oklahoman he had good reason to be suspicious of a Texan)—both of us careful here—and Mark Twain and the American vernacular, though our idiom was closer to the elaborate period of Henry James than the direct speech of Twain or Hemingway, not to mention the varieties of the spoken word Ralph had grown up on in Oklahoma City and I up the line in New Haven. All the while, we punctuated our sentences with more than an occasional "Mr. Ellison" and "Mr. Callahan."

Then, at precisely five minutes to 5, he slapped the glass table with his palm, looked at me with those warm, defiant brown eyes and said, "Well, John, would you like a drink?" Whether we'd come through the ritual of the academic or the therapeutic hour I was unsure. But once I'd gotten my voice to record over "Mr. Ellison" and say "yes" and

"Ralph" in the same breath, he disappeared into the kitchen and in a few minutes returned with a glass and a bottle of Irish whiskey for me and a glass and a bottle of bourbon for him.

We went from there, Fanny's lovely, cool, crystal, sneak-up-on-you martinis held for another occasion, having the special good time you have when you know the friendship developing is more compelling and easeful than what you counted on, hoped for or imagined would be the case. It was, I should add, a three-cornered friendship that evening and for the next 16 years. From the first, Mrs. Ellison—Fanny McConnell Ellison—was exceedingly good company. Witty, pithy, as stylish as her husband and an even more ungladsome sufferer of fools, she kept Ralph and me honest then and on many subsequent occasions.

We lingered a long time after dinner at an elegant Italian marble table, watched over by an early Romare Bearden collage in space much less hemmed in by books and stacks of papers than would be the case in succeeding years. Over brandy and cigars—evil, enormous Dominicans that Ralph had laid in after his Cubans ran out—and for Fanny, slender Schimmelpinnicks from Holland, we talked of growing up, Ralph in Oklahoma City, Fanny in Pueblo and Chicago, I in New Haven. I remember half-striding, half-weaving through an arch between the dining room and Ralph's study off the living room arguing with him about the Vietnam War in my stocking feet. And I remember their solicitude about me finding my way downtown well after midnight. Over my protests, both put on light coats and Ralph a sporty fedora from the 1940s or 1950s, and they walked me up the hill to Broadway and put me in a cab.

"Yellow Cab," Fanny said. "John, always take a Yellow Cab in New York." I remember forgetting the shaving brush belonging to Al Smith that Ralph had offered to give me much earlier in the evening. Most of all, I had the feeling of having been at home with Ralph and Fanny and felt what Ralph, speaking about writing, called that "same pain, that same pleasure." In my case, the feeling came from a sudden awareness that feeling at home and being home were not the same thing, strive as we may to answer the question Ralph posed musing on the death of his father. "But what quality of love sustains us in our orphan's loneliness?"

II

"Be your own father," the WWI vet tells Invisible Man as they ride a bus toward their exiles North. Now Ralph never gave that kind of advice. Not directly anyway. But for some of my generation—a few are here today, on a day's notice from the ends of the country—Ralph accepted the office of fatherhood. I suppose he did that first by telling us about how as a boy of two or three he'd go with his father, Lewis Ellison, on an ice and coal wagon in Oklahoma City during the first World War. He spoke with a son's helplessness and sorrow and a storyteller's detachment of watching when his father fell delivering a block of ice to Mrs. Salters' grocery store where, he said, the only entry to the dirt cellar was down through the metal plates on the sidewalk—if there were sidewalks then in Oklahoma City—where all was dark and slippery so three-year-old Ralph saw his father disappear, then heard the ice thudding on the dirt floor and his father, too, falling as the ice cut into his ulcer. Then Ralph would come back into the present, and clasp and unclasp his fingers as he told of the horse-drawn ambulance wagon taking his father to the hospital.

In "Tell It Like It Is, Baby," an essay on the Civil War and civil wars among other themes, Ralph wrote movingly about his last glimpse of his father. His mother, Ida, didn't believe him when he told her he'd seen his father through the swinging doors in the surgery room after her last sight of him and before she led her young son from the hospital not suspecting she'd seen her husband for the last time. Ralph told, too, that for years he believed his father would return and didn't accept his passing until he was thirteen or fourteen.

"Be your own father": how charged and mysterious those words must have been for the man and the novelist who put them into the mouth of the Negro World War I veteran in *Invisible Man*. "My father," Ralph would tell his friends, "not only fought in the Philippines; but he was one of the American troops sent to China during the Boxer Rebellion."

Certainly, that line about fatherhood has been the stuff of restless dreams for me. In his remembrance of his father in "Tell It Like It Is, Baby," Ralph speaks of "our orphan's loneliness"; his phrase conveys the immense space he had to try to fill after the loss of his father. His phrase also speaks of the American condition—"orphan" is Ishmael's last word in *Moby Dick*—perhaps especially for young men of my generation who came of age in the 1960s. Thinking of Ralph this morning and now months later, as I elaborate on what I said at his funeral service, I see him vividly across the sixteen years I knew him—a man of sixty-four, though he didn't look it, when I first met him in 1978. Then he looked (and was) in the full force of his prime, a fatherly but also brotherly presence. Gradually he became an elder, became grandfatherly, especially as I knew him with my daughters. As I feel Ralph's presence again over the years I knew him and think of fatherhood's office, I realize there's a link between his fatherly and patriotic impulses.

He was a patriot in as complex and perhaps ambivalent a way as he was a father. *Pater and patria*: "heart mysteries there," as Yeats wrote in the late 1930s when Ralph was rereading the Irish writers, Joyce and Synge and Yeats and O'Casey he'd first discovered along with T.S. Eliot at Tuskegee. I realize that Ralph put me and maybe others of my generation who knew him—Jim McPherson, Leon Forrest, Bob O'Meally, Michael Harper and Robert Stepto, whose father passed in Chicago on the very morning of Ralph's going—in touch with that double impulse: the need to love your country and your father. Ralph was a patriot in much the same way he was a father—unconditionally, with the critical perspective that comes only from love. How unfashionable it was in the circles of the educated, aspiring young, black, and white, in the 1960s to admit to any patriotism. Writing now I realize what an insular, convenient, partial, and provincial truth that was for me and so many others deferment-anxious students at a time when many other young Americans embraced or at least accepted the patriotic office and served in the Vietnam War. Oh, that service was sometimes, but not as often as we tended to say, an antithetical, deceived expression of patriotism. I can't walk away from that conviction. On that score my views haven't changed much, but I hope my sense of others' impulses has grown more tolerant and compassionate and, yes, more complex, and for partly selfish reasons, because my belief in my integrity is bound up with a willingness to grant that of those who fought. No, there's more; there's the ability to grieve over their service and their fate as I grieved when unawares I came across my name on the wall of the Vietnam Memorial a few years ago.

John F. Callahan, the letters read, each one a sharp tiny bamboo spear thought of the mysterious double I would never know. Had he been as scared as I when I woke up night after night running from a dark pagoda into a jungle lit up by rifle reports from Vietcong in black pajamas? Or had my unknown kinsman died feeling more at peace with himself than I had waking up cold and wet in the sweat of recurring nightmares?

Equally, for the young in my camp during the 1960s, fighting a civil war with your father made you a member in good standing of that generation in revolt. Though I didn't know it, the generational pull made it easier to shirk the responsibility of knowing my father on my most private, intimate terms as well as his, if, that is, you ever know others on their terms. But perhaps if you're honest, you can know someone else truly on your terms.

As a son and a writer, who had lost his father through fate and the gods, found him again many times through acts of memory and imagination, and so could not afford to lose him through neglect or passing rebellion, perhaps Ralph Ellison was brooding about the mysteries of kinship when he wrote that outrageous line, "Be your own father." Again I call to mind Melville—the madness he saw in his father which returned in suicidal form to his son. In "The Try-Works" chapter Ishmael briefly transcends his "orphan's loneliness." He wishes only "to sit down and break the green damp mould [of earth's secret flesh] with unfathomably wondrous Solomon." There was something of that wonder and communion in Ralph's recollection of his father. Once when I repeated his line, "be your own father," he seemed almost embarrassed. "Ah yes," he said, and looked away remembering his father or perhaps dreaming of other prose, for, after all, fatherhood and kinship are such profound themes in his second novel since the manuscript calls to mind Joyce's progression to *Ulysses* from *Portrait of the Artist As a Young Man*. At any rate, I felt Ralph was telling his younger friends that to be your own father and your own person, you had to embrace all your fathers, including and perhaps starting with your unsought, unchosen natural father.

Like others who *seemed* to come of age in the 1960s, I had trouble with citizenship, trouble embracing this nation as my country with all the attendant responsibilities, privileges, and, duties. There was a similar mix of shame and unworthiness that, unplumbed, settled like volcanic ash on father and country."America love it or leave it" a certain provoking bumper sticker from the 1960s read. And it took a while for many to resist saying I'll leave it and begin to say, with Ralph: "All right, damn it, I'll love the country in my own way. I sure as hell won't leave it; no, by God, I'll change it." Leaving fathers was also too easy then, perhaps because it is impossible it, as Ralph insisted needed to be the case for Americans, we chose a conscientious consciousness. I remember leaving my father—shame was there, perhaps because I wasn't yet my own man—in spirit and then geography as I went first to Illinois and then to Oregon. When I lighted in Oregon, as if in response, my father left this world for good, dying suddenly November 22nd, 1967, the evening before Thanksgiving and four years after John F. Kennedy, whose assassination my father never got over."Oregon? As far away as you could get, huh?" my father's boss, an elegant black man, observed to me at my father's wake back in New Haven. He was fast on his feet and on my case partly, he told me, because of his strife with his own twenty-five-year-old son. "So it goes," Ralph said when I knew him well enough to tell him this and turning his head, he looked out at a gull wheeling across the Hudson unsure whether to plunge on upriver or turn back toward the safe harbor.

Back in Oregon after a night flight in which I dreamed my just dead and buried father was a passenger passing on an approaching jetliner that exploded as it pulled parallel to mine and before I could wave to him, I watched on the evening news a clip of a graying senator named McCarthy declaring his presidential candidacy. In an act of deflected grief I pursued my lost country and maybe sought my lost father in the Protean shapes of Eugene McCarthy's presidential campaign. Along the way, as if I and not Death were in Samarra, I kept a tortuous, jagged rendezvous with myself. Jagged: that word summons Ralph's description of the blues as "an impulse to keep the painful details and episodes of a brutal experience alive in one's aching consciousness, to finger its jagged grain, and to transcend it." Some of that shoe of Ralph's fit; I had to finger the jagged, destructive grain of my past to embrace my father and my own potential for fatherhood and citizenship. Coming back to Ralph, as a man and a friend, he kept all that open. Never lecturing or prescribing, at least not on that subject, he allowed his younger friends to become better fathers than we would have been without him and without our sometimes silent pursuit of the old sundered kinship with our fathers. He taught me to attend to unfinished business and took a lovely interest in my two daughters on their terms and his. Somehow Ralph remembered and summoned in a new time and place that mingling of authority and tenderness bequeathed him long ago by his father in the less than three years he knew him.

III

That Ralph and Fanny Ellison had no children, was a sadness to them, a grief. Nevertheless, they loved and respected the children of their friends. In some lovely mysterious way, without children of their own, they knew my daughters on my daughters' terms, and so I want to tell you a story about Ralph and my daughters, Eve and Sasha. (Others have talked about Ralph as a storyteller, and that's true enough. He could weave spells, whether telling stories about changing a tire, as Dick Lewis claimed; the power of suction to make a reluctant horse drink at the water's edge as I heard him do; Southern matters like dogs and whiskey as Bill Styron has told us, or, as I've heard Ralph in his mimicking Southern black female voice, stories of "country matters" with a risqué rural spin.) Today though, I want to tell you about Ralph's lovely knack of loosing his imagination gently upon children, as if his voice were a pet come to lick their cheeks.

"Memories are old identities," Yeats has said, and my memory of Ralph and my daughters celebrates his identity as a storyteller in the old way of Aesop and Charles Chesnutt's Uncle Julius combined with a finely tuned contemporary sense, which in their time and place the old storytellers had, of how to hold a child's attention until she, in this case, my three-year old Sasha, bursts into participation. Call-and-response indeed. So I'd like to tell you the story of a story Ralph made up and spun out in Plainfield, in 1980 when my wife, two daughters and I were there for the first time. Now I know many of you visited the Ellisons in their Berkshire summer home at one time or another from the 1960s till the mid or late 1980s. By 1980 the awful aura of the 1967 fire which burned up *both* copies of Ralph's nearly finished second novel had all but dissolved, at least when company came and he was working well. 1989 or 1990, I think, was the last summer they got up there, Ralph was so unswervingly fixed on finishing his book which he'd resumed full-time work with a vengeance after *Going to the Territory*. "I won't leave here, John, even to go to Plainfield," he told me once when I hadn't asked, gesturing toward his computer and the wall of books in his study, "till I get this book done." Perhaps, I remember feeling it was his way of talking to Fanny more than to me.

I want to take you back to 1980 when Eve was six and Sasha three, almost four. These were August dog days with Ralph on his tractor mowing the meadow and Fanny tending flowers, especially her sunflowers so tall and strong they remind me of "Jack and the Beanstalk." Or, thinking of dinner, she might be testing an ear of corn or a head of lettuce in her vegetable garden. We arrived on a hot Saturday in the middle of August, stopped in, went to get settled at the Whale Inn, Fanny's recommendation two towns over, and came back for dinner. My wife, Susan, and the girls still knew the Ellisons only through Fanny's notes and cards and Ralph's voice on the phone at Christmas and Thanksgiving. The next day there was a benefit reading at the Cummington Library by Ralph, Dick Wilbur and William Jay Smith followed by dinner afterwards at Ralph and

Fanny's for everyone including the girls.

But Saturday night was for getting acquainted, especially the girls and Ralph. Already, in the afternoon, Fanny had won their hearts by stealth showing them the haunts of the local animals. Two especially in the person of a fox and a wondrous porcupine (the Porc U Pine a.k.a Porky, of her subsequent cycle of letters to the girls) she had designated *genii loci*. Meanwhile, Ralph had stayed inside with Susan and me. After dinner Eve and Sasha put on their red Chinese pajama tops and bottoms, and asked for a story, in the familiar, easy cozy way of sisters who were best friends. Ralph was relaxing in his chair, sitting back puffing on his pipe. Though they hadn't specifically asked Ralph for the story, the girls were looking up at him fascinated by the wreaths of smoke he began to blow in the air. And then he told a story.

"One night, girls," he began,...and told of how he and Fanny had retired, and were comfortable in bed. Just as Ralph was more or less cozy and drifting off, Fanny leans over and says, "Ralph, there's a noise on the roof." And Ralph, as he told it, had said something like, "Oh, yes, sure, dear, I imagine there is a noise on the roof." Staying right with him, Fanny said, "No, really Ralph, there's someone on the roof." And Ralph said in his characteristic tone of easy resignation and stubborn refusal to concede defeat or claim victory: "Well, let's see what happens."

A little later Fanny tells him again, "Ralph, dear, there really is someone on the roof." And Ralph said—I imagine the dear got him—"All right, I'll see about it."

Now remember, Ralph is telling this story to two little girls. (With so many novelists here, I have to keep the frame in mind.) He's talking to two little girls who are sitting down just beginning to lean forward toward him and his story.

So Ralph described getting up. He wasn't about to go up on the roof in his pajamas and robe. He wanted, I think, to impress on Fanny the seriousness of this enterprise, this sacrifice, this potential "last measure of devotion" he was about to give to her. He pulled on some trousers and a shirt, he told the girls, put on a hat, took a lantern, and then, in battle array, grabbed up his weapon. I forget what it was; maybe one of those wonderful improvised tools you use to pick apples off the higher branches of trees, I'm not sure, but one of those things Ralph, who came by honestly his "thinker-tinker" phrase in *Invisible Man*, would have had handy. Anyway, Ralph proceeded to climb up toward the roof.

By now, the little girls' faces were tilted upward to where Ralph's words mingled with the smoke from his pipe on its way toward the ceiling. As he got up on the roof, he said, he started to slip a little but not enough to fall and not loud enough to worry Fanny. The moon was out, he told the girls, and, safe on the roof, he looked around feeling he was not alone. And sure enough, he saw a face with goggles on. Behind the face he saw a cloudy shape of white or gray. "A parachute," he told them. "I couldn't believe it, it was a damn parachute," he said, pleased with his phrase then a little sheepish as if his "damn" were not appropriate for two little girls. But their grins told him otherwise.

And then he'd said in that special, low chuckling voice of his, "for God's sake, what's a damn aviator doing on our roof?" He paused to let the girls' eyes widen still further. "I wanted to shout to Fanny," he said, "but she wouldn't have been able to hear me. She was downstairs in bed, and I knew I had to deal with this myself."

Well, Ralph carried this tale on, for, good God, 20 or 30 minutes. It was a yarn of impeccable weave, woof and warp indistinguishable, a tall tale in the southwestern tradition like Mark Twain's "Blue-Jay Yarn." Little by little, as Ralph described the features he made out from this face with goggles on and the rest of the scene on the roof, and maybe a hint of fuselage in the trees beyond, the little girls started to giggle and laugh.

They were in complete cahoots with Ralph and also Fanny who had sat down between them unnoticed by me until this point in the story.

Finally, the smaller girl, plump and round and red of the face, not Eve, the young woman you've seen and heard play here today but her younger sister, Sasha, started to speak. For a while giggles stifled her words, but like Ralph, Sasha is stubborn and she kept on.

"Ralph, Ralph," she cried waving her arms in delight, "it was a raccoon!"

She was right. You know that. She and Eve were on Ralph's frequency and he theirs. I wish you could have been there as Ralph regaled these girls and created for them out of that fullness he seemed able to put into whatever he did, whether it was writing, building a hi-fi, taking and developing photographs, or making coffee, or, as he was to do the next morning, teaching six-year-old Eve to make coffee.

IV

There are so many memories dancing through me like Sasha's eyes when she was delivering the punch line, but the last one I'll speak about is the most recent, the simplest, and the most profound. It happened at the private dinner Random House tendered Ralph on his 80th birthday, March 1, 1994. Several people had toasted him—Al Murray and one or two others—and at a certain point he rose to his feet. Before speaking, he looked around the table, not to find his bearings (he had those) but to survey the faces, linger on a few, and move on in order to locate the image he sought as vividly in sight as it was in his mind. He came to rest on Fanny's face. His eyes met hers, hers met his and they looked at each other a long time. Every woman and every man would be looked at that way. "And Fanny," was all he said. "Fanny." This was his way of acknowledging things which could not be said but had been experienced and were remembered, and which he would dare to imply in a word and a tone before going on to acknowledge and, as he almost always did, explore a territory beyond what had been thought and said by those around him.

V

Ah, there are so many images of Ralph Ellison. Perhaps seeking one true to his complexity, I remembered his fondness for birds. Anyone who has sat with him in his apartment knows he was drawn to birds. That fondness for birds goes way back to his days in Oklahoma City, to his time in Abbeville, South Carolina, when, months after his father's passing, a relative took him to see his grandfather, Big Alfred Ellison, a heroic figure in the Reconstruction and post-Reconstruction South. There Ralph got up in the morning after a storm and saw "a nest of fledgling birds" like himself maybe, "that had been blown from their home in a tree." Birds came to his rescue, too, in Dayton during the desolate winter of 1937—after his mother's swift, unexpected passing—pheasant and quail, flickers and a cardinal red as fresh blood. Always and everywhere there were birds: Birds up the Hudson beyond the woods where he and Tucka Tarby hunted at Bard College; birds: hawks and swallows, in Plainsfield; robins, gulls, sparrows and Canada geese tracked with binoculars from his window on Riverside Drive. His imagination went out to the birds so fully you thought he had the power to summon them.

As I was brooding and smiling, no, grinning, over Ralph's fascination with birds, crows too (he was democratic about birds as about so many things), I recalled a passage from Melville. Was it from Melville Ralph got his penchant for beginning a sentence with

"And"? From Melville a little of the courage to exclude nothing and include every voice and idiom in his vernacular American prose? (Recently I came across a volume of *Moby Dick* Ralph gave Fanny in 1944, before they were married, inscribed simply, "For my beloved Fanny": now what other man have you known who would have given the woman he loved *Moby Dick* as a gift?) In *Moby Dick*, which Ralph loved and whose eloquence and greatness he aspired to in his novels, there are these words and who knows but that on some mysterious frequency Herman Melville had the likes of Ralph Ellison in mind? "And there is a Catskill eagle in some souls that can alike dive down into the blackest gorges and soar out of them again and become invisible in the sunny spaces. And even if he forever flies within the gorge, that gorge is in the mountains, so that even in his lowest swoop the mountain eagle is still higher than other birds upon the plain, even though they soar."

In the rush of his prose I feel Ralph Ellison's soul dive and soar. "And it is this which frightens me," he wrote with brave complexity at the end of *Invisible Man*: "Who knows but that, on the lower frequencies, I speak for you?"

VI

Grieving for Ralph Ellison, I grieve for myself. Remembering him, knowing something of his foibles and quirks as well as his gifts, generosities and, above all, his inviolable integrity as a writer, I re-experience the rush of reading *Invisible Man* for the first time. In 1960, just before the student sit-ins stirred my generation's roots, I sat in the deep New England dark in a dormer of Fenwick Hall at the College of the Holy Cross and read till dawn, yes, and till midmorning too, cutting a Latin Tacitus class in which I was holding on for dear life to a passing grade.

Yes, that's me, I felt when I finished *Invisible Man*. When I thought about my feeling, I was surprised. It was one thing to identify with Fitzgerald's Irish Catholic young man in *This Side of Paradise* or Joyce's in *Portrait of the Artist*, but now I was transformed because of Ellison's intensely particular rendering of Invisible Man's experience as a Negro in the South, in Harlem, and sometimes drawing rooms and even a posh bedroom in downtown Manhattan. Because I was an Irish Catholic from New Haven who nevertheless felt out of place at Jesuit Holy Cross—my father's college where I was supposed to feel at home—I found a kinsman in Invisible Man, who was somehow an outsider at his Negro college, where he was supposed to feel at home. ("You and Ralph were lucky to go to Holy Cross and Tuskegee," Fanny Ellison told us one evening a few years ago. "You might have had your heads turned at Harvard or Yale. You might not have become who you are." And I thought of Ishmael's remark that a whaling ship was his Harvard and Yale, and how the true American is also, inevitably and always, a provincial looking for the way home.)

Neither did I put down *Invisible Man* in a kinship of alienation, that fashionable and oh so provincial reflex of the time. Rather, I was exhilarated then as I am now by Invisible Man's emergence, his self-mocking, qualified and therefore all the more convincing resolve to engage the world. Invisible Man's coming out, his embrace of "the possibility of action" was a precious personal resolve for me. If he can do it, hurt more than I, "hurt to the point of abysmal pain," I felt, so can I. Though, come to think of it, I went underground in a manner of speaking, perhaps because I could not have survived exposed in the world, only to emerge in the tumult of the 1960s. Sometimes I think we Americans are most visible underground and most invisible when we emerge. That may be part of what Ellison was getting at with Invisible Man's wonderful, complex phrase about the need to affirm the "beautiful absurdity of [our] American identity."

But that's another story—though here, too, Ralph's imagination would not rest. In "Brave Words for a Startling Occasion," his 1953 address in response to the National Book Award, he associates the American quest with a mysterious fusion of deepest personal and national yearnings. "The way home we seek," he wrote, making the *Odyssey* a fable for the American predicament, "is that condition of man's being at home in the world, which is called love, and which we term democracy." To the end, love and democracy were Ellison's touchstones for the way home. Like Jefferson, who did not say "happiness" but "the pursuit of happiness," Ellison spoke not of home but the way home. Perhaps we are never truly home, and that, too, is another story.

For now, it's enough to say that a great writer and a great and good soul is gone. For me, a friend and a father is gone, too; but as Ralph said of his own father, "He only perished, he did not pass away." So, too, with Ralph. In life and legacy he was a true American kinsman, and he lives on through his nourishing words. Like Melville's catskill eagle descending and ascending, his spirit quickens the pulse and beckons us home to the lower and the higher frequencies of America.

NOTES

This essay is an expanded version of a eulogy delivered at Ralph Ellison's funeral, April 19, 1994 in New York City. Portions of it were published in *Willamette Week*, May 11-May 17, 1994.

From *Callaloo* 18.2 (1995), 298-309.

The Achievement of Ralph Ellison

James W. Tuttleton

For by a trick of fate (our racial problems not withstanding) the human imagination is integrative—and the same is true of the centrifugal force that inspirits the democratic process. And while fiction is but a form of symbolic action, a mere game of "as if," therein lies its true function and its potential for effecting change. For at its most serious, just as is true of politics at its best, it is a thrust toward a human ideal. And it approaches that ideal by a subtle process of negating the world of things as given in favor of a complex of man-made positives.

—Ralph Ellison, "Introduction to *Invisible Man*"

Although Ralph Ellison (1914-1994) died last year and is now personally lost to us, he has perhaps never been more visible to those with an eye for distinguishing American fiction and criticism. And certainly his work has never been more necessary to American literary culture than it is today. The salient sign of his visibility is of course his one—and only—novel, *Invisible Man* (1952), a work that won him the National Book Award. It is in my view the best novel ever written by an African-American, and it may well be the best novel written since World War II. Certainly, millions of copies of it have been sold and read; and it has become an inevitable assignment in school and college courses in the American novel, thanks to its splendid narrative account of the apprenticeship of a young black boy struggling to be seen, struggling to define himself against the forces of poverty, educational incompetence, white racism, political manipulation by Communists and black nationalists, and even personal exploitation by sex-crazed white women.

I do not mean to suggest that *these* subjects lifted *Invisible Man* to international importance. But Ellison's mastery in the handling of scene and dialogue, his vivid characterization and plotting, and his dazzling repertory of styles and symbolic devices—all of these elements of his tragicomic poetry made for stunning intellectual richness and an aesthetic delight greatly superior to anything produced by the "Harlem Renaissance" novelists (Claude McKay, Jean Toomer, Zora Neale Hurston, et al.) or even by the prolix Richard Wright or William Attaway during the 1930s and 1940s.

Although he wrote only one novel, I think it fair to say that Ellison also towered over his near contemporaries James Baldwin, LeRoi Jones, (Imamu Amiri Baraka), William Melvin Kelley, and John A. Williams. Indeed, compared to Ellison's great achievement, the more recent contemporary adulation of Jamaica Kincaid, Alice Walker, and Toni Morrison seems grotesque. If these comparisons segregate Ellison from white fiction and seem to diminish him as merely "a credit to his race," let me go further and say that, in my view, *Invisible Man* towered over anything produced by Mailer, Bellow, Malamud, Roth, Updike, Cheever, Barth, Vonnegut, Pynchon, Hawkes, and Barthelme.

I shall have more to say about *Invisible Man* in due course. But another sign of Ellison's intellectual presence—and pertinence for literary culture now at the end of our century—is the new Modern Library edition of his nonfiction prose. *The Collected Essays of Ralph Ellison*[1] includes all of Ellison's published and unpublished expository writing. Readers familiar with his already available volumes *Shadow and Act* (1964) and *Going to the Territory* (1986) will find these books completely reprinted here. In addition, more than a score of other, previously uncollected writings have been brought together to complete this huge volume. In all there are some sixty-one essays expressive of Ellison's thinking about a wide range of cultural subjects. Aside from autobiographical reminiscences and interviews with journalists and editors, there are a great many celebrations of American music.

In his youth Ellison had a deep desire to play the trumpet and majored in music at Tuskegee Institute; but though he never made it as a musician, his love of spirituals, the blues, jazz, and classical music shines on nearly every page. We also have here recollections of (or reflections on) memorable performers like Mahalia Jackson, Charlie Parker, Jimmy Rushing, Simon Estes, and Jessye Norman. There are likewise observations on the visual arts (especially the work of Romare Bearden); appreciations of other writers (Mark Twain, Richard Wright, Stephen Crane, Alain Locke, Bernard Malamud); several lectures and addresses at colleges and universities; the original working notes for—and a thirtieth-year introduction to—*Invisible Man*; a great many reflections on race in America; and extensive commentary on the indivisibility of American culture as a fusion (to be celebrated) of distinctive ethnic, racial, and cultural elements.

There is so much richness here that it is impossible to summarize the book. A simple way to view it would be to say that it is the work of a midcentury American artist and intellectual reflecting seriously on elements of both high and low culture in the public life. Nowadays the term "intellectual" stands in derision, as it is associated with power- and publicity-hungry freaks in the academy. But Ellison came to his maturity as a writer just after World War II, when the term had some dignity as a vocation and it was still possible to aspire to be one. His conception of the life of the mind and art was shaped by T.S. Eliot, Henry James, André Malraux, Kenneth Burke, W.E.B. DuBois, Richard Wright, and the writers then associated with *Partisan Review*. He did not always agree with them about politics, race, and culture, but he conducted his arguments with great seriousness, personal dignity, and an actual knowledge of racial and cultural experience in the America to the west of the Hudson River.

Perhaps some sense of this remarkable writer's mind can be suggested by attention to several themes that run through this definitive collection. First, a great many essays deal with how American culture has been and is being formed and shaped as a dynamic process that fuses into one entity a wide range of human activities. Ellison was always preoccupied in some part of his mind with the way elements of any race's cultural expression filter into the mainstream of (and thus help to form) American culture. Ellison thought black American culture immensely rich, as indeed it is. But in the 1930s black culture had been grossly oversimplified by white American leftists and others who reduced blacks to the stereotype of the wretched of the earth. Segregated and excluded from the inner circle of American life, blacks were supposedly so desperate for a better life that they could and should be manipulated to bring about the socialist revolution. In this struggle, black artists were supposedly useful agents. Ellison saw how the Communists had seduced and abandoned black writers like Richard Wright, and he had no intention of being co-opted by the Left. Later, in the Sixties civil-rights movement, in order to further the cause of desegregation, political liberals (both black and white) once again reduced blacks to this stereotype of the racial victim who has been excluded from American culture.

Ellison was drawn to the radical Left in the Thirties and Forties (he even wrote for *The New Masses*) and was supportive of integration and black civil rights in the Fifties and Sixties. But he would not let this reductionist stereotype of black culture go uncriticized. Black life was too positive and various in its engaging forms. As he remarked in "That Same Pain, That Same Pleasure: An Interview": "I have no desire to write propaganda. Instead, I felt it important [in *Invisible Man*] to explore the full range of American Negro humanity and to affirm those qualities which are of value beyond any question of segregation, economics or previous condition of servitude. The obligation was always there and there is much to affirm."

As their essays make plain, whatever the legal condition of slavery and desegregation may have meant, in the domain of culture and society blacks had always been fully involved in the national life. Many blacks had long been reduced to menial work as cooks, domestics, share-croppers, yard-boys, and manual laborers. But over the years there emerged a great many important black ministers, teachers, lawyers, musicians, editors, businessmen, union leaders, and college presidents—all of them defining and expressing a rich and diverse and creative black culture. In their preoccupation with black victims, few liberal whites seemed to notice these blacks or to speak about their contributions to American life. Indeed, this complex black culture was so diverse that not even any single *black* could speak for it.

Not only was North American black culture immensely diverse, it was also so rich and influential that, in Ellison's view, many of its forms had already entered the mainstream culture of America and had been assimilated into the consciousness of whites long before many whites were even aware of it. Much of Ellison's essay-writing was devoted to showing this contribution blacks had made to the national experience in its broadest terms, that is, in both high culture and the popular culture. But his point was never merely a pride in individual black achievement. What interested Ellison most was how a national culture gets formed in the first place. In these essays he shows that the forms of folk culture (white as well as black) are invariably already integrated in America. Spirituals, the blues, and jazz were originally distinctive forms of more or less anonymous black folk consciousness. But such was their moral and aesthetic power, despite the fact that no one person had "originated" them, that they permanently changed mainstream popular music. But it hardly ends there.

Folk culture, which is this already intermixed and continually integrating amalgam of creative elements, was itself for Ellison the fertile seedground of superior artistic genius. Spirituals, the blues, and jazz, for instance, did not merely influence mainstream popular music but also re-emerged in transfigured form in the musical expression of brilliant individual composers like George Gershwin, Aaron Copland, and Igor Stravinsky, to name just a few.

Ellison, for many years the Schweitzer Professor of the Humanities at New York University, was a colleague and friend of mine. And when he learned that I knew John Lewis, the founder and director of the Modern Jazz Quartet, he was keen to meet him. Lewis had also been trained in the conservatory tradition of classical music. Bach, Mozart, and Stravinsky were as familiar to Lewis as Duke Ellington, Satchmo, and "Bird" Parker. And Lewis's jazz compositions—and not merely those in the "Third Stream" phase—were brilliant realizations of Ralph Ellison's tenaciously held belief that the lines of creative influence flow from black culture into white and back again, and from low culture into high and back again, all this producing a single, unified, dynamic national culture. In fact, for Ellison, American culture was a rich, seamless tapestry of varicolored elements in which there were so many black contributions that, after a while, it was sometimes impossible to identify them as such.

A second theme running through these essays is the role of the writer in America. Ellison certainly saw himself as a figure in the continuum of black writing. But, more broadly, he knew himself to participate in a wider current of mainstream American fiction. Beyond that, he saw himself as a citizen of the republic of letters that included the Frenchman Malraux, the Pole Joseph Conrad, the Russian Dostoevsky. Since "white literature" was continually influenced by black writing, and vice versa, he did not believe in the segregation of black literature in college courses like "The Negro Novel," etc. During his Schweitzer Professorship, I chaired the English department, worked out with him an annual program of lectures, and used to talk to him at great length about the American masters who were our common pedagogical concern. As a teacher, his was truly a "rainbow curriculum" of various writers exploring the multicultural aspects of American life in a democratic polity. But his choice of books and writers was always based upon considerations of art rather than race.

During the Sixties, when the black-power movement got going in earnest, Ellison's lectures and essays on the unity of an American culture to which blacks had made an inseparable contribution brought him under shrill and sometimes raucous censure from radical separatist blacks who thought him too subservient to racist honky culture, which they wanted to demolish. Some black radicals could never forgive him for his portrait of Ras the Exhorter, the black nationalist rioter in *Invisible Man*, who romantically solicited and indeed incurred his own destruction. The abuse Ellison suffered in those years of the New Left, as a so-called "Uncle Tom," was wholly undeserved, as *Invisible Man* and his nonfiction works are one long brilliant protest against the continuing forms of American racism. But the courage and dignity with which he bore insult from even his own people—evident in the interview "Indivisible Man"—were signs of great personal magnanimity.

As a black novelist and intellectual, Ellison saw his role as the affirmation and celebration of American life as a whole. This also put him at odds with white radicals, who wanted him to sign off and merely denounce America for her history of slavery and continuing racism. Socialists like Irving Howe and some of the others in the *Partisan Review* crowd wanted Ellison to reproduce Richard Wright's savage denunciations of white racism in *Native Son* (1940), *12 Million Black Voices* (1941), and *Black Boy* (1945). In "Black Boys and Native Sons" (1963), Howe excoriated "accommodationists" like Ellison"

> In response to Baldwin and Ellison, Wright would have said (I virtually quote the words he used in talking to me during the summer of 1958) that only through struggle could men with black skins, and for that matter, all the oppressed of the world, achieve their humanity. It was a lesson, said Wright, with a touch of bitterness yet not without kindness, that the younger writers would have to learn in their own way and their own time. All that has happened since bears him out.

But did it? I don't think so, nor did Ellison, who had been befriended by Wright. In *Invisible Man* Ellison, like Wright in *Native Son*, dealt frankly, comically, and horrifyingly with the forms of white racism. But at the same time he knew that Wright's posture of despair, alienation, and feverish militancy was not the only stance for the black writer. Hence he refused to reduce his unnamed protagonist to the subhuman condition of Wright's Bigger Thomas, and he deplored Wright's dismissal of what Wright had called "all that art for art's sake crap." For Ellison, fiction was not racial propaganda. As he remarked in "The World and the Jug," "what an easy con-game for ambitious, publicity-hungry Negroes this stance of 'militancy' has become." And he liked to quote—of all people—President Lyndon B. Johnson's remark that art is not a social weapon. For Ellison, the demand—whether made by white or black critics—that the Negro writer subordinate his art to anti-racist propaganda denies the writer his own vision:

> For I found the greatest difficulty for a Negro writer was the problem of revealing what he truly felt, rather than serving up what Negroes were supposed to feel, and were encouraged to feel. And linked to this was the difficulty, based upon our long habit of deception and evasion, of depicting what really happened within our areas of American life, and putting down with honesty and without bowing to ideological expediencies the attitudes and values which gave Negro American life its sense of wholeness, and which render it bearable and human and, when measured by our own terms, desirable.

He said that for this reason black writers often failed "to achieve a vision of life and a resourcefulness of craft commensurate with the complexity of their actual situation. Too often they fear to leave the uneasy sanctuary of race to take their chances in the world of art." It was in the world of art and according to aesthetic standards that Ralph Ellison wanted *Invisible Man* judged. And his artistic standards were so high and exacting that he was never able to complete a second novel (especially after a fire in his summer house destroyed his working manuscript).

A third theme that runs through this volume is the praise of the American language as a vernacular medium adequate to the highest art. Few American writers, white or black, have been as sensitive as he to the evolution of the American language out of the whirling maelstrom of immigrant experience. He immensely admired Twain's ear for Southern speech, studied the Mississippi dialect in Faulkner's prose, and listened for and learned from James's vernacular locutions. Ellison was naturally sensitive to the speech of blacks as a distinctive idiom of our "American version of English." In a speech to Haverford students in 1969, he noted how "the American language owes something of its directness, flexibility, music imagery, mythology, and folklore to the Negro presence." In "Going to the Territory," he called the slaves and their successors ingenious in developing the linguistic skills necessary to communicate in a mixed society, and he particularly praised blacks for their "melting and blending of vernacular and standard speech and a grasp of the occasions in which each, or both, were called for." In fact, Ellison called the vernacular style "the American style":

> But by "vernacular" I mean far more than popular or indigenous language. I see the vernacular as a dynamic *process* in which the most refined styles from the past are continually merged with the play-it-by-eye-and-by-ear improvisations which we invent in our efforts to control our environment and entertain ourselves. This is not only in language and literature, but in architecture and cuisine, in music, costume, dance, tools, and technology. In it the styles and techniques of the past are adjusted to the needs of the present, and in its integrative action the high styles of the past are democratized. From this perspective the vernacular is, no less than the styles associated with aristocracy, a gesture toward perfection.

Richard Kostelanetz once called Ellison a "brown-skinned aristocrat." This sounds like "reverse color prejudice" to me, as well as class prejudice; and it implies that he was too "white" to be a black. Many blacks do have white ancestry, through no responsibility of their own. Ellison even had Cherokee ancestry, and when he learned that I too was from the South and had a Cherokee grandmother, it sealed our friendship. In his own selfhood he was the living personification of the interrelation of racial and cultural elements in America that was his dominating theme. And he saw me in that light as well.

Was he an aristocrat? Indeed, he did carry himself as if he were A Visible Somebody. He was an aristocrat, but only in the way that every American man and woman is an heir to incalculable cultural wealth. Ellison's whole career, insofar as I understand it, was devoted to making clear that elements of the high style—like elements of popular culture—are available to *everyone for everyday life*. He had started out as a poor boy in Oklahoma, looking at magazines like *Vogue* and *Harper's*, recognizing in them a style higher and better and more distinguished than what he saw around him. It was like the difference between his daily clothes and his Sunday go-to-meeting clothes. The boy decided that he wanted to wear glad rags every day of the week, and so he became one of the most elegantly dressed men I have ever known.

Further, as a youth he found in Conrad, Hemingway, and Eliot a literary imagination superior to that of the best sellers and poetasters, and he wanted what these artists had to give. Mozart and Rossini were his inheritance—as available to him (or to any black boy) as to Marian Anderson. High culture, the fusion of black and white influences and much else besides, was his for the taking. He was as comfortable—clad in a tuxedo, listening to chamber music in the staid, large reading room of the Century Club, to which Henry James had also belonged—as he was in an all-black jazz nightclub toe-tapping to local riffs. Indeed, in every aspect of life Ellison worked to bring the high style, the patrician, the best, into our common everyday possession; and to lift vital, worthwhile folk creations into general consciousness as values in themselves and as a common American legacy offering inspiration to rising genius. This was, for Ralph Ellison, what a democratic culture was all about.

NOTES

1. *The Collected Essays of Ralph Ellison*, edited with an introduction, by John F. Callahan. Preface by Saul Bellow. The Modern Library, 856 pages, $20.

From *The New Criterion,* December 1995, 5-10.

Juneteenth: Ralph Ellison's National Narrative

Robert J. Butler

Like its extraordinary central character Alonzo Z. Hickman, Ralph Ellison's long-awaited second novel, *Juneteenth*, has finally "arrived." A major achievement, it has proven well worth the long wait. It is a robust novel centered in a deep and resonant vision of the American experience and is written in a distinctively Ellisonian style which is noteworthy for its lyrical power, rhetorical extravagance, and formal control. It is clearly a book which can only add to Ellison's reputation as a major writer who has masterfully integrated American, African American and modern traditions.

Readers will immediately discern in this novel features which have become Ellison trademarks. Elaborate use is made of African American folk traditions rooted in the Brer Rabbit folktales, blues music, and sermons. (Indeed, Hickman himself drinks deeply from all three wells, starting out as a blues musician, becoming a revivalist minister, and presenting himself to the reader as a gifted story teller who is well aware of the importance of trickster heroes in black folklore.) The novel is also artfully interwoven with motifs found in Ellison's previously published fiction, especially ocular imagery, avian symbolism, and subtle allusions to classical mythology and American myth. The search for a usable past which is at the center of *Invisible Man* and "Flying Home" is also a critically important concern in *Juneteeth*. As Hickman reminds us late in the novel as he tries to make sense of his own life and the historical experience of his country, "It's all a matter of time" (276). Like invisible man and Todd from "Flying Home," he must connect his past and his present in a vital Bergsonian continuum if he is to open the doors to a liberating and humane future. The past for Hickman, as is the case with all of Ellison's mature characters, can be a "threat" if misunderstood or denied but it can also be a "touchstone" and a "guiding star" (16) if properly imagined, emotionally assimilated, and thus connected to a living present and an open future.

One could go in listing other formal and substantial parallels between this book and Ellison's previous work. (As Irving Howe in an early review of *Invisible Man* rightly observed that no white man could have written that novel, we can say with equal firmness that *only* Ralph Ellison could have written *Juneteenth*.) But it is also important to note that *Juneteenth* represents new directions in Ellison's art and vision since it is in several significant ways strikingly different from *Invisible Man* and Ellison's short stories, especially "Flying Home" and "King of the Bingo Game." For while these extraordinary fictions are centered in alienated figures attempting to make meaningful contact with outward social experience by assuming viable public roles, *Juneteenth* is, in the best sense of the word, a "national" narrative which is centered in a heroic figure who successfully takes "the next step" (*Invisible Man,* 575) which invisible man talks about by actually assuming the "socially responsible role" (*Invisible Man,* 581) which Ellison's nameless character seeks. Father, minister, and citizen, Hickman is no underground figure afflicted with twentieth-century *anomie*; rather, he is a public figure whose personal story is part of a larger national narrative.

This novel, therefore, has a historical sweep and public resonance either missing or indirectly alluded to in Ellison's previously published fiction. It is a sustained and wise meditation on America as a nation with a special destiny which is symbolized by the Juneteenth celebration, a time when news of the Emancipation Proclamation was brought to the Oklahoma territories, a critically important moment when the full promise of American democracy, so betrayed by slavery, was temporarily redeemed for all Americans. The Juneteenth sermons, recreated so powerfully in Chapter 7, relate the story of American slavery in fuller detail and with more directness than do the dream sequences in the Prologue of *Invisible Man*. And the story of blacks during the Reconstruction period and in the early days of the twentieth century are rendered in exacting detail, focusing on Hickman's life as an itinerant preacher.

Unlike Ellison's previous fiction which generates its meanings by placing tortured individuals in very private spaces such as the underground, *Juneteenth* is filled with important scenes which are enacted in public settings which resonate with meanings which define the experience of the nation. The novel opens in Washington, D.C. in the early 1950s, a time when the United States assumed new global responsibilities as a nation and when the civil rights movement was on the verge of transforming American society. The speech which Senator Sunraider delivers on the floor of the United States Senate is replete not only with a racist diatribe which reveals America once again betraying its national promises, but also is filled with mythic images and ideals from the nation's past which can revitalize American society. Reminding his audience that "we become victims of history only if we fail to evolve ways of life that are more free, more youthful, more human" (19), Hickman invokes the mythic image of America as a new world "Eden" (20) in order "to make manifest our lovely dream of progressive idealism" (20). Central to this vision of American democratic possibility is creating a social world "which will allow each and every one of us to rise high above the site of his origins, and to soar released and ever reinvigorated in human space" (19).

Here the very public setting of the United States Senate is an altogether appropriate background for Senator Sunraider to meditate on the national destiny in the historically crucial period of the Cold War. His speech clearly outlines two basic options for America in the second half of the twentieth century: 1) We can become "victims of history" by not fulfilling the principles of American democracy or 2) We can be "reinvigorated by space" if we remain true to the "principles" (*Invisible Man,* 580) which invisible man enigmatically ponders but which *Juneteenth* spells out in lucid detail. For America to fulfill its historic role, it must answer what Sunraider characterizes as "three fatal questions" which "history has put to us": How can the many be one? How can the future deny the past? And how can the light deny the dark? (20) The answer to all three questions lay in developing "a willed and *conscious* balance" (20) which requires Americans to embrace "unity in diversity" (20). Such a consciousness will enable us not only to achieve temporal balance (infusing the ideals of the American past with the present and thus creating a liberating future) but also a racial brotherhood which can harmonize the "light" with the "dark". The net effect of both forms of unity is to reinvent the nation envisioned by the Founding Fathers, a society where the rights of the individual (the "one") are held in balance with social responsibility (the needs of the "many"). Sunraider therefore calls for "citizen individualists" (24) to renew the American dream in the second half of the twentieth century. Such people are well aware of "our national ambiguities" and will not "falter before our complexity" (20). They will provide the "creative momentum" resulting in the "creative action" (20) which America needs to restore its historic purpose and renew itself as a nation.

But the violence and chaos that soon erupts in this scene when Sunraider is shot by a nameless assassin reveals the essential problem faced personally by the senator and culturally by Cold War America. Instead of achieving a "willed and conscious balance," (20) which unifies ideals and action, individuals and society, and people of all races and backgrounds, the people in this scene degenerate to forms of behavior and thought which result in their becoming the "victims of history" (19) which Sunraider had warned against earlier in his speech. After he makes some grossly racist remarks at the end of his talk deploring what he calls the "dark side" (22) of American life which elicit "enthusiastic rebel yells" (24), a nameless man rises up in the gallery and shoots him. The scene thus becomes an epiphany dramatizing what is wrong with America in the post-World War II period. Espousing high-flown ideals of making the world a more democratic place, America, like Sunraider, contradicts these ideals in the early 1950s by endorsing both the *de jure* segregation of the Jim Crow South and the *de facto* segregation of the urban North, thus creating an environment which will erupt in great violence during the 1960s and 1970s.

This scene of personal and national failure is balanced by two other scenes of personal and national promise, both which are also enacted in strikingly public settings. Midway through the novel, the Juneteenth celebrations in the early days of Oklahoma statehood are powerfully rendered in a series of sermons which serve as the thematic core of the novel. This scene, which is presented as a memory called up by the wounded Senator Sunraider, pictures him as a six-year old assistant to Rev. Hickman as they conduct a revivalist show which is described as a mixture of "the Resurrection, minstrel shows, and vaudeville routines" (117). In remembering this episode from his past, Sunraider is given a hint of what is necessary for his salvation, for Hickman's sermon is about finding "a blessing laced up with a calamity" (119), that is, discovering the heroic story of how African Americans transcended slavery by creating a distinctive New World culture of their own which resulted in their rebirth as a people. As Sunraider imaginatively re-lives the extraordinary call-response sermon which he and Hickman delivered at Juneteenth, he momentarily ceases to be the deeply conflicted Senator Sunraider and becomes for a few moments Hickman's assistant Bliss as they celebrate the triumph of African American will and spirituality:

> They had us bound but we had our kind of time, Rev. Bliss. They were on a merry-go-round that they couldn't control but we learned to beat time from the seasons. We learned to make this land and this light and darkness and this weather and their labor fit us like a suit of new underwear. With our new rhythm, amen, but we weren't free and they still kept dividing us. There's many a thousand gone down the river. Mamma sold from papa and chillun sold from both. Beaten and abused and without shoes. But we had the Word, now, Rev. Bliss, along with the rhythm. They couldn't divide us now. Because anywhere they dragged us we throbbed in time together. If we got a chance to sing, we sang the same song. If we got a chance to dance, we beat back hard times and tribulations with the clap of our hands and the beat of our feet, and it was the same dance. Oh, they come out here sometimes to laugh at our way of praising God. They can laugh but they can't deny us. They can curse and kill us but they can't destroy us all. This land is ours because we come out of it, we bled in it, our tears watered it, we fertilized it with our dead. So the more of us they destroy the more it becomes filled with the spirit of our redemption (131).

Unlike Sunraider's speech on the floor of the Senate which rhetorically calls for the American need for "balance" between the individual and community but contradicts these abstract sentiments with racist remarks, Hickman's sermon provides compelling evidence that American blacks have achieved this balance in their historical experience. Not only do Hickman and Bliss become psychologically and spiritually fused in their shared sermon but their call-and-response technique joins them to the crowd of over 5,000 people physically present and also with all American blacks of the past, the "many thousands gone" who symbolize the historical experience of black people in America. Hickman's masterful sermon, unlike Sunraider's speech at the outset of the novel, is more than mere rhetoric since it is composed and delivered by a true "citizen-individualist" (24) which Sunraider can verbally describe but has failed to become. For Hickman's art joins outwardly detested individuals into an inwardly triumphant community which shares the same "rhythm," the "same song" and the "same dance." Because they "throbbed in time together," they have transcended the dehumanizing forces of slavery and have become a human community which can serve as a model of what Americans should become in the present, a people joined by "the spirit of our redemption."

The final episode in this triad of scenes which help to structure the novel is Hickman's meditation before the Lincoln Memorial late in the book. Once again, Ellison employs a very public setting to convey meanings which resonate beyond the lives of individuals and define the historical and cultural experience of the nation. Contemplating "the great brooding eyes" of Lincoln, Hickman comes into close imaginative contact with Lincoln's "distant vision" (282) of equality, freedom, and justice. Lincoln therefore becomes, in Hickman's mind, a resonant symbol of the unity between blacks and whites in America:

> *So yes, he's one of us, not only because he freed us to the extent that he could but because he freed himself of that awful inherited pride they deny to us, and in so doing became a man and he pointed the way for all of us who would be free - yes!* (282)

To be sure, this scene is surrounded by ironies which complicate Hickman's vision. He is clearly mindful of Lincoln's "contradictions" (283) and is also painfully aware that Lincoln "could only take one step along the road that would make us free" (282). Moreover, as he considers the figure of the dying Senator Sunraider physically before his eyes as he considers the memory of his visit to the Lincoln Memorial earlier that afternoon, he is clearly reminded of how Lincoln's mythic vision of America as a "vista of perpetual dawn" (282) has been dimmed in many ways by a subsequent history of racial division and violence. As an American pragmatist who has known much hardship in his own life, Hickman is surely aware that there is indeed "much grit in the spiritual greens" (280) of his own personal life and the life of the nation. But these ironies are not finally reductive because they do not obscure the fact that Lincoln's "ideals" are "sublime" (283) and that these ideals from the past are a viable source of hope for Americans in the present. Admitting that post-Civil War American history has been "crazy" since it has contradicted the principles upon which the country was founded, Hickman nevertheless asserts that ...part of that craziness contains the hope that has sustained us for all these many years...We just couldn't get around the hard fact that for a hope or an idea to become real it has to be embodied in a man...(286)

It is precisely the image of Lincoln as an embodiment of American ideals that gives Hickman the ability not to lose faith in Bliss/Sunraider who, by this point in the novel, has come to symbolize both American possibility and the betrayal of such possibility. Lingering over the memory of Lincoln's brooding eyes, Hickman gazes at the dying Sunraider who, like Lincoln, was brought low by an assassin's bullet and thinks "I'll have to stay close to him and seek him out" (286). The momentary "loss of empathy" (285) he had experienced earlier passes and he renews his ties with his adopted son.

Part of the power of *Juneteenth* grows out of the fact that hope for the nation is represented not only in the mythic figure of Lincoln whom Hickman envisions as a kind of "Father" (283) of the country but also in Hickman himself who becomes a heroic "citizen-individualist" (24) by effectively assuming a number of public roles, most notably as a human father to Bliss and a spiritual father to his congregations. Hickman thus becomes not only one of Ellison's most remarkable characters but a rarity in modern literature, a genuinely public hero who fulfills himself by actualizing social roles which are essential to the health of the nation.

The turning point in Hickman's life is when he assists in Bliss's birth and then immediately shoulders the responsibility for raising the child. Realizing at this precise moment "that was the end of the old life for me" (313), he abandons a highly individualistic life as one who "rambled and gambled out in the Territory" (292) and becomes, like American figures such as Lincoln and classical heroes such as Odysseus, a person who is capable of assuming the enormous "weight" (313) of fatherhood. Freely giving up the "heathen freedom" (316) of a picaresque wanderer, he finds his "way" (316) to a larger and more meaningful freedom grounded in love and social responsibility.

The relationship between Hickman and Bliss therefore becomes a metaphor of how Ellison sees the relationship between whites and blacks in America. Born out of injustice and violence (Bliss's white mother has been involved in the lynching of Hickman's brother Bob who could well have been Bliss's father), it becomes a relationship grounded in what Melville would call "moral inter-indebtedness" (416). When Hickman is first confronted with the nameless white woman who asks him to deliver her baby, he has become "a man full of hate" with "murder in [his] heart" (307). Indeed, he is reduced to a condition of being "deaf and blind" (309), wanting to kill both mother and child as revenge for the lynching of his brother. But he also feels a mysterious connection between himself and the unborn child, a "cord of kinship stronger and deeper than blood, hate or heartbreak" (304), taking on the "awful burden" (317) of first delivering and then raising Bliss as his son.

This surprising and mysterious relationship between a black man and a boy of indeterminate racial origins leads the way to personal salvation for Hickman and suggests the possibility of cultural redemption for America. For the bloody delivery of the child becomes "Eden and Christmas squeezed together" (307) - a recovery of innocence where Hickman turns from being a man dominated by hatred to a loving father and a minister who can assist others (both black and white) on their way to redemption. Even though Bliss is first perceived by Hickman as "fruit of all this cancerous wrong" (306), the racism which has resulted in the lynching of his brother, he eventually becomes for Hickman a kind of Christ child offering redemption. (It is altogether appropriate that the role which Bliss plays in the revivalist act he shares with Hickman is rising out of a coffin, being resurrected from the dead.) Like America itself, Bliss is a "beginning" (307) leading to a new life. When Hickman assumes the responsibilities for raising Bliss, he undergoes a kind of conversion from a free but morally limited life of picaresque wandering to a much more meaningful life as a public hero who can help others to achieve the same kind of liberating transformation.

Bliss's story, like Hickman's, functions on two levels, personally and nationally. His early life with Hickman, like the Edenic life enjoyed by Huck and Jim on the raft, is a recovery of racial harmony or "bliss." But his adult life, initiated by the trauma of being claimed at a revivalist meeting by a white woman who identifies herself as his mother, is a "fall" from grace which clearly parallels the national fall from grace in the period following Reconstruction when the freedom, justice, and equality promised at the Juneteenth celebration is withdrawn and replaced by new forms of slavery in the Jim Crow period. It is for this reason that Hickman sees the wounded Senator Sunraider as a symbol of modern America when he observes "...there lies the nation on its groaning bed" (318). Like America, Bliss has been corrupted, first by a career as a maker of cheap films and later by the political power extended to him as a U.S. senator.

But Ellison does not present Bliss's story nihilistically as symbolizing a national disaster brought on by racial injustice and conflict. Although Bliss has chosen to desert Hickman and their vocation as preachers assisting blacks and whites along the road of "salvation" and eventually becomes Senator Sunraider, a virulent segregationist who fans the flames of racial discord, Hickman chooses to view him as a prodigal son rather than a damned soul. His deeper wisdom and powers of love motivate him neither to forget Bliss nor resent him for betraying their relationship but instead to pursue him faithfully because of the "promise" he represents:

> "...we kept the faith through all these watchful and graveling years. We held steady, stood firm in the face of everything; even after he ran away and we picked up his trail. I had been claimed by then and they loved him. Foolish to do but all those from the old evangelizing days felt the same need I felt to watch him travel and to hope for him and to learn. Yes, I guess we've been like a bunch of decrepit detectives trailing out of love. We didn't have to think about it or talk it over, we all just missed him and kept talking about him and seeking for him here and there. Lord, but we missed little Bliss. We missed his promise, I guess, and we were full of sorrow over his leaving us that way, just up and gone without a word. So we kept looking for him and telling all those who had heard him when he was traveling with me throughout the country to keep a lookout. Some thought he had been kidnapped and some that he was dead, and others that his people had come and taken him away. . .(316-17)

It is important to realize the "promise" which Bliss represents, like Bliss himself, is wounded but not "dead." And although, like the Prodigal Son, he has wandered away from his home, he is not truly lost because he is pursued by Hickman and others who are characterized as "decrepit detectives" who are "trailing [him] out of love." Moreover, Bliss himself desires a reunion with the family he has deserted - when he is shot in the novel's second chapter, he immediately thinks back to his days as a revivalist preacher with Hickman, finally thinking at the end of the chapter "Bliss be-eeee thee ti-ee that binds..." (32). The remainder of the novel consists of his trying to re-establish the ties that bind him to Hickman as both he and Hickman attempt to call up in memory a world of human love centered in family and community. Their meditations dramatize in a powerful way the passage from Eliot's "Little Gidding" which prefaces the novel:

> This is the use of memory:
> For liberation - not less of love but expanding
> Of love beyond desire, and so liberation
> From the future as well as the past. Thus, love of country
> Begins as attachment to our own field of action
> And comes to find that action of little importance
> Though never indifferent. History may be servitude,
> History may be freedom. See, now they vanish,
> The faces and places, with the self which, as it could, loved them,
> To become renewed, transfigured, in another pattern (ix).

The acts of memory shared by Hickman and Bliss in *Juneteenth* are liberating, not enslaving, because they flow from love which moves beyond simple "desire" and "our own field of action" to something broader and more enriching, a love of others and, finally, a "love of country." Bliss, who has been enslaved during his adult years by the wrong kind of love, a lust for money and power, can finally be "renewed" and "transfigured" by the kind of deeply spiritual love which Hickman offers him.

The novel, therefore, presents substantial hope in both its personal and national narratives. And such hope is impressively rendered in the interior monologue which constitutes the book's final chapter. In this extraordinary sequence Sunraider "strained" (324) to hear Hickman's liberating voice and, although he can not literally talk with him in any outward way, he does commune with Hickman's spirit as they re-live important moments of the past. Like the protagonist of *Invisible Man* in the hospital episode, he is outwardly immobilized but inwardly alive as he envisions the deeper meanings of his life. Imagining himself atop a train speeding West, he revisits both his personal and cultural past. And as "he moved with inward turning eyes" (332), he sees his own life and the life of the nation in sharp, lucid ways. Looking at an airplane skywriting "Niggers stay Away from the Polls" (332), he experiences the injustices of being a black person in the segregated South. He then views a scene of great national waste, a pigeon shoot in Oklahoma which greatly resembles the equally prophetic slaughter of pigeons in the opening scene of Cooper's *The Pioneers*. Ellison here links the irrational destruction of nature with another American "sin," racism. One bird, which refuses to make himself vulnerable to such senseless killing by staying under cover, is described by an outraged shooter as "a malignant nigger in the woodpile" (339). Significantly, Bliss identifies with the bird: "he felt responsible for the pigeon's life but was unable to do anything about it" (339). As he witnesses the bird eventually being flushed from his cover and shot, he becomes the bird: "As the bird dropped from site the Senator seemed to fall within himself" (340). In this epiphany Sunraider finally acknowledges his mixed racial origins - he too has been a "nigger in the woodpile" who has been flushed from his cover and "shot" as he tries to fly away from his origins.

As the sequence develops, Sunraider continues to discard the false facades he has used throughout his adult life and embraces his true self as "Bliss." At a key point he envisions a "small handsome boy…A fine grand rascal of a little boy" (341) and feels the "impulse to sweep the child into his arms," sensing that he "looks awfully familiar" (341). The boy clearly represents his earlier self as "Bliss," the self he repressed by becoming "movie man" a maker of cheap popular films driven by a lust for money and later Senator Sunraider, a person corrupted by a mania for power. Although he tries to connect with the boy, he is instead rebuffed by the child's "hot black eyes" (342) and a number of emphatically obscene gestures which he addresses to him before moving "silently into the crowd" (343).

Sunraider is likewise reproached in the subsequent episode by an elderly black woman who characterizes him as a "slack asted piece of peckerwood trash" and who tells him "You is simply nothing gone to waste…You ain't no eagle, fox, nor bear. You ain't a rabbit, or a skunk or a wheel in a wheel! You ain't nothing…(344-45). When he tries to defend himself from this bleak indictment by saying "I know who I am and, for the time being at least, I am a senator" (345), the reader remains convinced of both the boy's and the woman's negative assessment. By assuming the false roles as an adult, which have gotten him so much money and political power, Sunraider has become a "walking personification of the negative" (344). Interestingly, his word choice here is taken exactly from Chapter 3 of *Invisible Man* where the vet in the Golden Day episode describes invisible man as a "walking personification of the Negative" (9).

However, the novel does not conclude with the woman's harangue reducing Sunraider to "nothing" or with his own voice admitting that his life is a hopeless negation but instead the book closes with the intriguing image of "Hickman's consoling voice, calling from somewhere above" (350). This voice offers substantial hope, particularly when Sunraider recalls directly after his encounter with the boy and the woman, Hickman's sermon to a congregation terrified by a lightning storm which had "plunged the church into darkness" (345). At the exact point where the choir had "faltered in their singing and the women began to scream," Hickman transforms such "noisy confusion"

(345) into a place of "joyful and unearthly radiance" (346) with a powerful song about Christ's resurrection:

He 'rose...
Heroes!

He 'rose
Heroes!

He 'rose
Up from the dead! (346)

The song indeed provides a "comfort" (346) to the senator because it not only returns him to his earlier and truer self as Bliss who helped others by preaching the gospel of resurrection but it also reminds him that he too is worthy of salvation even in his currently degraded state. As he vividly experiences such "teasing fragments of memory long rejected," he opens "inward-searching eyes" (346) to both parts of his divided life. He is thus calmed and consoled by two lyrical images of church life he once shared with Hickman, a "choir of girlish voices lifted in vesperal song" and a muted trombone playing the "lyrics of some ancient hymn" (346).

Counterpointed with these powerful images of spiritual communion and transcendence are nightmare images of modern American culture descending into chaos and madness - the gigantic automobile bedecked with both an American flag and the stars and bars of the confederacy. Driven by nihilists intent on senseless violence, such "a rolling time bomb" (349) becomes a frightening symbol of the kind of racially divisive and self-destructive culture which Sunraider as an adult has helped to build. But it is significant that he clearly rejects this symbol of American decline, reducing it to "junkyard construction" which has been built by "clowns" (350). Turning away from this apocalyptic symbol of cultural decay, he moves his attention at the very end of the novel to Hickman's "consoling voice" which calls from "somewhere above" - a voice of love which leads the way to transcendence and new life. Just as Hickman had earlier served as a mid-wife who brought him into life because he thought "he deserves a chance" (311) to live, Hickman now assumes the role of minister offering him a new life of the spirit.

****

Although *Juneteenth* was written sporadically over a long period of time dating back to the 1950s, it is in a very real sense Ellison's gift to the present, a late-twentieth century America longing for revitalized community on many levels - family, marriage, neighborhood, and nation. The voice of this extraordinary novel, like Hickman's voice is "consoling" because it points to a way out of the cultural confusion America has been mired in for the past thirty years. According to the authors of *Habits of the Heart: Individualism and Commitment in American Life*, American society in the second half of the twentieth century has been damaged by a "radical individualism" (21) which has eroded social institutions and commonly held values to the point where forms of community have been weakened, producing a "socially unsituated self" (55) leading to cultural anarchy and a painful alienation of the individual. *Habits of the Heart*, like many other studies of late twentieth century American culture, has a two-fold purpose, first diagnosing the precise nature of this destructive individualism and them attempting to define a solution to the problem:

> The central problem of our book concerns the American individualism that Tocqueville described with a mixture of anxiety and admiration...We are concerned that this individualism may have grown cancerous - that it may be

> destroying those social integuments that Tocqueville saw as moderating its more destructive potentialities, that it may be threatening the survival of freedom itself. We want to know what individualism in American looks like and feels like, and how the world appears in its light.
>
> We are also interested in those cultural traditions and practices that, without destroying individuality, serve to limit and restrain the destructive side of individualism and provide alternative models for how Americans might live. (vii)

Juneteenth is likewise concerned about the destructive effects of late twentieth century American individualism and seeks an alternative to it in "cultural traditions and practices" dating back to the early days of the American experience. Senator Sunraider is consumed by a "cancerous" egoism which prompts him to value the money and political power which aggrandize the isolated self at the expense of his responsibilities to the social world. In deserting Hickman and denying his racial identity, he indeed becomes what Robert Bellah calls a "socially unsituated self" (55) luxuriating in a freedom which enables him to make money and gain outward control over people but which, in the final analysis, empties his life of meaning. Alonzo Hickman, on the other hand, rejects such an empty "heathen freedom" (305) in assuming the social roles of father, minister, and citizen and, in so doing, becomes the novel's true hero, a "citizen-individualist" (24) who can successfully harmonize a potent self with equally powerful commitments to community, and nation. In so doing, he drinks deeply from two nourishing cultural streams, an African American religious tradition which connects the self to God and the community and also an American political tradition best exemplified by Lincoln which unifies the one and the many, thus vitally connecting the individual self to all people.

Ellison's voice in *Juneteenth*, like Hickman's voice, has a special power and resonance for Americans at the end of the twentieth century because it not only lucidly diagnoses our cultural problems but also suggests in imaginatively compelling and concretely dramatized ways, strategies for creatively handling and perhaps solving such problems. In this sense, it rises well above most modern and postmodern fiction which is brilliant as a diagnostic tool but usually disappointing as a curative force. Centered in an extraordinary character of unusual depth and richness, it also uses myth and symbol wisely to become that rarity in late twentieth-century literature, a robust national narrative.

Works Cited

Bellah, Robert, Richard Madsen, William Sullivan, Anne Swidler, and Steven Tipton. *Habits of the Heart: Individualism and Commitment in American Life*. New York: Harper and Row, 1985. For other studies of the loss of community brought on by an excessive individualism in late twentieth century American life see Amitai Etzioni's *The Spirit of Community: The Reinvention of America's Society* (New York: Simon and Schuster, 1993) and Robert Hughes's *The Culture of Complaint: The Fraying of America* (New York: Warner Books, 1993).

Ellison, Ralph. *Invisible Man*. New York: Random House, 1952.
__________. *Juneteenth: A Novel*. New York: Random House, 1999.
Melville, Herman. *Moby Dick*. New York: Bobbs Merrill, 1964

Selected Bibliography

PRIMARY WORKS

Novels

Invisible Man. New York: Random House, 1952. 30th Anniversary Edition, New York: Random House, 1982. Franklin Center, Penn.: Franklin Mint Corp., 1980.

Juneteenth. New York: Random House, 1999.

Short Fiction

"Afternoon." *American Writing,* edited by Otto Storm and others, 28-37. Prairie City, Ill.: J.A. Decker, 1940.

"And Hickman Arrives." *Noble Savage* 1 (1960): 5-49. Reprinted in *Black Writers of America,* edited by Richard Barksdale and Keneth Kinnamon, 693-712. New York: Macmillan, 1972.

"Backwacking: A Plea to the Senator." *Massachusetts Review* 18 (Autumn 1977): 411-Reprinted in *Chant of Saints,* edited by Michael S. Harper and Robert B. Stepto, 445-50. Urbana: University of Illinois Press, 1979.

"The Birthmark." *New Masses,* 2 July 1940, 16-17.

"Cadillac Flambé." *American Review* 16 (1973): 249-69.

"A Coupla Scalped Indians." *New World Writing* 9 (1956): 225-36.

"Did You Ever Dream Lucky?" *New World Writing* 5 (April 1954): 134-45.

"Flying Home." In *Cross Section,* edited by Edwin Seaver, 469-85. New York: Fischer, Reprinted in *Dark Symphony*: *Negro Literature in America,* edited by James A. Emanuel and Theodore L. Gross, 254-74. Toronto: Free Press, 1968.

"In a Strange Country." *Tomorrow* 3 (July 1944): 41-44.

"Invisible Man." *Horizon* 16 (October 1947): 104-18.

"Invisible Man: Prologue to a Novel." *Partisan Review* 19 (January-February 1952): 31-40.

"It Always Breaks Out." *Partisan Review* 30 (Spring 1963): 113-28.

"Juneteenth." *Quarterly Review of Literature* 14 (1965): 262-76.

"King of the Bingo Game." *Tomorrow* 4 (November 1944): 29-33.

"Mr. Toussan." *New Masses*, 4 (November 1941): 19-20.

"Night-Talk." *Quarterly Review of Literature* 16 (1969): 317-29.

"Out of the Hospital and Under the Bar." In *Soon, One Morning*, edited by Herbert Hill, 242-90. New York: Knopf, 1963.

"The Roof, the Steeple and the People." *Quarterly Review of Literature* 10 (1960): 115-28.

"Slick Gonna Learn." *Direction* (September 1939): 10-11, 14, 16.

"A Song of Innocence." *Iowa Review* 1 (1970): 30-40.

"That I Had the Wings." *Common Ground* 3 (Summer 1943): 30-37.

Collected Short Fiction

Flying Home and Other Stories, edited by John F. Callahan. New York: The Modern Library, 1995.

Collected Nonfiction

The Collected Essays of Ralph Ellison, edited by John F. Callahan. New York: The Modern Library, *1995.*

Going to the Territory. New York: Random House, 1986.

Shadow and Act. New York: Vintage Books, 1964.

SECONDARY WORKS

Bibliography

Covo, Jacqueline. *The Blinking Eye: Ralph Waldo Ellison*. Metuchen, N.J.: Scarecrow Press, 1974.

Collections of Essays

Benston, Kimberly W., ed. *Speaking for You: The Vision of Ralph Ellison.* Washington, D.C.: Howard University Press, 1987.

Bloom, Harold, ed. *Ralph Ellison.* New York: Chelsea House Publishers, 1986.

Gottesman, Ronald, ed. *The Merrill Studies in "Invisible Man."* Columbus: Merrill, 1971.

Hersey, John, ed. *Ralph Ellison: A Collection of Critical Essays.* Englewood Cliffs, N.J.: Prentice Hall, 1970.

O'Meally, Robert G., ed. *New Essays on "Invisible Man."* New York: Cambridge University Press, 1988.

Parr, Susan Resneck, and Pancho Savery, eds. *Approaches to Teaching Ellison's "Invisible Man."* New York: MLA, 1989.

Reilly, John M., ed. *Twentieth Century Interpretations of "Invisible Man."* Englewood Cliffs, N.J.: Prentice-Hall, 1970.

Trimmer, Joseph, ed. *A Casebook on Ralph Ellison's "Invisible Man."* New York: Thomas Y. Crowell, 1972.

Special Issues of Journals

Carleton Miscellany 18 (1980).

CLA Journal 13 (March 1970).

Delta (Montpellier, France) 18 (1984).

Parts of Books and Chapters in Books

Baker, Houston A., Jr. *Blues, Ideology, and Afro-American Literature: A Vernacular Theory.* Chicago: University of Chicago Press, 1984.

__________. *The Journey Back: Issues in Black Literature and Criticism.* Chicago: University of Chicago Press, 1980.

__________. *Singers at Daybreak.* Washington, D.C. Howard University Press, 1974.

Baumbach, Jonathan. *The Landscape of Nightmare: Studies in the Contemporary American Novel.* New York: New York University Press, 1965.

Bone, Robert. *The Negro Novel in America.* New Haven: Yale University Press, 1965.

Bryant, Jerry. *The Open Decision: The Contemporary American Novel and Its Intellectual Background.* New York: Free Press, 1969.

Butler, Robert. "The City as Psychological Frontier in Ralph Ellison's *Invisible Man* and Charles Johnson's *Faith and the Good Thing* in *The City in African-American Literature,* ed. Yoshinobu Hakutani and Robert Butler. Teaneck, N.J.: Fairleigh Dickinson University Press, 1995.

Byerman, Keith. *Fingering the Jagged Grain: Tradition and Form in Recent Black Fiction.* Athens: University of Georgia Press, 1985.

Callahan, John F. *In the African-American Grain: The Pursuit of Voice in Twentieth Century Black Fiction.* Urbana: University of Illinois Press, 1988.

Cooke, Michael G. *Afro-American Literature in the Twentieth-Century: The Achievement of Literacy.* New Haven: Yale University Press, 1984.

Dixon, Melvin. *Ride Out the Wilderness.* Urbana: University of Illinois Press, 1987.

Gates, Henry Louis, Jr. *Figures in Black: Words, Signs, and The Racial Self.* New York: Oxford University Press, 1989.

__________. *The Signifying Monkey: A Theory of African-American Literary Criticism.* New York: Oxford University Press, 1988.

Harper, Michael S., and Robert B. Stepto, eds. *Chant of Saints: A Gathering of Afro-American Literature, Art, and Scholarship.* Urbana: University of Illinois Press, 1979.

Hassan, Ihab. *Radical Innocence: Studies in the Contemporary American Novel.* Princeton, N.J.: Princeton University Press, 1961.

Klein, Marcus. *After Alienation.* Cleveland: World Publishing Corp., 1965.

Klotman, Phyllis Rauch. *Another Man Gone: The Black Runner in Contemporary Afro-American Fiction.* Port Washington, N.Y.: Kennikat Press, 1977.

Margolies, Edward. *Native Sons: A Critical Study of Twentieth-Century Negro American Authors.* Philadelphia: J.B. Lippincott Co., 1968.

Murray, Albert. *The Omni-Americans.* New York: Avon, 125-30.

Petesch, Donald A. *A Spy in the Enemy's Country.* Iowa City: University of Iowa Press, 1989.

Rogers, Lawrence R. *Canaan Bound: The African-American Great Migration Novel.* Urbana: University of Illinois Press, 1997.

Rosenblatt, Roger. *Black Fiction.* Cambridge, Mass.: Harvard University Press, 1974.

Scruggs, Charles. *Sweet Home: Invisible Cities in the Afro-American Novel.* Baltimore: The Johns Hopkins Press, 1993.

Smith, Valerie. *Self-Discovery and Authority in Afro-American Literature.* Cambridge: Harvard University Press, 1987.

Stepto, Robert B. *From Behind the Veil: A Study of Afro-American Narrative.* Urbana: University of Illinois Press, 1979.

Tanner, Tony. *City of Words.* New York: Harper and Row, 1971.

Books

Busby, Mark. *Ralph Ellison.* Boston: Twayne, 1991.

Dietze, Rudolf F. *Ralph Ellison: The Genesis of an Artist.* Nuremberg: Verlag Hans Carl, 1982.

Gray, Valerie Bonita. *Invisible Man's Literary Heritage: "Benito Cereno" and "Moby Dick."* Amsterdam: Editions Rodopi, N.V., 1978.

List, Robert N. *Dedalus in Harlem: The Joyce-Ellison Connection.* Washington, D.C.: University Press of America, 1982.

McSweeney, Kerry. *"Invisible Man": A Student's Companion to the Novel.* Boston: Twayne, 1988.

Nadel, Alan. *Invisible Criticism: Ralph Ellison and the American Canon.* Iowa City: University of Iowa Press, 1988.

O'Meally, Robert G. *The Craft of Ralph Ellison.* Cambridge: Harvard University Press, 1980.

Sundquist, Eric. *Cultural Contexts for Invisible Man.* Boston: St. Martin's Press, 1995.

Watts, Jerry Gafio. *Heroism and the Black Intellectual: Ralph Ellison, Politics, and Afro-American Intellectual Life.* Chapel Hill: University of North Carolina Press, 1994.

Articles

Abrams, Robert E. "The Ambiguities of Dreaming in Ellison's *Invisible Man.*" *American Literature* 49 (Jan., 1978), 592-603.

Anderson, Jervis. "Going to the Territory." *New Yorker,* 22 (Nov. 22, 1976), 55-108.

Baker, Houston. "To Move Without Moving: An Analysis of Creativity and Commerce in Ralph Ellison's Trueblood Episode." *PMLA* 98 (Oct. 1983), 828-45.

Benston, Kimberly. "Ellison, Baraka, and the Faces of Tradition." *Boundary* II:6 (Winter, 1978): 333-54.

Blake, Susan L. "Ritual and Rationalization: Black Folklore in the Works of Ralph Ellison." *PMLA* 94 (1979), 121-136.

Bone, Robert. "Ralph Ellison and the Uses of the Imagination." In *Anger and Beyond.* Ed. Herbert Hill (New York: Harper and Row, 1966), 86-111.

Bucco, Martin. "Ellison's Invisible West." *Western American Literature* (1975), 237-38.

Butler, Robert. "Dante's *Inferno* and Ellison's Invisible Man: A Study in Literary Continuity." *CLA Journal* 28: 1 (Sept. 1984), 54-77.

_________. "Patterns of Movement in Ellison's *Invisible Man.*" *American Studies* 31: 1 (Spring, 1980), 5-21.

_________. "Down from Slavery: Invisible Man's Descent into the City and the Discovery of Self." *American Studies* 29:2 (Fall 1988), 57-67.

_________. "The Plunge into Pure Duration: Bergsonian Visions of Time in Ellison's Invisible Man." *CLA Journal* 33:3 (March 1990), 260-279.

Callahan, John F. "Democracy and the Pursuit of Narration." *The Carleton Miscellany* 18:3 (Winter 1980), 51-69.

___________. "Frequencies of Eloquence: The Performance of Composition of *Invisible Man.*" In *New Essays on Invisible Man.* Ed. Robert O'Meally (New York: Cambridge University Press, 1988), 54-94.

___________. "Piecing Together Ralph Ellison's Unfinished Work." *The Chronicle of Higher Education* (Sept. 20, 1996), B3-B4.

Chisholm, Lawrence. "Signifying Everything." *The Yale Review.* 54:3 (Spring 1965), 450-454.

Christian, Barbara. "Ralph Ellison: A Critical Study." In *Black Expression* ed. Addison Gayle, Jr., (New York: Weybright and Tally, Inc., 1969), 353-65.

Clipper, Lawrence J. "Folklore and Mythic Elements in *Invisible Man.*" *CLA Journal* 13 (March 1979), 239-254.

Cohn, Deborah. "To See or Not to See: Invisibility, Clairvoyance and Re-visions of History in *Invisible Man* and *La casa de les espiritus.*" *Comparative Literature Studies* 33:4 (1996), 372-95.

Collier, Eugenia. "The Nightmare Truth of an Invisible Man." *Black World* 20 (Dec.1970), 12-19.

Deutsch, Leonard. "Ellison's Early Fiction." *Negro American Literature Forum* 7 (Summer 1973), 53-59.

_____________. "Ralph Waldo Ellison and Ralph Waldo Emerson: A Shared Moral Vision." *CLA Journal* 16 (1972), 160-173.

Dietze, Rudolf F. "Ralph Ellison and the Literary Tradition." In *History and Tradition in African-American Culture.* Ed. Gunter H. Lenz., (Frankfort: Campus Verlag, 1984), 18-29.

Dixon, Melvin. "O Mary Rambo, Don't You Weep." *Carleton Miscellany* 78 (Winter 1980), 98-104.

Doyle, Mary Ellen, S.C.N. "In Need of Folk: The Alienated Protagonists of Ralph Ellison's Short Fiction." *CLA Journal* 20:2 (Dec. 1975), 165-72.

Dupre, F.W. "On *Invisible Man.*" *Book Week* 26 (*Washington Post*), September 1965, 4.

Fass, Barbara. "Rejection of Paternalism: Hawthorne's 'My Kinsman, Major Molineux' and Ellison's *Invisible Man.*" *CLA Journal* 14 (1971): 317-23.

Forrest, Leon. "Luminosity from the Lower Frequencies." *The Carleton Miscellany* 18:3 (Winter 1980), 82-97.

Frank, Joseph. "Ralph Ellison and a Literary 'Ancestor': Dostoevski." *New Criterion* (Sept. 1983), 140-52.

Goede, William. "On Lower Frequencies: The Buried Men in Wright and Ellison," *Modern Fiction Studies* 15 (1969), 483-501.

Gordon, Gerald T. "Rhetorical Strategies in Ralph Ellison's *Invisible Man.*" *Rocky Mountain Review* 41 (1987), 199-209.

Harding, James M. "Adorno, Ellison, and the Critique of Jazz." *Cultural Critique* 31 (Fall 1995), 129-158.

Harris, Trudier. "Ellison's Peter Wheatstraw: His Basis in Folk Tradition." *Mississippi Folklore Register* 6 (1975), 117-26.

Herman, David. "Ellison's 'King of the Bingo Game': Finding Naturalism's Trap Door." *English Language Notes* 29: 1 (Sept. 1991), 71-74.

Horowitz, Floyd. "Ralph Ellison's Modern Version of Brer Bear and Brer Rabbit in *Invisible Man.*" *Midcontinent American Studies Journal* 4 (1963), 21-27.

___________. "The Enigma of Ellison's Intellectual Man." *CLA Journal* VII (Dec. 1963), 126-32.

Howe, Irving. "Black Boys and Native Sons." In *A World More Attractive* (New York: Horizon Press, 1963), 98-122.

Hyman, Stanley Edgar. "Ralph Ellison in Our Time." *The New Leader* 47:22 (Oct. 26, 1964), 21-22.

Kaiser, Ernest. "A Critical Look at Ellison's Fiction and at Social and Literary Criticism by and about the Author." *Black World* 20: 2 (Dec. 1970) 53-9; 81-97.

Kent, George. "Ralph Ellison and the Afro-American Folk and Cultural Tradition." *CLA Journal* 13:3 (March 1970), 265-276.

Kostelanetz, Richard. "The Politics of Ellison's Booker: *Invisible Man* as Symbolic History." *Chicago Review*, XIX, 2 (1967), 5-26.

Lee, Kun-Jong. "Ellison's *Invisible Man*: Emersonianism Revisited." *PMLA*, 107:2 (March 1992), 331-44.

__________. "Racial Variations on American Themes." *African American Review* 30:3 (Fall 1996), 421-40.

Lewis, R.W.B. "The Ceremonial Imagination of Ralph Ellison." *Carleton Miscellany* 18: 3 (Winter 1980), 34-38.

Lieberman, Marcia R. "Moral Innocents: Ellison's *Invisible Man* and *Candide*." *CLA Journal* 15 (Sept. 1971), 64-79.

Lyne, William. "The Signifying Modernist: Ralph Ellison and the Limits of the Double Consciousness." *PLMA* 107:2 (March 1992), 319-30.

Marvin, Thomas F. "Children of Legba: Musicians at the Crossroads in Ellison's *Invisible Man*." *American Literature*, 68:3 (Sept. 1996), 587-608.

McPherson, James Alan. "Indivisible Man." *The Atlantic.* 226:6 (Dec. 1970), 45-60.

Mengeling, Marvin. "Walt Whitman and Ellison: Older Symbols in a Modern Mainstream." *Walt Whitman Review* 12 (Sept. 1966), 67-70.

Neal, Larry. "Ellison's Zoot Suit." *Black World.* 20:2 (Dec. 1970), 31-50.

O'Meally, Robert G. "The Rules of Magic: Hemingway as Ellison's 'Ancestor.'" *Southern Review* 21 (1985), 751-69.

Ostendorf, Berndt. "Ralph Ellison's 'Flying Home': From Folk Tale to Short Story." *Journal of the Folklore Institute* 13:2 (1976), 185-99.

______________. "Ralph Waldo Ellison: Anthropology, Modernism, and Jazz." In *New Essays on Invisible Man.* Ed. Robert O'Meally (New York: Cambridge University Press, 1988), 95-122.

Parrish, Timothy. "Ralph Ellison, Kenneth Burke, and the Form of Democracy." *Arizona Quarterly*, 51:3 (Autumn 1995), 117-48.

Pinckney, Darryl. "The Drama of Ralph Ellison." *New York Review of Books*, XLIV: 8 (May 15, 1997), 52-60.

Reed, Brian. "The Iron and the Flesh: History as Machine in Ellison's *Invisible Man*." *CLA Journal* 37:3 (March 1994), 261-73.

Reilly, John M. "The Testament of Ralph Ellison." In *Speaking for You: The Vision of Ralph Ellison.* Ed. Kimberly W. Benston (Washington, D.C.: Howard University Press, 1987), 49-62.

Richardson, Brian. "White on Black: Iconography, Race and Reflexivity in Ellison's *Invisible Man.*" *Southern Humanities Review*, 30:2 (Spring 1996), 139-50.

Rovit, Earl H. "Ralph Ellison and the American Comic Tradition." *Wisconsin Studies in Contemporary Literature* 1 (1960), 34-42.

Sale, Roger. "The Career of Ralph Ellison." *Hudson Review* (Spring 1965), 124-28.

Sanders, Archie. "Odysseus in Black: An Analysis of the Structure of *Invisible Man.*" *CLA Journal* 13 (March 1970), 217-228.

Schafer, William J. "Ralph Ellison and the Birth of the Anti-Hero." *Critique: Studies in Modern Fiction* 10 (1968), 81-93.

Schaub, Thomas. "Ellison's Masks and the Novel of Reality." In *New Essays on Invisible Man*. Ed. Robert O'Meally (New York: Cambridge University Press, 1988), 123-156.

Schultz, Elizabeth A. "The Illumination of Darkness: Affinities between *Moby Dick* and *Invisible Man.*" *CLA Journal* 32 (Dec. 1988), 170-200.

Scruggs, Charles. "Ralph Ellison's Use of *The Aeneid* in *Invisible Man.*" *CLA Journal* 17 (March 1974), 368-78.

Sisney, Mary F. "The Power and Horror of Whiteness: Wright and Ellison Respond to Poe." *CLA Journal* 29 (Sept. 1985), 82-90.

Skerrett, Jospeph T., Jr. "The Wright Interpretation: Ralph Ellison and the Anxiety of Influence." *Massachusetts Review* 21 (1980), 196-212.

Smith, Valerie. "The Meaning of Narration in *Invisible Man.*" In *New Essays on Invisible Man.* Ed. Robert O'Meally (New York: Cambridge University Press, 1988), 25-54.

Staples, Brent. "In His Own Good Time." *New York Times Book Review*, 3 August 1986, 15.

Stepto, Robert. "Literacy and Hibernation: Ralph Ellison's *Invisible Man.*" *The Carleton Miscellany.* 18:3 (Winter 1980), 112-141.

Tate, Claudia. "Notes on the Invisible Woman in Ralph Ellison's *Invisible Man.*" In *Speaking for You: The Vision of Ralph Ellison.* Ed. Kimberly W. Benston (Washington, D.C.: Howard University Press, 1987), 163-72.

Trimmer, Joseph. "Ralph Ellison's 'Flying Home.'" *Studies in Short Fiction* 9 (Spring, 1972), 175-82.

Tuttleton, James W. "The Achievement of Ralph Ellison." *The New Criterion* 14:4 (Dec. 1995), 5-10.

Vauthier, Simone. "Not Quite on the Beat: An Academic Interpretation of the Narrative Stance in Ralph Ellison's *Invisible Man.*" *Delta* 18 (April 1984): 69-88.

Vogler, Thomas. "Somebody's Protest Novel." *Iowa Review* 1 (Spring 1970), 64-82.

Walling, William. "'Art' and 'Protest': Ralph Ellison's *Invisible Man* Twenty Years After." *Phylon* 34 (June 1973), 120-34.

Walsh, Mary Ellen Williams. "*Invisible Man:* Ralph Ellison's Wasteland." *CLA Journal* 28 (1984), 150-58.

Wilner, Elenor R. "The Invisible Black Thread: Identity and Nonentity in *Invisible Man.*" *CLA Journal* 13 (1970), 242-57.

Wright, John. "Dedicated Dreamer, Consecrated Acts: Shadowing Ellison." *The Carleton Miscellany.* 18:3 (Winter 1980), 142-199.

__________. "The Conscious Hero and the Rites of Man." In *New Essays on Invisible Man*. Ed. Robert O'Meally (New York: Cambridge University Press, 1988), 157-186.

Interviews

Carson, David L. "Ralph Ellison: Twenty Years After." *Studies in American Fiction* 1 (Spring 1973): 1-23.

Cohen, Ted, and N.A. Samstag. "An Interview with Ralph Ellison." *Phoenix* 22 (Fall 1961): 4-10.

Garrett, George, ed. *The Writer's Voice: Conversations with Contemporary Writers.* New York: William Morrow & Co., 1973.

Geller, Allen. "An Interview with Ralph Ellison." In *The Black American Writer. Vol. 1: Fiction,* edited by C.W.E. Bigsby. Baltimore: Penguin Books, 1969.

Graham, Maryemma and Amritjit Singh. *Conversations with Ralph Ellison.* Jackson, Miss.: University of Mississippi Press, 1995.

Hersey, John. "A Completion of Personality': A Talk with Ralph Ellison." In *Speaking for You,* edited by Kimberly W. Benston. (Washington, D.C.: Howard University Press, 1987): 285-307.

O'Brien, John. *Interviews with Black Writers.* New York: Liveright, 1973.

Reed, Ishmael, Quincy Troupe, and Steve Cannon. "The Essential Ellison." *Y'Bird Reader* 1 (1978): 126-59.

Remnick, David. "Visible Man." *New Yorker,* (March 14, 1994): 34-38.

Stepto, Robert B., and Michael S. Harper. "Study and Experience: An Interview with Ralph Ellison." In *Chant of Saints,* edited by Michael S. Harper and Robert B. Stepto. (Urbana: University of Illinois Press, 1979): 451-69.

Welburn, Ron. "Ralph Ellison's Territorial Vantage." *Grackle* 4 (1977-78): 5-15.

Index